Baedeker

Tuscany

www.baedeker.com

Verlag Karl Baedeker

TOP ATTRACTIONS ★ ★

The list of sights is almost endless, but where are the highlights in Tuscany? Cultural sites, the finest scenery and the prettiest seaside resorts – we have summarized them, so that you know what not to miss.

1 ★★ Alpi Apuane
An area with much to offer: interesting combination of mountains and coast
▶ page 140

2 ★★ Lucca
The former city of silk merchants is a pearl among all the beautiful Tuscan cities.
▶ page 273

©Baedeker

1 Alpi Apuane

2 Lucca

3 Florenz

4 Medici-Villen

6 Pisa

5 La Verna

7 Chiantigiana

9 Volterra

8 Arezzo

10 Siena

11 Cortona

12 Monte Oliveto Maggiore

15 Massa Marittima

14 Pienza

13 Montepulciano

16 Sant' Antimo

17 Monte Amiata

18 Roselle

19 Elba

20 Parco Naturale della Maremma

21 Giardino dei Tarocchi

22 Giglio

3 ✶✶ Florence
Quite simply the tourist highlight of Tuscany – the history of the Renaissance and humanism is close enough to touch here. ► page 211

4 ✶✶ Medici Villas
Noble residences of the wealthy family around Florence ► page 257

5 ✶✶ La Verna
St Francis is said to have received the stigmata here. ► page 156

6 ✶✶ Pisa
Everyone thinks of the »Leaning Tower« – but the city on the Arno has much more to offer. ► page 326

7 ✶✶ Chiantigiana
Wine region and cultivated landscape par excellence ► page 180

8 ✶✶ Arezzo
Fascinating: the famous fresco cycle by Piero della Francesca ► page 143

9 ✶✶ Volterra
Home of alabaster – and souvenirs galore ► page 410

10 ✶✶ Siena
Built on seven hills like Rome – and for many the most beautiful city in Tuscany ► page 377

11 ✶✶ Cortona
Enchanting location on the slopes of Monte San Egidio ► page 194

12 ✶✶ Monte Oliveto Maggiore
Romanesque monastery with beautiful frescoes ► page 300

13 ✶✶ Montepulciano
Has a reputation not only among wine lovers but also among music lovers! ► page 316

Siena
Swirling banners at the Palio

14 ✶✶ Pienza
Was intended to be the ideal Renaissance city. ► page 323

15 ✶✶ Massa Marittima
»Jewel of the Alta Maremma« ► page 292

16 ✶✶ Sant' Antimo
One of the wealthiest monasteries in Tuscany ► page 298

17 ✶✶ Monte Amiata
Beautiful area for hikers and bikers ► page 303

18 ✶✶ Roselle
Necropolis of a former Etruscan city ► page 262

19 ✶✶ Elba
Holiday paradise for water-sports fans, hikers and mountain bikers ► page 199

20 ✶✶ Parco Naturale della Maremma
Once a swamp – today fertile farming and pasture land ► page 290

21 ✶✶ Giardino dei Tarocchi
Tarot Garden full of giant mythical creatures and glittering towers ► page 310

22 ✶✶ Giglio
Rocky island that attracts divers and swimmers ► page 258

THE BEST BAEDEKER TIPS

Of all the Baedeker tips in this guidebook, here is a selection of the best. Experience and enjoy Tuscany at its most beautiful!

▊ Golf: an experience for all the senses
That is certainly what awaits golfers on the Punta Ala course. Get ready for a surprise! ► page 102

▊ How about some wild mountains?
Near Botri, about 13km/8mi north of Bagni di Lucca, is the entrance to a rock gorge that is part of the Riserva Naturale dell' Orrido di Botri. ► page 143

White as marble ...
... lardo, bacon from Colonnata

▊ Lost and found
Antique lovers will certainly find something in the shops or large antique market of Arezzo. ► page 148

▊ Homemade
Traditional delicacies like herbal liqueurs and aromatic ointments – the monastery pharmacy in Camaldoli is the right address for this. ► page 155

▊ Art Nouveau in Tuscany?
Sometimes you find masterpieces of a building style exactly where they are least expected. The town hall of Borgo San Lorenzo is a good example of this. ► page 161

▊ Lardo di Colonnata
According to an old tradition white bacon is stored in marble jars for up to six months before it is served cut into paper-thin slices. It tastes best on unsalted bread and served with a glass of Tuscan wine! ► page 174

▊ Locanda La Palazzina
This accommodation is absolutely fabulous – the beautiful villa, its wonderful location and the breakfast buffet are incomparable. ► page 192

▊ Natural bathtubs
How about a trip to cooling waters? The natural granite sea-water pools between Fetovia and Seccheto are a wonderful place to relax. ► page 204

▊ Take the bus!
The panoramic road to Fiesole gives a unique view of Florence. Enjoy this cheap and comfortable treat on bus no. 7! ► page 207

▊ Why wait? Book ahead!
Queuing up at the Uffizi? Not necessary! ► page 228

Just a little hungry?

Visit the covered market in Florence and pick up a bite to eat. If you like tripe, try the Florentine specialty »panino con lampredotto«. ► page 245

Picnic with a view

The perfect place for a picnic is about 10km/6mi south of Livorno.
► page 269

Cowboys up close

Watch the cattle drovers at work in the Maremma. ► page 288

Howl with the wolves

Parco Faunistico dell'Amiata and its wolves – not just for children page
► page 306

Cheese lovers: don't miss it!

The pecorino from Pienza is something special. ► page 323

Off to the factory!

The factory outlets of Prato are heaven for money-conscious fashion fans.
► page 357

Free bath

You have to find them first, but it is worth the effort to relax in the luminous turquoise pools at Bagno Vignoni!
► page 372

Good timing is …

… if you come to Siena in September or early October, as the unique floor of the cathedral can be seen in its entirety only then. ► page 382

Thermal baths
are one of the pleasures of Tuscany.

*Pinocchio, the most famous
long nose in the world*
► **page 40**

BACKGROUND

PRACTICALITIES

Price categories

Hotels
Luxury: from €160/£110
Mid-range: €65 – 160/£45 – 110
Budget: under €65/£45
for one night in a double room

Restaurants
Expensive: from €50/£35
Moderate: €25 – 50/£18 – 35
Inexpensive: up to €25/£18
For one main dish
(Secondo piatto)

TOURS

SIGHTS
from A to Z

Tasty olives
► **page 84**

Beach life, Tuscan-style
► **page 406**

Lorenzo, one of the famous Medici
► **page 238**

Sometimes the cliché does fit: picture-post-card scenery with fields of sunflowers in Val d'Orcia
► **page 372**

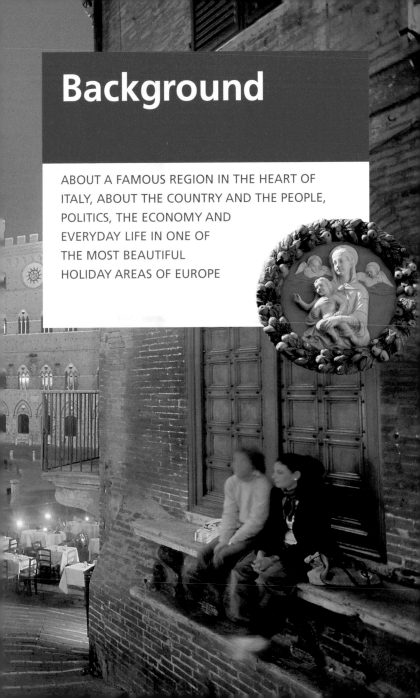

Background

ABOUT A FAMOUS REGION IN THE HEART OF
ITALY, ABOUT THE COUNTRY AND THE PEOPLE,
POLITICS, THE ECONOMY AND
EVERYDAY LIFE IN ONE OF
THE MOST BEAUTIFUL
HOLIDAY AREAS OF EUROPE

BELLA TOSCANA

Some travel destinations really make it difficult. Tuscany, for example: its image as the ideal place for culture and scenery is not the best starting point when trying to take a critical look at the region.

For lovers of art and Italy the gently rolling hills between Florence and Siena have always had an irresistible attraction, but in recent years they have not been only ones to rave. Whole villages in Tuscany have been taken over by second-homers from Britain, Germany and elsewhere, Tuscan olive oil can be found in every kitchen and everyone has become an expert on the proper cooking time for pasta.

It is seemingly impossible to talk about Tuscany without going into

raptures and repeating what everyone says when they come back from a holiday in the region: that one or two visits are simply not enough. Is it possible to claim this in a guidebook without losing all objectivity as a lover of Italy? It is possible, even necessary, because the weight of evidence is simply overwhelming.

A Wide Range of Charms

The importance of this region, which produced geniuses like Leonardo da Vinci and Michelangelo, Brunelleschi and Dante, Petrarch and Boccaccio, is indis-

Michelangelo's David
The original of the famous statue was moved from Piazza della Signoria into the Accademia in 1873.

putable. Humanism and the Renaissance developed here between the 14th and the 16th century – and fundamentally changed European art and culture. It is not just a question of the absolute highlights like Florence, Siena, Lucca or Montepulciano, whose fascination cannot be denied. The countless treasures of architecture and art that lie within their walls would be reason enough to sing the praises of the region.

However, this alone does not explain what is so special about Tuscany. Leave the art gallery, the church or the palazzo, sit at a table in a street café a few steps away, and enjoy an espresso or a cappuccino. Wander through medieval lanes that wind up to the highest point of the town; drive along winding roads through the countryside and

Gentle hilly landscape
As soon as you get away from the coast, the land becomes green and restful.

Tuscan cuisine
offers all sorts of delicacies.

Sandy beaches
like this are typical for the Maremma.

Picturesque light
makes the landscape appear even more like a dream.

Important wine region
The most famous wines of the region are Brunello di Montalcino, Vino Nobile di Montepulciano and Chianti.

Pleasant accommodation
Historic villas, elegant town houses, small family-run bed and breakfasts, mountain cabins, youth hostels and holidays on the farm

stop to admire the view over vineyards and meadows, small villages and remote farms. Have a picnic under olive trees or enjoy a plate of homemade pasta and a glass of red vino da tavola in the evening – and any doubts about whether or not to love Tuscany will be wiped away, without a trace.

The Right Balance

Tuscany is ideal for everyone who likes to balance culture and good food with physical activity. Joggers, hikers and cyclists have opportunities on all sides to take exercise in lovely surroundings, and ambitious mountain bikers will appreciate challenging trails like those in the Monti Metaliferi and Chianti. Horse lovers can find stables in the whole region, and Tuscany is slowly turning into a golfer's paradise, too. On the coast swimmers and sunbathers can of course try out every kind of water sport. Diving is particularly recommended in the Arcipelago della Toscana. Visitors who really want to pamper themselves in spas have a wide range of choice. This is actually a tradition in Tuscany. Some of the hot springs were already used by the Etruscans and the Romans, others in the Middle Ages. The most famous spas are the elegant 19th-century facilities at Montecatini Terme and Chianciano Terme in southern Tuscany.

There are many ways to have a wonderful holiday in Tuscany. You can do almost anything, but you do not have to. The important thing is to get the right balance. Because all visitors should discover and experience this unique region for themselves and in their own way ...

Enchanting corners *like this one can be found in the smallest villages.*

Facts

What is the mezzadria? Where are Tuscany's highest mountains? Why is Prato called »rag city«? Where has iron ore been mined since the Middle Ages? Where was Italy's best-known female rock singer born?

Nature

Regione Toscana

Tuscany is a historical and geographical landscape and one of the 20 regions of Italy (Regione Toscana). In the west it extends to the Mediterranean Sea, in the north and east it borders on Liguria, Emilia-Romagna and the Marche, in the south on Umbria and Latium. The seven islands of the Tuscan archipelago (Arcipelago Toscano), of which Elba, Giglio and Capraia are the biggest, also belong to the region's territory.

Scenery

At the mention of Tuscany olive groves, vineyards and cypress avenues winding along gently rolling hillsides come to mind. But the scenery is more varied than this – and by no means always as charming as the picture postcards suggest. Most of the region is hilly, and the north-west is actually mountainous, but in the south-west, in the Maremma and on the coast, the landscape is flat: this area was once marshy and is now partly a nature reserve. The densely populated belt between Pisa and Florence in the north contrasts with the less densely populated areas of fields, forests and isolated farms that mainly lie in the south.

Apennines and Apuan Alps

The Apennines, a mountain range which runs through all of Italy, form the mountainous backbone of Tuscany, and are here called the Tuscan or Etruscan Apennines. Northern Tuscany is characterized by the so-called Northern Apennines, which are formed of grey sandstone and have their highest peak, Monte Cimone (in Emilia-Romagna, 2,165m/7,103ft), just north of Tuscany.

The Apuan Alps lie to the south-west of the Apennines. Their rocky formations reach almost 2,000m/6,600ft and are reminiscent of high mountain ranges. They rise steeply from a coast famous for its marble, which is quarried near Carrara and Massa among other places.

Valleys in the north, hills in the south

The basins that formed between the Apennines and the coast in northern and central Tuscany are valleys today: the Lunigiana, for example, Garfagnana, Mugello, Casentino and Valdarno as well as Val di Chiana.

South of the Arno the Tuscan landscape is completely different. Although the elevations in the Colline Metallifere are in part quite high, the area is characterized not by connected mountains but by gently rolling hills from which individual mountains rise. Erosion has made some of the slopes very steep, forming deep gorges and erosion channels, as can be seen near Volterra or the so-called Crete of Siena. The ground is very fertile and is intensively used for agriculture. The highest peak in Tuscany is the 1,734m/5,689ft-high Monte Amiata, an extinct volcano in the extreme south-east.

← *A break in a Tuscan idyll*

Picture-postcard Tuscany: gentle hills and remote farms

Coastal plains   Tuscany has a coastline of about 300km/190mi. In the north the coastal plain is a narrow strip before the Apuan Alps, with long, sandy beaches and a well-developed infrastructure for tourism. From the mouth of the little Cecina River southwards to Civitavecchia in **Maremma ▶** Latium the coastal plain is known as the Maremma. This straight sandy coast was feared for centuries because it was infested with malaria. The Maremma was cultivated and densely populated during the Etruscan period, and then again from the 19th century.

Tuscan islands   The Tuscan archipelago consists of seven main islands and several small ones, which lie off the Tuscan coast in the part of the Tyrrhenian Sea that is bordered by the Italian mainland in the east and the French island of Corsica in the west. Social and economic life in the archipelago is limited for the most part to four islands: Elba, Giglio,

Giannutri and Capraia. Gorgona, the site of an Italian prison, may only be visited with special permission. In 1990 parts of the Tuscan archipelago were made into a national park to protect the flora and fauna. In 1998 the entire islands of Montecristo (►Elba), Gorgona (Livorno), Pianosa and Giannutri, 85% of Capraia, 55% of Elba and 50% of Giglio were placed under protection.

Several rivers flow through Tuscany, all of them from the Apennines **Rivers** or the hills to the Mediterranean. The Arno, Tuscany's longest river, rises north of Arezzo at Monte Falterona and flows through Florence and Pisa almost 250km/155mi to the sea. The other major rivers are the Magra, Serchio, Cecina, Ombrone and Fiora. Extreme differences in water level during the course of the year are typical of all these rivers for climatic reasons.

Plants

Tuscany is an area of ancient settlement, and the plants and animals **Man-made** originally native to this area have accordingly been pushed into the **landscape** margins. Outside the cities and tourist areas most of the land is used for agriculture; olive groves, vineyards and wheat fields predominate. The three characteristic trees of the region are the olive tree with its green-silver shiny leaves, the slender, dark-green cypress and the stone pine with its umbrella-like crown.

Tuscany was originally covered with dense forests – oak, beech or fir **Macchia** trees depending on the elevation. However, for the most part these forests were already cleared during ancient times. The erosion that followed washed away the earth and in many parts of the mountains left bare rock without any plant cover. On the hills and in the valleys between the foothills the ground that was not used for agriculture was soon covered by macchia: evergreen, low shrubs with small, often leathery leaves which protect the ground from evaporation and form an impenetrable and thorny thicket. Just like the Mediterranean heath which can often be found at higher altitudes, macchia is characteristic of the Tuscan landscape. In the spring it is transformed into a colourful sea of flowers. Many plants contain aromatic resins and essential oils that produce an intense perfume. The main plants of the macchia are varieties of heather, broom, laurel, sage, arbutus, juniper, cistus, myrtle, mastic, pistachio and bramble.

Tuscany has been reforested since the early 20th century, especially **Forests** since the end of the Second World War. Today 37% of the region is forest, making it now one of the Italian regions with the most tree cover. These efforts have been concentrated in the Apennines and other mountainous regions, where today beech, oak, ash, fir, spruce and larch are growing again. Chestnuts, too, can often be found up to elevations of about 900m/2,950ft. In the Tuscan coastal areas pine,

Maremma cattle are white and have long, curved horns.

ITALY'S WILD WEST

Life in the Maremma is far from the romantic image of the Wild West. Yet there are a few parallels: sparsely populated land, horses and cattle roaming free, and cattle drovers.

The Maremma is actually **swampland**. The Etruscans were the first to drain and settle it. They constructed drainage channels and founded the cities of Rusellae and Vetulonia. In Colline Metallifere, the hilly, ore-rich landscape south of Cecina , they mined minerals. The Romans took over this Etruscan heritage and distributed the fertile land to veterans, but when their empire fell apart the drainage channels decayed. The land became swampy again and malaria was rife. The settlers fled from the deadly illness into the hills, where they built their spiritual and secular centres of power. During the Middle Ages and under the Habsburg grand dukes there were repeated efforts to drain the land, but the Maremma remained a poor and unpopulated region with a high crime rate until well into the 19th century – Italy's »Wild West«.

While most of the Maremmani had to work in the fields of the estate owners, the romantics in distant Livorno and Florence developed an idealized picture of the life of the Maremma farmers in the middle of **unadulterated nature**. Landscape painters captured on canvas idyllic scenes of cattle herds and half-wild horses. The building of the railway line along the coast in 1860 created new jobs, but also caused more malaria – the water-filled pits that were excavated for the railway were ideal breeding places for the dreaded mosquitoes. Large parts

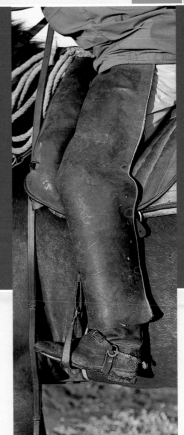

of the Maremma were completely drained only from the 1930s. The land reform twenty years later also contributed to changes in the landscape. Today barley, maize, fruit, vegetables and wine are grown in the fertile plains.

Cowboys of the Maremma

The Maremma has its characteristic way of breeding cattle. White longhorn cattle are raised here on the open range. They are particularly robust, resistant towards disease and very undemanding. The half-wild Maremma horses, Maremmanos, are more rare. Both the Maremmanos and the Maremma cattle are herded through the swampy plains by »butteri«, cattle drovers on horseback – with the reins in one hand and the long drover's staff, the uncino, in the other. Day in, day out the butteri tend their herds, which are gradually decreasing year on year.

The mounted cattle drovers of the Maremma who drive cattle across rough territory and swampy plains are called »butteri«.

Anyone interested in a closer look at the day-to-day life of the Maremma cowboys and their skill on horseback should go either to the »torneo dei butteri« in August or to one of the large cattle drives that take place several times a year. It is also possible to watch the cattle drovers at work. These »meetings« are arranged by the Azienda Regionale Agricola di Alberese (tel. 05 64 40 71 80).

cedar, black and white poplar as well as local eucalyptus trees have also been planted. In the southern coastal and hilly regions cork oaks can occasionally be found.

Animals

The natural fauna has been pushed back even more than the plant world in Tuscany. Thus of the once rich stocks of game – deer, wild boar, rabbits – the only significant remaining populations live in less accessible mountainous regions. Not only dense human habitation, intensive use of land and disappearance of the original forests have drastically reduced the original fauna; air and water pollution and the popularity of shooting, which claims the lives of many birds every year, have also played a part. About 30,000 white long-horn cattle live in herds in the Maremma, where they are herded by cattle drovers (butteri). The horses of the butteri have adapted completely to the climate of the Maremma.

The Maremma is also known for raising sheep and pigs.

Population · Economy · Politics

Tuscany is Italy's fifth-largest region and has had partial autonomy since 1970. It has been sub-divided into ten provinces since 1992.

Regione Toscana

With a population density of 153 residents per sq km (396 per sq mi) Tuscany lies considerably below the Italian national average of 192 residents per sq km (497 per sq mi). But there are great variations within the region. About 70% of the inhabitants live in the densely populated urban areas of the Versilia and northern Tuscany, which together account for about 20% of the land area. The hills of southern Tuscany, above all the provinces of Siena and Grosseto, as well as the Apennines, are sparsely populated. Here above all – as in Tuscany as a whole – the population has declined in the past decades. Migrants from other parts of Italy and other European countries compensate this somewhat.

Population

Today there is still a distinct division into traditional urban and rural areas. On the one hand the historic cities like Florence, Pisa and Luc-

Cities, villages and fattorie

In Carrara anarchism and communism have a long tradition: two members of the Circolo Communista Giuseppe Ulivi.

Facts and Figures *Tuscany*

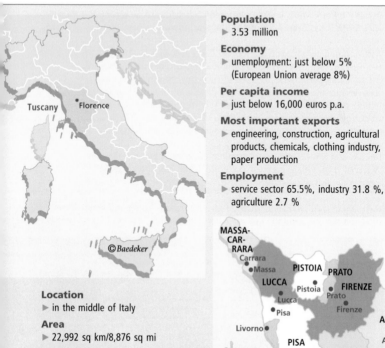

Population
► 3.53 million

Economy
► unemployment: just below 5%
(European Union average 8%)

Per capita income
► just below 16,000 euros p.a.

Most important exports
► engineering, construction, agricultural
products, chemicals, clothing industry,
paper production

Employment
► service sector 65.5%, industry 31.8 %,
agriculture 2.7 %

Location
► in the middle of Italy

Area
► 22,992 sq km/8,876 sq mi

Regione Toscana
► Tuscany is one of the 20 regions of
Italy. In 1992 it was divided into ten
provinces. These are Arezzo, Firenze,
Grosseto, Livorno, Lucca, Massa-
Carrara, Pisa, Pistoia, Prato and
Siena.

Capital
► Florence (Firenze)

ca have an urban culture and lifestyle that have developed over centuries, while on the other hand there is a typical rural settlement pattern in the valleys and remote hilly regions, with villages and many
individual farms that lie in the middle of their fields. The villas of
landowners from the cities, which were mostly only occupied during

the summer and the hunting season, connected the urban and rural lifestyles. They were part of the »fattoria«, the estate, while as part of the »mezzadria« (»half-lease«) system the land was placed in the hands of farmers whose farmhouses (casa colonica) were in the middle of their fields. Even though the mezzadria system has now been abolished and the rural population (currently about 5–6% of the total) has been reduced drastically by the exodus to the towns, this settlement pattern is still characteristic of southern Tuscany in particular. Today many fattorie are used as holiday apartments or second homes.

Economy

Tuscany, like the neighbouring Umbria, lies on the border between the wealthy industrialized north of Italy and the poorer south, the mezzogiorno. Within Tuscany, too, there is an **economic divide** between the north with its large cities and the sparsely populated south. The region has a very versatile economy. Like everywhere else, the number of people employed in agriculture is declining drastically and is presently less than 3%. About 32% work in industry or as craftsmen, more than 65% in the service sector. Florence is not only politically important as the capital of Tuscany but also economically as a centre of commerce and trade fairs, and as the home of large publishers as well as an excellent science centre.

Economic structure

Agriculture remains the economic factor that marks the face of the region. For centuries the system of mezzadria dominated agriculture. The landowners lived in the cities and turned over the land to farmers in a system by which the owners paid half of the costs (for example for seed) in return for half of the crop and other services. Farms tended to be mixed farms, with grain, wine and olive or fruit trees. These have all but disappeared today. Old leases were dissolved and many small businesses that supplied additional income were closed. This led to the formation of modern medium-size to large businesses with high degrees of specialization.

Agriculture Mezzadria

Tuscany mainly produces grain, sugar beets, olives, wine (for example in the famous Chianti region between Florence and Siena), fruit, vegetables and sunflowers. The EU-wide overproduction of wine and sugar are a problem here as elsewhere. Livestock (cattle, pigs) plays less of a role, as does fishing, which is mainly concentrated in the harbour of Livorno.

The production of metals, marble and clay has a long tradition in Tuscany. Iron, copper, lead, zinc and other ores (mercury, antimony) have been mined in the **Colline Metallifere**, on Elba and at Monte Amiata since the Middle Ages. Both mining and smelting have now largely stopped. Only manganese and pyrite are still mined. However, the marble quarries near Carrara and Massa in the Apuan Alps and

Mining

Next to wine, olives are the most important produce …

the processing of marble continue to be important. The quarries for the world-famous white marble go back to antiquity, but today face tough foreign competition (► Baedeker Special p.414). Lignite mining at Ombrone has all but stopped. Geothermal energy from the Colline Metallifere is increasingly being used and converted to electricity in a large power plant near Larderello.

Industry Agriculture is the basis for multi-faceted **industrial activity**. This includes production of sugar, edible oils, leather and shoes as well as wine, and also wood-processing industries such as furniture and paper factories on the edge of the forested mountain ranges.

The textile industry has a long tradition as well – Tuscany is to this day one of the centres of the Italian **textile and clothing industry**, which consists mostly of small and mid-sized businesses concentrated around Florence and especially Prato. New fabric was produced from old clothing in Prato after the Second World War, which earned it the unflattering nickname »rag city«. Today Prato is known both for its leading role in the textile industry, and for high-quality fabrics that are used in artisan production. Both mass and craft production exist in the traditional **glass and ceramics industry** in the Elsa valley near Siena, as well as in the making of gold and silver jewellery in Arezzo. The capital goods industry, above all machine and auto manufacturing, is located mainly in the industrial belt from Pistoia to Prato and Florence, as well as along the Arno valley via Pontedera to the coast near Livorno.

… in the Tuscan countryside

In a region with so many centres of the arts and such natural beauty, **Tourism** tourism plays a large economic role. In recent years an average of 6 million guests (of them 2.5 million from abroad) have visited Tuscany every year. Historic cities like Florence, Pisa, Siena, Lucca and Arezzo, but also the seaside resorts, above all Viareggio, Forte dei Marmi, the resorts on the Etruscan Riviera to the south and the island of Elba, are the main destinations for visitors to Tuscany. Montecatini Terme, Chianciano Terme and other spas are also popular.

? DID YOU KNOW ...?

■ About 20,000 objects of cultural value have been counted in Tuscany – more than in any other Italian region.

History

When it is claimed that urban culture has its roots in Italy, Tuscany is probably the region that best fits the bill. The successors to the autonomous Etruscan cities were medieval city states, whose architectural heritage shapes the appearance of the region to this day.

Prehistory and Early History

The earliest archaeological finds date from the Stone Age. Remains of primitive stone tools and bones from the Palaeolithic age were found near Arezzo and in the Apuan Alps.

During the Bronze Age an autonomous culture, the so-called Belvedere-Cetona culture, developed among the **first settled Tuscans**. Near Chiusi on Monte Cetona, which gave this culture its name, the remains of a late Bronze Age village (1500 to 1000 BC) were discovered.

Between 1000 and 800 BC the transition took place to early Iron Age culture, which reached its zenith in the 8th century BC. This civilization, which spread through northern and central Italy, was named after Villanova near Bologna, the site of the main finds. The last phase of Villanova culture is also the first phase of Etruscan culture, which was later to develop into the first advanced civilization of Italy.

Villanova culture

Etruscans and Romans

Etruscans

9th century BC	Etruscans appear on the Apennine peninsula.
From the 6th century BC	Etruscan city states in the area of modern Tuscany and Latium
Late 5th century BC	Greeks end Etruscan naval domination.
3rd century BC	Decline of the Etruscan states

The first inhabitants of the core area of Tuscany who are known by name are the Etruscans. The Greeks, who were probably the people most closely related to the Etruscans, called them Tyrrhenoi, while their Roman neighbours called them Tusci or Etrusci. Their own name for themselves was Rasenna. Even though well over 10,000 inscriptions are known from the Etruscan period, the origins of this people remain a mystery. They were probably a mixed culture formed from the indigenous Villanova civilization that inter-married with Indo-European migrants, and settlers from eastern Greece and Asia.

Who were the Etruscans?

← *Piazza della Signoria in Florence when it was still open to traffic*

The Etruscans spread

Wherever the Etruscans came from, they did not conquer by force the regions they settled. It can be proved that they lived in the coastal area around the modern towns of Cerveteri and Tarquinia. From the 6th century Etruria extended north to the Po valley and soon after south to Campania.

They do not want a state ...

Most of the population were farmers, serf tenants or slaves; they were ruled by a land-owning aristocracy. The Etruscans did not want to form a state, but instead founded a loose league of cities, in which every city (and the surrounding territory) pursued its own political goals. The higher level of organization was the **twelve-city league**. Six of these main Etruscan cities lay in modern-day Tuscany: Arezzo, Chiusi, Cortona, Ruselle, Populonia and Volterra. The religious centre of the city league was the sanctuary Fanum Voltumnae (shrine of Voltumna) near Bolsena, where the delegates of the city rulers held a council once a year. Etruria was densely populated; Volterra, for example, had more than 50,000 residents.

... and they trade in the entire Mediterranean region

The Etruscans owed their power and wealth above all to their skill at working iron, copper and silver-bearing lead. Their **mining** operations for the most part concentrated on Elba, Etruscan Ilva (= iron), and the coastal region around Populonia. Etruscan metal products were greatly prized in the ancient world and extensive trade relationships existed. They penetrated northern Europe by land and shipped their precious goods throughout the Mediterranean region to Iberia, Gaul, Carthage and to the Near East. Thus there was no lack of trade-based conflicts. After victory over the Greeks around 540 BC in a sea battle near Alalia (Corsica) the Etruscans gained control of the Tyrrhenian Sea.

Rome brings the Etruscans to their knees

In the 5th century BC the Etruscans lost important sea battles against their Greek and Phoenician rivals. Their rule over the Tyrrhenian Sea was long finished when the Romans conquered the first Etruscan city, Veii, in 396 BC. The Etruscan league came more and more under the influence of the expanding Roman state. The lack of solidarity among Etruscan cities was advantageous for Rome. However,

Etruria was allowed to remain autonomous and to continue processing metals for Rome, which used force only when opposition grew in Etruria and the league joined an anti-Roman coalition. The Samnite wars from 343 to 290 BC led to the **collapse of the Etruscan city states**. Etruria was conquered and became an unhappy ally of Rome.

Romans

3rd century BC	Rome expands into Etruscan territory.
From 88 BC	Roman citizenship for residents of Etruria
AD 297	Etruria and Umbria together become the fifth region of the Roman state.

In the 3rd century BC the Etruscan cities lost their autonomy to Rome. Unlike the Etruscans the Romans set about subduing all of central Italy. In order to create the necessary infrastructure for this, **military bases, bridges and roads** were first built. The Via Aurelia, which was begun in 241 BC, ran along the Tyrrhenian coast to Pisa; the Via Cassia via Bolsena, Chiusi and Arezzo to Fiesole; other military roads were added. A few cities, especially Volterra, Arezzo and Fiesole, enjoyed a renaissance. They acquired Roman **temples, theatres, thermal baths and aqueducts**. As an ally of Rome, Etruria suf-

First military bases, then temples and thermal baths

Stones with a history: the Roman road in the Etruscan necropolis Roselle

fered in the Roman wars against Carthage, Gaul and the kingdoms of the Diadochi to the east. The territory made a substantial contribution to the alliance in the form of soldiers and finances. In the legendary battle against Hannibal at Lake Trasimeno (217 BC) the involuntary allies and the enemies of Rome gained new hope, for the Carthaginians inflicted a crushing defeat on Rome. Yet they did not gain the final victory.

Economic decline The 2nd century BC brought the first signs of economic decline in Etruria. The import of grain from Roman colonies led to the abandonment of agriculture and consequently to strong migration from rural areas. Mining, long the wealth of the region, stagnated. The coastal region became swampy and malaria spread.

After the so-called Social Wars from 91 to 88 BC, rights of Roman citizenship were granted to Etruria, but the consequent status of political equality also meant the end of any independence. The exodus from the land increased dramatically. Equipped with the new citizenship, thousands moved to the steadily growing city of Rome.

Octavian, who took the name Augustus after 27 BC, was the first to try to halt the decline of Etruria, which threatened the cities too, by means of a land reform and administrative measures. Etruria then

Who is top dog? The noble families of San Gimignano competed in the Middle Ages for the tallest tower.

became the seventh region of Roman territory, together with the northern parts of Latium, but the situation improved only a little.

In late antiquity Emperor Diocletian redrew the boundaries of his empire. In AD 297 the old area of Etruria together with Umbria became the fifth region of the Roman Empire, named Tuscia – the term »Toscana« only appeared in the 13th century. The region was almost ruined by massive imports of grain from Egypt and Sicily. Mining and processing of ore were hardly important any longer.

3rd century BC Region of Tuscia

With the fall of the western Roman Empire – officially in the year 476 – urban life all but extinguished in the region of Tuscia. Soon only the ruins of great temples, amphitheatres, baths and aqueducts testified to Roman rule.

Fall of the western Roman Empire

Middle Ages

6th century	Lombard Duchy of Tuscia
8th–9th century	The Franks conquer the Lombard kingdom and make Tuscia into a march.
12th–13th century	Cities prosper economically and become politically autonomous; conflicts between Guelfs and Ghibellines.
14th century	Florence becomes a financial centre.

The end of the western Roman Empire left a power vacuum that was at first filled by tribes who were looking for new areas to settle. With the Lombards, who entered northern Italy from 568 under Alboin, better times arrived. As an agrarian people they revitalized **agriculture** and took over Roman administrative structures. The capital of the Lombard Duchy of Tuscia was Lucca. The peaceful rule of the Lombards lasted about two hundred years. It brought traders, pilgrims and craftsmen into the area.

Lombard period

Charlemagne expanded the kingdom of the Franks towards the end of the 8th century into northern and central Italy and subjugated the Lombards. He had himself crowned as Roman emperor in 800 in Rome and became the protector of the papal state. Tuscia became a march, a border county, in order to secure the imperial boundaries. From this time Frankish counts resided in Lucca and San Miniato.
From the 10th century the Holy Roman emperors tried to increase their political power in northern Italy, and made use of the bishops for imperial political purposes. Moreover the **march of Tuscia**, which belonged to the rulers of Canossa from the 11th century, became

Franks in central Italy

stronger. Countess Matilda of Tuscia, in particular, was adept at increasing her holdings and using them politically. She mediated during the Investiture Controversy in 1077 between Holy Roman Emperor Henry IV and Pope Gregory VII in the castle of Canossa. After Matilda died in 1115 – she had willed all her property to the pope – the conflicts between pope and emperor went on for generations. At first local nobles like the Guidi near Florence, the Gheradesca between Pisa and Volterra and the Berardenga between Siena and Arezzo profited politically.

Rise of the cities   Maritime and long-distance trade led to an increase in the political and economic importance of the cities. Textile production flourished in Arezzo, Lucca and Florence, in Siena financial institutions grew, and Pisa took on the role of a powerful naval republic with property and trading privileges in almost all major neighbouring countries on the Mediterranean. Parallel to the economic recovery the Tuscan cities also gained **political autonomy** for the first time; public assemblies were formed, consuls and podestà (mayors) elected.

Neither the emperor nor the pope could prevent the growing self-determination of the cities. The policies of both Emperor Frederick Barbarossa and Emperor Frederick II were defeated by the bitter resistance of communes, which developed into city states and were thus increasingly faced with conflicts between rival noble and patrician dynasties. Communes adopted the tactic of gaining the support of the emperor or the pope. The opposing parties in the communes during the struggle of individual families for political power were named after the battle cries »**Ghibellines**« (the imperial party) and »**Guelfs**« (the papal party). There were constant rivalries between the urban centres of power. Florence, above all, was continually at odds with Siena. At the end of the 13th century Pisa's glory as a naval power had already been extinguished. Its rivalry with Genoa ended in disaster, when Pisa lost its entire fleet in the naval battle of Meloria in 1284.

Pisa loses,   Florence profited more than Lucca and Siena from Pisa's defeat. The
Florence wins   harbour of Pisa silted up and the centre of power in Tuscany moved inland to republican Florence. Meanwhile banking developed on the basis of trade and manufacturing, and the rich guilds of merchants and craftsmen formed an **urban oligarchy** which determined the course of politics from then onwards. In the second half of the 14th century Arezzo, Pistoia, Prato, Cortona, Volterra, San Gimignano and Colle di Val d'Elsa became economically dependent on the Guelf city of Florence, even though they were not subdued by military means.

In 1406 Florence finally officially extended its control over Pisa. Only Lucca and Siena remained independent, and by the time Siena was forced to surrender its autonomous status in 1559, Florence too had ceased to be a city state.

From the Medici to the Habsburgs

Early 15th century	Cosimo founds the Medici dynasty.
1569	Cosimo I becomes Grand Duke of Tuscany.
1737	The Medici dynasty dies out; the Grand Duchy of Tuscany passes to the Habsburgs.
1799	Napoleon Bonaparte takes over Tuscany. In 1814 he is exiled for one year on Elba.
1848	Grand Duke Leopold II flees to Naples from civil unrest.

The Rule of the Medici

At the beginning of the 15th century the noble families in Florence fought over political control of the city. At first Rinaldo degli Albizzi gained control and sent his opponent Cosimo de' Medici (1389–1464) into exile. A year later Cosimo Il Vecchio (the elder) returned amidst popular jubilation, exiled his opponents and increased his political influence by placing people loyal to him in the most important city offices. Cosimo increased the wealth of his family business, but kept the good of the city in mind and established numerous charitable foundations (►Baedeker Special p.238).

Cosimo Il Vecchio

The funerary chapel of the Medici grand dukes in San Lorenzo in Florence

Lorenzo Il Magnifico

After Piero de' Medici's short time in office Lorenzo Il Magnifico entered (1449–1492) the political stage. More than any other person of his time he embodied the manner of governing, lifestyle, world view, education and patronage of the Renaissance man. At the same time he secured for Florence the cultural and political lead in Tuscany by making use of Medici bank funds to the point of bankruptcy. Lorenzo died in 1492 at the age of 44.

The »magnificent« was followed by the »unlucky« Piero, who was driven out of the city because of his compliant attitude towards King Charles VIII of France. The Dominican monk Girolamo Savonarola seized the moment and proclaimed a theocracy, which failed in 1498 due to the resistance of the people and the papacy. Savonarola was executed and Florence again had a republican city government.

Alessandro

Only in 1512 did the Medici return, with the help of foreign troops. Their political success was at first mixed until Emperor Charles V elevated the young Alessandro de' Medici to the title of Duke of Florence in 1531. The murder of Alessandro in 1537 at the hands of a relative brought Cosimo I (son of the legendary condottiere Giovanni delle Bande Nere) to power.

Cosimo I

The expansionist policies of Cosimo I (1519–1574) were aimed above all at the neighbouring city of Siena, which continued to defend its independence. But Cosimo's goal was to create a state including the whole of Tuscany. He made skilful use of the rivalry between Spain, Germany and France and arranged the conquest of

Leonardo's vehicles were built from his designs in the museum of Vinci.

Siena in 1555 by imperial troops. The ennoblement of the Medici reached its pinnacle when they were awarded the title of **Grand Duke of Tuscany** in 1569 by Pope Pius V.

With Francesco I and Ferdinando I a weaker phase of the Medici era had already begun. They concerned themselves only with lucrative dynastic policies that would secure their power and great **splendour at court**. Cosimo II and Ferdinando II allowed their mothers and wives to take the reins of power from their hands. Cosimo III, a religious fanatic, tormented his subjects with merciless taxation policies. The dynasty died out in 1737 with the death of the last, childless Medici ruler, Gian Gastone. During the Medici era Tuscany lost its position as the centre of European textile trading, despite a renewed flowering of the arts. Trade and credit banking were affected, too. In the 16th century the urban moneyed aristocracy looked for low-risk investments and rediscovered land and large estates – the picturesque man-made landscape of Tuscany slowly began to take shape, albeit in the shadow of feudalism.

The dynasty dies out

? DID YOU KNOW ...?

■ where the spheres on the Medici coat of arms come from? They symbolize pills, for the name of the most famous Tuscan dynasty means »doctors«. The patron saints of the Medici were the two early Christian doctors Cosimo and Damian.

Tuscany under the Habsburgs

The Habsburgs with Franz Stephan of Lorraine, who ruled from Vienna as Emperor Franz I, succeeded the Medici as grand dukes of Tuscany. Austria needed soldiers for its power politics and recruited many young Tuscans for the army. However, the rule of the foreign Habsburgs was open to reform in the period of the Enlightenment. The traditional sectors of the economy were revived and a **new legal system** established the equality of all citizens before the law. Agriculture with its feudal structures remained a problem: the land reform provided tenants with no more than the right to be consulted.

Foreign rule and Enlightenment

The son and successor of Franz I was **Archduke Leopold**, who ruled from 1747 to 1792 and resolutely continued his father's policy of reform. He dissolved the Inquisition and confiscated clerical estates in Tuscany. The abolition of torture and the death sentence was a further virtually revolutionary measure. He did not achieve the legal transformation of tenants into landowners, but after failed harvests and famines great efforts were made that transformed swampy agricultural regions like the Maremma and Val di Chiana into arable land again.

In 1790 the popular archduke left his residence in Florence to succeed his childless brother Emperor Joseph II in Vienna. **Ferdinand III**, the son of Leopold, took over as ruler of Tuscany and

Archdukes Leopold and Ferdinand

proved to be much more reactionary. His policy of neutrality was interrupted abruptly by the French revolution and Napoleonic wars.

**From Napoleon
to the
restoration**

In 1796 Napoleon Bonaparte conquered northern Italy, and in 1799
also annexed Tuscany after Ferdinand III fled to Vienna. Napoleon
turned Habsburg Tuscany into a **puppet state** called the »Kingdom of
Etruria«, which was in part ruled by his sister Elisa Baciocchi-Bona-
parte. After the collapse of the French empire Napoleon spent one
year in exile on the island of Elba in 1814. The **Congress of Vienna**
(1814–1815) re-drew the political map of Europe. Ferdinand III returned and ruled the Archduchy of Tuscany until his death (1824) with a
policy of restoration. The principality of Lucca went to the Bourbons.

Popular revolt

Leopold II (1797–1870), son of Ferdinand III, had little opportunity
for restoration policies because of the socio-political impulses of the
French revolution in the early 19th century. Everywhere in Europe
nationalist liberation movements rebelled against the old powers and
dynasties, against feudal structures and princes. Leopold II also felt
the wind of change known as the **Risorgimento**, the Italian movement for unity and independence. From 1830 unrest increased in all
the larger cities of the region. The press supported the Risorgimento
movement, and democrats demanded an assembly that would write
a constitution. Archduke Leopold II was soon forced to accept the
reform proposals of Florentine liberals led by Bettino Ricasoli. During the first Italian war of independence against Austria in 1848/
1849, Leopold II sought the protection of the king of Naples. In Florence a republican civilian government took power. Leopold returned to Florence in 1852 with the help of Austrian troops. All pro-
gressive elements were against him. However, the Florentine-Tuscan
independence movement felt unable to bring about the renewal with
its own resources and thus sought the solidarity of Piedmont and its
chief minister, Camillo Benso di Cavour.

Tuscany in United Italy

1860	Tuscany joins the newly founded Kingdom of Italy.
1921	Founding of the Communist Party of Italy in Livorno
1940	Italy enters the Second World War.
September 1943	Italy surrenders. Villages and cities in Tuscany are plundered and destroyed during the German withdrawal.
1966	The river Arno floods the old city of Florence.

In the decisive war of independence in 1859 Austria lost northern Italy. Leopold II abdicated on 27 April 1859. Under the ruling house of Piedmont, the only liberal constitutional state in Italy at that time, the unification of Italy was completed in 1859–1861: L'Unità. On 15 March 1860 Tuscany joined the young kingdom under Vittorio Emmanuele II. **Florence was the capital of Italy** from 1865 to 1871, when the king moved to Rome.

L'Unità

At this time the industrial age arrived in Tuscany. Heavy industry was established in Livorno, Florence, Pistoia and Piombino. Prato became a centre of the textile industry. The economic upswing also politicized of the labour force. The **Socialists** gained ground, but in the second half of the 19th century liberal democratic politicians held office in most city halls in Tuscany. Despite industrialization Tuscany remained for the most part – thanks to the agrarian policies of the Habsburgs – an agricultural region that was still farmed in the centuries-old system of tenancy.

Industrialization

Tuscany in the 20th Century

In 1915 Italy entered the First World War on the Allied side against the partners in the former Triple Alliance, Germany and Austria. Between 1914 and 1918 the heavy industry of Tuscany worked at full capacity.

First World War

After the end of the war Italian soldiers streamed back to their home provinces but faced immediate unemployment. Labour strikes and rural unrest in the whole region soon caused the ideological radicalization of the political parties. On 21 January 1921 the Communist Party of Italy (PCI) was founded in Livorno, Tuscany. A year and a half later the Fascist movement under Benito Mussolini, later known as Il Duce, prepared to take over government. After the »March on Rome« in October 1922, paramilitary organizations of the Fascists occupied all key positions in the region and the king nominated Mussolini prime minister. The antifascist resistance was stronger in Tuscany than in other places but Fascist forces prevailed. Mussolini's populist policies enthralled the masses, and the labour programmes of the 1930s brought about an improvement in the economy. The construction of the central line of the Italian railways (Florence-Bologna) was celebrated as a heroic feat. The monarchy continued to exist only on paper.

1920s and 1930s

In 1940 Italy entered the war. Tuscan cities, especially Pisa, were partially destroyed in Allied bombing raids. In 1943 the Allies landed in southern Italy. The Grand Fascist Council deposed Mussolini, who was arrested in July 1943. When Italy surrendered in September 1943, the German forces disarmed the Italian army but met with resistance from partisans in northern and central Italy. The Italian

Second World War

Resistenza lasted almost two years. During the German retreat the SS destroyed whole villages in the provinces of Pisa, Arezzo, Siena and Florence.

On 2 June 1946 a plebiscite proclaimed the **Italian Republic** with a clear majority. Vittorio Emmanuele III abdicated. The Christian Democratic party (DC) won the first national elections, followed by the Socialist Party (PSI) and the Communist Party (PCI). Florence became the official capital of the Regione Toscana. The PCI won the first regional elections with an overwhelming majority and took the position of mayor and the top communal positions in almost all Tuscan cities and communities. The PCI remained the strongest political party in Italy until the late 1980s. In 1950 the Sila Law provided for the partial dispossession of Tuscan large landowners – the farmers finally owned their own land.

Catastrophic flood 1966
Florence suffered the worst flooding in its history on 4 November 1966. The Arno burst its banks and the water level in the old city reached six metres (20ft).

1990s
On 27 May 1993 six people were killed by a bomb in the historic quarter of Florence. The massive detonation damaged the southern and western wings of the Uffizi considerably. After years of renovation the Uffizi were restored to their former splendour by 1998.

Since 2001
In late 2001 the restoration of the Leaning Tower of Pisa was completed. It once again became possible to climb the world-famous campanile.

! Baedeker TIP

Tuscany during the war
The Val d'Orcia is an idyllic place, the estate La Foce an enchanting site whose gardens attract tourists from all over the world. It is difficult to believe that war raged here.
The diary of Iris Origo, the former owner of La Foce who made Tuscany her adopted home, brings these memories back to life. She tells of the hardships of the population, of their sympathy with the partisans, of the revenge of the retreating Germans and of the fearful wait for the arrival of the Allies. Iris Origo: *War in Val D'Orcia 1943–44.*

← *A popular photo motif in Pisa: holding up the Leaning Tower …*

Art and Culture

About 20,000 cultural monuments have been counted in Tuscany – more than in any other region in Italy. This includes graves from the Etruscan period as well as medieval city palaces, churches and chapels, Renaissance villas, wonderful parks and private gardens.

Etruscans and Romans

The first period of advanced civilization in Italy was that of the Etruscans. They settled in the area between the Arno, the Tiber, the
ridge of the Apennines and the Tyrrhenian Sea from about 900 BC.
Between the 8th and the 5th century BC they were organized in a federation of 12 cities: Arretium (Arezzo), Velathri (Volterra), Curtuns
(Cortona), Perusia (Perugia), Clusium (Chiusi), Rusellae (Roselle),
Vatluna (Vetulonia), Volsinii (Orvieto), Vulci, Tarquinii (Tarquinia),
Caere (Cerveteri) and Veii (Veio). The dividing line between Etruscan and Roman art cannot be determined in space or time.

First period of advanced civilization

There are no examples of Etruscan temples in Tuscany, but they deserve mention. Unlike Greek temples they were not placed in the
surroundings like monuments, but were embedded into the landscape with sensitivity for spatial planning. Temples rested on a po-
dium, faced a courtyard and had a deep portico. This spatial accent
developed into a trademark of Roman architecture in the following
centuries.

Temples

Etruscan art has been passed down above all through finds from
necropolises. The end of the 8th century BC saw the emergence of
the **chamber grave**, which has several rooms or even large areas for
dances and games, just as an aristocratic house would have had.
Only in the course of the 4th century did the chamber grave make
way for the spacious, richly painted burial hall (Tomba dei Rilievi
in Cerveteri). Vases filled with wine, oil or grain, gold jewellery and
small art objects which were placed in the graves as funerary goods
testify to the Etruscan belief in an afterlife. In Volterra and Chiusi
ash urns of alabaster and tuffstone were produced and decorated
with reliefs. Mythological themes or festivities were depicted, often
framed architecturally with columns or lintels. Their expressiveness
lies in the representation of the figures, which are turned and stret-
ched, rather than in their spatial depth and detail. The Guarnacci
Museum of Volterra and the Etruscan museums of Chiusi, Cortona
and Florence have extensive collections of urns of the Hellenistic
period (4th–1st century BC).

Necropolises, grave finds

Even though the Bronze Warrior in the Museo Archeologico in Florence is an example of Greek influence, Etruscan culture achieved at
least partial independence in the area of sculpture too. Marked
examples for the archaic character of Etruscan sculpture are the Chimera, also in Florence, as well as the Capitoline Wolf, which was
created in the 5th century BC and which stands in the Palazzo dei
Conservatori in Rome today. Typically for the time, the expressive

Sculptures

← *Art for the living room …*

strength of both figures lies in the type and not in individual characteristics. In the 2nd century BC the originality of Etruscan art was lost in the wake of Roman mixed culture. An example is the Arringatore (speaker) from the Museo Archeologico in Florence: the inscription and typical stiffness are Etruscan, but the posture and clothing are Roman.

Painting Etruscan painting has been documented since the 6th century BC and shows – in the burial cult too – **depictions from life**: hunting, fishing and banquets were part of the repertoire of the tomb paintings. An impressive example is the giant of the Tomba del Tifone in Tarquinia / Latium (late 2nd century to early 1st century BC). Without the example of Hellenistic art the great pathos of movement, the passionate facial expression, the modelling of the body and the rich colour spectrum would have been unthinkable.

Rome prevails From the 5th century BC Rome began to expand its sphere of influence and conquer the Etruscan cities, until the last one fell in 280 BC. A new **system of roads** was built, connecting Rome to the main cities of Tuscany. It corresponds essentially to the modern roads. The Romans profited from the Etruscans' technical knowledge, as in the construction of vaults or in water engineering. Cities like Volterra,

The Roman theatre in Volterra:
the builders used the steep slope as spectator seating.

Arezzo and Fiesole flourished. Temples, theatres and thermal baths were built, often using material from demolished Etruscan monuments. The strict axial outlines of Roman cities can still be seen clearly in the colony of Lucca: the two main streets, cardo and decumanus, intersect at the forum, which is Piazza San Michele today. The streets that divide the city into islands of houses (insulae) have also remained. Since the destroyed amphitheatre was used as the foundation for houses in the Middle Ages, its elliptical form is still clearly visible today.

Middle Ages

Romanesque period

Tuscan Romanesque style is also called **Proto-Renaissance** since – unlike the Romanesque style in France, Britain and north of the Alps – it prepared the way and was a model for the Renaissance, just as antiquity was.

Forerunner of the Renaissance

Two buildings in **Florence**, both dating from around the middle of the 11th century, mark the beginning of the Proto-Renaissance: the baptistery of the cathedral and the church San Miniato al Monte. The baptistery, which was begun in 1059, is an eight-sided, two-storey central-plan building with a choir chapel. It is so close to the architectural concepts of ancient times that the Renaissance architect Filippo Brunelleschi in the early 15th century copied the structure, assuming that it was really a building from ancient Rome. The façade of San Miniato al Monte is thoroughly inspired by antiquity. With its green-white marble covering and its geometric decorations it is reminiscent of a reliquary.

Architectural history was made not only in Florence but also in Pisa, where from 1062 the largest and architecturally most important Romanesque cathedral was built. Its concept of a **church in the form of a cross with a transept** and a dome above the crossing, which goes back to Byzantine models, was new. Typical features of Pisan architecture include the blind arcades with rhombus-shaped patterns on the ground floor and the rows of pilasters with architrave on the upper floors, which refer to ancient models. The dwarf galleries of the choir are high Romanesque. Elements of the most diverse styles and cultural regions melded in the cathedral of Pisa to a new architectural language, which became the model for urban ecclesiastical buildings in the 12th and 13th centuries. This can be seen especially clearly in the church San Michele in Foro in Lucca, which not only adopts the floor plan of a columned basilica with transept, but also the system of decoration with blind arcades and marble facing around the entire building.

In the cathedral of Pisa: the marble stripes above the arcade emphasize the horizontal and recall eastern architecture.

Rural churches From the 11th century many parish churches were built outside the villages. These simple small churches, called pieve, follow the basilica pattern and have one or three apses, simple square pillars, and no decoration or divisions of the walls.

Sculpture Architectural sculpture plays a minor role in Italian Romanesque style, except for the capitals. Guglielmo made the figurative decorations on the upper part of the façade of Pisa, whose style – influenced by the Lombard region – shows a love of rich decorative effects and reveals influences from Byzantine, Islamic and ancient art. There were numerous commissions for sculptors for interior furnishings: baptismal fonts, pulpit and altar balustrades.

Nicola Pisano ▶ In the mid-13th century Nicola Pisano from southern Italy received the commission for the pulpit of the baptistery in Pisa. The artist, whose name is in the inscription around the pulpit, here laid the foundation for Italian sculpture. He departed from the traditional square pulpit form and created a free-standing hexagon, which was covered with panels of relief sculpture. From then on many pulpits in Tuscany followed this principle. The concept of reliefs that take up the entire height of the parapets was also new. The figures no longer stand out like silhouettes from the relief background; instead they overlap and give an impression of depth. The **intense study of antiquity** by the sculptor is evident not only in the direct adoption of particular figures and changed conception of relief sculpture, but also in the natural depiction of many individual figures.

Painting on panels did not have a continuous tradition. A change in **Painting**
the liturgy had far-reaching consequences for painting: the priest no
longer celebrated mass from behind the altar, but rather in front of
it. The altar could now be decorated with a painted panel, known as
a retable. This resulted in a new task for painters. The oldest panels
show Christ surrounded by scenes from his life; later saints were added. Guido da Siena completed a retable in 1260 on which the Virgin
is surrounded by four saints. Christ on the cross was another common subject. Byzantine influence can be seen in the fact that the figure of the living Christ was replaced with the dead Christ, his body
turned slightly to the left, and in the strictly hieratic composition of
the figures on all of the early panels.

In the late 11th century the economic rise of the cities began. Family **Palazzi and**
towers were built as the emblem of individual noble families. Their **family towers**
height showed the owner's importance – 15 of the original 72 towers
have survived in San Gimignano. The **palazzo comunale** added another important building task in the 13th century; it was the office of
the podestà and other political organs. The Palazzo Pubblico in Siena
and Palazzo Vecchio in Florence impressively demonstrate the increased power of the urban population. The **Piazza Signoria in Florence** took its present form when many houses were torn down in
the 14th century. A monumental axis was built between the Piazza
Signoria and the cathedral and adorned with important buildings
like the Palazzo Vecchio, the Loggia dei Lanzi, Orsanmichele, the
campanile and the cathedral.
The city inhabitants took an active part in shaping their surroundings: in Florence there was a tradition from the late Middle Ages of
holding a competition for the best design, which was open to everyone, when a public building or artistic decoration of a building was
planned. Another Florentine characteristic was to entrust the construction, care and repair of individual buildings to various guilds. In
Siena a municipal commission for the beautification of the city was
founded. It was responsible for the adornment of streets and
squares.

Gothic Period

The beginning of the construction of the Cistercian abbey San Galga- **Churches**
no (today in ruins), which was built from 1224 as a basilica with ribbed vaulting, a transept and a choir without an apse, is considered to
be the beginning of the Gothic period in Tuscany. In this respect it
followed the **model of Burgundian Cistercian churches**, while the
structuring of the walls with arcades, false triforia and lancet windows showed innovation. The forms used in this church had great influence on the major building projects of the time. Above all the
churches of the mendicant orders made use of this new repertoire of
forms, as can be seen in San Domenico in Arezzo and elsewhere.

Siena and Florence

Siena was to Gothic architecture what Florence and above all Pisa were to the Romanesque style. The Sienese first planned to give their Romanesque cathedral a new look in the early 13th century. At the east end the renovation affected the transept, the straight choir wall, the square side chapels of the choir and the massive dome over the hexagonal crossing. Vaults were added to the unusually high nave. The façade, which was renewed from 1284 by **Giovanni Pisano**, was intended to simulate a larger church through its height and rich sculptural decoration on the three doorways. About 50 years later an even more ambitious plan was made, which did not prove to be viable: the main part of the existing cathedral to become the transept of a new, much larger nave. After part of the aisle was built, significant constructional defects were found by consultants and the enlargement was stopped.

In Florence the campanile of the cathedral was the defining building project for two decades. It was begun in 1334 by Giotto, who constructed the plinth, and continued from 1337 by **Andrea Pisano**. Pisano gave the storey for the sculptural decoration a strong vertical alignment, which was continued on higher storeys. Construction was completed by Francesco Talenti who reverted to cubic storeys with an increasing number of windows with each further storey.

Sculpture
Giovanni Pisano ▶

The sculptural decoration of the cathedral façade of Siena is among the most important figural works of the Italian Gothic period. Inspired by the sculpture of south-west France, Giovanni Pisano and his studio created a complete series of sculptures whose theme was the story of the Virgin and the coming of Christ. Unlike French models, where the figures are part of the architecture, in Siena they stand as an independent element. The architecture became a backdrop in front of which the sculpture developed. On the pulpit of the cathedral of Siena the Pisani developed even further what had been achieved with the pulpit in Pisa cathedral: the basic form was expanded to an octagon. Scenes with many small figures predominate and seem to wind around the entire balustrade. Under the influence of French sculpture the figures are more supple with softer robes and expressive features.

Arnolfo di Cambio and **Tino da Camaino**, who were the assistants and successors of the Pisani, allowed themselves to be influenced more by international Gothic style, so that their sculpture lost individuality and expression. The works of Jacopo della Quercia reveal a more exact imitation of nature and a close study of antiquity, combined with a high standard of Gothic stylization.

Painting
Cimabue, Duccio di Buoninsegna ▶

From the mid-13th century the two main centres of painting, which continued to be strongly influenced by Byzantine art, were Florence and Siena. Their most important representatives were Cimabue and Duccio di Buoninsegna. The style of painting of the Florentine Cimabue shows an otherworldly abstraction. He tried to capture a vision of the transcendental world on a panel. The Sienese Duccio depicts the Virgin Mary in the *Maestà*, which he created for the cathedral in Siena in 1311 (today in the Museo dell'Opera), and the *Madonna Rucellai* (Florence, Santa Maria Novella) in 1285 as unaffected, elegant, almost graceful. His human image is defined by classical standards, and the bodies of his figures are quite sophisticated in form. While Duccio found his models in Byzantium, his colleague Simone Martini, who together with the brothers Pietro and Ambrogio Lorenzetti created the large altar paintings for Sienese churches, took French Gothic as his inspiration.

Giotto took a step that gave a new direction to the development of painting: in his frescoes for the Peruzzi chapel and the Bardi chapel in Santa Croce (Florence), in a constant striving for harmony of proportion and balance he tried to grasp and convey a new consciousness. Realistic detail and rich colours mark the paintings of this artist, who became famous in his own lifetime, and whose influence no artist in Florence could escape.   ◀ Giotto

The painting of the large wall of the Camposanto in Pisa was no ordinary task. Around the middle of the 14th century Francesco Traini worked on the fresco, only part of which remains today, on the subject of the joy of life and certainty of death, with depictions of the Last Judgement, paradise and hell as well as the encounter with death of knights and ladies of the court. The Great Plague of 1348 was the motivation for detailed study of this subject.   ◀ Painting of the Camposanto in Pisa

A crowded scene on the reliefs of the Sienese cathedral pulpit, which Nicola Pisano carved in marble

Renaissance and Baroque

Renaissance

Beginnings of the Renaissance in the quattrocento

Florence was the centre of the early Renaissance in Italy, which developed in the first decades of the 15th century, the quattrocento. The artists were interested above all in the physical world. They tried to describe it realistically with the aid of scientific methods but at the same time to give it an ideal character. Renaissance artists took the works of ancient times for their models. A leading idea of the enthusiasm for antiquity was that the »dignity and excellence of mankind« was based on his individuality, not on divine salvation. Every person was accorded an individual sphere of knowledge and action. This had far-reaching consequences for the arts. The artist, previously no more than a simple craftsman, now saw himself as a humanist, who by the power of his »virtù«, his ability, formed individual ideas into individual works. And in truth artistic creations achieved a level of scientific, artistic, compositional and contextual intent that went far beyond the concept of craftsmanship.

Architecture: Brunelleschi and Alberti

Two persons had a definitive influence on Renaissance architecture: Brunelleschi and Alberti. Filippo Brunelleschi (► Famous People), the builder of the dome of the cathedral in Florence, is considered to be the man who renewed architecture. Clear composition, geometrically proportioned forms, balanced spatial arrangement (in reference to lighting, too), the use of ancient motifs and the adoption of elements of Byzantine tradition mark his work. Leon Battista Alberti, a humanist scholar who also worked as an architect and adviser to princely courts, provided, so to speak, the theoretical superstructure with his writings on the theory of architecture.

Churches

The classical Renaissance façade was developed at Santa Maria Novella in Florence which, with its monumental blind arcades in the ground floor and the white-green facing, tied in to the Florentine Proto-Renaissance. Its features included large volutes, added as a connection between the nave and the lower aisles. The church Santa Maria dei Carceri in Prato, designed by Giuliano da Sangallo, was a pioneering work. Its central plan revisited the old theme of martyrs' churches.

Secular buildings

The search for style manifested itself more strongly than ever in secular architecture. The castle-like residences of the nobility were replaced by the city palaces of princes and the leading families of the quattrocento (15th century). Palazzi were designed to look like monuments with their regular composition, clear division of storeys and a symmetrical arrangement of the façade. An important change in the floor plan was to move the stairs from the courtyard to the in-

Fountains and famous statues decorate Piazza della Signoria in Florence. The most famous is the copy of Michelangelo's »David«.

side of the building. This permitted the evolution of square **arcaded courtyards**. Coats of arms and allegorical references in friezes, capitals, door and window frames glorified the owner of the building. The three-storey façade of Palazzo Rucellai in Florence (begun around 1457) adopted the order of columns of the Colosseum in Rome, with pilasters that had Doric capitals on the ground floor, Ionic capitals on the first floor and Corinthian capitals on the second floor.

In Tuscany the influence of Giovanni Pisano dominated until the end of the 14th century. At the beginning of the quattrocento, however, a **fundamental change** took place. In Florence unfinished buildings required completion: the bronze doors of the baptistery, the cycle of statues on Orsanmichele, the decorations for the cathedral and the campanile – all were challenging projects for sculptors who were expected to express the new ideas about humankind in visual form. Consequently independent, free-standing sculpture was developed, a pioneering innovation that was taken up outside Italy only much later.

Sculpture

One of the first examples of a free-standing sculpture was Donatello's *David* around 1430–1433 (Florence, Museo Nazionale del Bargello). Thorough study of a living model was the prerequisite for rendering posture and surfaces of the body on which bones, muscles and tendons appear. The sensual beauty and nudity of the figure were completely new. The sculptor learned from antiquity

◀ Donatello

without copying it; he knew how to apply it in an individual manner. Donatello changed the structuring of reliefs in a fundamental way by making the background a spherical three-dimensional space.

Lorenzo Ghiberti ▶   With Lorenzo Ghiberti this stylistic change can easily be comprehended: in the 28 reliefs on the bronze doors of the baptistery (Florence, 1403–1424) he created a work that remains strongly related to the Gothic period and takes up early Renaissance subjects only hesitantly. In contrast the Renaissance forms of the bronze statuette of St Stephen for Orsanmichele (Florence 1427–1428) are highly sophisticated: the young martyr radiates stillness and grace.

Andrea della Verocchio, Luca della Robbia ▶   Andrea del Verrocchio's work for Orsanmichele, including the bronze group *Christ and St Thomas*, was mostly executed on behalf of the Medici. Luca della Robbia and his nephew Andrea adapted the technique of faience to large sculptures and created numerous works in majolica. At first they limited themselves to figures in white relief on blue backgrounds; later the terracottas became colourful, as in the frieze on the Ospedale del Ceppo in Pistoia.

Michelangelo ▶   The universal artist Michelangelo Buonarroti (▶ Famous People) worked mainly but not only as a sculptor. Probably the most famous of his works are the much-copied marble *David* (Galleria dell'Accademia, Florence), the painting *The Holy Family* (Uffizi, Florence) and the **Medici funeral chapel** at San Lorenzo in Florence. Numerous Italian artists came to the city on the Arno to learn from Michelangelo's example before settling down in their native regions.

Masaccio's frescoes in the Brancacci chapel in Florence

When Masaccio began to decorate the Brancacci chapel in Florence in 1427, most of his colleagues still worked in the international Gothic style. His Brancacci frescoes and the painted funerary monument with the Holy Trinity in Santa Maria Novella (Florence) initiated a radical change: the **rules of perspective** were followed with scientific correctness, the figures are fixed in a space and shown in rounded detail by means of light and shade. The composition of a scene as a space in perspective was adopted by Paolo Uccello, Filippo Lippi and Andrea Castagno and developed further, while outside Florence the international Gothic style was still in use for years. From 1438 Domenico Veneziano enriched the draughtsmanlike, linear orientation of Florentine painting with intense colours. In the mid-15th century painting also became more open to influences from antiquity.

Painting, Masaccio

Antonio del Pollaiuolo was fascinated by complex ancient motifs of movement, which he tried to capture in his works. Space and atmosphere were intended to emphasize the expressiveness of his figures. The Carmelite monk Fra Filippo Lippi idealized Biblical events in his works by means of worldly beauty, as in the fresco cycle created between 1452 and 1466 in the cathedral of Prato and his *Annunciation* in San Lorenzo in Florence. The frescoes of Fra Angelico in the Florentine monastery of San Marco show astonishing **spatial depth and realism** and are marked by a deep faith. Piero della Francesca is considered to be the great master of perspective. His fresco cycle in the church of San Francesco in Arezzo, which was executed between 1452 and 1466, is one of the most expressive works of Renaissance painting.

◄ Pollaiuolo

The Florentine Sandro Botticelli painted figures and forms that were full of atmosphere and represented ideal types. He placed numerous portrait figures in his paintings and emphasized linear elements of composition. His pagan mythological pictures are filled with a dreamy melancholy; they include the famous *Birth of Venus* and *Primavera*, both in the Uffizi Gallery in Florence. Leonardo da Vinci was a pivotal figure in the establishment of high Renaissance painting (► Famous People). As an »uomo universale« he devoted himself to intense scientific and technical studies, designed architectural plans and also constructed stage machinery.

◄ Botticelli, Leonardo da Vinci

After a period of absolute artistic flowering came a century marked by plague, poverty and war. During the high Renaissance artists mastered the classical world of forms and ideas. The understanding of ancient art had reached a high standard; materials and technique were used to perfection. Florentine art began to liberate itself from the strict model of nature. The perfect balance of classical art was no longer the main goal. Artists were challenged by decay, sensuality and death, while at the same time invention, imagination and expressiveness became important concepts. New genres in painting, such as the landscape and still life, emerged. Next to the church the most important clients were the ducal house and the nobility. Theoretical

Mannerism

interest in the history of art awakened, as the **writings of Giorgio Vasari** on the life and work of Italian artists testify. An example is Giambologna's well in the park of the Medici villa Pratolino near Florence. Its personification of a mountain range was given the form of an ancient giant whose limbs and beard melt into the rock out of which he was sculpted. The boundary between art and nature blurs as they become united as equals.

Founding of the Uffizi

In Florence as early as 1582 a museum had been established in the Uffizi – which Vasari had originally designed as an administrative building – in order to house cultural treasures of the city which no longer had a liturgical function and works of the 14th to 16th centuries, as well as to present examples of Umbrian, Emilian and Venetian, Flemish and German art.

Baroque

Tuscany an artistic backwater

The Italian centres of the Baroque were Rome, Bologna and Naples. Florence never wanted to be a Baroque city, but preferred to hold on to its Renaissance urban features. The few Baroque new or remodelled buildings there were rather sober and reserved. They lacked expansive staircases, ballrooms with ornate decorations and richly appointed door and window frames. The **late Baroque style in Florence** flourished for a short time under Archduke Cosimo III, who employed a few artists in his archducal workshops. Palazzo Pitti was one of the few buildings that was redesigned in the Baroque style; it was enlarged and newly decorated in the 17th century. The much-occupied painter and architect Pietro da Cortona, a master of illusionist ceiling painting, decorated the rooms in the piano nobile. In the second half of the 17th century Pier Francesco Silvani and Antonio Ferri gave Palazzo Corsini a monumental staircase and a richly decorated and stuccoed ballroom, which made the building closer to Roman than to Florentine Baroque. The painting of the choir of Santa Maria Maddalena dei Pazzi by Pier Francesco Silvani and Cirro Ferri is rich but comparatively crude. All in all neither Tuscan Baroque painting nor its architecture achieved the quality of Roman Baroque.

19th and 20th Centuries

19th century

The status of Tuscany in the Baroque period as an artistic backwater did not change in the 18th and 19th centuries. The discovery of Roman antiquities and their reception by artists put Rome and archaeological excavations in southern Italy at the centre of attention. In the second half of the 19th century art schools and colonies formed in various places, as everywhere in Europe. In the late 1860s

*The art of the Tuscan garden:
the park of Villa Garzoni near Lucca*

the Macchiaioli group of artists formed around Giovanni Fattori, who taught at the academy in Florence from 1847. They developed an independent early impressionism that was influenced by the work of Camille Corot.

20th century, art nouveau

Art nouveau left more traces in Tuscany than might have been expected in this region. Art nouveau buildings and interesting architectural details of this style – window frames, painted façades or shop windows – can be found today above all in **Viareggio**, where after a large fire in 1917 almost the entire seaside promenade was rebuilt in a new style, as well as in Lucca, Florence, Pistoia, Pisa and Montecatini Terme. The most famous representative of art nouveau in the region was the Florence-born **Galileo Chini** (1873–1956), who founded a ceramics factory in 1896 and soon gained international attention with his decorations. He owed many of his inspirations to a two-year stay in Bangkok, where he helped decorate the royal palace. Chini later moved his factory from Florence to Borgo San Lorenzo. The close cooperation between Chini and the architect Alfredo Belluomini brought forth the famous, oriental-style Caffè Margherita in Viareggio.

Painting

In Italy, too, avant-garde art emerged from the cities, since artistic movements like Futurism were inextricably connected with the experience of urban life and the industrialization of society. Most young talent was drawn to the cities: Gino Severini, for example, who was

born in Cortona in 1883 and with Umberto Boccioni was responsible for developing Futurism in painting. Amadeo Modigliani (► Famous People), born in 1884 in Livorno, also found the inspiration for his art not in his home town but above all in Paris, which attracted artists from all over Europe in the early 20th century. One of the few internationally recognized artists to remain closely connected to his Tuscan homeland was Marino Marini (1901–1980) from Pistoia. There is now a museum of the sculptor's works in Pistoia, as in Florence too.

Even though Tuscany is not a region where many modern or contemporary artists have worked, their art can nevertheless be found in a number of places. An especially prominent example is the Giardino dei Tarocchi, a fairytale park with fantasy sculptures near Capalbio by Niki de Saint Phalle, who died in May 2002. The sculpture park has now become a magnet for visitors to southern Tuscany. Saint Phalle's artist colleague Daniel Spoerri has followed this example and constructed an interesting sculpture garden close to Seggiano.

Modern and contemporary art in Tuscany

Prato, the otherwise rather »unartistic« neighbour of Florence, has specialized in contemporary art: since 1988 the Centro per l'Arte Contemporanea Luigi Pecci has shown works by Richard Baquié and Willi Kopf as well as Anne and Patrick Poirier. The collection of the textile dealer Giuliano Gori in Montale near Pistoia can be seen only by appointment (tel. 05 74 53 17). Gori transformed his villa and his park into an eldorado for contemporary art. He enriches his collection of classics, including Umberto Boccioni, Giorgio de Chirico, René Magritte, Fernand Léger and Pablo Picasso, by inviting internationally renowned artists to come and work there for several months in the summer.

There are few excellent examples of urban planning and architecture of the 20th century in Tuscany, since most cities of the region have a complete historic urban fabric and thus little room for large new projects. Between 1933 and 1936 the railway station Santa Maria Novella was built in Florence. Its elements of modernist style make it one of the most important large buildings of Italian functionalism, but its marble facing is a continuation of local tradition. One of the architects responsible was Giovanni Michelucci from Pistoia, who is now honoured in his hometown (like Marini) with a permanent exhibition.

Architecture

The opportunities are greater for conversions or restorations of existing buildings. A successful example is Pietro Carlo Pellegrini's conversion of the cathedral museum in Lucca, which was re-opened in 1994. He united four buildings from different eras into one complex, without blurring the architectural individuality of each one.

Restorations

← *Art nouveau architecture: Caffè Margherita in Viareggio*

Famous People

Brunelleschi, Boccaccio, Macchiavelli and Leonardo – most people know that they came from Tuscany. But what about Gianna Nannini, Roberto Benigni and Amadeo Modigliani?

Roberto Benigni (born 1952)

Some consider him to be the modern Charlie Chaplin. It is indisputable that Roberto Benigni, born in Misericordia near Arezzo in 1952, is one of the greatest multi-talented individuals of the cinema today. The **comedian, entertainer, actor and film maker** was raised a Catholic, but (or maybe for that reason) the Roman Catholic church has been a favourite target for his comedy and satire since his first appearance on stage. He began his acting career in the early 1970s in Rome with fringe theatre and one-man shows. He made his film debut in 1977 in *Berlinguer ti voglio bene* by Giuseppe Bertolucci, the brother of the star director Bernardo. Nine years later he had his international acting breakthrough in the comedy *Down by Law* by Jim Jarmusch. His greatest success so far, *La vita è bella* (*Life is Beautiful*, 1997), in which he played the leading role and directed, brought him the highest artistic honours and international film prizes, including three Oscars.

Comedian and more ...

Giovanni Boccaccio (1313–1375)

Boccaccio was probably born in Paris as the illegitimate son of a well-to-do merchant from Certaldo. He grew up in Florence and first entered his father's occupation. Business took him to Naples, where he decided to study classical languages. He remained there for many years and became the author of works of literature in Latin and Italian. Around 1340 he was in Florence again, where he met the humanist and scholar Petrarch and with him tried to revitalize the Latin and Greek languages and literature.

His famous cycle of novellas ***Il Decamerone*** (*The Decameron*), which today is considered to be the origin of Italian prose, was written under the influence of the Great Plague of 1348. In the 100 stories, which are told by ten people on ten days, questions on the morals of love are discussed before the backdrop of a catastrophe that nullifies the restrictions imposed by the law, religion and morality. Boccaccio was an admirer of Dante, and also wrote a *Vita di Dante* (around 1360), along with other works, and in 1373 received the first public professorship from the city of Florence for his interpretation of the *Divine Comedy*.

Creator of *Il Decamerone*

Filippo Brunelleschi (1377–1446)

The Florentine architect and sculptor Brunelleschi is considered to be the true creator of Renaissance architecture. He was inspired to

Renaissance architect

← *The wooden puppet with the long nose is a childhood memory – and it makes a popular souvenir.*

his innovations by ancient monuments, which he studied in Rome together with his friend, the sculptor Donatello. He applied his new insights to the two Florentine churches San Lorenzo and Santo Spirito, among other projects. In a daring synthesis of the early Christian basilica and elements of ancient architecture (columns, pilasters, capitals, entablature) Brunelleschi created spaces with balanced proportions, bathed in light, in which the spatial whole is engaged in constant interplay with individual forms. Among Brunelleschi's great feats of engineering is moreover the massive, self-supporting, double-skin construction of the cathedral dome in Florence. But Brunelleschi also proved to be a pioneer for his painting colleagues: from Euclidian optical teachings he developed central perspective projection, i.e. the scientifically exact depiction of a three-dimensional space on a surface, which opened unforeseen possibilities for painting.

Dante Alighieri (1265–1321)

Author of the Divine Comedy

The offspring of a respected Florentine patrician family, Dante grew up in a part of the city close to the cathedral at a time when battles between the Ghibellines and Guelfs raged in the cities of northern Italy. The young nobleman studied law and then went into politics. In the year of his election to the Signoria (1300), bloody battles broke out again between the noble factions in the city, and the pope sent the French prince Charles of Valois to Florence. The Guelfs were convicted of conspiracy and their leaders were banished from the city. As their supporter Dante was sentenced to exile for life; the sentence was later changed to a death sentence. Embittered and dependent on help from others, Dante lived in northern Italy and later in Ravenna until his death in 1321.

His most important work was done during his exile years, including the *Commedia* in the Tuscan dialect, the fore-runner to the Italian national language. The word »Divina« was added later (*Divine Comedy*). The allegorical poem, which is composed of 100 songs in verse form, takes as its subject fundamental questions on theology and philosophy, church and state as well as the socio-political situation in Italy in Dante's time.

Donatello (around 1386–1466)

Sculptor

Donatello (actually Donato di Niccolò di Betto Bardi) is considered to be the most important sculptor of the 15th century. In his time he was unsurpassed in expressiveness, diversity of subjects and richness of creativity. As an apprentice Donatello worked in the atelier of Ghiberti, as a master he produced statues in his home town of Florence for the cathedral as well as for the church Orsanmichele. Contact with Roman antiquity then brought him far beyond the medieval understanding of art. His *David* (1430, today in the Museo Nazionale del Bargello in Florence), was the first nude figure; his *Gattamelata* in Padua the first equestrian statue; and his *Judith Kills Holofernes* in front of the Florentine Palazzo Vecchio the first completely free-standing group sculpture. The Medici honoured the sculptor by having him interred in the crypt of Cosimo the Elder in San Lorenzo in Florence.

Galileo Galilei (1564–1642)

It took the church a long time to admit its mistake: in 1993 it lifted the ban on Galileo Galilei – exactly 360 years after it had condemned his teachings as heretical.

»And yet it moves!«

The mathematician, physicist and philosopher received a professorship in mathematics in Pisa, the city of his fathers, when he was only 25. He is thought to have conducted experiments here that led him to epoch-making discoveries: the candelabra in the cathedral induced him to experiment with the motion of a pendulum; the Leaning Tower helped him to examine free fall. He developed the laws of acceleration in Padua, where he taught from 1592. In 1609 he made a copy of the telescope which was invented in Holland a year earlier and used it to explore the heavens. Galileo's public support for the heliocentric model of the universe proposed by Copernicus brought him into conflict with the official opinion of the church, which banned his teachings in 1616. A text which Galileo composed in 1632, in which he described the earth as a

ball that rotates around the sun, brought on a court trial. The sentence was pronounced on 22 June 1633: to recant his teachings and unlimited imprisonment, which he spent in Arceteri with a few interruptions. Galilei's famous statement is legendary: »And yet it (the earth) moves.«

Catherine of Siena (1347–1380)

Along with Francis of Assisi, Catherine of Siena is probably **one of the most prominent saints** in all of Italy, and certainly one of the most venerated in Tuscany. The daughter of a wool dyer took a vow of chastity at the age of seven. At the age of twelve she refused to marry, but her family allowed her to enter the Dominican order only after numerous humiliations. She devoted herself to the sick and poor as a lay sister, but also to extreme acts of penance in which she experienced states of ecstasy and visions. Outside the convent walls she worked for the return of the popes to Rome from Avignon,

One of the most honoured saints of Tuscany

where they had been living since 1309. On 29 April 1380, at the age of only 33, Catherine collapsed and died in Rome. She was declared a saint by Pope Pius II 81 years later. Catherine's body was buried in Rome in Santa Maria sopra Minerva; her head rests in San Domenico in Siena.

Leonardo da Vinci (1452–1519)

Engineer, artist and scientist

The Italian Renaissance produced numerous many-sided personalities, but only the genius Leonardo da Vinci united excellence as a painter, sculptor and architect with achievements as a scientist and engineer. Leonardo entered the painters' guild in Florence at the age of 20. From 1482 until 1498 he worked at the court of Duke Lodovico Sforza in Milan. He lived in Florence again from 1500 to 1506, then in Milan and from 1513 to 1516 in Rome, until he accepted the invitation of King François I to France in 1517. Probably the most famous painting by da Vinci is the *Mona Lisa* (1503–1505) with her mysterious smile of wonderful grace. It hangs in the Louvre in Paris today, as does the *Virgin and Child with St Anne*. Da Vinci also worked as a builder of fortresses and devoted himself intensely to scientific tasks. He dissected cadavers, wrote an essay on the anatomy of the human body and illustrated it with drawings. He performed experiments on flight, observed the flight of birds, examined the laws of air and water currents and did botanical and geological experiments. His many drawings, the studies of the movement of the human body, naturalistic observations, designs of buildings and technical projects all prove his universality.

Niccolò Machiavelli (1469 –1527)

Defender of »raison d'état«

As a historian Niccolò Machiavelli was the greatest chronicler of his home town of Florence. As chief secretary of the republic of Florence (1498–1512), despite internal political divisions he was a confirmed advocate of the republican system, in which he saw the best chance of personal development for citizens. The Roman republic, which had placed the common good of all citizens before personal good, served as a his model, as he elaborated in his *Thoughts on Politics and Government* (*Discorsi*). The analysis of his own time led him to penetrating but discouraging **insights on the rules of politics.** Thus his famous writing *The Prince* (*Il Principe*) reads: »The ruler who is best able to act like a fox has always had the advantage. But whoever has this ability must know how to keep it a secret and must be a skilled hypocrite and swindler.« During his lifetime the writings of Machiavelli were known only to a small circle of intellectuals. It was their effect on posterity that made him famous as an advocate of raison d'état, even though Machiavelli merely demystified the religious embellishments of the medieval state and exposed their power mechanisms.

Michelangelo Buonarroti (1475– 1564)

Caprese is a small village in Casentino, a quiet part of Tuscany off the beaten paths. Here, over 630 years ago, the painter, sculptor, architect, poet and scientist Michelangelo was born. He began his career at the age of 13 as an apprentice in the workshop of the Florentine painter Domenico Ghirlandaio. Along with his affinity to painting he increasingly developed a passion for sculpture. In 1489 the young Michelangelo was accepted by the sculpture academy of the Medici Gardens. In 1494 he left Florence to spend the following four decades travelling between Florence, Bologna and Rome. After that he lived in Rome until his death, with only short interruptions. In Tuscany the work of this great universal artist can be found mainly in Florence, for example in the Galleria dell' Accademia, where the original of the famous *David* is exhibited and in the Uffizi, where his *Holy Family* can be admired.

Universal genius

Amadeo Modigliani (1884–1920)

The port city of Livorno is the home of the painter and sculptor Modigliani. After studying art in Florence and Venice he lived mostly in Paris from 1906, where he met Picasso and other contemporary artists. He started sculpting through his acquaintance with the Romanian sculptor Brancusi. He developed his unmistakeable style under the influence of Cubism. His portraits typically depict oval faces, long necks, eyes slightly out of position and lifeless, contorted bodies. Like many of his artist colleagues Modigliani lived his life apart from bourgeois standards. Marked by illness, alcohol and drugs, he died of a cold at the age of only 36 on 25 January 1920.

Livorno's most famous son

Gianna Nannini (born 1956)

Italy's most famous **female rock singer** was born on 14 June 1956 in Siena. She wrote her first song at the age of 14 and in order to earn money she worked in her family's traditional confectioner's shop while studying piano. At the age of 19, immediately after graduating from secondary school, she was accepted by the faculty of philosophy in Milan, performed as a singer in bars and got her first recording contract. Her first LP appeared in 1976. After the hit *America* in 1980 her name was known all over Europe. Gianna Nannini's trademark is her powerful, somewhat rough voice. Her music, in which she often advocates human rights, solidarity and liberty, ranges from hard rock to Italian folksongs to sensitive ballads.

Rock singer

Iris Origo (1902–1988)

Historian and Tuscan by choice

Many people have adopted Tuscany as their home, but Iris Origo is one who also commemorated the region in literature. Her preferred subject was the medieval history of Tuscany, to which she dedicated two books: *The Tuscan Saint*, a monograph on Bernardino of Siena, and *In the Name of God and Business*, a study on the merchant Francesco di Marco Datini. She was a well-travelled historian of Anglo-American descent, who married Marchese Antonio Origo in 1924 and moved with him to the estate La Foce near Montepulciano. She lived there until her death in 1988 – also during the Second World War when German troops devastated the region during their retreat. Iris Origo and her husband supported the partisans and prisoners of war who escaped German captivity. In her diary she recorded this period in detail (▶Baedeker Tip p.41).

Petrarch (Francesco Petrarca; 1304–1374)

One of the founders of humanism

On the transition from the Middle Ages to the Renaissance a figure of enormous significance appeared: Francesco Petrarca, poet and scholar, lover and researcher of classical antiquity, and thus one of the founders of humanism. His family lived in Avignon, the residence of the popes at that time, because of his father's occupation. Francesco studied law, first in Montpellier, then in Bologna, and then returned to Avignon. He soon became famous, travelled and gained influence as the friend of Cardinal Colonna. A key experience not only for him but also for the attitude of an entire age was to climb Mont Ventoux in 1336, the first known ascent of a mountain for its own sake in modern times. Later Petrarch withdrew to his estate near Avignon and devoted himself to his literary work. From 1362 he lived in Italy again.

Pinocchio

The story of the long-nosed **marionette that came to life** has been a hit for generations, both as a novel and as a film – most recently in 2002 by Roberto Benigni. The funny long-nosed figure comes from the pen of

Carlo Lorenzini, who wanted to remain anonymous and thus named himself Carlo Collodi after his hometown. The theatre critic and founder of the satirical journal *Il Lampione* (*The Lantern*) first wrote the Pinocchio stories as a serial novel for the *Giornale per i Bambini*, a children's magazine. In 1878 the episodes were collected into a novel and published under the title *The Adventures of Pinocchio*. Translated into more than 80 languages today, the book has become a classic of children's literature.

Giacomo Puccini (1858–1924)

During his own lifetime the **composer Puccini became a music legend** and was celebrated by critics and audiences alike. His moving melodies were adored by the middle class at the end of the belle époque and have retained their fascination to this day. As scion of a respected musical family from Lucca, he became organist of the churches in Lucca at the age of 14. When he was present in 1876 in Pisa at a performance of Verdi's *Aida* he resolved that he too would compose operas. He passed the entrance examination for the conservatory in Milan with honours in 1880. From 1884 he was the protégé of

? DID YOU KNOW ...?

■ Since the maestro himself wanted his operas to be performed outdoors, his friends took up the idea. For over 50 years the Puccini Festival has been held in Torre del Lago on a stage by the sea in July and August.

the famous publisher Giulio Ricordi. His private life was more complicated, as he fell in love with Elvira Gemignani, a married woman from Lucca, who followed him to Milan. The relationship was made legal only 19 years later. In 1893 the opera *Manon Lescaut* brought his breakthrough, in 1896 *La Bohème* followed, in 1900 *Tosca*, and in 1904 the touching love story *Madame Butterfly* made him world famous.

Most of Giacomo Puccini's operas were composed in his art nouveau villa Torre del Lago. Puccini is buried in the chapel next to his study.

Practicalities

WHAT ARE THE TUSCAN CULINARY SPECIALTIES? WHAT IS THE SPEED LIMIT ON ITALIAN MOTORWAYS? WHAT SHOULD YOU DEFINITELY NOT LEAVE AT HOME? READ IT HERE, IDEALLY BEFORE THE TRIP!

Accommodation

Wide choice

Tuscany offers a broad spectrum of accommodation, which ranges from city hotels with a long tradition and luxurious or simple country hotels to holiday flats and cheap private accommodation. However, the high prices also show that this is one of the most popular holiday regions of Italy. It is possible to negotiate quite low prices in hotels on the coast in the low season.

Bed & Breakfast

Bed & Breakfast Italia, the leading agent for private accommodation in Italy, is a recommendable alternative to a hotel. It offers everything from a room with use of a bath (2 stars) to accommodation in renowned historic buildings with private bath etc. (4 stars).

Information at: B & B Italia, Corso Vittorio Emanuele II., 282, I-00186 Roma, tel. 066 87 86 18, fax 066 87 86 19, www.bbitalia.it.

Guest Houses

Accommodation in monasteries

Accommodation offered by religious communities is an affordable alternative to hotels. What was originally only intended for pilgrims has become very popular among »normal« tourists, since the guest houses of monasteries are generally good value (accommodation with half board between 20 and 40 euros). A minimum stay of two days is often required. A list of guest houses can be obtained from the tourist information offices (▶Information).

Hotels

Hotel categories

Hotels in Italy are officially divided into five categories, from luxury hotels with five stars to simple accommodation with one star. Beyond that there is also smaller, unclassified accommodation of an acceptable standard. The number of stars only gives limited information on the actual comfort and prices of the house, which can vary greatly depending on the season and region. Thus the prices in the summer on the coast or in Florence for a double room are up to three times as high as in the interior. Many hotels on the coast are only open from April to October. Since most guests stay for more than one or two nights, special rates are offered for stays of at least three nights, as well as the chance to book full board (pensione completa) or half board (mezza pensione).

i **Price categories**

■ The hotels recommended in this guide in the chapter »Sights from A to Z« are divided into the following price categories (double room per night without breakfast):
Luxury: from €160/£110
Mid-range: €65 to €160/£45 – 110
Budget: under €65/£45

Florence, Lucca, Pisa and Siena have many visitors all year round, above all at Easter and Whitsun, during the high season (May to September) and for trade fairs, so that **reservations** are always necessary. In most other cities it is essential to book ahead only in the high season.

Agriturismo

Agriturismo can best be translated as »holiday in the country«. The variety of accommodation is broad: from camping and rooms on farms to comfortably appointed apartments and holiday houses in rural settings. In 1999 Tuscany was the first region in Italy to begin evaluating the standards of farms and holiday resorts which are suited for this special kind of tourism. The classification goes from one ear of

Stylish country accommodation – like La Foce near Montepulciano (information at www.lafoce.com).

grain for basic accommodation and service to five ears of grain for especially comfortable accommodation. The classification is increased if the hosts have personnel trained in tourism, environmental specialists or wine experts available as well as typical regional specialties like honey, wine or olive oil. Currently the programme includes 1,400 locations.

Camping and Caravanning

Most camp grounds in Tuscany are situated along the coast and on the island of Elba, but can also be found in the interior and near almost all larger cities. On Elba alone there are more than 30 camp sites, some of them extremely pleasant and beautiful. The relatively high cost of accommodation in Italy also applies to camping: the average price for a tent and two people is 15 euros per night. The tourist information office of Regione Toscana in Florence (► Information) publishes a free camping brochure every year *Campeggi e Ostelli per la Gioventù in Toscana*. Information on camping can be found at local tourist offices and from the Italian Camping Union (see below).

Large selection

Wild camping is not allowed. Anyone travelling in a caravan may spend one night parked at the roadside, in a parking lot or rest stop if it is not specifically prohibited.

Free camping, caravanning

USEFUL ADDRESSES

AGRITURISMO

► **Agriturist Toscana**
Via degli Alfani, 67
I-50121 Firenze
Tel. 055 28 78 38

► **Terranostra Regionale**
Via della Demidoff, 64 / D
I-50127 Firenze
Tel. 055 324 50 11
Fax 055 324 66 12

► **Turismo Verde Toscana**
c/o Agricoltori
Via Verdi 5
I-50122 Firenze
Tel. 055 200 22
Fax 055 234 50 39

► **www.agriturismo.regione.
toscana.it**
Detailed and well-informed website on the various
addresses for agriturismo in
Tuscany

CAMPING

► **Federazione Italiana del
Campeggio e del Caravanning**
Via Vittorio Emanuele II
I-50041 Calenzano / Firenze
Tel. 055 88 23 91
Fax 05 58 82 59 18

► **Internet**
www.touringclub.it

YOUTH HOSTELS

► **Associazione Italiana Alberghi
per la Gioventù**
Via Farini, 52
I-00185 Roma
Tel. 06 48 90 68 86
Fax 06 48 90 77 40
www.travel.it/hostels
www.ostellionline.it

► **Arezzo**
Villa Severi, Via F. Redi 13
Tel. 05 75 29 90 47
Fax 05 75 30 04 42

► **Cortona**
San Marco, Via F. Maffei 57
Tel. 05 75 60 13 92

► **Florence**
Villa Camerata
Viale A. Righi 2 / 4
Tel. 055 60 14 51
Fax 055 61 03 00
Santa Monaca
Via Santa Monaca 6
Tel. 055 26 83 38
Fax 055 28 01 85
www.ostello.it

► **Lucca**
San Frediano
Via della Cavallerizza, 12
Tel. 05 83 46 99 57
Fax 05 83 46 10 07

► **Marina di Massa**
Apuano, Via delle
Pinete –
Partaccia 237
Tel. 05 85 78 00 34

► **Pisa**
Madonna dell'Acqua
Via Pietrasantina 15
Tel. 050 89 06 22

► **Prato**
Villa Fiorelli
Via di Galceti, 64
Tel. 05 74 69 07 86

► **San Gimignano**
Ostello della Gioventù
Via delle Fonti 1
Tel. 05 77 94 19 91

Fax 05 77 94 19 82
Open: March to October

▶ **Siena**
Guidoriccio, Via Fiorentina 89
Tel. 057 75 22 12
Fax 057 75 20 77

▶ **Volterra**
Ostello della Gioventù
San Pietro
Via del Poggetto 4
Tel. 058 88 55 77
Open: March to mid-October

Youth Hostels

There are about 20 youth hostels in Tuscany. An international youth hostel identity card is necessary to stay in a youth hostel. The prices are generally between about 8 and 15 euros per person per day. Reservations are highly recommended in the high season. The youth hostels below are, when not stated otherwise, open all year.

Arrival · Before the Journey

By Air

The most important Tuscan airport is Aeroporto Galileo Galilei (www.pisa-airport.com), just over one mile outside Pisa. There are connections to Pisa from the following destinations in the United Kingdom and Ireland: Belfast International (Jet2.com), Bournemouth (Ryanair, Tomsonfly), Bristol (easyjet), Coventry (Tomsonfly), Dublin (Ryanair), Doncaster (Ryanair, Tomsonfly), East Midlands (Ryanair), Edinburgh (Jet2.com), Glasgow Prestwick (Ryanair), Leeds-Bradford (Jet2.com), Liverpool (Ryanair), London Gatwick (British Airways, easyjet) and Stansted (Ryanair), Manchester (Jet2.com) and Newcastle (Jet2.com). Intercontinental flights land at Leonardo da Vinci airport in Rome. The small Amerigo Vespucci Airport (www.aeroporto.firenze.it) lies 6km/3.5mi outside Florence in Peretola. The airline Meridiana (www.meridiana.it) flies there from London Gatwick.

By Train

For those who do not like flying, the train is an option for getting to Tuscany, but is **less suitable for local travel**, since many small towns have no train connections. Florence is a major rail hub, and can be reached from London via Paris in about 17 hours as an overnight trip. There are also good direct connections from Germany, Austria and Switzerland. The main routes between Florence and Rome circle

The start of a restful holiday in the south

around Tuscany. The coastal line runs from Pisa via Livorno and Grosseto to Rome, the interior line from Pisa via Florence to Rome. Local lines are Empoli–Siena–Grosseto; Siena–Chiusi; Asciano–Grosseto and Cecina–Volterra. Most of the Italian rail network is maintained by the Italian national railway, the Ferrovie dello Stato (FS); this is complemented by several private lines (schedules in the FS timetable). There are different kinds of trains: Regionale (slow local train), Interregionale (mainline train) and Espresso (express train). Intercity, Eurocity, Eurostar and the Pendolino, a high-speed luxury train, require seat reservations; there is also a surcharge on the regular fare (supplemento). There are one-way (andata) and return tickets (andata e ritorno) for first (prima) and second (seconda) class (classe). International tickets are valid for two months, and the journey may be interrupted as often as the traveller wishes. For tickets bought in Italy the following applies: for distances up to 200km/125mi the ticket is valid for 6 hours, for journeys over 200km/125mi for 24 to 48 hours.

Don't forget: tickets must be validated at the departure station! There are special rates for groups, senior citizens over 60 years, young people under 26 years and families.

By Car

From the west There are no car-carrying »motorail« trains from Calais or Paris to Italy, so motorists will normally need to make the long journey on European highways. For those driving from the UK south-east through France the most obvious route is to go south to Lyon, then cross the Alps on the E70 to Turin; or, alternatively and further north, to pass Geneva and take the Mont Blanc tunnel to Turin (European route E25), then south to Genoa and along the coast into Tuscany. The coastal route is the E80 from the south of France parallel to the shore of the Mediterranean to Genoa, La Spezia and Livorno.

Drivers who have been in the Swiss or Austrian Alps before travelling to Tuscany or are coming from Germany or other points further north have a number of options. One is to take the St Bernard Pass, entering Italy at Chiasso, and on to Milan and then either via Bologna on the E35 to Florence, or on the E62 to Genoa and then via the E80 to La Spezia and south to the Tuscan coast. Alternatives from Switzerland are the Simplon Pass and St Gotthard Pass. Further east there is the route E45 from Munich to Innsbruck and the Brenner Pass, then on past Verona to Bologna and west into Tuscany.

From the north

In Italy tolls are charged to use the motorways – either in cash, with a credit card or with the so-called Viacard. This card is available from automobile clubs, at main toll stations, at petrol stations and rest stops on the motorway.

Tolls

 ## ARRIVAL INFORMATION

AIR TRAVEL

▶ **Alitalia**
Lungarno Acciaiuoli 10/12 R
I-50123 Firenze
Tel. 05 52 78 81 (Mon–Fri
9am–4.30pm) or
tel. 848 86 56 43 (24 hours)
Fax 055 27 884 00
www.alitalia.it
Aeroporto Galileo Galilei
I-56100 Pisa
Tel. 050 50 07 07
www.pisa-airport.com

▶ **Meridiana**
Aeroporto Amerigo Vespucci
Tel. 05 53 02 49 10, 199 11 13 33
(7.30am–9pm) or
Aeroporto
Galileo Galilei
Tel. 05 04 30 48
www.meridiana.it

RAIL TRAVEL

▶ **In London**
Rail Europe Travel Centre
178 Piccadilly
London W1V 0BA
Tel. 0870 8 37 13 71
www.raileurope.co.uk

▶ **In Italy**
Trenitalia
Tel. 848 88 80 88
(toll-free)
www.fs-on-line.com

BUS

▶ **Eurolines**
Bookings online and in UK
through National Express, tel.
087 05 80 80 80; www.eurolines.
com and www.nationalexpress.
com

By Bus

Bus tours directly to Florence, Pisa and Siena or which include these cities as part of a tour of Tuscany are offered by many tour operators. These are mostly group tours. The Euroline buses which connect many European cities have no direct link from London to Tuscany; with changes in Paris and Milan the journey time to Florence is about 28 hours. Arrival by bus may be convenient for travellers who are moving on to Tuscany from other parts of continental Europe. Even then, the journey can take some time: for example, the trip from Munich takes about 14 hours, changing in Milan.

Immigration and Customs Regulations

Travel documents

The identity cards and passports of EU citizens are often no longer checked. However, since random inspections are carried out at the border and identification is required at airports, visitors should be able to show their **passports** when they enter the country. Children under 16 years of age must carry a children's passport or be entered in the parent's passport.

Car documents

Always carry your driving licence, the motor vehicle registration and the international green insurance card. Motor vehicles must have the oval sticker showing their nationality unless they have a Euro licence plate.

Pets and travel

Those who wish to bring pets (dogs, cats) to Italy require a new **pet pass**. Among other things, it contains an official veterinary statement of health (no more than 30 days old), a rabies vaccination certificate that is at least 20 days and no more than eleven months old, and a passport photo. In addition, the animal must have a microchip or tattoo. A muzzle and leash are required at all times for dogs.

Customs regulations for EU citizens

The European Union member states (including Italy) form a common economic area, within which the movement of goods for private purposes is largely duty-free. There are merely certain maximum quantities which apply (for example 800 cigarettes, 10 litres of spirits and 90 litres of wine per person). During random inspections customs officers must be convinced that the goods are actually intended for private use.

Customs regulations for non- EU citizens

For travellers from outside the EU, the following duty-free quantities apply: 200 cigarettes or 100 cigarillos or 50 cigars or 250g of tobacco; also 2 litres of wine and 2 litres of sparkling wine or 1 litre of spirits with an alcohol content of more than 22% vol.; 500g of coffee or 200g of coffee extracts, 100g of tea or 40g of tea extract, 50ml of perfume or 0.25 litres of eau de toilette. Gifts up to a value of €175 are also duty-free.

Travel Insurance

Citizens of EU countries are entitled to treatment in Italy under the local regulations in case of illness on production of their **European health insurance card**. Even with this card, in most cases some of the costs for medical care and prescribed medication must be paid by the patient. Upon presentation of receipts the health insurance at home covers the costs – but not for all treatments. Citizens of non-EU countries must pay for medical treatment and medicine themselves and should take out private health insurance.

Health insurance

Since some of the costs for medical treatment and medication typically have to be met by the patient, and the costs for return transportation may not be covered by the normal health insurance, additional travel insurance is recommended.

Private travel insurance

Beaches

The Tuscan Mediterranean beaches are for the most part flat and have fine-grained sand. The coastline is rocky near Piombino and Populonia as well as around Monte Argentario. Sunbathers and swimmers are mainly attracted to the beaches on the Versilia coast at Forte dei Marmi, Lido di Camaiore and Viareggio. Other destinations at the top of the list are **Elba** and **Isola del Giglio**. The Riviera degli Etruschi between Livorno and Piombino and the coast of the Maremma, where the nicest beaches are at Punta Ala and on the peninsula Monte Argentario, are less frequented.

Beaches

Children in Tuscany

Italians love children; this applies to Tuscany too. Here is a selection of activities that children and adults will enjoy:

 SELECTED TIPS

▶ **Capalbio**
Colourful fantasy park – the Tarot garden by Niki de Saint Phalle (see p.310) is a treat for children. In a huge park eccentric fabled creatures live in a fantasy land.

▶ **Collodi**
Every child knows the long-nosed rascal! Pinocchio's amusement park lies between Pistoia and Lucca in a side valley (see p.287). Children can play here in a labyrinth,

explore the pirates' grotto or climb on the corsair's ship.

▸ **Florence**

Florentine museums are generally very child-friendly, and more and more of them offer creative activities which introduce children to history, science, art and culture in a playful way. The following are recommended: Museo per Ragazzi (see p.222) in Palazzo Vecchio, Museo di Storia della Scienza (p.230), Museo Stibbert (p.257) and the peculiar wax figure museum La Specola (p.235).

▸ **Mondobimbo**

Amusement park for children from 2 to 10 years in Via Ponte Rosso (tel. 05 55 53 26 46).

▸ **Siena**

A museum in Siena is devoted exclusively to children up to 11 years old. Here small children are introduced to art and its history through theatre performances and workshops. The children are taught to look at paintings and to »read« pictures. Too bad that the instruction is in Italian!
Museo d'arte per bambini
Via dei Pispini 164
Tel. 05 77 465 17
www.comune.siena.it/bambinimus

▸ **Treno Natura**

A trip on the »Treno Natura« through the Sienese countryside is especially entertaining for children. Old engines or steam locomotives are used. The route goes through the Crete, Val d'Orcia, around Monte Amiata and into Valle dell'Ombrone – untouched regions that will delight even the little ones.
Information under:
Trena Natura, Ferrovia Val d'Orcia
Tel. 05 77 20 74 13
www.ferrovieturistiche.it

Electricity

Italy uses 220 volt electricity; an adapter is generally necessary.

Emergency

▸ **General emergency numbers**
Tel. 113 (national)

▸ **Police emergency number**
Tel. 112 (national)

▸ **Fire department**
Tel. 115 (national)

▸ **Accident and medical emergency**
Tel. 118 (national)

▸ **Breakdown service of the ACI**
Tel. 80 31 16; 800 116 800 (mobile phone)

Etiquette and Customs in Tuscany

Bella figura, a beautiful appearance, is a deep-seated need for most Italians. Everyone who goes out in public likes to dress up, even for a trip to the post office or market, following Coco Chanel's motto: always be dressed to meet the love of your life. When there is a choice, money is always spent on fashion (and good food) rather than furniture or a coat of paint for the façade. »Unlabelled« tourists who stroll into cathedrals with flip-flops on their feet, wear shorts to visit the art gallery, sit in a restaurant in sandals or even dare to stroll through the old city with a naked chest – something not even the tifosi, soccer fans from Juventus Turin, Lazio Roma or Sampdoria Genoa, would consider – are looked down upon with amusement or a complete lack of comprehension.

What is acceptable in Italy and what isn't?

Take an example of bella figura every morning from the baristi, who play the leading role in hundreds of thousands of bars up and down

Coffee bars

When is the best moment to merge?

the country: to prepare steaming espresso they usually wear smart waiter's jackets and snappy little caps; they are the sovereign rulers of the public standing before them, handing out foamed cappuccini, freshly-baked cornetti and of course glasses of fresh water with matchless elegance. A sit-down bacon-and-eggs breakfast is boring by comparison! Break out of the hotel routine at least once and treat yourself to a colazione all'italiana with a slice of Tuscan life thrown in. And leave a few coins for the men behind the counter – service jobs are often badly paid.

Taking photos Bella figura also makes life easier for photographers. Most Italians are happy to get in front of a lens – this reveals their love of theatre. Take the opportunity for a chat, which can quickly develop into a spontaneous casting session. Often the next-door neighbour will want to join in, the children wave over their whole class for the photo session and the padrone insists that the entire brigade of waiters gets into the picture. A photo is always a public event, an expression of joy, of being chosen.

Traffic Italians are also spontaneous behind the wheel. Although the government of Silvio Berlusconi decided to introduce a points system for traffic offences in 2004, southern Italians in particular constantly prove their mastery of the art of living, airily attempting to overtake on the wrong side or parking their Fiats three deep – it's a relief when the chaos then unsnarls and as many people as possible join in with all the gestures at their command. Then the street becomes a living piazza, the machine-like routine of day-to-day life is interrupted. The purpose of all this is to communicate, and only rarely to be proved right, a fact proven by the Italians' chivalrous regard for pedestrians, which is a pleasing contrast to other Mediterranean countries.

? DID YOU KNOW …?

■ A vino or grappa with a cigarette – smokers have had to go without since January 2005 in restaurants and bars. Except in a closed, separately ventilated room. Don't rely on the proprietor taking an accommodating attitude: the fines go up to 2,200 euros.

Arrangiarsi To enjoy life in Italy, approach individual Italians and let them know through a smile or a gesture just how much you appreciate dealing with such a competent and winning counterpart. Do not hesitate to ask for the waiter's first name, and call out a »bravo«, »grande« or »bello« too many rather than one too few.

And if things are not working out, bring the ancient Italian art of »arriangiarsi« into play. With Tuscans and Romans, Milanese and Neapolitans, a sympathetic compliment is usually more effective than a threatening attitude, which – you guessed it – is detrimental to the bella figura. This is a nation that prefers to be adored than to be told what to do.

Festivals · Holidays · Events

 FESTIVAL CALENDAR

HOLIDAYS

1 January: New Year's Day
(Capodanno)
6 January: Epiphany
(Epifania)
25 April: Liberation Day 1945
from the German army
(Anniversario della Liberazione)
Easter Monday
(Lunedi di Pasqua)
1 May: Labour Day
(Festa dei Lavoratori)
2 June: Republic Day
(Fondazione della Repubblica)
15 August: Assumption of the
Virgin (Ferragosta)
1 November: All Saints' Day
(Ognissanti)
8 December: Immaculate Con-
ception (Immacolata)
25 / 26 December:
Christmas Day/Boxing Day
(Natale)

FEBRUARY / MARCH

▶ **Viareggio and Pisa**
Carnival parades with magnifi-
cently and imaginatively decorated
floats.

MARCH / APRIL

▶ **In many places**
Palm Sunday: blessing of the palm
branches with procession.

▶ **Florence**
On Easter Sunday residents and
visitors go to the Piazza del
Duomo for »Scoppio del Carro«.
An igniter shaped like a dove
shoots on a rope from the cathedral altar to a festively decorated
cart in order to set it alight.

▶ **Prato**
Parade and display of the Holy
Belt (also 1 May, 15 Aug, 8 Sept
and 25 Dec).

APRIL / JUNE

▶ **Florence**
Maggio Musicale Fiorentino,
Italy's oldest music festival

MAY

▶ **Alberese**
Merca del Bestiame (1–3 May), a
festival of the butteri, the »cowboys of the Maremma«, with
rodeo. The young Maremma cattle
are branded on this day.

▶ **Cortona**
Giostra del Archidado:
Archers' festival with
historic costumes.
At the end of May elected repre-
sentatives of the various parts of
Cortona compete for a 15cm/6in
dice, the so-called Dado.

MAY / JUNE

▶ **Pisa/Torre del Lago**
Puccini opera season

JUNE

▶ **In many places**
Corpus Christi processions

▶ **Fiesole**
Estate Fiesolana: music, theatre,
dance and film festival, from mid-

June until the beginning of August.

▸ Arezzo

Giostra del Saraceno on the third Sunday in June: a somewhat dangerous equestrian tournament, first mentioned in 1593. The festival is repeated on the first Sunday in September (see p.144).

▸ Pisa

Regatta di San Ranieri: Rowing regatta on the Arno between the four parts of the city, annually on 17 June in honour of the patron saint of Pisa. The rowers compete in historical costumes.

On the last Sunday in June the Ponte di Mezzo is transformed into the site of the Gioco del Ponte, a colourful competition between historically costumed representatives of the northern and southern banks of the Arno.

▸ Florence

Calcio in Costume: ball game in historical costumes on the Feast of St John on the Piazza della Signoria.

JULY

▸ Arezzo Wave

High-quality free open-air festival with excellent artists from the international music scene (www.arezzowave.com).

▸ Siena

Palio delle Contrade: famous historic horse race on the Campo (▸Baedeker Special p.394).

▸ Grosseto

International Jazz Festival.

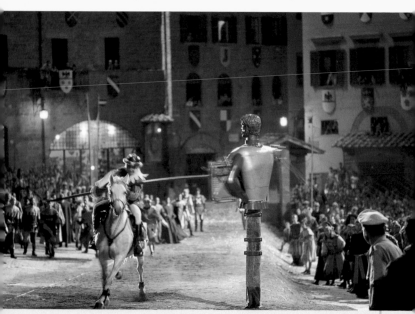

Arezzo: giving his all in the battle against the Saracen king!

► Pistoia
Summer festival with the biggest Italian blues and rock festival. On 25 July Giostra dell'Orso – historical equestrian games.

► San Gimignano
Concert and opera performances on the cathedral square.

► Volterra
Open-air theatre performances.

JULY / AUGUST

► Montepulciano
Bravio delle botti: a horse race just like the Palio in Siena, which has taken place on 29 August in honour of the patron saint of Montepulciano, San Giovanni Decollati, since 1372. Today it is no longer carried out on horseback, but with 80kg/176lb barrels, which are rolled down the main street by representatives of the different parts of town. Beforehand there is a colourful parade with more than 200 knights and noble ladies, banners and weapon-bearers in historical costumes.

► Montichiello
Teatro Povero: the whole village performs in a play which was also written by the inhabitants.

► Siena
Jazz concerts and workshops.

AUGUST

► Montalcino
Sagra del Tordo: on the second Sunday in August every year the hunting season is opened with the Thrush Festival. Pipers, drummers, knights in festive costumes and ladies of the castles form a historic parade, which goes up to the Fortezza, where the best archers of the quartieri (quarters) compete.

► Massa Marittima
Balestro del Girifalco: town festival with archery contest in medieval costumes.

► In many places
Processions and fireworks on 15 August for the Assumption of the Virgin.

► Cortona
Sagra della Bistecca on 15 August: large culinary festival with market in Porto Santo Stefano.

► Siena
16 August: Palio delle Contrade (►Baedeker Special p.394).

► Alberese
Torneo dei Butteri: equestrian competition of the butteri (cowboys) on 15 August.

SEPTEMBER

► Arezzo
Giostra del Saraceno: this competition goes back to the crusades (see June, p.144 and photo p.80).

► Pienza
Fiera del Caio: sheep's cheese festival on the first Sunday.

► Sansepolcro
Palio della Balestra: historical crossbow competition on the second Sunday in September.

► Lucca
Luminaria di Santa Croce: torch-light procession on 13 September.

▶ **Forte dei Marmi**
Satire festival with cabaret, talk shows and video shows – unique in Italy.

SEPTEMBER / OCTOBER

▶ **Impruneta**
Festa dell'Uva:
largest wine festival in the Chianti region on the last Sunday in September.

▶ **In many places**
Almost every village in Chianti holds its own wine festival at the end of September / beginning of October.

DECEMBER

▶ **In many places**
Enchanting Christmas crèches.

Food and Drink

Tuscan cuisine
The worldwide spread of Italian cooking means that Italian food is eaten and the ingredients for an Italian meal are available almost everywhere. However, food cooked locally by local chefs always tastes better. Every region has its own recipes and specialties, depending on what kinds of produce are available. Tuscan cuisine is hearty and very tasty. It relies above all on fresh ingredients – garden vegetables, herbs, legumes, olive oil, chicken, rabbit, pork, fish and lots of beef.

Eating habits
As far as eating habits are concerned, Italy has a few peculiarities. Italian breakfast (colazione) is often limited to cappuccino, espresso or caffè (a strong espresso) with baked goods. But hotels are generally prepared for the habits of their foreign guests and offer a more ample breakfast buffet. Lunch (pranzo) is usually eaten around 12.30pm or 1pm, but dinner is almost never available before 8pm. Lunch and dinner always consist of several courses. They begin with an appetizer (antipasto), followed by the first course (primo) with pasta or soup and a second course (secondo) with a meat or fish dish. They finish with cheese (formaggio), a piece of cake or another sweet (dolce), ice cream (gelato) or fruit (frutta).

Tipping
In hotels and restaurants service is included, but 5–10% of the bill is generally expected as a tip. In bars or cafés service is not included, in which case 10–15% is given as tip. In taxis just round up the fare.

Typically Tuscan

Antipasti
Tuscan ham (prosciutto toscano) is delicious and saltier than Parma ham. Tuscan salami (salame toscano) is spicy and prepared with large pieces of fat and peppercorns. **Crostini**, small slices of bread grilled with a topping, are also very popular – the classic topping is a tasty, warm paste made of chicken liver, sardines, onions and herbs

in white wine. Finocchiona looks at first like a large salami, but is younger and tastes of the fennel seeds used to make it.

Pappa al pomodoro is a tempting paste made of bread and tomatoes, with fresh basil and olive oil. One fantastic cold summer dish is **panzanella**, a salad made of hard bread soaked in water, ripe tomatoes, onions, sometimes cucumbers, seasoned with olive oil, basil, pepper and salt. **Ribollita** is a thick soup that has simmered for hours and is brought to boil again before it is served; the ingredients vary with the region. But Tuscan kale always plays an important part, and white beans are mostly included, too (winter dish). **Zuppa di pane** or **pancotto** is bread soup with tomatoes, garlic, basil and olive oil. **Farinata** is a corn soup with cabbage. A rich variety of various pasta shapes and recipes, which change from season to season and one region to another, can be added.

Primo

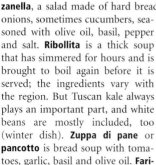

i **Price categories**

- The restaurants recommended in this guide in the chapter »Sights from A to Z« are divided into the following price categories (3-course dinner without wine):
  Expensive: over €50/£35
  Moderate: €25 to €50/£18 – 35
  Inexpensive: under €25/£18

Fagioli (white cooked beans) are a classic side dish and are seasoned with olive oil and pepper. **Fagioli all'uccelletto** is a soup made of beans and tomatoes with sage. Local fresh vegetables (verdure) like spinaci (cooked spinach leaves), quickly sautéed in hot garlic-olive oil, or courgette chunks fried in olive oil taste best. Two especially tasty dishes are **fiori fritti** and **carciofi fritti**, courgette flowers and artichoke quarters in bread dough, fried in olive oil.

Contorni
(side dishes)

Arrosto misto is generally rather dry, a platter of various types of fried meats (chicken, rabbit, guinea fowl, pork chops, beef etc.). The famous Florentine T-bone steak (**Bistecca Fiorentina**) usually comes from Argentina today – seldom is it a genuine Chianina cow raised in Tuscany. Pieces of rabbit dipped in bread dough and fried in olive oil (**coniglio fritto**) are often served with carciofi fritti. **Arista** is spicy oven-roasted pork with rosemary, **cinghiale in dolce e forte** is a sweet-and-sour wild boar stew cooked in Chianti, with celery, rosemary, pine nuts and raisins.

Secondo

The best Tuscan cheese (formaggio) is sheep's cheese (**pecorino**) from southern Tuscany. Fresh (fresco) and matured (stagionato) pecorino of excellent quality are sold in the shops in Asciano, Pienza, Montepulciano and Montalcino.

Cheese
(formaggio)

Bread features in almost every Tuscan meal. It is eaten with ham or cheese, with antipasto, even with pasta, meat, vegetables – but not for breakfast. And the bread is unsalted so that it does not clash with

Bread (pane)

Olive oil is one of the ingredients in healthy Mediterranean cuisine and is getting to be more and more popular in the rest of Europe. The use of good, aromatic olive oil turns even a simple dish into a treat.

A CULINARY MIRACLE

We can envy the Tuscans for many reasons: the mild climate, good wine, food, their lifestyle, the rich culture. But maybe their olive trees are the biggest reason to be envious. Without olives something would be missing from the Tuscan landscape, and Tuscan cooking would also lack one vital ingredient: olive oil.

Olives contain a high-quality oil which can be extracted through simple cold pressing. It is the only oil that can be consumed without any treatment. It may be surprising to learn that Tuscans regard wine as a normal foodstuff. But olive oil is much more important to them. They appreciate the work that goes into making just one litre, because they know how little the trees bear and that it takes many years for them to yield fruit at all. Every Tuscan has »his« oil press (frantoio), where he gets his year's supply around Christmas time. Consumption is high: an Italian family of four uses one litre a week.

Harvested by Hand

Many experts consider Tuscan olive oil to be the best of all. The climate and soil quality are vital, as well as the dense network of oil presses, which make it possible to press the olives immediately after harvesting and also to choose the time and method of harvesting. The quality of the oil depends on the ripeness of the olives when they are harvested. In the Tuscan hills the harvest usually begins in early November and runs until Christmas. At this time the olives are not yet ripe and taste best. The difficulty comes from the fact that the green, red-green or black-red olives have to be picked by hand because they still cling to the branches and can only be persuaded with difficulty to fall into the nets that are spread out below. Beating the trees would damage the olives and the exposed oily flesh would lose its quality and fine taste by starting to oxidize and ferment.

Olives appear to have been culti-vated in the Near East as much as 8,000 years ago. The Phoenicians and the Greeks contributed to their spread but the Romans were doubtless their greatest promoters.

To the Press – as Quickly as Possible

The worst thing for the quality of the oil would be to leave the olives lying on the ground or in the nets. Ideally, olives should go to the press 48 to 72 hours after being picked. The less time they spend in jute sacks, crates or spread out on a wooden or terracotta floor, the less free oleic acids they will develop and the more of their fruity taste will remain. In the frantoio the leaves are removed, the olives are washed, ground and pressed. Some swear by heavy old millstones and intermittent pressing, while others are convinced of the superiority of modern mechanical mills and continuous centrifugal pressing. Both methods produce high-quality oil, provided that attention is paid to strict cleanliness in the traditional method, and that the temperatures are not set too high in the modern process in order to extract more oil.

Strict Laws

Attributes like »cold pressed« and »first pressing« sound good but are only meant to increase sales. They say nothing about the quality of the oil. According to European Union regulations Olio d'Oliva Extravergine (»extra virgin olive oil«, the highest quality level) must be cold-pressed from fresh olives and may not contain more than 1% of free oleic acids.

The same applies to Olio d'Oliva Vergine (»virgin olive oil«), but with a maximum level of free oleic acid of 2%. Olio d'Oliva (olive oil) is a mixture of refined and virgin olive oil (max. 1.5 % free oleic acids). Olive oil is getting to be more and more popular and it has almost more benefits for health than in terms of taste.

Apart from the fact that it is easy to digest and has a high content of vitamin E, olive oil also reduces the risk of heart attacks. While polyunsaturated fats such as those in sunflower, maize or soy bean oil reduce both LDL cholesterol and HDL cholesterol in equal measure, the oleic acids in olive oil reduce only the harmful LDL cholesterol.

So enjoy olive oil, and do something for your health at the same time …

Summer, sun, good food and pleasant company – what more could you want?

the taste of the meal. Dante said: »The foreign bread really tastes salty.« Fortunately most bakers take pity on foreigners and offer one kind of bread with salt (pane salato). A specialty is the Tuscan flat loaf (castagnaccio toscano), made of chestnut flour, olive oil, raisins and pine nuts.

Sweets (dolci) Almonds are one of the most important common ingredients in Tuscan pastries. They are vital in one the best known Tuscan sweet products, the **cantuccini** of Prato, the pretty almond biscuits which are said to taste best when dipped in Vin Santo. The almond biscuits bruti ma buoni (»ugly but good«) also come from Prato. Castagnaccio, baked from fresh, roasted chestnut flour, a tasty flat bread, is at home in all of Tuscany. Almost every restaurant and every pastry shop (pasticceria) sells **torta della nonna** (grandmother's tart) made of shortcrust pastry, vanilla cream, pine nuts and almonds. But every larger town has its own dolce, which the residents are very proud of. For Lucca it is **buccellato** (»soldier's bread«), an egg and yeast dough with orange peel, aniseed and raisins; in Volterra **cavallucci**, round honey cakes with nuts, candied fruit and aniseed: in Montalcino **ossi di morto** (»dead men's bones«), a dry, flat biscuit made of egg whites and hazelnuts; in Poggibonsi **pan co'santi**, sweet bread with sultana raisins and nuts; in Lamporecchio (near Vinci) **brigidini**, paper-thin, crispy aniseed waffles, and in Siena the legendary **panforte**, similar to gingerbread with almonds and candied fruits.

Not everything called gelato tastes good. Gelati that live up to their name are only a few hours old. So the best ice cream comes from ice-cream shops (gelateria) that make their own (produzione propria) and have a fast turnover.

Ice cream (gelato)

Anyone who doesn't want to drink wine with their meal can order beer or mineral water. To conclude a meal everyone in Italy drinks **caffè espresso**. Among foreign travellers to Italy **cappuccino**, a strong coffee with lots of hot milk topped with the famous milk foam, is much more popular than caffè. There's nothing better than a cappuccino during an early morning stroll through town. But beware: if you order cappuccino after lunch, you will be marked down as a tourist at first sight. Italians only drink it in the morning.

Drinks

Grappa is the proper conclusion to a rich meal. Nothing comes after it, except perhaps a cigar. Grappa has to be strong and dry and pleasantly fruity. However, good grappa is rare in Tuscany because the culture of distilling is centred on northern Italy. Tuscany actually has only one first-class grappa distiller: Giovacchino Nannoni in Paganico (not far from Montalcino). Nannoni distils for many wine producers in Chianti and in Montalcino. His spirits are found not in his own name but in those of the winegrowers (for example Altesino, Gabbiano, Nittardi, Mastroianni, Monte Vertine, Poggio Antico, Ornellaia or Verrazzano). If in doubt look for the names of well-known northern Italian spirits.

A grappa to finish off

Health

In many places there is a Guardia Medica for medical help. The medical emergency service at night (8pm–8am) and on holidays is provided by the Guardia Medica notturna e festiva. Medical emergency help or first aid (pronto soccorso) outside hospitals (ospedali) comes from the White Cross (Croce Bianca), Green Cross (Croce Verde) and Red Cross (Croce Rossa Italiana), whose addresses can be found on the first pages of the telephone book (Avantielenco). Dentists can be found in the telephone book under »medici dentisti«.

Medical help

Pharmacies (farmacie) are generally open Mon–Fri 9am–1pm and 4–7.30pm. They are closed on alternate Wednesdays or Saturdays.

► **Medical emergency service**
Tel. 118

► **24-hour medical service (English spoken)**
Tel. 055 47 54 11

Every pharmacy displays in the window or door a list of pharmacies (farmacie di turno) which are open at night and on holidays.

Information

▶ USEFUL ADDRESSES

▶ **Italian National Tourist Office ENIT (Ente Nazionale Italiano per il Turismo)**
www.italiantourism.com

IN AUSTRALIA

▶ **Italian Government Tourist Office**
Level 4, 46 Market Street
NSW 2000 SIDNEY
Tel. 02 92 621 666

IN CANADA

▶ **Italian Government Tourist Office**
175 Bloor Street E, Suite 907
Toronto M4W 3R8
Tel. 416 925 48 82

IN UK

▶ **Italian State Tourist Board**
1 Princes Street
London W1B 2AY
Tel. 207 408 12 54

IN USA

▶ **Italian State Tourist Board**
630 Fifth Avenue, Suite 1565
10111 New York
Tel. 212 245 48 22

INTERNET

▶ **www.turismo.toscana.it**
To get started: overview of the region, events, excursions, accommodation and much more.

▶ **www.emmeti.it**
Descriptions of museums and accommodations in the larger towns in Tuscany.

▶ **www.tuscany.net**
Short introduction to the most important destinations and accommodation.

▶ **www.turismoverde.com**
Tips and lots of background information on Siena and surroundings: Along with the usual tourist information there are, for example, legends associated with the region.

▶ **www.chianti.it**
Everything about the Chianti region, for example, wineries, gastronomy, accommodation and cultural highlights.

▶ **www.hotelsearch.it/alberghi/ campeggi-toscana.htm**
Overview of hotels, guest houses and camp grounds.

▶ **www.rivieratoscana.com/en/ct**
Sightseeing attractions on the Tuscan coast, many practical tips.

▶ **www.arca.net/uffizi**
The Uffizi gallery in the net

IN TUSCANY

▶ **Assessorato Regionale al Turismo**
Via di Novoli 26
I-50127 Firenze
Tel. 05 54 38 21 11
Fax 05 54 38 30 64
www.regione.toscana.it
There are tourist offices in all of the larger communities in Tus-

cany, the Aziende di Promozione Turistica (APT). See addresses under Sights from A to Z

EMBASSIES AND CONSULATES IN ITALY

► **Australian Embassy in Rome**
Via Antonio Bosio 5
Tel. 06 85 27 21
www.italy.embassy.gov.au

► **British Embassy in Rome**
Via XX Settembre 80A
Tel. 06 422 00 001
www.britishembassy.gov.uk

► **British Consulate in Florence**
Lungarno Corsini 2
Tel. 055 28 41 33

► **Canadian Embassy in Rome**
Via Zara 30
Tel. 06 44 59 81
www.canada.it

► **Embassy of the Republic of Ireland in Rome**
Piazza Campitelli 3
Tel. 069 697 91 21
www.ambasciata-irlanda.it

► **New Zealand Embassy in Rome**
Via Zara 28
Tel. 06 441 71 71
www.nzembassy.com

► **United States Embassy in Rome**
Via Vittorio Veneto 119
Tel. 06 4 67 41
www.usis.it

► **United States Consulate in Florence**
Lungarno Amerigo Vespucci 38
Tel. 055 26 69 51

Language

Many Italian dialects can be heard in Tuscany. However, communication is not a problem compared with other regions, since the Tuscan dialect is the foundation for written Italian. Anyone who tries to speak a little Italian – no matter how ungrammatical and incorrect – usually gains much support and is rewarded with a sincere »brava« or »bravo«, which means »well done«.

Italian Phrases

At a glance

Sì / No	Yes / No
Per favore / Grazie	Please / Thank you
Non c'è di che	You're welcome
Scusi! / Scusa!	Excuse me!
Come dice?	Pardon?
Non La / ti capisco	I don't understand you

Parlo solo un po' di ...	I only speak a little
Mi può aiutare, per favore?	Could you help me?
Vorrei ...	I would like ...
(Non) mi piace	I (don't) like that
Ha ...?	Do you have ...?
Quanto costa?	How much does it cost?
Che ore sono? / Che ora è?	What time is it?
Come sta? / Come stai?	How are you?
Bene, grazie. E Lei / tu?	Fine, thanks. And you?

Travelling

a sinistra	left
a destra	right
diritto	straight ahead
vicino / lontano	close / far
Quanti chilometri sono?	How far is it (in kilometres)?
Vorrei noleggiare ...	I would like to rent ...
... una macchina	... a car
... una bicicletta	... a bicycle
... una barca	... a boat
Scusi, dov'è ...?	Excuse me, where is ...?
la stazione centrale	the main railway station
la metro(politana)	the underground
l'aeroporto	the airport
all'albergo	to the hotel
Ho un guasto.	I had a breakdown.
Mi potrebbe mandare ...	Could you send me ...
... un carro-attrezzi?	... a tow truck?
Scusi, c'è un'officina qui?	Is there a garage here?
Dov'è la prossima stazione di servizio?	Where is the next petrol station?
benzina normale	normal petrol
super / gasolio	super / diesel
deviazione	detour
senso unico	one-way street
sbarrato	closed
rallentare	drive slowly
tutti direzioni	all directions
tenere la destra	drive right
zona di silenzio	honking not allowed
zona tutelata inizio	no parking zone
aiuto!	help!
attenzione!	careful!
Chiami subito ...	Please call ... quickly
... un'autoambulanza	... an ambulance
... la polizia	... the police

Going Out

Scusi, mi potrebbe indicare ...?	Where is there ...?
... un buon ristorante?	... a good restaurant?
... un locale tipico?	... a typical restaurant?
C'è una gelateria qui vicino?	Is there an ice-cream shop here?
Può riservarci per stasera	Could I reserve a table for to-night
... un tavolo per quattro persone?	... for four people?
Alla Sua salute!	Cheers!
Il conto, per favore.	The bill, please.
Andava bene?	Did it taste good?
Il mangiare era eccellente.	The food was excellent.
Ha un programma delle manifestazioni?	Do you have a calendar of events?

Shopping

Dov'è si può trovare ...?	Where can I find ...?
... una farmacia	... a pharmacy
... un panificio	... a bakery
... un negozio di articoli fotografici	... a photography shop
... un grande magazzino	... a department store?

A beautiful setting: Piazza della Signoria in Florence

... un negozio di generi alimentari	... a grocery shop
... il mercato	... the market
... il supermercato	... the supermarket
... il tabaccaio	... the tobacconist
... il giornalaio	... the newspaper stand

Accommodation

Scusi, potrebbe consigliarmi ...?	Could you please ... recommend?
... un albergo	... a hotel
... una pensione	... a guesthouse
Ho prenotato una camera.	I have reserved a room.
È libera ...?	Do you still have ...?
... una singola	... a single room
... una doppia	... a double room
... con doccia / bagno	... with shower / bath
... per una notte	... for one night
... per una settimana	... for one week
... con vista sul mare	... with a sea view
Quanto costa la camera ...?	How much does the room cost ...?
... con la prima colazione?	... with breakfast?
... a mezza pensione?	... with half board?

Doctor and Pharmacy

Mi può consigliare un buon medico?	Could you recommend a good doctor?
Mi può dare una medicina per ...	Please give me medicine for ...
Soffro di diarrea.	I have diarrhoea.
Ho mal di pancia.	I have a stomach ache.
... mal di testa	... head ache
... mal di gola	... sore throat
... mal di denti	... tooth ache
... influenza	... the flu
... tosse	... a cough
... la febbre	... a fever
... scottatura solare	... sunburn
... costipazione	... constipation

Numbers

zero	0	cinque	5
uno	1	sei	6
due	2	sette	7
tre	3	otto	8
quattro	4	nove	9

dieci	10	quaranta	40
undici	11	cinquanta	50
dodici	12	sessanta	60
tredici	13	settanta	70
quattordici	14	ottanta	80
quindici	15	novanta	90
sedici	16	cento	100
diciassette	17	centouno	101
diciotto	18	mille	1000
diciannove	19	duemille	2000
venti	20	diecimila	10,000
ventuno	21	un quarto	1/4
trenta	30	un mezzo	1/2

Menu

Prima Colazione	*Breakfast*
caffè, espresso	small coffee, no milk
caffè macchiato	small coffee, a little milk
caffe latte	coffee with milk
cappuccino	coffee with foamy milk
tè al latte / al limone	tea with milk / lemon
cioccolata	hot chocolate
frittata	omelette/pancake
pane / panino / pane tostato	bread / roll / toast
burro	butter
salame	sausage
prosciutto	ham
miele	honey
marmellata	jam
iogurt	yoghurt

Antipasti	*Starters*
affettato misto	mixed cold meats
anguilla affumicata	smoked eel
melone e prosciutto	melon with ham
vitello tonnato	cold roast veal with tuna sauce

primi piatti	*pasta and rice dishes, soups*
pasta	noodles
fettuccine / tagliatelle	ribbon noodles
gnocchi	small potato dumplings
polenta (alla valdostana)	maize pudding (with cheese)
vermicelli	thin spaghetti
minestrone	thick vegetable soup

Wonderful Tuscan black olives (olive nere)

pastina in brodo	meat broth with thin noodles
zuppa di pesce	fish soup

Carni e Pesce	*Meat and Fish*
agnello	lamb
ai ferri / alla griglia	from the grill
aragosta	lobster
brasato	roast
coniglio	rabbit
cozze / vongole	mussels / clams
fegato	liver
fritto di pesce	fried fish
gambero, granchio	shrimp
maiale	pork
manzo / bue	beef / ox
pesce spada	swordfish
platessa	plaice
pollo	chicken
rognoni	kidneys
salmone	salmon
scampi fritti	fried langoustines
sogliola	sole
tonno	tuna
trota	trout
vitello	veal

Verdura	*Vegetables*
asparagi	asparagus
carciofi	artichoke
carote	carrot

cavolfiore	cauliflower
cavolo	cabbage
cicoria belga	chicory
cipolle	onions
fagioli	white beans
fagiolini	green beans
finocchi	fennel
funghi	mushrooms
insalata mista / verde	mixed / green salad
lenticchie	lentils
melanzane	aubergine
patate	potatoes
patatine fritte	French fries
peperoni	paprika
pomodori	tomatoes
spinaci	spinach
zucca	pumpkin

Formaggi	*Cheese*
parmigiano	Parmesan
pecorino	sheep's cheese
ricotta	cottage cheese

Dolci e frutta	*Sweets and Fruit*
cassata	ice cream with candied fruit
coppa assortita	mixed ice cream cup
coppa con panna	ice cream cup with whipped cream
tirami su	sponge with mascarpone cream
zabaione	egg cream
zuppa inglese	trifle

Bevande	*Beverages*
acqua minerale	mineral water
aranciata	orangeade
bibita	refreshment
bicchiere	glass
birra scura / chiara	dark / light beer
birra alla spina	draught beer
birra senza alcool	non-alcoholic beer
bottiglia	bottle
con ghiaccio	with ice
digestivo	after-dinner liqueur
gassata/con gas	carbonated
liscia/senza gas	not carbonated

secco	dry
spumante	sparkling wine
succo	fruit juice
vino bianco / rosato / rosso	white / rosé / red wine
vino della casa	house wine

Language courses in Tuscany

Various institutes offer Italian language courses in Tuscany. Both beginners' and advanced courses are available and generally last – depending on the intensity – from two to four weeks. Along with these regular courses there are also holiday courses which include hotel and full board along with the lessons.

FLORENCE

▸ **CDV Centro Pontevecchio**
Piazza del Mercato Nuovo 1
Tel. 055 29 45 11
Fax 055 238 68 87
info@cpv.it

▸ **Centro Koinè**
Via Pandolfini 27
Tel. 055 21 38 81
Fax 055 21 69 49
www.koinecenter.com

▸ **Macchiavelli**
Piazza S. Spirito 4
Tel. 055 239 69 66
Fax 055 28 08 00
www.centromachiavelli.it

▸ **Scuola Lorenzo de Medici**
Via Faenza 43
Tel. 055 28 73 60, fax 055 239 89 20
www.lorenzodemedici.it

MONTEPULCIANO

▸ **Il Sasso – Scuola di Italiano**
Via di Gracciano nel Corso 2
Tel. 05 78 75 83 11

Fax 05 78 75 75 47
www.ilsasso.com

PISA

▸ **Instituto Linguistico Mediterraneo**
Via C. Battisti 3
Tel. 050 50 03 99
Fax 050 481 57
www.ilm.it

SIENA

▸ **Saena Julia**
Via Monna Agnese 20
Tel. 05 77 441 55
Fax 05 77 28 31 62
www.saenaiulia.it

▸ **Scuola Leonardo da Vinci**
Via del Paradiso 16
Tel. 057 724 90 97
Fax 057 724 90 96
www.scuolaleonardo.com

VIAREGGIO

▸ **Centro Culturale Giacomo Puccini**
Via G. Vespucci 173
Tel. 05 84 43 02 53
Fax 05 84 96 12 75
www.centropuccini.it

Literature and Film

Boccaccio, Giovanni: The Decameron. Penguin Classics 2003. Collection of 100 stories, which were written after the great plague in Florence in 1348 and are considered to be the genesis of Italian prose.   Fiction

Collodi, Carlo: The Adventures of Pinocchio. Simply Read Books 2002. The imaginative story of the long-nosed wooden puppet, wonderful for old and young.

Dante Alighieri, The Divine Comedy. Everyman's Library. Dante's chief work, an allegorical epic poem in the Tuscan dialect composed from 1311, contains many references to current events and contemporaries of Dante.

Forster, E. M.: Room with a View. Bantam Classics 1988. Florence 1907: an Englishwoman on a cultural journey falls in love with a young aesthete. At first she denies her feelings, but then she finds the courage to choose against all conventions.

Fruttero, Carlo und Lucentini, Franco: An Enigma by the Sea. Chatto and Windus 1994. A detective thriller set on the Tuscan coast, one of a series of gripping mysteries by the successful duo.

Nabb, Magdalena: Death of an Englishman. Soho Crime 2001. Thrill crime novel with the somewhat slow Inspector Maresciallo Guarnaccia as the focus.

Origo, Iris: The Merchant of Prato. David R. Godine 1986. The diary of Francesco di Marco Datini, a businessman from Prato in the early Renaissance.

 Tuscany in the movies

- Eight and a Half: an amusing self-portrait by Fellini with Marcello Mastroianni.
- The English Patient: set in the last days of World War II in the deserted and mined Villa San Girolomo in Tuscany, among other places.
- Life is Beautiful: Benigni succeeded here in making the tragedy of the Holocaust the subject of a bittersweet comedy.
- Tea with Mussolini: a group of English ladies who have been interned in Tuscany believe themselves to be under Mussolini's special protection.
- Room with a View: very beautiful, atmospheric adaptation of E.M. Forster's novel. Incidentally, there were Baedeker guidebooks back then too: when young Lucy Honeychurch strolled through the streets of Florence she always had the red guidebook with her to satisfy her thirst for knowledge.

Origo, Iris: War in Val D'Orcia: An Italian War Diary, 1943-1944. David R. Godine 1995. Description of the war years in Val d'Orcia (▶ Baedeker Tip p.41).

Pratolini, Vasco: A Tale of Poor Lovers. Monthly Review Press, 1988. Life and love in Florence in Fascist times.

Mayes, Frances: Under the Tuscan Sun. Broadway Books 1999. Autobiographical, romantic love story; an American declaration of love for Tuscany!

Non-fiction **Hibbert, Christopher**. The Rise and Fall of the House of Medici. Penguin Books. Readable account by a leading cultural historian.

Hibbert, Christopher: Florence: The Biography of a City. Penguin Books 1994. An excellent account of the history of the city.

Burke, Peter: The Italian Renaissance: Culture and Society in Italy. Polity Books 1999. A standard work on a great period in the history of Tuscany

Vasari, Giorgio: The Lives of the Artists. Oxford World's Classics 1998. Around 1550 Vasari wrote his entertaining short biographies of the famous artists of his time.

Media

Daily *La Repubblica*, Italy's biggest-selling daily newspaper, is published in
newspapers Florence with a local section. *Corriere della Sera* is the number two national newspaper. *La Stampa* and *Il Secolo XIX* from Turin are leading newspapers read outside their home region.
La Nazione is the largest Tuscan daily newspaper and published in Florence, followed by Livorno's *Il Tirreno*, which is mainly read along the Tuscan coast. Leading European newspapers are available in the larger cities and in popular tourist locations.

Calendar The monthly *Firenze Spettacolo* in Florence has information on all
of events important events. The tourist information centres and the hotels also have the twice-monthly *Firenze Concierge Information*. It is published in English and Italian.

Money

Euro On 1 January 2002 the euro became the official currency of Italy.

Currency Citizens of EU members countries may import to and export from
regulations Italy unlimited amounts in euros.

Banks With few exceptions the banks are open Mon–Fri 8.30am–1pm; afternoons vary (about 2.30–3.30pm). On days before holidays (prefestivi) the banks close at 11.20am.

HELPFUL INFORMATION

LOST CARD?

In the event of lost bank or credit cards contact the following offices in Italy or the number given by the bank in your home country:

► **Eurocard/MasterCard**
Tel. 800 / 87 08 66

► **Visa**
Tel. 800 / 81 90 14

► **American Express**
Tel. 800 / 86 40 46

► **Diners Club (Rome office)**
Tel. 06 / 35 75 33 3
Have the bank sort code, account number and card number as well as the expiry date ready.

EXCHANGE RATES

► **1 € = 1.35 US$**
► **1 US$ = 0.74 €**
► **1 £ = 1.47 €**
► **1 € = 0.68 £**

Cash is available at ATM machines without problems round the clock by using credit and debit cards with a PIN. Credit cards have limits.

ATM machines, debit cards

Loss of a card must be reported immediately.
Most international credit cards are accepted by banks, hotels, restaurants, car rentals and many shops.

Credit cards

In Italy customers are required to request and keep a receipt (ricevuta fiscale or scontrino). It can happen that a customer is asked to show a receipt after leaving a shop. This is intended to make tax evasion more difficult.

Receipts

Post · Communications

Italian post offices offer regular mail and package delivery services as well as postal banking services. They are open Mon–Fri 8.25am–1.45pm and Sat 8.25am–noon. Post offices close at noon on the last day of the month.

Post offices

Postage stamps (francobolli) can be bought in post offices or – more quickly – in tobacco shops, which have the »T« sign (tabacchi). In towns the next tobacco shop is never far away.
Letters up to 20g/0.7oz and postcards within Italy and to EU countries cost 0.41 euros, airmail 0.62 euros.

Postage stamps

COUNTRY CODES

▶ **From Italy**
to other countries: 00 followed by the country code, e.g.
to UK: 0044
to USA: 001

▶ **From other countries to Italy:**
+39

CITY AREA CODES

The local area codes are part of the Italian telephone numbers. Both in local calls and when calling from foreign countries, the area code including the 0 must also be dialled.

TELEPHONE DIRECTORY INQUIRIES

In Italy tel. 12
Abroad tel. 4176

FEES

Cheaper rates apply daily from 10pm to 8am and on weekends.

Telephoning | Phone calls to other countries can be made from public telephone booths with an orange telephone receiver symbol. They work with coins (only a few) or with telephone cards (carta telefonica), which can be bought in bars, newspapers stands or tobacco shops.

Important | Area codes are part of the Italian telephone numbers. This means that the area code including the initial 0 must always be dialled when calling from another country as well as locally.

Mobile phones | The use of mobile telephones from other countries is generally problem-free in Italy. The two most frequented telephone networks are Telecom Italia Mobile (Number 2 22 01) and Omnitel Pronto Italia (Number 2 22 10).

Prices and Discounts

In Tuscany there are unfortunately no significant tourist discounts such as a special Tuscany Card. Entrance fees and opening hours can be found in the internet at www.firenzemusei.it or www.sbas.firenze.it.

▶ WHAT DOES IT COST?

Three-course meal
€20–35

Simple meal
€8 – 12

Espresso
from €1.50

Petrol
about €1 per litre

Shopping

For shoes or clothing, electrical appliances, pasta or wine, in markets, in boutiques or in factory outlets – Italy in general and Tuscany in particular are a shopper's paradise.

Visitors who like to preserve their holiday memories with something culinary will be spoiled for choice by the huge selection of tasty foods and delicious local products. Tuscan wines come first ►wines, above all the top vintages of Chianti Classico (► Baedeker Special p.114), Brunello di Montalcino and Vino Nobile from Montepulciano.
Tuscan olive oil is also famous (► Baedeker Special p.84), as are the cheeses, especially the various kinds of pecorino, the air-cured wild boar ham and the delicious sausages. Nibblers will love the countless pastries and cakes, including the famous Sienese panforte and the Luccan chestnut bread. Gourmet products and other fresh foods can be bought on markets, which are still an important institution of Tuscan community life.

The region is famous for exquisite fashion and beautifully made leather products – from shoes to belts and bags to wallets or gloves –

A special treat: the famous Sienese panforte

but also for fine accessories, wonderful fabrics and jewellery. Especially in Florence and Prato, but also in Siena, Pisa or Lucca the well-known labels have their own shops. The factory outlets in Prato are famous for bargains (▸Sights from A to Z, Prato).

Wine ▸p.110.

Kitsch or art?
No matter whether it's a miniature *David* or a somewhat more original work of art – marble products from Carrara or Pietrasanta and alabaster work from Volterra are probably the best-known crafts to be bought locally, sometimes even directly from the workshop. Pottery has a long tradition in Tuscany and a high level of craftsmanship. The selection of pottery for everyday use and ornaments of all kinds is large, and ceramics with traditional patterns and motifs are especially in demand. Tuscany is also known for its wrought-iron work, basketry, handmade furniture and antiques.

Sports and Outdoors

Golf
Golfers can choose between 20 different golf courses in Tuscany. The brochure *Tuscany and Golf* can be obtained from the Italian tourist information office (▸Information). The Federazione Italiana di Golf publishes annually a list of Italian golf courses with a schedule of tournaments (Viale Tiziano 74, I-00196 Roma, tel. 06 36 85 1, www.federgolf.it).

The fact that Mario Cipollini and Francesco Casagrande were born in Tuscany and learned to ride a **bicycle** there should speak for itself. Tuscany really does offer good conditions for cyclists, even if there are not as many cycle routes as in other European countries. Most side roads offer a pleasant ride. A bicycle is also popular and practical for exploring towns. All mid-size to large holiday places now have bike and even mountain bike rentals. From the Regione Toscana mountain bikers can order the information brochure *Viaggio in Toscana – Tuscany by Mountain Bike* (▸ Information), which lists some routes.

Riding schools and horse farms (maneggi) can be found in almost all areas of Tuscany, but above all in the south, in the Maremma. The addresses listed under Agriturismo

STABLES IN THE MAREMMA

GROSSETO

▶ **Alberese Natura Srl**
Spergolaia, 58010 Alberese
Tel. / fax 05 64 40 71 00
www.alberese.com

▶ **Il Marruchetone**
Dello Sbirro
58040 Roselle
Tel. / fax 05 64 40 10 01

CAMPAGNATICO

▶ **Poggio Caiano**
Loc. Poggio Caiano, 76
58042 Campagnatico
Tel. 05 64 99 55 56
Fax 05 64 99 58 00
www.poggiocaiano.it

CAPALBIO

▶ **Vallerana**
Str. della Sgrilla, 23
58011 Capalbio
Tel. 05 64 89 20 25
www.agriturismo-vallerana.com

▶ **Oasi Botanico Naturalistica Capalbio**
Borgo Carige
58100 Borgo Carige
Tel. / fax 05 64 86 41 95

CASTIGLIONE DELLA PESCAIA

▶ **Fontevecchia**
Loc. Fontevecchia
58040 Vetulonia
Tel. / fax 05 64 94 80 96

▶ **La Luciana**
Loc. Andreina
58043 Castiglione della Pescaia
Tel. 05 64 94 40 90

CIVITELLA PAGANICO

▶ **Terranova**
Podere Magenta, 23
58030 Monte Antico
Tel. / fax 05 64 99 10 65

MANCIANO

▶ **Le Morelle**
Loc. Le Morelle
58014 Manciano
Tel. 05 64 60 29 41
Fax 05 64 60 21 28

ORBETELLO

▶ **Doganella**
Loc. Doganella, 151
58010 Albina
Tel. 05 64 87 81 71

as well as the local tourist offices have further information. The brochure *Ippovia Toscana* with suggested routes is available from Regione Toscana (▶Information).

Hiking conditions in Tuscany have improved in recent years. The number of marked trails has increased and almost all APT offices give free hiking and trekking maps to holidaymakers. The Garfagnana in the north-east (ideal starting point is Bagni di Lucca) and Monte Amiata, where fit hikers can manage the ascent to the summit at 1,739m/5,700ft, are especially beautiful hiking areas with relatively good waymarkers.

Hiking and trekking

► DIVING SCHOOLS ON ELBA

► **Associazione Circoli Subaquei**
Lo. Antiche Saline
Tel. 05 6559 30 46

CAPOLIVERI

► **Centro Sub Corsaro**
Loc. Pareti
Tel. 05 65 93 50 66

CAVO

► **Sporting Club**
Loc. Pareti
Tel. 05 65 93 93 11 60
Fax 05 65 94 99 60

LACONA

► **Blue Immersion**
Camping Lacona
Tel. 34 79 14 08 81
Fax 05 65 96 43 30

PORTO AZZURRO

► **Orso Reale Diving**
Loc. Reale
Camping Reale
Tel. 05 65 92 11 69

► **SubMaldive**
Lungomare
A. de Gasperi 18
Tel./fax 05 65 92 02 39 and
055 67 22 12
www.submaldive.com

PORTOFERRAIO

► **Enfola Diving Center**
Spiaggia dell'Enfola
Tel. 33 57 07 71 88

SECCHETO

► **Diving Service Center**
Hotel La Stella
Tel./Fax 05 65 98 70 82

Chianti, where walks of varying degrees of difficulty are offered, is also becoming increasingly popular as a hiking area. Information on longer tours, called trekking in Italy, can be obtained from Club Alpino Italiano (CAI, Via del Studio 5, I-50100 Firenze, tel. 055 29 85 80).

Sailing, surfing and diving
The Tuscan mainland coast at Viareggio, Forte dei Marmi, Punta Ala, Castiglione della Pescaia, the Monte Argentario peninsula and the island of Elba are ideal areas for sailing and surfing.
Elba also offers excellent conditions for divers. There are many diving schools; when choosing one, make sure it belongs to the official »Associazione Circoli Subaquei«.

Boating
Foreign boating licences are recognized in Italy. For boats with motors of more than 3HP a third-party insurance is required; an international association certificate is accepted as identification.

Winter sports
In 1904 the aristocrat Farina Cini came back from Norway with two bent wooden boards and was the first to decide to ski in Tuscany. Today the most popular site for winter sports is **Abetone** in the pro-

vince of Pistoia. Around the village of 800 inhabitants at 1,388m/ 4,554ft altitude there are about 40 ski slopes and lifts up to 1,940m/ 6,365ft. **Monte Amiata** in the south of the region also has several ski lifts.

Spas

There are countless hot springs in Tuscany, which are used for health purposes. Of the several places with »Bagno« or »Bagni« in their names, most have modest, sometimes a bit old-fashioned spa facilities. Modern thermal baths with swimming pools and wellness areas do not exist. However, in some places in southern Tuscany bathing in natural warm-water pools is possible, for example Saturnia and Bagni San Filippo. In the north of the region the two spas **Montecatini Terme** and **Bagni di Lucca** were fashionable places frequented by the nobility and high society in the 19th century. Montecatini Terme is along with the modern **Chianciano Terme** – which Fellini immortalized in the film *Eight and a Half* – today also the most popular spa in Tuscany, with stylish old hotels, parks and all facilities that a spa needs. Spa guests who can do without entertainment and are primarily looking for rest and recuperation should go to the south, to the pretty little **Bagno Vignoni**, where the thermal bath is right in the middle of the town (swimming in the modern thermal pool in Hotel Posta Marcucci), to **San Casciano dei Bagni** or to the tiny **Bagno San Filippo**.

Unusual spa ambience: the grottoes of Montesummano Terme

● THERMAL BATHS

▶ **Terme di Montecatini**
Montecatini Terme
Viale Verdi 41
Tel. 05 72 77 84 18
Very formal, elegant state spa – the
largest in Tuscany and one of the
most famous in Europe.

▶ **Terme di Saturnia**
58050 Saturnia
Tel. 05 64 60 10 61
Fax 05 64 60 12 66
Singularly beautiful natural pools,
open for a relaxing swim free of
charge.

▶ **Terme di Bagno Vignoni**
San Quirico d'Orcia
Piazza del Moretto
Tel. 05 77 88 73 65
Idyllic spa with a large
15th-century pool.
A small natural pool below Bagno
Vignoni is free of charge.

▶ **Terme di San Filippo**
Castiglione d'Orcia
Loc. San Filippo 23
Tel. 05 77 87 29 82
Outside the tiny spa town in a
wooded valley is the charming
waterfall Fosso Bianco. The warm
water is an inviting place for a
swim.

▶ **Terme di Chianciano**
Chianciano Terme, Via delle Rose
Tel. 057 86 81 11
Fax 057 86 06 22
www.termechianciano.it
Modern, popular
spa, famous for its
thermal springs.

▶ **Bagni di Lucca**
Tel. 058 38 72 21
Open April until 20 Nov.
Ancient spa, very popular in the
belle époque among intellectuals,
artists and the aristocracy.

Time

Italy is in the central European time zone (CET), one hour ahead of
Greenwich Mean Time. For the summer months from the end of
March to the end of October European summer time is used
(CEST = CET+1 hour).

Transport

Motorway   Almost all motorways (autostrada) in Italy charge tolls (pedaggio).
The tolls can be paid either in cash, with a credit card or with the
so-called Viacard. They are available in Italy from the automobile
clubs, the ACI offices at the borders, motorway entrances, in tobacco
shops as well as at petrol stations.

The import and transport of petrol in jerry cans is not allowed. Unleaded petrol (95 octane, benzina senza piombo or benzina verde), super petrol (97 octane) and diesel (gasolio) are available. Petrol stations are generally open from 7am until noon and from 2pm until 8pm. Along the motorway they are usually open 24 hours. Automatic petrol pumps are available on weekends, increasingly also during the midday hours and at night.

Petrol stations

In summer 2002 some new traffic regulations were introduced in Italy. The permitted alcohol level was reduced from 80mg to 50mg of alcohol per 100ml of blood. On motorways dipped headlights are required during the daytime and the speed limit in rain has been reduced to maximum 68mph (110 km/h) from 80mph (130 km/h)! Beyond that the following limits apply. Cars, motorcycles and campers up to 3.5 t: within city limits 30mph (50km/h), outside city limits 55mph (90 km/h), on four-lane roads (2 lanes in each direction) 68mph (110 km/h), on motorways (autostrada) 80mph (130 km/h); cars and campers over 3.5 t: outside of city limits 50mph (80 km/h), on four-lane roads 50mph (80 km/h) and on motorways 62mph (100 km/h). Anyone caught breaking the speed limit can expect heavy fines. Important: **safety vests** are required in Italy for motorists who have a breakdown.

Traffic regulations

Private towing is not allowed on motorways. If a car breaks down, foreign travellers in cars or on motorcycles will be towed to the next garage by the Italian automobile club. Helmets are required on motorcycles of over 50cc. If a vehicle is wrecked completely, customs must be notified since there might be an import duty on it.

Further regulations

Minibuses and expensive or relatively new cars are particularly vulnerable to break-ins or theft. The most important rule when parking a car is never to leave anything inside, especially not valuables, to empty the glove compartment and leave it open, and to remove the radio when possible. If you can, leave the car in a locked parking lot or garage overnight. If the worst happens anyway, always notify the police. This is absolutely necessary for the insurance claim!

Car theft

Parking

Most cities in Tuscany are closed to vehicles in the centre or only open for local residents. Almost all cities have parking lots outside the historic centre. From there the old city is generally within a few minutes walking distance or – more rarely – a bus ride away. But even if it is possible to drive into the town, this is not necessarily advisable, as the narrow streets require experience. Of course, there is too little parking space in almost all towns. Cars are safest in parking garages and guarded parking lots. No parking signs (zona tutelata INIZIO = beginning of no parking zone) should be followed uncon-

Lack of parking space

ditionally. Parking is prohibited in spaces marked in yellow (for example, reserved for taxis and busses), along herbs marked in black and yellow as well as in nature reserves.

Rental Cars

General In order to rent a car in Italy, you have to be at least 21 years old, have a credit card and have had a national driving licence for at least a year. Bookings can be made with the well-known international car hire firms, which are present in all larger cities, before travelling to Italy. This usually saves money. Local car rentals are in the telephone book under »Noleggio«.

AUTOMOBILE CLUBS

► **Automobile Club d'Italia (ACI)**
Via Marsala 8, I-00185 Roma
Tel. 064 99 81

► **Touring-Club Italiano (TCI)**
Corso Italia 10, I-20122 Milano
Tel. 02 8 52 61

► **Towing service - ACI**
Tel. 80 31 16; 800 11 68 00
(mobile phone)

LOCAL CAR RENTALS

► **Avis**
Florence, Lungarno Torrigiani 33
Tel. 05 52 34 66 68

► **Hertz**
Pisa, Aeroporto Galileo Galilei
Tel. 05 04 91 87

► **Europcar**
Pisa, Aeroporto Galileo Galilei
Tel. 05 04 10 81

CAR RENTALS IN ITALY

► **Avis**
Tel. (199) 10 01 33, www.avis.com

► **Budget**
Tel. (800) 472 33 25
www.budget-italy.com

► **Europcar**
Tel. (800) 01 44 10
www.europcar.com

► **Hertz**
Tel. (091) 21 31 12, www.hertz.com

► **Italy by Car**
Tel. (800) 84 60 83
www.italybycar.it

Railways ►Arrival, By Train

Buses Railways are the most convenient way to move between larger towns and cities. For small towns and villages, travellers without their own car will need to take local buses from the nearest major centre to outlying places. The local services are run by a large number of different companies. Ask at the nearest tourist information office for timetables.

Travellers with Disabilities

Although ancient Tuscan hill towns with steep cobbled streets are not an ideal place for those with disabilities, in general the provision of ramps and other services in hotels, museums and public facilities is improving in Italian cities. A number of travel companies cater for people with mobility problems or other special needs. See www.accessible-italy.com for details of tours to Florence and elsewhere. www.everybody.co.uk has information about airlines. The Italian railways have a brochure on *Services for Disabled People*.

 TOURS FOR THE DISABLED

UNITED KINGDOM

▶ **RADAR**
12 City Forum, 250 City Road,
London EC1V 8AF
Tel. (020) 72 50 32 22
www.radar.org.uk

USA

▶ **SATH (Society for the Advancement of Travel for the Handicapped**
347 5th Ave., no. 610
New York, NY 10016:
Tel. (21) 4 47 72 84
www.sath.org

When to Go

Tuscany lies on the edge of the Mediterranean climatic zone. Dry, hot summers and damp, mild winters are typical for this area. The temperatures along the Tuscan coast are more moderate than inland: in winter a little higher and in summer a bit lower. The Apennines and the Apuan Alps get the most rain, over 2,000mm/80in annually, while the coasts get less than 1,000mm/40in annually, and the interior has the driest climate (Florence 840mm/33in, Siena 860mm/34in annually).

The best time for hiking or cultural trips to Tuscany are the months April, May and June or September and October. It is possible to enjoy **spring** in April already, but there can be cool days with rain and wind just as in the **fall**.

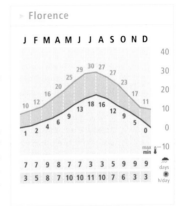

▶ Florence

J F M A M J J A S O N D

max / min

J	F	M	A	M	J	J	A	S	O	N	D	
7	7	9	8	7	7	3	3	5	9	9	9	days
3	5	8	7	10	10	11	10	7	6	3	3	h/day

! *Baedeker* TIP

What will the weather be like?

To check up on the weather right before a trip to Tuscany, see www.versilia.toscana.it/meteo for the Tuscan weather forecast.

In Florence the normal daily temperatures in May are 20–22°C (68–72°F). The months of May and June are considered to be ideal, when the poppies and gorse are in full bloom and the temperatures on nice days are warm enough to enjoy sitting on the piazza or a picnic outdoors. The large number of traditional festivals and events are also a reason to go in May/June, and the wine festivals, which are held mainly but not only in the Chianti region, are an argument for visiting Tuscany in the autumn.

Summer
From July to September the weather is mostly dry and very warm in Tuscany – the preferred time for a beach holiday on the coast or on one of the islands. In Florence temperatures vary in July between 28°C and 33°C (82–91°F) by day and between 18°C and 20°C (64–68°F) by night. In the towns at higher elevations there is always a breeze that makes the heat bearable in the warmest months.

Wine

Wine from Tuscany
A more traditional wine region than Tuscany is hard to imagine – at least in Italy. Some Tuscan wines are world famous, others are real insider tips, and others again don't need to be considered. Even though Tuscany is known mostly for red wine, its white wine tradition is much older. However, white wines have maintained their position only in a few regions like Montecarlo and San Gimignano. The coast near Livorno and around Pisa has interesting white wines from the local Vermentino grape, but the Trebbiano grape, which is still the dominant white variety, hardly yields satisfactory quality. Most of the successful new white wines are thus based mainly on Sauvignon and Chardonnay. The main variety for all traditional Tuscan red wines is Sangiovese in its various forms. Canaiolo is used often in Chianti; the growers aim to gain a more intense flavour from this grape. Colorino is added for colour, Malvasia Nera for a milder flavour. In areas directly influenced by the sea (the provinces Livorno, Pisa and Grosseto) Ciliegiolo mixed with Sangiovese or cultivated separately produces unique and remarkable red wines. Since Tuscany has an unusually broad range of microclimates – from fertile ground close to a warm coast to stony ground at a cool 500m/ 1,640ft in Chianti Classico or Rufina – many foreign varieties have been acclimatized here in recent decades. Cabernet Sauvignon and Merlot are the latest trend; more rarely are Pinot Nero and Syrah also grown.

Tuscany Wine regions

There are several levels of quality in Italian wine according to the **How to judge?**
most recent wine law of 1992. It begins with table wine (Vino Rosso
or Vino Bianco, without year or place of origin); the next class of

table wines gives the place of origin (for example Vino Rosso Tosca-no) and the best class contains the DOC and DOCG wines (control-led and guaranteed place of origin). DOC and DOCG wines are al-ways analysed and tasted before being sold. A new law, which has only partially been applied, controls and guarantees the declaration of sub-zone, commune, location, micro zone, wine and vineyard on the label.

The more exact the declaration, the stricter are the quality controls expected of the wine. Of the average 300 million litres (80 million US gallons) of wine produced in Tuscany annually almost 40% are labelled with a controlled origin (DOC and DOCG) – compared to Italy as a whole (about 17% DOC or DOCG) a high proportion.

Where to buy? Above all in Chianti, but also in other wine regions many wine-growers sell their products direct. The signposts to wineries are easy to find – cantina aperta (open cellar), degustazione vini (wine tas-ting), visita cantina (visit the cellar) or vendita diretta (direct sales) show the way. But it is a mistake to think that buying direct is chea-per: the prices at the wineries are often higher than in the shops (**enotece**) in the surrounding area!

Classic Wine Regions

Chianti General information on Chianti ▶Baedeker Special p.114

Montalcino In ancient times Montalcino was already famous for its (surprise) white wine! This is not unusual since red wine is a relatively new in-vention in the history of wine. In the mid-19th century a certain Cle-mente Santi recognized the advantages of the Tuscan **Sangiovese** variety. Against the customary practice of processing various kinds of grapes together into wine, his grandson Ferruccio Biondi-Santi culti-vated Sangiovese separately and called this robust wine, which was rich in tannin, Brunello. It was only over 100 years later, in the 1970s, that **Brunello** became a fashionable wine and fetched top pri-ces. In Montalcino everyone wanted to be a Brunello producer, and today there are more than 200. The Brunello that comes from lower sites in the south of Montalcino is heavy, dark and rich in tannin, while the wines from higher sites and those north of the town are marked by dense colour, elegance, high acidity and fruity character. If 20 euros for a bottle of Brunello seems too much, there is a more affordable alternative: the younger, somewhat lighter and more rustic Rosso di Montalcino is mostly a good buy!

The wines ▶ Brunello di Montalcino DOCG (type of grape: Sangiovese, also called Santo Grosso; prescribed storage time: 4 years, of this 3 in a wooden barrel, riserva 5 years). Rosso di Montalcino DOC (type of grape: Sangiovese; prescribed storage: 1 year; wood not required). Other wi-nes: Moscadello DOC (sweet desert wine), various white and red Vini da Tavola and – today more rare – Chianti Colli Senesi DOCG.

SELECTED WINEGROWERS

CHIANTI:
Barberino Val D'Elsa

► **Isole e Olena**
Località Isole 1
Tel. 05 58 07 27 63
Fax 05 58 07 22 36

► **Castello
di Monsanto**
Via Monsanto 8
Tel. 05 58 05 90 00
Fax 05 58 05 90 49

► **Casa Emma**
San Donato in Poggio
Tel. 05 58 07 28 59
Fax 05 71 66 77 07

► **Le Filigare**
Via Sicelle 35
Tel. 05 58 07 27 96
Fax 05 58 07 21 35

CHIANTI:
Castellina in Chianti

► **Castellare in Castellina**
Località Castellare
Tel. 05 77 72 0903
Fax 05 77 74 28 14

► **San Fabiano Calcinaia**
Localià Cellole
Tel. 05 77 97 92 32
Fax 0577979455

CHIANTI:
Gaiole in Chianti

► **Badia di Coltibuono**
Località Badia a Coltibuono
Tel. 057 77 44 81
Fax 05 77 74 92 35

► **Castello di Cacchiano**
Località Monti in Chianti
Tel. 05 77 74 70 18
Fax 05 77 74 71 57

► **Capanelle**
Località Capanelle 13
Tel. 05 77 74 511
Fax 05 77 74 52 33

► **Rocca di Montegrossi**
Località Monti in Chianti
Gaiole in Chianti
Tel. 05 77 74 79 77
Fax 05 77 74 78 36

CHIANTI:
Greve in Chianti

► **Castello di
Querceto**
Greve in Chianti
Tel. 05 58 59 21
Fax 05 58 59 22 00

► **Castel Ruggero**
Via Castel Ruggero 33
50011 Antella
Tel. und Fax 055 64 992 37

► **Viticcio**
Via San Cresci 12/ A

THE SIGN OF THE BLACK ROOSTER

The word Chianti has a long history. At first it was an Etruscan family name; in the Middle Ages it was a military alliance of the feudal lords of Radda, Gaiole and Castellina. Then it became the name of the region and later of its wines. Finally it became the generic name for a popular type of Tuscan wine.

The original Chianti territory included, according to Cosimo III's Bando decree of 1716, only the lands of Radda, Gaiole and Castellina. In 1932 parts of Greve, San Casciano and Tavernelle in the north and Castelnuovo Berardenga in the south were added. In 1967 the introduction of the DOC appellation brought legal recognition of a wine region which had meanwhile spread to cover almost all of Tuscany. The year 1841 was decisive; on his vast estate of Brolio Castle, Bettino Ricasoli then realized his vision of a modern Chianti with a mixture of Sangiovese, white Malvasia and Canaiolo grapes. Due to the great demand, high-yield Trebbiano was added to the Chianti mixture, the yield per acre was increased without consideration for quality and Chianti grapes were planted in unsuitable areas. All of this led to a large drop in Chianti consumption in the 1970s. In the following decade, however, broad-based improvements in quality made Chianti Classico one of the most sophisticated Italian wines and restored its international reputation.

Wines with Tradition

As early as the 14th century the famous »fiasco« bottles in braided straw were produced near San Gimignano. They became the trademark of Chianti in the whole world. Today the original bottle is increasingly being replaced by the Bordeaux bottle, but the sparkling fresh, fruity Chianti of the old days still exists. The naked pink cherub on the bottleneck is the promise of an uncomplicated, pleasant drink. Today even the simplest Annata Chianti wines are robust and contain tannins, so that it is advisable to store them for two or three years. The Riserva Chianti wines have even more body, mostly with a good dose of tannin and marked by wood when young. They are intended for longer storage. A black rooster on the bottleneck is the sign of Chianti Classico, produced by members of the Gallo Nero consortium.

Chianti Classico

Chianti (including all sub-zones) may be grown on about 23,000 ha/57,000 acres of the total 32,000 ha/79,000

Some Chianti Classico wine bottles have a black rooster on the bottleneck (on a gold background if it is a »riserva« – in a red ring if it is a young wine). The rooster is the trademark of the historic Chianti Classico consortium.

acres of the Tuscan DOC regions. Of the 90 million litres of Chianti produced, about half are ordinary Chianti without any additional appellation. Another 25 million litres are Chianti Classico, and the rest is from other sub-regions.

Neither the Rufina region east of Florence in the Sieve valley nor Montalbano west of Florence, nor the hills of Arezzo, Pisa or Siena have much in common with the actual Chianti region apart from the type of grape (Sangiovese). Nevertheless the wine politicians decided in an unhappy moment that these regions would be called Chianti, while the original regions would be elevated to Chianti Classico. Apart from a few Chianti Rufina and excellent Chianti Colli Fiorentini vintages, the best Chianti still comes from the Classico region.

Prime Locations

Chianti Classico is actually less of a wine than a forest region. Only one tenth of the 70,000 ha/173,000 acres are vineyards. The best locations for Chianti Classico are between 250m and 450m (800–1,500ft) above sea level in stony, unfertile alberese or galestro soil and on slopes facing south-east, south or south-west.

Good conditions can be found in the north, above all near Greve, and in the south around Castelnuovo Berardenga. The classic sites, where soil, microclimate, elevation and sunshine are ideal, and the Sangiovese vine can give its best, can be found in the sunny basin of Conca d'Oro near the village of Panzano, on the hills around Gaiole and further south in Monti, near Radda and around Castellina.

Very high locations produce rustic, strong, sometimes joyless wines, while lower, mostly more fertile and warmer locations produce a full-bodied, powerful but unrounded Chianti.

The new production regulations, which define the parameters of quality for Chianti Classico production, provide for the following varieties: Sangiovese (75–100 %), Canaiolo (up to 10 %), Malvasia and Trebbiano (up to 10%), other varieties (up to 15%). Riserva can be pressed only from red grapes. The prescribed period for maturing is one year for Annata, two years for Riserva.

Tel. 055 85 42 10
Fax 05 58 54 48 66

MAREMMA

▶ **Tenuta dell'Ornellaia**
Via Bolgherese 191
57020 Bolgheri
Tel. 05 65 71 811
Fax 05 65 71 82 30

MONTALCINO

▶ **Tenute Silvio Nardi**
Località Casale del Bosco
Tel. 05 77 80 82 69
Fax 05 77 80 82 69

▶ **Siro Pacenti**
Loc. Pelagrilli 1
Tel. 05 77 84 86 62
Fax 05 77 84 69 35

MONTEPULCIANO

▶ **Salcheto**
Via di Villa Bianca, 15
Tel. 05 78 79 90 31
Fax 05 78 79 97 49

MORELLINO
DI SCANSANO

▶ **Fattoria Le Pupille**
Loc. Istia d'Ombrone
Piaggie del Maiano 92a
58040 Grosseto

Montepulciano As a red-wine region Montepulciano is considerably older than its successful neighbour Montalcino. A good Vino Nobile is neither worse nor better than a Brunello or a Chianti Classico, just different. Maybe it is even the most approachable of the three Sangiovese classics from Tuscany. Its acidity is mostly embedded in a thick cushion of fruit and the tannin is balanced by strength and fullness. The main problem is the bottlers of Vino Nobile today: only a few can still be considered reliable. When it succeeds, the Nobile is a friendly, warm and lovable wine, which generally offers very good value. The situation with the affordable Rosso di Montepulciano is even more heterogeneous; stick to the well-known names.

The wines ▶ Vino Nobile di Montepulciano DOCG (type of grape: Sangiovese, also called Prugnolo, Canaiolo; prescribed storage time: 2 years in a wooden barrel, riserva 3 years). Rosso di Montepulciano DOC (type of grape: like Vino Nobile; prescribed storage time: 1 year, wood not required). Other wines: Vin Santo (dessert wine), white and red Vini da Tavola, Chianti Colli Senesi DOCG.

Carmignano The modest village of Carmignano lies west of Florence on top of the Montalbano ridge of hills and was always considered to be part of the city's zone of influence. Even though Montalbano could not devote large, connected areas to winegrowing because of its topography, its wine has numbered among the best and most expensive Florentine red wines since the 14th century. It ought to be mentioned that the amount of Cabernet in a Carmignano does not reflect modern fashion, but has been usual since the 18th century. Its admirers love its smoothness and elegance.

Carmignano DOCG (type of grape: Sangiovese, Cabernet / 15%, Ca-   ◄ The wines
naiolo / 15%; prescribed storage time 20 months, of which 1 year in
a wooden barrel, riserva 2 years). Other wines: Chianti Montalbano
DOCG, Barco Reale DOC (light red wine), Vin Santo DOC.

The rough, clefted Sieve valley east of Florence produces red wines   Rufina and
with body and acidity. Rufina wines are mostly very strong and   Pomino
equipped with a steely acidity; they are valued for their durability.
The region was forgotten except for two or three quality producers,
but in recent years has again been producing wines that can take
their place alongside other Tuscan wines. High above the Sieve valley,
in the mini-region Pomino (the only producer is Frescobaldi) an ex-
traordinary white and a red with individual character are produced.
Chianti Rufina DOCG (type of grape: Sangiovese, Canaiolo; prescri-   ◄ The wines
bed storage time: 8 months, riserva 3 years). Pomino Rosso DOC
(type of grape: Sangiovese, Merlot, Cabernet, Canaiolo; prescribed
storage time: 1 year). Pomino Bianco DOC (type of grape: Pinot
Bianco, Chardonnay, Trebbiano).

Lesser-Known Wine Regions

The original zone Colli Fiorentini includes a broad area to the south   Colli Fiorentini
and east of Florence and would even be much larger if the Floren-
tines had not given a large part of their Colli to the prestigious
Chianti Classico. As region of origin the Colli Fiorentini are very heterogeneous and seem to result more from a political compromise
than from an appraisal of growing conditions. However, a handful of
winegrowers in this part of Tuscany have retained their individuality
and aim to produce real top-quality red wines – some as Chianti,
some as Vino da Tavola.
Chianti Colli Fiorentini DOCG (types of grapes: Sangiovese, Canaio-   ◄ The wines
lo), Chianti DOCG (types of grapes: Sangiovese, Canaiolo), red Vini
da Tavola.

This wine with a melodious name comes from the warm, green hills   Montecarlo
of Lucca. The growing region is very small and the wines have not
always been worthy of attention. But recently it has been exciting to
follow the development in quality of some of the growers' red and
white wines.
Montecarlo Bianco DOC (type of grape: Trebbiano among others),   ◄ The wines
Montecarlo Rosso DOC (type of grape: Sangiovese, Canaiolo).

California is the name of a village on the so-called Etruscan coast   Coast south
south of Livorno, and the speedy development and type of wine   of Livorno
found there indeed seem to be Californian. Until a few years ago the
hinterland of Florence's favourite beach was a winegrowing no-
man's-land. But there was one prominent exception: the famous Sassicaia of the Marchese Incisa. In 1994 this »ringleader of the Tuscan

Vino da Tavola revolution« was given a legal status and since then has very properly called itself »Bolgheri DOC Sassicaia«. Only in the recent past were the Ornellaia of Lodovico Antinori and the Grattamacco of Meletti-Cavallari added, and very recently Piero Antinori with his Guardo al Tasso. But a considerable number of winegrowers in the DOC regions Bolgheri, Montescudaio and Val di Cornia are following suit and will soon be talked about. The warm coastal climate is proving to be very suitable for Cabernet and Merlot, which are the dominant element of the majority of wines here. They wines do not have the vegetable aromas sometimes evident in the bad years of the Cabernets of central Tuscany, or the often bitter tannins of the Merlot and Cabernet vintages from Friuli.

The wines ► Bolgheri DOC (white, rosé and red), Montescudaio DOC (white and red) and Val di Cornia DOC (white, rosé and red).

Vin Santo Once there was a delicious wine, which farmers kept in small amounts in their attics in wooden barrels for five, eight, even ten years. The wine was very sweet and strong and was served to guests as a special honour. The farmers would send a bottle of the »holy

Vineyards characterize the Chianti landscape, of course.
Conditions for the famous red wine are ideal here.

wine« to influential people on holy days when they needed favours. But they would never have stooped to selling their Vin Santo for money. Times have changed, and a caricature of what was once a fine wine can be found in every supermarket. The production of authentic Vin Santo is highly complicated. And how could it be other than enormously expensive, after being pressed from dry grapes, stored for years in small barrels and thus concentrated to a fraction of the original amount? An encounter with a really great Vin Santo – and that happens rarely – is an unforgettable experience, as hardly any other sweet wine can attain its variety in taste, its depth and harmony. Recommended producers with highly concentrated, in some years unforgettable Vin Santo are Avignonesi (Montepulciano), Capezzana (Carmignano), Isole e Olena (Barberino / Chianti Classico), Montellori (Fucecchio), Paterno & Corzano (San Casciano / Colli Fiorentini), Poliziano (Montepulciano), San Giusto a Rentennano (Gaiole /Chianti Classico) and Selvapiana (Rufina).

The growing region of Morellino di Scansano covers about 58,000 ha/143,300 acres in southern Tuscany between the rivers Ombrone and Albegna. This includes the entire community of Scansano (where the wine gets its name) as well as parts of the communes of Manciano, Magliano in Toscana, Grosseto, Compagnatico, Semproniano, Montemerano and Roccalbenga. Gently rolling hills with glowing colours and intense light are characteristic of the area. The usual elevation lies between under 100m and over 500m (330ft to over 1,650ft) above sea level and the soil varies greatly. The growing zone is marked by a clearly Mediterranean, warm and sunny climate. The summer is usually dry, fall is mild with generally not very much precipitation, which diminishes even more in January and February and becomes regular again in the spring. There is rarely any frost. Morellino di Scansano, which gained the DOC appellation in 1978, should be produced from at least 85% Sangiovese (called Morellino locally) and at the most 15% other red grapes of recommended or permitted varieties like Alicante, Ciliegiolo, Colorino, Merlot and Cabernet.

Morellino di Scansano

Tours

IF YOU DREAM OF STROLLING AROUND OLD TOWNS AND TRIPS ON WINDING COUNTRY ROADS THROUGH IDYLLIC SCENERY, THEN TUSCANY IS FOR YOU.

TOURS THROUGH TUSCANY

The suggested tours are as varied as Tuscany itself. No matter whether you like to visit cities rich in art and culture, or prefer to be out and about in natural surroundings – the choice is yours.

━━━ TOUR 1   **On side roads from the coast to Florence**
For all those who believe the journey is its own reward: the seaside resort of Viareggio on the Versilia coast is the starting place for this route, which touches Pisa, Pistoia and Florence, three of the most beautiful Tuscan cities.   ▶ **page 126**

━━━ TOUR 2   **In the footsteps of the hermits: through the Casentino**
An excursion to a varied mountainous region with remote monasteries and small towns that few tourists visit.   ▶ **page 128**

━━━ TOUR 3   **In the heart of Tuscany**
From Siena this tour passes through some of the most beautiful scenery, where pretty towns like Pienza, the world-famous wine region Montepulciano and spas large and small are relaxing and restorative places to stay.   ▶ **page 130**

━━━ TOUR 4   **Just follow the coast**
The Costa degli Etruschi stretches from Livorno to Piombino – a historic strip of land that owes its name to numerous archaeological finds from the Etruscan period.   ▶ **page 133**

━━━ TOUR 5   **Hot springs and Etruscans**
Etruscan necropolises, restful nature, swimming on the Monte Argentario peninsula or in the hot springs at Saturnia, and old towns on tuffstone cliffs are the attractions on this route.   ▶ **page 135**

Monte Argentario
*Refreshing and relaxing: a swim
in Cala Grande Bay.*

Florence
On mild summer nights enjoy the view of the city from the hills or stroll along the Arno River.

© Baedeker

Arezzo
Poetry fresco in Giorgio Vasari's house

Pisa
Everyone knows the Leaning Tower of Pisa

★ Viareggio
★ Collodi
Pescia
★ Pistoia
★ Montecatini Terme
Vinci
★ Poggio a Caiano
Florence
Consuma-Pass
★ Stia
★ Camaldoli
★ ★ Pisa
TOUR 1
★ Vallombrosa
Bibbiena
★ Poppi
★ ★ La Verna
★ I Pieve di Romena
Livorno
TOUR 4
TOUR 2
Rosignano Marittima
★ ★ Arezzo
Cecina
★ Bolgheri
Castagneta Carducci
Sassetta
Campiglia Marittima
★ ★ Siena
Asciano
★ ★ Monte Oliveto Maggiore
TOUR 3
Buonconvento
Pienza
★ ★ Montepulciano
★ Monticchiello
★ Montalcino
★ San Quirico d'Orcia
★ Chianciano Terme
★ Populonia
★ ★ Sant' Antimo
★ Vetulonia
TOUR 5
★ ★ Monte Amiata
Radicofani
★ ★ Roselle
★ Grosseto
Alberese
★ Saturnia
★ Sovana
Magliano
Talamone
Sovana
★ Pitigliano
Capalbios
★ Monte Argentario
★ Giardino dei Tarocchi

Travelling in Tuscany

The right means of transport

In Tuscany most holidaymakers still travel by car. There are reasons for this: as the train system does not cover every town, many places can only be reached by car. However, it is not impossible to travel through Tuscany by train (▶Arrival ▶Transport) – provided you are not too short of time and accept the fact that not every town is accessible. By using local buses it is possible to reach almost any place in the region, but this method of travel is extremely time-consuming. Visitors who have no car are well advised to make one of the larger cities – Florence, Siena or Lucca – their base and use local transport to explore the surrounding region. Tuscany is also an attractive area for walking and cycling holidays (▶ Sports and Outdoors). And lovers of art and architecture who enjoy city life can spend weeks in Florence and Siena without feeling the need to travel.

Beaches and culture

For those who want to enjoy the beaches and swimming in Tuscany, the coast and the islands are the right destination, of course. In Viareggio and most places along the Versilia coast, however, the prices are accordingly high.
The best place to combine the beach with the art is the northern part of the coast, where cities like Pisa, Lucca, Pistoia or even Florence are in easy reach via the motorway.

For nature lovers

Nature lovers might feel more at home on the coast south of Livorno, the so-called Etruscan Riviera with its long beaches and backdrop of pine forests. There are no quick motorway connections into the hinterland in southern Tuscany, and excursions to Chianti or Siena take a long time on winding roads.

In the heart ...

Florence and Siena with Chianti in between are the heart of Tuscany both geographically and in view of their importance – and thus come top in terms of accommodation prices, too.
What to do? It is easy to reach Florence from Prato, due to the good motorway connections, and visitors to Siena can easily find accommodation further to the west or south, for example in a town along the SS 2 motorway.

... or on the periphery?

If you are looking for a rest, the »border regions« of Tuscany are most suitable: Casentino and Pratomagno in the north-east, Garfagnana in the north-west, Maremma in the south-west or the area around Monte Amiata in the south. These parts of Tuscany still offer rural and reasonably priced accommodation that is often suitable for holidaymakers who want to stay longer.

In the high Middle Ages Abbazia Sant'Antimo near Montalcino →
was one of the wealthiest monasteries in Tuscany.

Tour 1 From the Coast to Florence on Side Roads

Start and finish: from Viareggio to Florence

Length: about 140km/90mi

The quickest way, but not the nicest, from the coast to Florence is the A 11 autostrada. The following route is recommended for those who want to enjoy the journey at leisure. The seaside resort Viareggio, centre of the Versilia coast and the Tuscan carnival, is the starting place for this route, which touches Pisa, Pistoia and Florence, three of the most beautiful Tuscan cities.

Viareggio, Pisa

❶ ✳ **Viareggio** is attractive for its beautiful beaches and an enormous selection of hotels and other accommodation. This holiday town with a long history lies a mere 20km/13mi north-west of Pisa, connected via the motorway and SS 1. In ❷ ✳✳ **Pisa** the legendary Leaning Tower has been open again since December 2001. But this university town has much to offer besides its famous monument – for instance an interesting historic centre on the banks of the Arno, student pubs in the university quarter and excellent shopping.

Stop in Certosa di Pisa

Leave Pisa heading north-east towards Calci and pass ✳ **Certosa di Pisa**, a site important in art history, with monks' cells from the 17th century. Endless olive groves spread out over the hilly landscape of Calci. The charming country road from Calci to Buti (17km/11mi) crosses the forested Monte Pisano range of hills (917m/3,001ft high).

Viareggio
Colourful floats in the famous Viareggio carnival parade

✳ Viareggio

Pescia

✳ Pistoia

✳ Collodi

✳ Montecatini Terme

✳ Poggio a Caia[...]

Vinci

✳✳ Pisa

Montecatini Terme
The exclusive thermal spa offers cures in high-class surroundings.

After Buti follow the SS 439 to Bientina and from there straight north via Altopascio, a station for medieval pilgrims, to the tranquil wine village Montecarlo (17km/11mi). It is surrounded by broad, vine-covered slopes. The SS 435 goes on to ❸ ✳ **Collodi**, birthplace of the long-nosed wooden puppet Pinocchio. Collodi is particularly attractive for families as the site of Pinocchio Park, which presents some of the adventures of the little rascal. In the neighbouring town of ❹ **Pescia** (4km/2.5mi) the medieval Piazza Grande is an inviting place to stop and stroll.

From Pescia drive via Vellano and Marliana to the world-famous hot springs at ❺ ✳ **Montecatini Terme** (30km/19mi). A wonderful panoramic road leads first through the Pescia valley and then through a densely forested area to Vellano (600m/1,970ft above sea level). This area is ideal for hiking and is known as »Svizzera pesciatina« because of the similarity to the lush green valleys of Switzerland. From Goraiolo drive through the hilly Nievole valley down to Montecatini Terme past expansive olive groves. After touring the large spa take the rack railway to ✳ **Montecatini Alto**, the old town centre, if only for the view.

Montecatini Terme

The SS 435 quickly leads to ❻ ✳ **Pistoia** 15km/9mi away. However, lovers of a medieval setting should stop in Serravalle, where time really has stood still! The small provincial capital Pistoia has a beautiful marketplace and cathedral square.

Pistoia

From Pistoia it is only about 40km/25mi on the autostrada to Florence. A small detour through the hills to ❼ **Vinci**, the birthplace of the famous Leonardo, offers variety. The house where he was born and two interesting museums are here. It is about 20km/13mi further to ❽ ✳ **Poggio a Caiano**, one of the most beautiful Renaissance villas of the Medici family. For the road from Poggio a Caiano to ❾ ✳✳ **Florence** there are several alternatives; the quickest route (and the easiest to find) to the city centre is the A 11.

At the gates of Florence

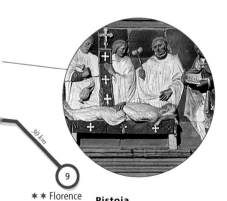

30 km

9

✳ ✳ Florence

Pistoia
Majolica frieze from the della Robbia workshop on the Ospedale del Ceppo

Tour 2 Through the Casentino

Start and finish: from Florence to Arezzo

Length: about 120km/90mi

The Casentino, headwater region of the Arno, is a forested mountainous area with remote monasteries and small towns that see few visitors. Only in the south of the Casentino, in the art city of Arezzo, does the route return to the tourist track.

Into the mountains!

Leave ❶ ✳✳ **Florence** on the south-eastern route (SS 67) towards Pontassieve, where medieval stone bridges cross the Sieve before it flows into the Arno. Then follow the winding SS 70 up to the ❷ ✳ **Consuma Pass**, where there is an optional detour to ❸ ✳ **Vallombrosa Monastery**. The 1,060m/3,478ft-high Passo di Consuma is the gateway to a fascinating mountain world. A panoramic road goes toward Poppi past dense forests, which slowly give way to meadows, vineyards and olive groves.

✳✳ Florence

1

Typical Casentino: Stia and Poppi

About 10km/6mi beyond Passo di Consuma a country road branches off from the SS 70 towards Pratovecchio and Stia (about 4km/2.5mi). The small detour is worth it not just because of Stia. Along the road, in the middle of wonderful scenery lies the medieval ❹ ✳ **Pieve di Romena** and the neighbouring Guidi Castello di Romena, which is however not open to the public. ❺ ✳ **Stia** has a small, very pretty old town – just like the next stop on the SS 70, a mere 11km/7mi away, ❻ ✳ **Poppi**. Poppi is a typical Casentino town, with the castle of the Guidi family rising above it. The former farm buildings of the castle have been restored and offer good food and accommodation.

First to the monks in Camaldoli ...

The journey from Poppi to the imposing monastery of the Benedictine Camaldolese order in ❼ ✳ **Camaldoli** (15km/9mi) is an interesting detour. Continue a further 4km/2.5mi to Serravalle or follow a beautiful but time-consuming route over Passo Fangacci (1,234m/4,049ft) to Badia Prataglia and then via the SS 71 to ❽ **Bibbiena** (9km/5.5mi), the industrial heart of the Casentino.

... and then to La Verna

From Bibbiena take the SS 208 (about 25km/16mi) to the beautifully situated Franciscan monastery ❾ ✳✳ **La Verna**. The route winds through pine forests and mixed areas of coniferous and deciduous trees. Here is an opportunity for a short detour from Chiusi della Verna (12km/7.5mi) to Caprese Michelangelo, the birthplace of a further major Renaissance artist next to Leonardo (museum in the house where Michelangelo was born). A route leads through charming scenery across the Catenaia Massif via Chitignano (thermal springs) to Rassina. From here the SS71 winds through the Arno valley to ➓ **∗∗ Arezzo**. Among many other attractions, the frescoes of Piero della Francesca in San Francesco church should not be missed.

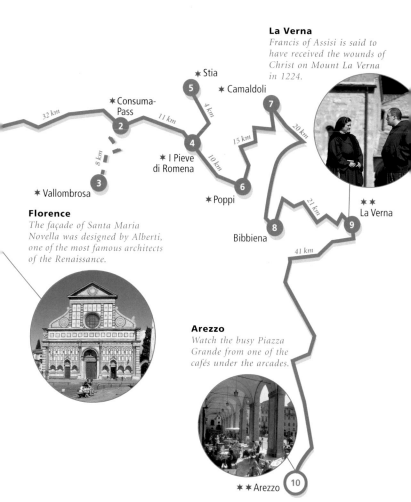

La Verna
Francis of Assisi is said to have received the wounds of Christ on Mount La Verna in 1224.

∗ Stia

∗ Camaldoli

∗ Consuma-Pass

∗ I Pieve di Romena

∗ Vallombrosa

∗ Poppi

Bibbiena

∗∗ La Verna

Florence
The façade of Santa Maria Novella was designed by Alberti, one of the most famous architects of the Renaissance.

Arezzo
Watch the busy Piazza Grande from one of the cafés under the arcades.

∗∗ Arezzo

The deep crevices in the earth around Siena look like moonscapes and are called »crete«.

Tour 3 In the Heart of Tuscany

Start and finish: circular tour starting from Siena

Length: about 150km/90mi

Siena is a good starting point for exploring south-eastern Tuscany since the city is easy to reach from the north via the autostrada (A 1). The described route passes through one of the most beautiful landscapes in Tuscany, through pretty towns like Pienza and the world-famous wine town Montepulciano, as well as spas large (like Chianciano Terme) and small (like Bagno Vignoni), ideal places to take a restorative break.

Start in Siena

Plan a couple of days for ❶✳✳ **Siena** – the city is full of important buildings and is also a seductive shopping town. Leave Siena on the SS 73 towards Arezzo. Immediately after the Arbia bridge the SS 438 turns off and meanders through the sparse landscape of the Crete region – beware of sheep on the road! ❷ **Asciano** is a centre for the production of pecorino cheese, but also the birthplace of the renowned Renaissance artists Domenico di Bartolo and Giovanni d'Asciano.

About 8km/5mi beyond Asciano is the monastery of ❸ ✶ ✶ **Monte Oliveto Maggiore**, a medieval Benedictine abbey with famous frescoes in the cloister. After 9km/5.5mi, near the brickworks town ❹ **Buonconvento**, the SS 451 meets the ancient Roman road Via Cassia (SS 2); 10km/6mi further south a winding road branches off near Torrenieri towards ❺ ✶ **Montalcino**. The well-tended vineyards give notice of the high-quality grapes ripening here. The dark red Brunel-

Monte Oliveto Maggiore, Montalcino

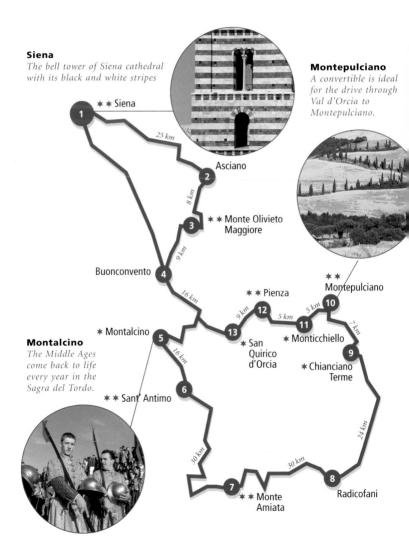

Siena
The bell tower of Siena cathedral with its black and white stripes

Montepulciano
A convertible is ideal for the drive through Val d'Orcia to Montepulciano.

✶ ✶ Siena

25 km

Asciano

8 km

✶ ✶ Monte Olivieto Maggiore

9 km

Buonconvento

16 km

✶ ✶ Pienza

✶ ✶ Montepulciano

9 km   5 km   5 km

✶ Montalcino

San Quirico d'Orcia

✶ Monticchiello

Montalcino
The Middle Ages come back to life every year in the Sagra del Tordo.

16 km

✶ Chianciano Terme

7 km

✶ ✶ Sant' Antimo

30 km

30 km

24 km

✶ ✶ Monte Amiata

Radicofani

lo di Montalcino is the top wine label of Tuscany, and the medieval town is like an open wine market.

Sant' Antimo, Monte Amiata

From Montalcino go to the abbey church of ❻✳✳ **Sant'Antimo** (10km/6mi), one of the most beautiful and largest Romanesque country churches of the region. It has a wonderful location at the end of a valley, surrounded by meadows and olive groves. From Sant'Antimo the road meanders further south. The landscape becomes more hilly and forested. About 800m/875yd beyond Seggiano, which stands atop a hill, a road turns off to the left to Daniel Spoerri's sculpture garden. After a stroll through the extensive grounds continue towards Arcidosso and ❼✳✳ **Monte Amiata**. The 1,738m/5,702ft-high peak of the extinct volcano, which often remains covered with snow until late spring, can be seen from far off. The mountain road to the peak goes through pine and mountain forest up to Alpine altitudes. Winding roads, now passing through forests of chestnut and beech, lead to the town of Abbadia San Salvatore, which lies below the interesting abbey that gave the town its name.

Abbadia San Salvatore

✳✳ **Abbadia San Salvatore** is only about 5km/3mi west of the Via Cassia (SS 2) as the crow flies. Follow this road 3km/1.8mi north and turn off on the narrow road towards Radicofani. The road is extremely winding but the views of the sparsely populated hilly countryside are rewarding. Hilltops farms with narrow roads leading up to them are the conspicuous features of the landscape. There are no towns here, and the only larger place is ❽**Radicofani**, which can be seen from far off thanks to its tall castle tower.

Chianciano Terme

The road between Radicofani and the tranquil spa Sarteano passes through charming scenery. From Sarteano it is only 10km/6mi to ❾✳ **Chianciano Terme**, the largest spa in Tuscany. Surprisingly the city, which does not seem very appealing at first sight with its large hotel complexes, has a pretty little old town.

Via San Quirico d'Orcia back to Siena

What Chianciano is for visitors to the spa, ❿✳✳ **Montepulciano** is for wine lovers. There is a pleasant alternative to the SS 146 for getting to Pienza, via ⓫✳ **Monticchiello**. This tiny village, which sits majestically on top of a hill, is a gem that no one should miss! This applies all the more to ⓬✳✳ **Pienza** about 5km/3mi away, a planned Renaissance town which rises above the surrounding hills. It is a further 10km/6mi to ⓭✳ **San Quirico d'Orcia** and the junction to the SS 2, which leads back to Siena.

! *Baedeker* TIP

Take a break?

On this tour there are many places to drink a cappuccino outdoors, but one of them is worth a detour: right next to the entrance to the tiny mountain village of Monticchiello there is a bar (La Porta) with a terrace on the old fortified walls.

Tour 4 Just Follow the Coast

Start and finish: from Livorno to Populonia

Length: about 120km/75mi

The Costa degli Etruschi, the Etruscan Riviera, stretches from Livorno to Piombino – a strip of land replete with history, which gets its name from numerous archaeological finds from the Etruscan period. Long stretches of coastline alternate with rich green Mediterranean macchia, pine forests and areas of swamp.

The SS 1 runs parallel to the coast. Follow it southwards from ❶ **Livorno** on the most striking section of coastline to ❷ **Rosignano Marittima**, a distance of no more than 26km/16mi. The old mountain village on a hilltop is visible from afar. After a short visit return to the SS 1 and drive southwards to ❸ **Cecina** (12 km/7.5mi). A visit to the fascinating prehistoric and Etruscan-Roman finds in Villa La Cinquantina 2km/1.2mi outside the town is well worthwhile.

Drive up to Montescudaio (7.5km/4.5mi) via a country road (no. 57). Signs here point to the »Strada del Vino« (wine route) and small wineries, which offer Montescudaio wines, and usually olive oil too, at reasonable prices. The panoramic road passes the villages of Guardistallo and Casale Marittimo and leads to the medieval Bibbona (10km/6mi). To the left and right of Via Bolgherese (strada provinciale no. 16), right through the wine growing region of the famous Ornellaia wine, look out for the unique cypress avenue of ❹ ✶ **Bolgheri** after about 5.5km/3.5mi. The tall cypresses form a proud line stretching more than 5km/

Livorno
Ferries run from the city harbour to Elba, the islands of the Arcipelago Toscano, Sardinia and Corsica.

Populonia
Pre-Christian graves are preserved in the former Etruscan necropolis.

Livorno

❶

26 km

Rosignano
Marittima
❷

12 km

27 km

❸
Cecina

✶ Bolgheri
❹

Castagneta
Carducci
❺
7 km

❻ Sassetta

14 km

23 km

❼
Campiglia
Marittima

13 km

✶ Populonia ❽

3mi from the church of San Guido, across the SS 1 and straight into the town. Every Italian knows the famous lines of the poet and Nobel prize winner Giosuè Carducci »Davanti a San Guido ...«, which described and immortalized Bolgheri.

Castagneta Carducci, Sassette and Campiglia Marittima

Between silver shimmering olive trees and fine vines continue along the SP 16 to ancient ❺ **Castagneta Carducci** (11km/7mi), which gets its name from the poet Carducci, whose former residence is now a museum with historical documents and exhibits. The tour winds along the SS 329 through dense forests of holm oak and chestnut. Be sure not to miss the charming village of ❻ **Sassetta** (7km/4.5mi), which is ideal for a longer stop. At the entrance to the village there is a large map with interesting hiking tours. A truly beautiful section of the wine route leads 13km/8mi to the magnificent medieval town of ✳ **Suvereto**, which goes back to before the year 1000, and after a further 10km/6mi to the picturesque ❼ ✳ **Campiglia Marittima**, which towers majestically above the sea and the surrounding countryside.

To Populonia

Towards Piombino the SS 398 passes through the lower Cornia valley to the small town of ❽ ✳ **Populonia** (18km/11mi). One of the most important Etruscan necropolises of Tuscany can be explored here – the archaeological park covers more than 80 ha/197 acres on the mountain ridge above the Gulf of Baratti. This is, incidentally, the best place for a dip in the sea – the lovely bay is certainly one of the most beautiful along this stretch of coast.

Traditional agriculture: a farmer brings in hay from his fields without machinery.

Tour 5 Hot Springs and Etruscans

Start and finish: from Vetulonia to Pitigliano   **Length:** about 150km/90mi

Etruscan burial sites, a restful, protected natural landscape, swimming on Monte Argentario peninsula or in the springs of Saturnia, and old towns on tuffstone cliffs are the attractions along this route.

This tour begins with a visit to the Etruscan excavations of ❶ ✳ **Vetulonia** (8km/5mi north-west of Grosseto) and ❷ ✳ ✳ **Roselle** (4km/2.5mi north). Afterwards eat lunch or go shopping in ❸ ✳ **Grosseto**, the capital of the Maremma. Leave Grosseto on the Via Aurelia (SS 1) southwards. After about 10km/6mi the narrow country road to ❹ **Alberese** and the marina of the same name turns off to the right. The access road is signed »traffico limitato«, which means that no more than 250 vehicles may pass per day, because Alberese is in the ✳ **nature reserve of the Maremma**, the Monti dell'Uccellina. This last refuge of free-roaming cattle and horses also includes a bird sanctuary and the coast. Hiking trails cross the natural pasture, macchia, swamp and coastal landscape. At the extreme south the nature reserve borders on the popular fishing and bathing village of ❺ **Talamone**, which can be reached on the SS 1 via Fonteblanda.

In the steps of the Etruscans

Back in Fonteblanda, leave the Via Aurelia (SS 1) and drive into the heart of the southern Maremma (Maremma Alta). This agricultural and pasture land has hidden charms. The lightly rolling plain rises over 100m/328ft only in a few places. With a little luck you will see longhorn cattle. Beyond Fonteblanda follow the zigzag country road (about 14km/9mi) to ❻ **Magliano**, which has an important Etruscan site and an almost intact medieval wall.

Home of longhorn cattle

A pleasant country road leads on to Orbetello and from there to the beautiful ❼ ✳ **Monte Argentario** peninsula, which is popular with locals and tourists alike for its beaches in little bays, yacht harbours and former fishing villages. Here Porto Santo Stefano has become a fashionable, bustling holiday resort.

Monte Argentario

The medieval town wall of ❽ **Capalbio** is a pleasant place to take a walk. About 3km/1.8mi south-east on the border to Latium, Niki de Saint Phalle's fantastic sculpture park ❾ ✳ **Giardino dei Tarocchi** is a remarkable sight. Afterwards follow the lonely road (20km/12mi) to La Sgrilla and from there the SS 74 further to Manciano. Right after the town the SS 322 turns off to the left towards Montemerano (4km/2.5mi), a nice town with a labyrinth of streets.

Capalbio, Giardino dei Tarocchi

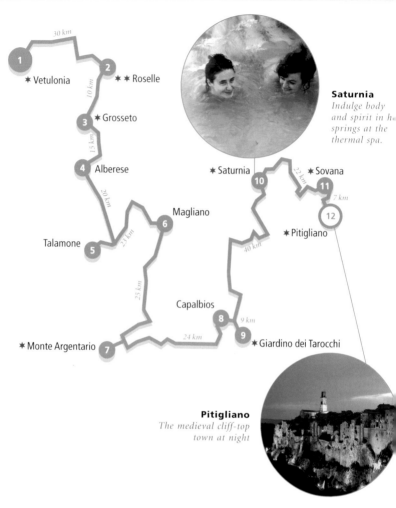

1 ✳ Vetulonia

30 km

2 ✳ ✳ Roselle

10 km

3 ✳ Grosseto

15 km

4 Alberese

20 km

6 Magliano

Talamone

5

23 km

25 km

Capalbios

8 9 km

7 ✳ Monte Argentario 24 km **9** ✳ Giardino dei Tarocchi

✳ Saturnia **10** 22 km ✳ Sovana **11** 7 km **12**

✳ Pitigliano

40 km

Saturnia
*Indulge body
and spirit in h…
springs at the
thermal spa.*

Pitigliano
*The medieval cliff-top
town at night*

Saturnia   The neighbouring spa ❿ ✳ **Saturnia** (12km/7.5mi) was mentioned
by ancient historians. No-one should pass through without indulging
themselves in the luxurious thermal bath. Those who prefer to bathe
outdoors follow the signs to the Cascate del Molino – here the waterfalls and sinter pools with steaming sulphuric water are open for
everyone at all times.

Sovana and   From Saturnia the road winds through a bizarre tuffstone landscape,
Sorano   which is lush green in places. The Etruscan ⓫ ✳ **Sovana** is an idyllic
elongated village with a massive ruined castle. In the immediate vici-

Dreamy impressions

nity of the village is an extensive Etruscan necropolis (marked paths lead to the most important burial chambers). The neighbouring ✳ **Sorano** stands gracefully on a rugged cliff. A winding road leads there (9km/5.5mi) through a craggy karst landscape. The columbaria (burial vaults) at the edge of Sorano are definitely worth seeing.

The final part of the route through the Etruscan-Roman border re- Pitigliano
gion is the picturesque ⑫ ✳ **Pitigliano**, where the houses rise from the green countryside like a sculpted crown (on the SS 74). The rock cellars under the town are still used to store Bianco di Pitigliano.

Sights
from A to Z

THERE IS LOTS TO DISCOVER IN TUSCANY: NOT ONLY HIGHLIGHTS LIKE FLORENCE AND SIENA, BUT ALSO PRETTY LITTLE VILLAGES AND PEACEFUL LANDSCAPES WITH ROLLING HILLS AND COLOURFUL POPPY FIELDS.

✶✶ Alpi Apuane · Garfagnana

E/F 3–6

Provinces: Massa-Carrara (MS),
Lucca (LU)

Everyone who enters Tuscany from the north-west should make a detour from Carrara (▶ Carrara • Massa) to the fascinating mountains of the Apuan Alps – a national park since 1985. Between the Apennines and this massif lies the Garfagnana, a mountain valley with isolated plateaus, chestnut forests, wild rivers and a famous dripstone cave – in short the ideal hiking area.

The name of the mountain range comes from the Ligurian Apuan people and was first used by Boccaccio for the mountain range parallel to the coast between the Tuscan-Emilian Apennines and the Versilian coastal plain. Monte Pisanino is the highest mountain (1,945m/ 6,381ft), but Monte Cavallo, Sagro, Tambura and Pizzo d'Uccello are also only just below 2,000m/6,600ft. Parallel to the Serchio River the SS 445 runs through the valley toward ▶ Lucca. Castelnuovo is a good starting point for hikes, mountain biking or horseback rides.

✴ Castelnuovo di Garfagnana

Heart of the Garfagnana

The heart of the Garfagnana, the valley of the Serchio River, which is flanked by the high ranges of the Apuan Alps on the west and the Apennines on the east, is the medieval town of Castelnuovo (population 6,000). From Piazza Umberto, which should be crossed quickly because of the through traffic, look up to the entrance of the **fortified old city**. Its castle with an enclosing wall and watchtowers, begun in the 13th century and later enlarged several times, is a witness to the warlike conflicts in the area.

Take the street on the right behind the city gate to get to the cathedral square with a nice view of the forested slopes in the background. The church was built in 1504 and is architecturally not very interesting, but it has a beautiful crucifix from the 14th century and a terracotta group *St Joseph and Two Angels* from the school of della Robbia. It is only a few steps to the second town square, Piazza delle Erbe, where there is a tourist information office with information on hiking trails and other activities. In Castiglione di Garfagnana, 5km/ 3mi north-east of Castelnuovo, Don Luigi Pellegrini's collection presents an overview of the traditional costumes and utensils and tools of the Garfagnana in 14 rooms.

Castiglione di Garfagnana ▶

Lago di Vagli, »sunken village«

The 13km/8mi detour from Castelnuovo di Garfagnana to Lago di Vagli is scenically beautiful (SS 445 to Poggi, then another 5.5km/ 3.5mi on a small country road). The **dammed-up lake** fills a narrow valley which was inhabited until 1953. The village that fell victim to the reservoir was called Fabbrica di Careggine. It can be seen every ten years – last in 2005 – when the lake is drained for cleaning – an eerie sight which draws many visitors.

✴ Barga

Barga, a town with a population of about 10,000 at 410m/1,345ft elevation, is for many the most charming place in the Garfagnana. Its cathedral is worth seeing and it has many proud palazzi, evidence of the town's former wealth. In the Middle Ages Lucca, Pisa and Florence fought over this fortress which controlled the narrow Serchio valley. They wanted to ward off the rulers of Modena (house of Este) in Castelnuovo further up the valley. At the parking lot near the entrance to the old city centre the Porta Reale remains from the former city fortifications – above the door is the city coat of arms with a barca (ship).

The observation platform in front of the cathedral of Barga commands a view over the housetops to the peaks of the Apuan Alps nearby.

✳
View ▶

A pleasant stroll through the **picturesque streets** of the centro storico leads up to the cathedral, where the square offers a wonderful
view of Barga and its surroundings. The only noteworthy feature on
the plain Romanesque façade of the church, which was built between
the 9th and the 15th century, is the 12th-century portal with a detailed relief depicting a grape harvest. Inside the church, the **marble
pulpit** from the second half of the 13th century, which is decorated
with reliefs, is the main attraction. It is set on four marble pillars of
which one stands on a crouching bearded man and two on lions.

✳ ✳
Grotta del Vento

☉

The detour from Barga (about 9km/6mi) to the Grotta del Vento
near Fornovolasco in the Parco Naturale delle Apuane is worthwhile.
The dripstone cave, which can be explored to a depth of 3.5km/
2.2mi, with bizarre stalactites and stalagmites along an underground
river, is the main tourist attraction of the Garfagnana. The various
routes through the grotto take from 1 to 3 hours (open: April–Sept
daily 10am–6pm, Oct–March only Sun and holidays; tel. 05 83 72 20
24).

Bagni di Lucca

Spa with
tradition

In Fornoli the SS 445 meets the SS 12 going toward Bagni di Lucca
(2km/1.2mi), a thermal spa visited mostly by Italians on the Lima
River, which flows into the Serchio not far to the west. The hot

▶ VISITING ALPI APUANE • GARFAGNANA

INFORMATION

Castelnuovo di Garfagnana
Via Cavalieri di Vittorio Veneto
Tel. 05 83 64 10 07
Fax 05 83 64 43 54

Barga
Pro Loco, Piazza Angelico 3
Tel. 05 83 72 34 99

EVENTS

During the »Rassegna Nazionale Artis-
ti di Strada« on the last weekend in
July or the first weekend in August
street theatre is performed throughout
the city for two days.

WHERE TO EAT

▶ Moderate
Osteria Vecchio Mulino
Castelnuovo di Garfagnana

Via Vittorio Emanuele 12
Tel. 05 83 621 92
Closed Mondays.
Rustic osteria that also sells traditional
regional products. Don't miss the giant
mortadella that they cut into cubes for
sampling.

WHERE TO STAY

▶ Mid-range
La Pergola
Barga
Via San Antonio 1
Tel. 05 83 71 12 39
Fax 05 83 71 04 33
Family hotel with pretty
rooms and a terrace for sunning.
With a little luck room
no. 43 will be available.

springs were already known in the high Middle Ages. During the belle époque nobles, artists and intellectuals met here, and Heinrich Heine recorded his stay in 1829 in the travel book *The Baths of Lucca*. Meanwhile the elegant charms of the world-famous spa, once so sophisticated, have become a bit **faded**.

As an alternative to a swim in the local waterfalls, there is a walk from the thermal baths in Bagni Caldi through dense chestnut forests to the hot springs. Of the thermal baths (38–54°C/100–129°F) only Villa Ada, Villa Demidoff and

<table><tr><td>! Baedeker TIP</td></tr><tr><td>A wild mountain region
In Botri, about 13km/8mi north of Bagni di Lucca, lies the entrance to a rocky canyon, part of the Riserva Naturale dell'Orrido di Botri. Two-hour and four-hour guided tours into the canyon are offered (beginning at 10am or 3pm, in Italian).</td></tr></table>

Jean Vorrand are still in use today for bathing, fango and sweating cures. The baths are only open from Easter to November.

From Bagni di Lucca the SS 12 runs through the lower Serchio valley to Borgo a Mozzano, where the spectacular 37m/40yd arch of the Ponte della Maddalena has spanned the river since the 12th century. The bridge takes its name from the Magdalene statue that once stood here and is now in the parish church. The unusual stone bridge is also called the devil's bridge by local people – probably because it was a masterpiece of engineering in its time which could only be understood as a work of the devil.

★ Borgo a Mozzano, Ponte della Maddalena

✦ ✦ Arezzo

| 14

Province: Arezzo (AR)
Population: 92,000

Altitude: 296m/971ft above sea level

It was no coincidence that Roberto Benigni used the squares and streets of Arezzo for the setting of his film *Life is Beautiful*: the sloping old city centre is among the most beautiful in Tuscany. But for art lovers there is another reason to visit the provincial capital on the edge of the broad plain of the ►Val di Chiana: the frescoes of Piero della Francesca in the church San Francesco, which can be viewed again after a restoration that took fifteen years.

Umbrians and Etruscans settled the hill with its fertile surroundings. The city belonged to the league of twelve main Etruscan centres. Under the Romans Arretium was founded in 294 BC as a military station on the Via Cassia. During the republican period a forum, theatre and baths were built. Arezzo became famous in the Augustinian

History

VISITING AREZZO

INFORMATION
APT
Piazza della Repubblica 28
Tel. 057 37 76 78
Fax 057 20 839
www.apt.arezzo.it

EVENTS
Giostra del Saraceno
Every year on the first Sunday in September eight representatives of the four parts of the city compete in a horse tournament, first documented in 1593, which is not without danger. Armed with lances they fight the wooden king Buratto of the Saracens. Pity the rider who gallops too long – he feels the long arm of the turning figure. The winner gets the »golden lance«.

WHERE TO EAT
▶ Moderate
② *Antica Osteria l'Agania*
Via Mazzini 10
Tel. 05 75 29 53 81
www.osteriagania.it
Closed Mondays.
Popular trattoria in the historic centre of Arezzo with typical Tuscan dishes, for example panzanella (bread soup) or ribollita (bean soup).

▶ Moderate
① *Buca di San Francesco*
Via San Francesco 1
Tel. 057 52 32 71
Closed Monday evenings and Tuesdays.
Charlie Chaplin and Salvador Dalí were pampered in this 14th-century palazzo.

③ *La Lancia d'Oro*
Piazza Grande 18 / 19
Tel. 05 75 21 033

Closed Sunday evenings and Mondays. In the warm season this restaurant is unsurpassable, as it has tables outdoors under the loggias of Vasari with a view of Piazza Grande.

WHERE TO STAY
▶ Mid-range
① *Villa Burali*
Gorello di Policiano
Tel. 05 75 97 90 45
Fax 05 75 97 92 96, 11 rooms
Notable 18th-century stately home, about 7km/4mi outside of town on the SS 71. The restaurant is highly recommended.

③ *Hotel Patio*
Via Cavour 23
Tel. 05 75 40 19 62
Fax 05 75 27 418
Something very special: a Tuscan palazzo in the old city of Arezzo conceals faraway, exotic worlds – inspired by the well-travelled author Bruce Chatwin. Choose between the tropics, an impressive Australian sunset and the Chinese emperor Wu-Ti's suite.

▶ Budget
② *B & B Tarussio*
Via Isonzo 41
Tel. and fax 05 75 90 10 35
Located in a side street behind the railway station, the Tarussio bed & breakfast which opened in 2004 is a real alternative to the somewhat expensive hotels of the old city.

Arezzo *Plan*

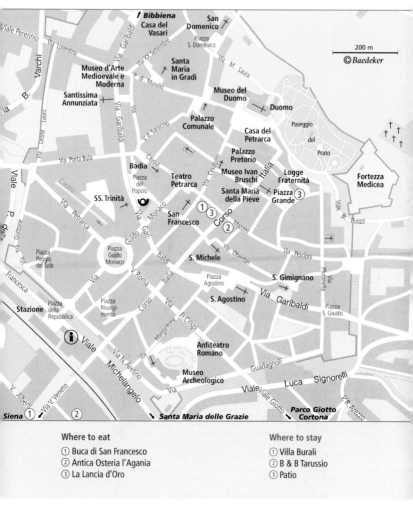

Where to eat
① Buca di San Francesco
② Antica Osteria l'Agania
③ La Lancia d'Oro

Where to stay
① Villa Burali
② B & B Tarussio
③ Patio

era for of its foundries and coral-coloured lacquered vases. From 1098 elected consuls ruled the city republic, which was able to stand up against Florence and Siena. Only in the battle of Campaldino (1289) was the former Ghibelline city, loyal to the emperor, defeated by the Florentines. In 1337 Arezzo was sold to Florence for 40,000 guilders and submitted to it from then on. The birthplace of the poet Petrarch had lost its independence, but its greatest artistic achievement, in the 15th century, was yet to come.

San Francesco

Opening hours:
Mon–Fri 9am–6pm,
Sat until 5.30pm
Sun 1–5.30pm

The old city of Arezzo lies on a slope and is accessible to non-residents only on foot. Thus no matter where you park the car, the way to the centre goes uphill first. The massive Franciscan church stands in the heart of the old city, where Via Cesalpino intersects Via Cavour, which expands to an oblong square with street cafés – including the famous Caffè dei Costanti. The unassuming, undecorated exterior of the church does not betray the world-class work of art hidden inside, which has been given new brilliance after a long restoration period. The church was begun in 1290 and finished in 1377 in the Tuscan Gothic style. The side chapels were added in the 15th century, the campanile in 1600.

Above the entrance is a round window by Guillaume de Marcillat. It portrays Pope Honorius III, who approved the order of St Francis. The 53m/174ft-long, aisle-less interior is remarkable for its murals. When the large Baroque altars were removed at the beginning of the 20th century remarkable frescoes by Spinello Aretino and his pupils came to light, including the *Meal with the Pharisee* (around 1440) by Parri di Spinello as well as the *Mystic Marriage of St Catherine*, the *Baptism of Jesus* and the *Annunciation* by Spinello Aretino himself, who also painted a cycle on the life of St Michael in the right choir chapel and a crucifixion group in the left choir chapel.

The *Annunciation* in the Capella Tarlati is attributed to Luca Signorelli, the depiction of the *Life of St Bernardino of Siena* (around 1460) on the right-hand wall and the *Legend of St Anthony of Padua* (around 1480) in the left side chapel are by Lorentino d'Arezzo.

★ ★
Fresco cycle by Piero della Francesca

A highlight of western art awaits visitors in the main choir chapel with the restored frescoes on the *Legend of the Cross* by Piero della Francesca (1420–1492). Since only a few visitors are allowed into the chapel at a time, it is best to order tickets in advance by telephone, at least during the tourist season (tel. 05 75 90 04 04). The ticket office is a few feet to the right of the church entrance. Or buy tickets online: www.pierodellafrancesca.it. Visitors are admitted every half hour. In the chapel itself audio guides are available in English. The commission to paint the chapel was given in 1447 by the wealthy merchant family Bacci to the Florentine Bicci di Lorenzo. He painted the triumphal arch wall (*Creation* to *Last Judgement*) and the dome of the choir (*Doctors of the Church*) up to 1452.

After his death Piero della Francesca continued the work on behalf of Giovanni Bacci. It was completed in 1464. The main master of the Italian early Renaissance took up the *Legenda Aurea*, which was composed in 1275 and narrates the fate of the cross of Christ. With this cycle he created one of the most expressive works of Italian Renaissance painting. The story goes from the death of Adam to the Persian War (7th century). The order of the pictures is not chronological – unlike the following description.

After Seth planted a tree branch on the grave of his father Adam at the direction of the archangel Michael, the shoot of the hope of salvation grew there.

◄ Right-hand wall, top

The kneeling Queen of Sheba recognized the sacred wood and prophesied that it would be the instrument of Christ's suffering. The handshake of the Queen of Sheba and King Solomon, wearing the hat of a Roman Catholic cardinal and the papal garments of the patriarchs of Constantinople, symbolized the unification of the church of the circumcision and the church of humankind to the people of God.

◄ Right-hand wall, middle

With a great effort three men carry the wood to Jerusalem for the building of the temple. There are no scenes from the New Testament. Neither did Piero della Francesca depict the crucifixion, since there was a 13th-century crucifix in front of the altar at that time already, which was included in the fresco cycle.

◄ Facing wall, right, middle

Before the decisive battle against Maxentius (312), the Roman emperor Constantine dreamt of the sign of the cross, under which he would be victorious. Using sophisticated light effects that include the choir windows as a source of light, Piero della Francesca here created **one of the first night scenes in European art**.

◄ Facing wall, bottom right

At Ponte Milvio Constantine – riding a white horse and carrying the cross – defeats Maxentius, who dies in the Tiber River.

◄ Right-hand wall, bottom

An angel tells Mary that she will die and ascend to heaven; the victory palm that the angel carried symbolized the incarnation of the Son of God.

◄ Facing wall, bottom left

Judas the Levite, who was tortured in a well, showed Helena, the mother of the emperor, the place where the true cross was buried.

◄ Facing wall, middle left

Three crosses were found on Golgotha but only the sacred cross could raise a dead person; Jerusalem in the background is actually Arezzo.

◄ Left-hand wall, middle

Chosroe II conquered Jerusalem in 614, stole the cross and had it made into a throne for himself, but the Byzantine emperor Heracleios won the cross back in a battle and condemned the defeated Persian king to death in front of his empty throne. Next to the shredded Moorish flag, the victorious banners of the crusades (white cross on red background) and the flags of the Holy Roman emperor wave in the centre of the picture; the green flag with a mystical bird postulates unity and love.

◄ Right-hand wall, bottom

Heracleios brought the cross back to Jerusalem. Adam's shoot bore fruit; the believers worshipped him. Two prophets conclude the cycle on the facing wall, top left and right.

◄ Left-hand wall, top

Around Piazza Grande

Follow Via Cavour to the east, cross the intersection with the broad shopping street Corso Italia and then walk uphill to Piazza Grande, the steeply sloping main square of Arezzo. Its stately old houses with opportunities for browsing in antique shops and second-hand book-

★ ★
Piazza Grande

shops make it the most beautiful square in the city.

The semicircular choir of the church Santa Maria della Pieve is an attractive architectural feature. To the right are the Renaissance façades of the Palazzo del Tribunale (palace of justice) and the elegant Palazzo della Fraternità dei Laici, both built in the 17th–18th centuries, while the north side of the square is dominated by Vasari's loggias. The restaurants and cafés under the shady arcades of the loggias are a wonderful place to take in the piazza at leisure.

Santa Maria della Pieve

(photo p.150) ►

The most important and also oldest church in the city is the parish church, simply called »la Pieve«. It already stood in the 12th century, was rebuilt after being destroyed in the 13th century and modernized in the 16th century by Vasari. The façade, which was built in front of an older one in the 13th century and faces the Corso d'Italia, is remarkable for the fact that it is not aligned with the nave, as in many other churches. In the dwarf galleries above the entrance the number of columns increases with every storey, which gives the impression that the building tapers.

A look up to the five rows of double windows of the campanile explains why this elegant torre, which was built around 1330, is called the »tower of one hundred holes«. The interior of the church has an austere clarity. Under the elevated presbytery, which was begun before 1200 and is the oldest part of the church, is the crypt with a reliquary bust of St Donatus, Arezzo's patron saint. The gilded silver bust, set with gems, is dated 1346. The polyptych of the Virgin above the altar, which was painted by the Sienese Pietro Lorenzetti, is noteworthy. Notice also the font in the baptistery under the tower with three relief scenes from the life of John the Baptist (around 1333).

Museo Ivan Bruschi

The medieval palazzo opposite the entrance of Santa Maria della Pieve (Corso Italia 14) was the home of the collector Ivan Bruschi, whose archaeological treasures are on display for the public.

Palazzo della Fraternità dei Laici

Adjoining the Palazzo del Tribunale is the Palazzo della Fraternità dei Laici, built by the charitable order of lay brothers Santa Maria della Misericordia in the 14th and 15th centuries. Its façade was begun by Baldino di Cino and Niccolò di Francesco in Gothic style and completed by Bernardo Rossellino in the Renaissance style. The belfry was added by Giorgio Vasari in the middle of the 16th century.

Palazzo delle Logge

The Palazzo delle Logge was also built to plans by Vasari, between 1573 and 1581 on the north side of Piazza Grande. It imitates ancient architecture. In front of the palazzo is a copy of a so-called pet-rone, a medieval pillory, where criminals were put on public display.

Only a few steps north of the church Santa Maria is Palazzo Pretorio, the former Palazzo Albergotti. Originally built in 1322 out of three patrician houses, the palace was altered considerably in the 15th and 16th centuries. The façade bears numerous coats of arm of the podestà and commissars of the 15th to 18th centuries. From 1404 to 1926 the palazzo was used by the judicial administration; today it houses the public library.

Palazzo Pretorio

The Casa del Petrarca (no. 28), presumed to be the birthplace of the poet Petrarch, is part of the same building block on Via dell'Orto. Francesco Petrarca (Petrarch) really was born in this street but the house was built in the 17th century, almost completely destroyed in World War II and rebuilt in 1948. Today it is the seat of the famous Accademia Petrarca di Lettere, Arti e Scienze, which guards the memory of the great humanist and has awarded the coveted Petrarca Prize for Literature since 1974 (hours: Mon–Fri 9.15am-12.45pm and 4–6.30pm, Sat mornings only).

Casa del Petrarca

The most beautiful place in Arezzo for a cappuccino: the arcades of the Piazza Grande

The semicircular choir of Santa Maria della Pieve illuminated at night

✳ **Duomo** Until the 13th century the cathedral of Arezzo stood outside of the city walls on Piota Hill where St Donatus was martyred and buried in 304. When the people of Arezzo demanded in 1111 that the bishop's seat be moved into the city a riot started and the medieval church was destroyed. In 1277 the building of the present cathedral was begun on the site of the former Benedictine church San Pietro Maggiore at the urging of Bishop Guglielmino degli Ubertini. Work continued in 1313 and 1510 but was not completed until the early 20th century.

In compliance with the rules of the mendicant orders the interior of the pillared basilica is plain. The main attraction is the wonderful large-scale stained glass by the French Dominican monk Guillaume de Marcillat (1467–1529) in the south aisle. Also worth seeing in the south aisle is the tomb of the Arezzan pope Gregory X (died 1276), which was made after 1320, and the burial chapel of Ciuccio Tarlati dating to 1334. The main altar holds the richly decorated late Gothic marble funerary monument with the relics of St Donatus. In the north aisle Piero della Francesca painted an impressive fresco with a depiction of the Magdalene (1459). After a miracle by the Virgin Mary the chapel Madonna del Conforto (Madonna of Consolation) was built between 1796 and 1817 at the northern aisle.

The cathedral museum in the former sacristy shows treasures of religious art, including valuable altar paintings, goldsmith work and an early Romanesque crucifix from the 11th century (hours: Thu–Sat 10am–noon or also upon request: tel. 05 75 239 91).

Museo del Duomo ⏱

After visiting the cathedral take a walk through the park of the Passeggio del Prato to the modern monument to Francesco Petrarca. The large park extends to the massive Medici fortress, which stands on 13th-century foundations. Grand Duke Cosimo I commissioned Giuliano da Sangallo in the mid-16th century to extend the old fortification and to give it a new wall and bulwarks. There is a fine panoramic view from the top.

Passeggio del Prato, Fortezza Medicea

A massive medieval tower marks the Palazzo Comunale west of the cathedral, formerly called Palazzo dei Priori. Today it is the city hall. It was built in 1333 as the office of the head of the guilds. After 1384 it was the residence of the administrative commissars from Florence, who also had the façade decorated extravagantly with their coats of arms.

Palazzo Comunale

Western Old City

There are more treasures of religious art north-west of the cathedral in the church San Domenico on the square of the same name. The Tarlati di Pietramala family donated the cost of the simple aisle-less church in 1275. It was completed shortly after 1300. The most valuable decoration was returned to its place in the apse in 2001: the crucifix by Cimabue dated 1260/1270, an early work by the famous artist which shows Byzantine influence. But with its image of a suffering Christ it is also a pioneering work. It is also worth taking a look at the frescoes by Arezzan painters, such as the scenes from the lives of St Philip and St James by Spinello Aretino on the entrance wall created around 1390, and the *Crucifixion* by his son Parri (around 1450). For information on the restoration of the Cimabue cross or to prepare to enjoy these works in person: www.cimabuearezzo.it. Tickets can be ordered in advance at tel. 05 75 90 04 04.

San Domenico

★
◀ Crucifix by Cimabue

The importance of the painter and architect Giorgio Vasari (1511–1574), apart from his architectural accomplishments, lies especially in his **biographies of Italian artists**, which are among the most important sources for Italian art history. In 1540 Vasari bought

★
Casa di Giorgio Vasari

Poetry according to Vasari

the two-storey house no. 55 in today's Via XX Settembre and painted the rooms (up to 1548). They were intended to depict one thing above all: the glory and importance of the arts. Vasari made use of allegorical images, for example the ceiling painting in the Camera Nuziale, or artists' portraits. The museum also has Vasari's model of the Palazzo delle Logge on Piazza Grande as well as paintings by contemporaries, including Jacopo Zucchi, Perin del Vaga and Francesco Vanni. Hours: daily except Tue 9am–7pm, Sun 9am–1pm.

The elegant Palazzo Bruni-Ciocchi or Palazzo della Dogana (there was a customs house here in the 19th century) in Via San Lorentino was designed around 1450 in early Renaissance style, presumably by Bernardo Rosselino. It was commissioned by Donato, the son of the famous Florentine chancellor Leonardo Bruni. Today the palace houses the **museum for medieval and modern art**. Visitors get an excellent overview of painting in Arezzo from its beginnings until the end of the 16th century, with works by Mar-

✳
Museo d'Arte Medievale e Moderna
⏱

garito d'Arezzo, Spinello Aretino and his son Parri, by Bartolomeo della Gatta, Luca Signorelli, Rosso Fiorentino and Vasari. The Tuscan masters of the 17th to 19th centuries include Cigoli, Fattori and Signorini. The museum also has valuable majolica, goldsmith work, ivory carvings as well as coins. Hours: daily except Mon 9am–7pm, Sat and Sun until 1pm.

Santa Maria in Gradi and Santissima Annunziata

Steps lead up to the church of Santa Maria in Gradi, built by the Florentine architect Bartolommeo Ammanati (1511–1592) on the foundations of a Romanesque church. Along with the bell tower built in 1631, in the interior a terracotta group (*Madonna of Mercy*) by Andrea della Robbia and the crypt of the original church deserve a look. Only a few steps south-west on Via Garibaldi Renaissance, Bartolomeo della Gatta and Antonio da Sangallo the Elder built the Church of the Annunciation between 1490 and 1520 on the site of a 14th-century oratory. The portal on the right is part of the previous Gothic building, as is the fresco of the annunciation above it (1370). The simple interior is remarkable for its glass window by Marcillat.

The second large Renaissance church in Arezzo is the abbey of St Flora and St Lucilla (also called Chiesa di Badia), which was originally founded in the 14th century by Benedictine monks from the monastery Monte Cassino. It got its present form when Giorgio Vasari undertook thorough renovations in the late Renaissance style in the mid-16th century. The monumental high altar is also his work (1562). **Andrea Pozzo** from Trento gave an excellent example of high Baroque mural painting in the tromp l'œil dome in the nave (1703): the skilled mixture of perspective, light and shade create a convincing impression of a massive dome.

Sante Flora e Lucilla (Chiesa di Badia)

Southern Old City

In front of the main railway station is the trademark of Arezzo, the wild chimera. The strength of a lion, the cleverness of a snake and the stoic temperament of a goat are united in the demonic fabled creature. The bronze monument is a copy of an Etruscan statue from the 4th century BC, which is in the Archaeological Museum of ► Florence today.

Chimera

The remains of the amphitheatre (entrance in Via F. Crispi) bear witness to the Roman period. The elliptical construction, which was built between the 1st and 2nd century, once held between 8,000 and 10,000 spectators. It was 121m/132yd long and 68m/74yd wide. The theatre fell into decay later when it was used as a stone quarry.

Anfiteatro Romano

The former monastery San Bernardo, which was built in 1547 by Olivet monks on the ruins of the Roman amphitheatre in a part of the stands, now holds the collections of the Museo Archeologico Mecenate (Via Margaritone 10). The archaeological museum displays numerous **finds from the Etruscan and Roman periods**, including terracotta decorations from a temple of the 5th century BC, Etruscan reliefs and votive offerings, Roman small bronze figures and mosaics as well as typical Arezzan »vasi corallini«, coral-coloured ceramic vases with terra sigillata decoration which were a popular export item during the imperial Roman period (hours: Mon–Sat 8.30am to 7.30pm).

✴ Museo Archeologico Mecenate

About 2km/1.3mi south of the old city, the late Gothic pilgrimage church of Santa Maria delle Grazie is surrounded by an expansive lawn. According to tradition St Bernardino of Siena came 1428 to this place, where there was a sacred spring from ancient times. He had the remains of the pagan cult removed and built a chapel. In 1449 the present building was begun in honour of the Madonna of Mercy (Madonna delle Grazie); in 1478 Benedetto da Maiano added a graceful portico. Toward the end of the 15th century Andrea della Robbia created the extravagant main altar with a pietà of marble and terracotta.

Santa Maria delle Grazie

Bibbiena • Casentino

G 13

Province: Arezzo (AR)   **Altitude:** 425m/1,394ft above sea level
Population : 11,500

Bibbiena, on a hill near the place where the Archiano flows into the Arno, 30km/19mi north of ▶Arezzo, is a good place to start excursions into the Casentino, the mountain range that borders the north-east of the Arno valley. Here visitors will find a densely forested but fertile mountain landscape, largely untouched nature and solitude.

Embattled city The city was probably founded by the Etruscans and was the object of heated conflicts well into the 15th century because of its location. Florence and Arezzo both claimed the valley pass in the extreme north-east of Tuscany for themselves and fought hard-contested battles here. Already in the early Middle Ages small monastic communities were founded in complete isolation in the Casentino. They included the hermit monastery Camaldoli and the famous Franciscan monastery La Verna, today an important place of pilgrimage. West of the Casentine source of the Arno lie the Pratomagno mountains with wonderful chestnut, pine and beech forests.

Sights in Bibbiena Bibbiena offers no sensations, but a **complete old town**, in which souvenir shops are so far rare. Via G. Borghi runs almost straight to Piazza Tarlati, the high main square with a clock tower and Palazzo Vecchietti Poltri. Among the city palaces in the centre, the most notable is Palazzo Dovizi, a Renaissance structure built in 1498 for Cardinal Bernardo Dovizi in the street with the same name. Dovizi, who was born in Bibbiena, served as secretary to Cardinal Giovanni de'Medici (the later Pope Leo X). The palazzo is privately owned and can only be viewed from the outside. Opposite it lies the church of San Lorenzo, where terracottas from the workshop of the della Robbias can be seen.

Excursion to Camaldoli

Mother house of the Camaldolese Order Camaldoli Abbey, the centre of the Camaldolese order, lies in the middle of a glorious forest landscape about 20km/13mi north of Bibbiena in the mountains of the Casentino. It was founded at the start of the second millennium in the course of the great western church reform. The members of the order retreated to places that were as isolated as possible so that they could meditate in peace. Here in the Casentino, Count Maldolo d'Arezzo gave St Romuald and his brothers in faith a piece of land where he built the founding monastery in 1012. The house was named Ca(sa di) Maldolo, »House of Maldolo«, after its donor. A short while later some monks moved higher up in

VISITING BIBBIENA • CASENTINO

INFORMATION

Piazza Matteotti 3
Tel. 05 75 59 30 98
infocasentino@apt.arezzo.it

WHERE TO EAT

► Inexpensive

Foresteria del Monastero
Camaldoli, rel. 05 75 55 60 13
www.camaldoli.it
Good food at a reasonable price is offered here, but reservations are requested (just tell them in the attached bar of the foresteria). Out-side of spiritual seminar weeks there is cheap and good accommodation in the Monastero.

► Moderate

Il Bivio
Loc. Bivio di Banzena
Tel. 05 75 59 32 42, closed Mondays.
Local cuisine at its best and for moderate prices in a modest-looking restaurant on the road from Bibbiena to La Verna.

WHERE TO STAY

► Budget

Il Mulino
Faltona, La Villa 32A
Tel. / fax 05 75 51 28 78
This is the right place for everyone who wants to really relax and get out into nature. The restored mill is situated romantically in a side valley of the Arno in the Casentino, the forested north-east of Tuscany. The German owners rent two holiday flats for two to four people.

► Mid-range

Falterona
Stia, Piazza Tanucci 85
Tel. 05 75 50 45 69
Fax 05 75 50 49 82, 15 rooms
Charming little city hotel in the middle of Stia in an old palazzo. The rooms are tiny, but furnished taste-fully.

order to be completely isolated at 1,100m/3,609ft in today's Eremo di Camaldoli. After the pope approved the order in 1113 the Camal-dolese community flourished.

The monastery complex today consists of a cloister, convent buildings, pilgrims' hospice (foresteria) and church. The monastery church was built in from 1509 to 1524 in place of a previous church and got its Baroque appearance in the late 18th century. Giorgio Vasari did several paintings for the interior. A visit to the **pharmacy**, a rare surviving ex-ample with its hand-carved shelves and furnished laboratory, is an abso-lute must. The pilgrims' hospice is completely booked almost all year round, since conferences and semi-nars are held here on a regular basis.

Monastero di Camaldoli

 Baedeker TIP

Homemade

Herbal liqueurs distilled from traditional recipes, varieties of tea, jams and aromatic ointments are only a few of the delicacies to be bought in the monastery pharmacy.

Eremo di Camaldoli

Shortly after the founding of the monastery St Romuald and a few monks moved higher up into the mountains in search of even greater solitude. Thus in 1027 on the »pleasant field« surrounded by woods, the Eremo di Camaldoli, a group of monks' cells with a church dedicated to the redeemer, was built. The Chiesa del Salvatore owes its Baroque appearance to renovations carried out in the years 1658, 1708 and 1714. 17th-century frescoes on the walls of the church show scenes from the life of St Romuald. The **20 monks' cells** are small huts standing in five rows, each with a small garden. According to tradition five were built by the founder of the order. Others go back to illustrious donors, like Pope Leo X's cell, where Maria de Medici is supposed to have lived once, and the cell of Duke Ranuccio Farnese. The modest cell of St Romuald, with a tiny chapel and study, is reached through the Foresteria Vecchia opposite the church.

Excursion to La Verna Monastery

Famous place of pilgrimage

Only about 20km/13mi separate La Verna from Bibbiena, but the winding road means that the trip takes some time. The monastery lies in the middle of expansive pine forests on the slope of Monte Penna (1,300m/4,265ft) above a steep cliff. The most famous Italian saint, Francis of Assisi, retreated to the isolation of the Casentino mountains after relinquishing the leadership of the Franciscan order. In 1213 Count Orlando Cattini of Chiusi, who had heard the preaching of the beggar monk, gave La Verna mountain to the saint and his followers. Here the Franciscans lived in simple huts at first. According to tradition Francis received the wounds of Christ here on 14 September 1224, two years before his death. Since then La Verna has been considered a holy place. Large numbers of pilgrims come here, especially on 14 September and 3 October, the day on which St Francis died..

From the parking lot in the woods walk about 500m/550yd to the entrance of the extensive monastery complex with its rustic stone buildings. The path leads to a broad square called Quadrante at the cliff, from which the most important attractions of the sacred site can be reached. In 1348 at the order of Count Tarlato di Pietramala the building of the large church (Chiesa Maggiore) was begun. It was completed in the early 16th century. The beautiful **terracottas by Andrea della Robbia** are notable: *Madonna with Saints* and *Adoration of the Child* (1479), *Annunciation* (1480), *St Anthony Abbas and St Francis* and *Ascension* (1499). The little adjoining church Santa Maria degli Angeli is older. St Francis himself laid the foundation stone for it in 1216. The following centuries brought considerable changes and extensions to the church. Inside are some terracotta works from the workshop of the della Robbias, and a memorial for the donor Count Orlando Cattani.

Magnificent view: the monastery of La Verna has a wonderful view over the forests of the Casentino.

The »Walk of the Stigmata«, decorated with frescoes on the life of St Francis, leads from the Quadrante to a group of chapels with the main attraction, the Chiesa delle Stimmate (Chapel of the Wounds). Halfway there a door leads into a cleft in the rock where St Francis set up spartan sleeping quarters for himself. In the Stimmate chapel, which was built in 1263, a marble frame in the floor shows the place where Francis is supposed to have experienced the **miracle of the stigmatization**. Ceiling and walls were originally painted with frescoes, which were lost or removed in order to make room for the large altar by Andrea della Robbia (1481). Before returning step out of the chapel of the cross, which lies in front of the Chiesa delle Stimmate, where a narrow but safe path leads around the cliff–in good weather there is a wonderful view of the Casentino. A beautiful hiking trail leads to the peak of the 1,283m/4,209ft-high Monte Penna.

✷
Chiesa delle Stimmate

A winding road connects La Verna with Chiusi della Verna 2km/ 1.3mi away. From there it is another 10km/6mi south to Caprese Michelangelo, which offers wonderful views of the craggy mountain world of the southern Casentino. The town with a population of 1,600 would probably attract no attention if it were not the birthplace of Michelangelo Buonarroti (▶Famous People). Of course this has only been certain since 1875 when a copy was found of the artist's birth certificate, made for Michelangelo's father Lodovico, at that time mayor of Caprese. That ended the quarrel between Caprese and the town of Chiusi della Verna, which also claimed to be the great man's birthplace.

Caprese Michelangelo

Casa Natale di
Michelangelo ► The house situated at the highest point in the town, the 14th-century Casa del Podestà, is considered to be the house where Michelangelo was born on 6 March 1475. Today a museum dedicated to the artist exhibits copies and photographs of his world-famous sculptures (hours: June–Oct daily except Mon 9.30am-6.30pm, Nov–June 10am–5pm).

Franciscan encounter

Via Poppi to Vallombrosa

From Bibbiena follow the Arno valley upstream with its meadows, vineyards and olive groves for 6km/3.5mi to Poppi (population 6,000). From the lower town on the river cross the old stone bridge and go up the wooded hill to the charming upper town with its straight, cobbled main street. The **beautiful old arcades** keep visitors dry here even in rainy weather. The Corso widens to a square, irregular but all the prettier for that, with the domed 17th-century oratory.

A steep ascent leads from the centre of Poppi up to a strong castle from which there is a **wonderful view of the hilly landscape of the Casentino**. The powerful Guidi counts had the castle built in the 13th century above today's town. The two-storey wings of the building surround an elegant inner courtyard with a boldly curved

Poppi staircase, wooden galleries and the coat of arms of the Florentine governor on the gatehouse. The castle chapel is well preserved with 14th-century frescoes, which are thought to be by Taddeo Gaddi. The library has precious incunabula and manuscripts. The former utility buildings of the castle today house the Casentino Hotel and its restaurant.

Castello Romena About 10km/6mi north of Poppi, near Romena, the Guidi had a 600m/1,950ft-high hill on the western bank of the Arno fortified with a mighty triple-walled castle, which fell to Florence in 1357. Today the castle is privately owned. It numbers Dante Alighieri, who mentioned it in his *Divine Comedy*, among its illustrious guests. The

Pieve di
San Pietro ► castle cannot be viewed at present, but the small Romanesque country church San Pietro, nestled in an idyllic landscape a few hundred yards below the castle, is open to visitors. Inside the church, which

was built around 1150, the **capitals** deserve attention. They are richly decorated with plants, heads of wild demons and scenes from the life of the apostle Peter.

Stia, just 11km/7mi north-west of Poppi, is one of those typical Casentino towns that offers no sensational sights, but is worth a stop for its wonderful atmosphere and harmonious appearance. Cross the river with its weir from the modern to the old city of Stia. Immediately behind the town gates is the heart of the town, the ascending Piazza Bernardo Tanucci with its **pretty old arcaded houses**. Just like the main square in Poppi this square has a rather »un-Tuscan« but still pleasant atmosphere. A Baroque façade with an open pediment conceals another example of Romanesque architecture, the 12th-century parish church of Santa Maria Assunta. According to legend it was built on behalf of Countess Matilda of Canossa. As in the Pieve di San Pietro the capitals of the church are wonderfully decorated with animal and plant motifs.

✷ Stia

About 13km/8mi west of Romena via the 1,060m/3,478ft-high Consuma Pass is the lonely forest region of Pratomagno, where nature lovers and hikers can find unforgettable scenery. Mountain trails lead to Monte Secchieta and the Falterona Massif, the headwater region of the Arno.

✷ Passo di Consuma

From the top of the pass a road to the left leads to the village of Montemignaio, 8km/5mi to the south. According to tradition its **Romanesque parish church** was commissioned by Countess Matilda of Canossa.

Montemignaio

In the early 11th century two monks from Settimo monastery settled as hermits in the lonely forests about 14km/9mi further west at the foot of Monte Secchieta. In 1028 the Florentine nobleman Giovanni Gualberto de Visdomi joined them and a short time later had a chapel built in Valle Ombrosa. In 1038 Gualberto founded the **Vallombrosan order**, which was confirmed in 1055 by the pope. Gualberto was canonized only 20 years after his death in 1073. In the 12th century the monastery properties grew through large donations, and in the 15th century the abbots even received the secular title of Marquess of Canneto and Monteverdi. The fortified monastery, which was later plundered, was built between 1450 and 1470. At the end of the 16th century the impressive monastery library and the small cloister were added. In the mid-17th century Gherardo Silvani gave the façade its present appearance. In 1866 the monastery was secularized, and monks did not move in again until 1963. The Romanesque monastery church is adorned with frescoes and paintings on the life of the founder of the order. In the left transept the chapel of the founder, Giovanni Gualberto, holds a shrine (around 1500) with an arm relic of the saint.

✷ Vallombrosa

Borgo San Lorenzo • Mugello

F 11

Province: Florence/Firenze (FI)   **Altitude:** 193m/633ft above sea level
Population : 16,000

Borgo San Lorenzo lies in the heart of the Mugello, a landscape in the north-east where the two artists Giotto and Fra Angelico were born and the Medici had two of their most beautiful country villas built.

The medieval town lies about 30km/19mi north of ▶Florence in the upper Sieve valley (Val di Sieve). The Sieve and its numerous tributaries meander through the Mugello hill and mountain landscape. The agricultural upper Sieve valley rolls gently while the forest and mountain landscape of the so-called Mugello Alto clearly has the character of the Apennine mountain range.

History   During the high Middle Ages Borgo San Lorenzo was part of the lands of the **Ubaldini**, who were able to resist the domination of Florence for a long time. The fate of Borgo San Lorenzo was sealed from 1290, when Florence acquired all rights to the Mugello region for 3,000 gold florins. In the mid-14th century the Florentines emphasized their claim by building a fortified wall around the city. The Albizi, the most stubborn opponents of the Medici, occupied Borgo in 1440. From 1529 to 1530 imperial troops built a military camp in Borgo and conquered Florence from here after an eight-month siege.

 VISITING BORGO SAN LORENZO

INFORMATION

Comunità Montana del Mugello
Via P. Togliatti 4
Borgo San Lorenzo
Tel. 055 849 53 46
Fax 055 845 62 88
www.turismo.mugello.toscana.it

WHERE TO EAT

▶ **Moderate**
Cosimo de' Medici
Barberino di Mugello
Viale del Lago 19
Garden restaurant with typically Tuscan cuisine, especially game specialties.

WHERE TO STAY

▶ **Mid-range**
Casa Palmira
Via Faentina 4
Loc. Feriolo / Polcanto
Tel. and fax 055 840 97 49
www.casapalmira.it
Stylish rural accommodation, but nevertheless close to Florence (16km/10mi). The owners, Assunta and Stefano, take especially good care of their guests
(cooking courses, fresco workshops, excursions in the region etc.).

What to see in Borgo San Lorenzo

The main attraction in Borgo San Lorenzo is the Romanesque parish church in Via San Francesco, which was first mentioned in 941. An inscription with the date 1263 reveals when the Romanesque-Gothic campanile was built. In the 16th century the adjoining monastery was built. The church gets its unmistakeable appearance from the **six-sided brick bell-tower**, which rises above the main apse. The interior has the typical outline of an early Christian basilica without transept. The decorations consist mainly of panel paintings and terracotta work of the 15th to 17th centuries.. The most important of these works is the »Black Madonna« of 1290, which is attributed to the famous Giotto.

✴ **Pieve di San Lorenzo**

> **!** **Baedeker TIP**
>
> **Art nouveau in Tuscany?**
> Sometimes examples of an architectural period can be found exactly where they are not expected. The city hall of Borgo San Lorenzo with art nouveau decoration by Tito Chini from 1931 is such a case. It is situated on Piazza Dante – for anyone who wants to take a look inside.

The oratory in Piazza Cavour was built between 1714 and 1743 to plans by the Florentine architect Girolamo Ticciati to hold a wooden crucifix which was revered for miraculous works (14th century).

Oratorio del SS. Crocifisso dei Miracoli

A little further eastwards the patrician Villa Pecori Giraldi houses the Museo della Manufattura Chini. The most famous offspring of the Chini artist family was **Galileo Chini** (1873–1956), who founded a ceramics factory in Borgo San Lorenzo in 1896 and influenced art nouveau in Tuscany with his decorations (hours: tel. 05 58 45 67 230).

Museo della Manufattura Chini

The former Palazzo del Podestà on Piazza Garibaldi contains the city library today. The façade is decorated with coats of arms of the podestà made of grey sandstone and majolica tiles. Inside the palazzo next to the entrance to the library is a small chapel.

Palazzo Pretorio

Only two of the five original gates remain in the medieval city fortifications, which were built in 1351: Porta Fiorentina, which has a rare type of Sienese round and pointed arch, and Porta dell'Orologio, which has a square bell-tower with a clock.

Porta Fiorentina and Porta dell' Orologio

Excursions into the Mugello • Val di Sieve

In Scarperia, 10km/6mi north-west of Borgo San Lorenzo, **the best knives in Italy** are supposedly made. But many people now know Scarperia for a completely different reason: about 1km/0.5mi east of the town is the Mugello racetrack (Autodromo Internazionale del Mugello), a track over 5km/3mi long where international car and motorcycle races have been held since 1974.

Scarperia

Buongiorno signori – a good start to a conversation with the two gentlemen ...

★
Museo dei Ferri
Taglienti ▶

🕐

The massive Palazzo Pretorio (or Castello del Vicario) stands on the town's main square, built in 1306 to plans by Arnolfo di Cambio and once the office of the Florentine vicars, whose stone and majolica coats of arms decorate the outer walls. The knife museum which is housed here is an attractive presentation of local craftsmanship – Scarperia was already known as the »city of knives« in the 15th century (hours: June–Sept Wed–Fri 3.30–7.30pm, Sat–Sun 10am–1pm, 3.30–7.30pm, otherwise only Sat and Sun 10am–1pm and 3 to 6.30pm). A walk through the town is an opportunity to glance into some of the workshops and look over the shoulders of the knife makers. Opposite the palazzo is the **provost's church** (Chiesa della Prepositura), which belonged to the adjoining Augustinian monastery until 1812. The showpiece of the church is a marble relief with a *Madonna and Child.*

★
Pieve di
Sant'Agata

From Scarperia a small country road leads to the neighbouring town of Sant'Agata (4km/2.5mi), where there is a fine example of Romanesque church architecture. The parish church was built almost completely of light stone (pietra alberese). Six slender columns divide the interior into a nave and two aisles and support the wooden roof. The eight-sided baptismal font (1503) is made from a single sandstone block (pietra arenaria). The baptistery is framed with filigreed relief panels, which decorated a pulpit in the 12th century. The delicate tabernacle, which shows the *Enthroned Madonna and Child*, is attributed to Giovanni della Robbia.

The medieval town 5km/3mi west of Borgo San Lorenzo on the Sieve distinguished itself after the Ubaldini were driven away as the most loyal ally of the Medici, who built two of their most beautiful country villas in the immediate surroundings of San Piero a Sieve in the 15th century and financed the expansion of Bosco ai Frati monastery near the town. In San Piero itself the Medici architects Baldassarre Lanci and Bernardo Buontalenti built **San Martino fortress**. On top of a hill above the town centre, it was the largest military complex of the Renaissance in the Mugello, even if it was of little use since no large defensive battles were fought here. The Medici fortress is privately owned today and unfortunately not open to the public.

San Piero a Sieve

About 3km/1.8mi north of San Piero a Sieve lies Bosco ai Frati, one of the oldest monasteries in Tuscany. Monks still live there today and it is open to the public. It was probably settled as early as the 6th century by Latin Basilian monks. The Ubaldini di Soli founded the monastery and turned it over to Franciscan monks in 1206. In 1420 Cosimo de Medici bought the complex. The court architect of the Medici, Michelozzo di Bartolomeo Michelozzi, finished the renovations and expansion of the monastery in 1438. It was converted to Baroque in the 17th century under Ferdinand II de Medici. On the plain façade and inside the church the **Medici coat of arms** (turtle and/or 6 spheres) can be seen several times. Even the gilded main altar (1626) displays the Medici symbols of worldly power. In the small Museo d'Arte Sacra the showpiece is a wooden crucifix by Donatello.

✶
Bosco ai Frati monastery

The fortified country estate of the Medici is accessible from San Piero a Sieve via the SS 65 towards Florence (turn off to the right after about 1km/0.6mi). This well-preserved country estate, which Cosimo il Vecchio built in the middle of the 15th century, stands in a dense cypress wood on a hill. Its fortress-like character with tower and ramparts is reminiscent of the Medici villa in Careggi near Florence. The adjoining garden is a rare example of a late medieval garden. The extravagantly furnished villa and the fabulous park can only be viewed by appointment (tel. 05 58 45 87 93).

Castello di Trebbio

This strong country castle of the Medici stands directly on the SS 65 between San Piero a Sieve and Barberino di Mugello. The surrounding meadows, vineyards, orchards and forests give an impression of the charming landscape of the time when the Medici court moved here in the summer to escape the city heat – Villa di Cafaggiolo was **the favourite country residence of Cosimo il Vecchio**. Michelozzo began it in 1451, after Castello di Trebbio was completed. In the 16th century the outbuildings of the villa housed a famous ceramic and porcelain factory. Unlike Villa di Trebbio the interior was almost completely changed by Cafaggiolo in the 19th century. The main

Villa di Cafaggiolo

⊙ halls got an antique-like décor (hours: summer Wed and Fri 2.30–6.30pm, Sat 10am–12.30pm and 2.30–6.30pm, otherwise only Sat and by appointment tel. 05 58 45 87 93)

Barberino di Mugello The town of Barberino di Mugello lies by the motorway exit with the same name on the Firenze–Bologna autostrada. Its castle on a hill on the north-eastern edge of town is worth a visit. In the Middle Ages the small fortress belonged to the Ubaldini and the Cattani di Cambiate; the coats of arms of these dynasties can still be seen undamaged in the walls. During the 17th century the Cattani heirs turned the castle into a fattoria (not open to the public).

East of Borgo San Lorenzo

Vicchio About 8km/5mi east of Borgo San Lorenzo lies Vicchio, where the painters Giotto and Fra Angelico were born. They did not stay at their birthplace long: Fra Angelico entered the Dominican order in Fiesole, Giotto moved to Florence, where he left important works in the Peruzzi chapel and the Bardi chapel in Santa Croce. Giotto's birthplace is in Vespignano, halfway between Borgo San Lorenzo and Vicchio. A small exhibition documents Giotto's artistic life (hours: summer Tue, Thu, Sat and Sun 10am–noon, 4–7pm, in the winter only Sat, Sun). The famous Florentine goldsmith **Benvenuto Cellini** also lived in Vicchio between 1559 and 1571. He does not appear to have been very welcome since he barely survived a poisoning attempt. On the house where he lived, Casa di Cellini next to the oratory, a memorial stone commemorates his stay. Giotto by contrast is honoured with a larger than life-size bronze statue on the central piazza. The Museo di Arte Sacra e Religiosità Populare »Beato Angelico« reopened in 2000. Its displays include frescoes from the school of Giotto and terracotta work from the school of della Robbia (Viale Beato Angelico 7; hours: summer Thu, Sat and Sun 10am–noon, 4–7pm; winter only Sat and Sun).

Giotto's birthplace ▶

Museo di Arte Sacra e Religiosità Populare ▶

⊙

San Godenzo At the foot of the Alpe di San Benedetto, about 20km/12mi east of Vicchio, San Godenzo lies on a densely forested slope. A conspiracy without consequences made this little mountain town famous: on 8 June 1302 the exiled Ghibelline leader **Dante Alighieri** met the rulers of the Mugello here, the Ubaldini, in order to make plots against Guelf Florence which failed in the end. St Gaudenzio lived here in the 6th century. Bishop Jacopo il Bavaro founded the local Benedictine abbey on his hermit's grave in 1028. Comparisons are drawn between the outwardly plain Romanesque columned basilica (in the centre of town) and the basilica of Fiesole as well as San Miniato al Monte in Florence. The precious furnishings include a Madonna polyptych from the school of Giotto and a wooden statue of St Sebastian by Baccio d'Agnolo (1507). The mummified corpse of St Gaudenzio rests in the crypt.

6km/4mi south-east lies the mountain village of Castagno d'Andrea, the birthplace of the Renaissance painter Andrea del Castagno (1423–1457), who is honoured only with a small monument. Wonderful hiking trails lead up to the 1,654m/5,427ft-high Monte Falterona. Finds from the Etruscan period were discovered on its slopes. Follow the course of the Sieve on the SS 67 toward Rufina to reach the largest wine region of the Mugello. Enormous **vineyards in fields and terraces** cover the fertile lower Sieve valley with a carpet of vines. About 4km/2.5mi before Rufina it is worthwhile to make a detour to the 992m/3,255ft-high Monte Giovi, a charming but also somewhat time-consuming drive on a small country road via Tamburino. The partisans of Mugello, around which heavy fighting raged, retreated to Monte Giovi at the end of World War II: the Gothic Line, the last German defensive line, ran along here. Today the slopes of Monte Giovi are part of a nature reserve.

Castagno d'Andrea

There is a reason for good olive oil being expensive: olives are still harvested by hand in nets, not with machinery.

Rufina

★

Villa di Poggio Reale ►

🕐

In the centre of this wine region numerous enoteche offer wine for sale along with wine tastings. After a generous tasting session a walk up to the Renaissance villa Poggio Reale (16th century), which is often mistakenly called a Medici villa, is recommended. It belonged to the Mormorai counts and later to the Berardi. The villa houses, among other things, the **Museo della Vite e del Vino**, a museum on wine and varieties of grapes that is well worth visiting (hours: Tue to Sun 10am–1pm and 2pm–7pm). The museum also has an enoteca.

Pontassieve

The name of the town at the confluence of the Sieve and Arno indicates that there must be a historic bridge here. The charming, double-arched brick bridge over the Sieve is easy to find. It was built under Cosimo I in 1555 to plans by his architect Bartolomeo Ammannati.

★ Carrara • Massa

E 3

Province: Massa-Carrara (MS)
Population : 65,000 (Carrara), 68,000 (Massa)

Altitude: 80m/262ft above sea level

Carrara, a busy and today mostly modern city, is one thing above all: the capital of the marble industry. The city owes not only its worldwide fame but also its name to the precious white stone: »car« means stone.

Carrara, which sits in a basin between the coast and the Apennines, spreads out on the western slope of the ► Alpi Apuane and in the south merges almost seamlessly with Massa, capital of the province Massa-Carrara. Massa has more ties with its famous neighbour than just geographical proximity. Both cities belonged to the **Malaspina** family from the 15th to the 18th century and later to the Lunigiana (and thus feel themselves to be part of Liguria rather than Tuscany), and both are characterized to this day by marble quarrying.

»David« for every household: Carrara without marble is unthinkable.

The beginnings of Carrara go back to pre-Roman times. Its first written mention is in a charter of donation of Emperor

VISITING CARRARA • MASSA

INFORMATION

Lungomare Vespucci 24
Marina di Massa
Tel. 05 85 24 00 46, fax 05 85 86 90 15
www.massacarrara.turismo.it

EVENTS

Simposio di Scultura

The chance to look over a sculptor's shoulder – once every two years in Carrara (always odd years) from the end of July until the middle of August at the Simposio di Scultura, when Piazza Gramsci, Piazza Erba and Via Plebiscito become one large open-air studio.

WHERE TO EAT

► Moderate

La Petite Cusine
Via Verdi 4
Tel. 058 57 02 26, closed Sun
Pretty little restaurant with light cuisine. Large selection of fish dishes.

Venanzio Colonnata
Località Colonnata

Piazza Palestro 3
Tel. 05 85 75 80 62
Closed Thu and Sun evening.
Ideal place to try Lardo di Colonnata, the famous regional bacon, when taking a trip to the marble quarries.

WHERE TO STAY

► Luxury

Maremonti
Viale Lungomare di Levante
Marina dei Ronchi
Tel. 05 85 24 10 08
Fax 05 85 24 20 09, 22 rooms
Cultivated hotel in a 19th-century villa with an enchanting garden and pool. Rooms facing the back are quiet, rooms facing the front have a terrace and a view of the sea.

► Mid-range

Michelangelo
Corso Fratelli Rosselli 3
Tel. 05 85 77 71 61
Fax 05 85 74 54 45
Every room is stylishly furnished with items from various periods.

Otto I to the bishops of the neighbouring city Luni in 963. In the 11th century Carrara fell to Pisa, which got its marble here to build the Campo dei Miracoli. This began its unstoppable rise to become the centre of Italian marble quarrying. In 1322 the town passed to Lucca, in 1329 to Genoa, in 1343 to the Visconti and in 1442 together with Massa to the Malaspina counts.

What to See in Carrara

The appearance of Carrara is marked mainly by the 19th and 20th centuries. The oldest part of the city lies relatively high up near the river Carrione, between the building of the Accademia di Belle Arti, the pretty **Piazza Alberica**, which is lined by Baroque palazzi, and the cathedral. The cathedral, a marble-clad basilica begun in the 11th and finished in the 14th century, is hemmed in by other buildings

★
Old town, Duomo
Sant'Andrea

◄ Cathedral

The flowing lines make it hard to believe that the draped fabric was chiselled out of hard stone.

CARRARA MARBLE

From a distance they look like fields of snow – the gigantic steps of the white marble quarries above Carrara, which go up to a height of over 3,000 feet in the massif of the Apuan Alps. No other natural stone is valued as highly as fine-grained white marble.

The name comes from the Greek word »mármaros«, meaning »broken stone«. In chemical terms, marble is a type of limestone. The Apuan Alps were covered by the sea more than 200 million years ago. The remains of shellfish and organic substances were compressed by the weight of the water above them and crystallized to an unusually pure limestone. When the African and European continental plates were pushed one over the other 50 million years ago, the region sank and the limestone was turned into marble by extreme pressure and high temperatures. After further millions of years the Apuan Alps were raised up and the marble in the almost 2,000m/6,500ft-high massif was exposed. The main characteristic of the hard, homogeneous stone is its durability. It stands up to every kind of weather and thus to the ravages of time. Foreign particles change the originally snow-white marble to striped, flame-patterned, spotted, marbled, veined and coloured marble. Traces of metallic salts cause discolorations during the process of formation: iron oxide causes red colouring, iron sulphide blue-black, while limonite, iron and manganese carbonate and iron hydroxide lead to yellow and brown tones, and ferrous silicates produce green colouring. Thus in Carrara more than 60 diffe-

rent types of marble are quarried in addition to the much-praised white »statuario«.

Tuscany's White Gold

It takes blood, sweat and tears to extract from the Apuan Alps the treasures that nature created in millions of years. Emperor Augustus sent slaves to the quarries of Carrara in order to gain marble for the triumphal arches and splendid villas of ancient Rome. The orders placed in Ligurian Luni, the centre of marble processing at that time, decreased with the decline of the Roman Empire from the 4th century AD. In 1185 the marble quarries of Carrara were mentioned as the suppliers of Genoa and Pisa, but became really famous only in the Renaissance, when sculptors and architects looked for perfect white blocks here for their sculptures, palaces and churches. Pisani, Bernini, Donatello or Henry Moore – they all wanted the »Tuscan white gold«. Michelangelo insisted on picking the best stone on site himself for his *David*. But even today leading architects are conscious of the impressive effect of this valuable stone, which has been used at the seat of government in Brasilia and, with conspicuous symbolism, for marble palaces in the desert sand of Saudi Arabia. Current estimates claim that the marble reserves will last at least another 300 years. The marble industry employs almost 3,500 people, including 1,200 persons in 300 quarries. The price per cubic metre for marble of average quality is about 1,000 euros. A medium-sized sculpted column now costs upwards of 20,000 euros.

Carrara marble has been coveted by sculptors for centuries.

From the Iron Chisel to the Wire Saw

The first »marmische«, as the workers are called here, made use of natural clefts in the rock by driving in spikes made of fig-tree wood which were then soaked in water, so that the expanding wood split the rocks. In Roman times iron wedges were bored into the rock along the cutting line in order to cut it from the mountain. In the mid-19th century the 3,000 or so workers in 600 quarries still extracted raw marble in this way. A motor-powered wire saw introduced in 1885 represented a major improvement. Annual production then climbed to almost 200,000t. In this method, which is still used today, a spiral wire with a thickness of 4mm to 6mm is guided over rollers in a circular path parallel to the stone layer at a speed of 5m to 6m (16ft to 19 ft) per second. It penetrates the stone and carries the actual cutting and sanding material –

gravel sand – while being sprayed with water. It can cut about 20cm/8in into the rock in an hour. The massive blocks (bancata) with a weight of up to 400t are then cut with diamond saws to a size suitable for transport. Recent efforts to cut marble with laser technology have proven to be too expensive.

Work in the marble quarries was always dangerous – there was a good reason why slaves and prisoners worked there in ancient times. One of the most hazardous jobs in the pre-industrial period was the transport of the gigantic marble blocks with the help of primitive wooden sleds, which rolled downhill on wooden poles that were greased with soap and secured only with hemp ropes. There were frequent fatalities when one of the giant blocks got out of control and buried workers underneath it. The »buccine« horns still sound in the valley today when the marble has

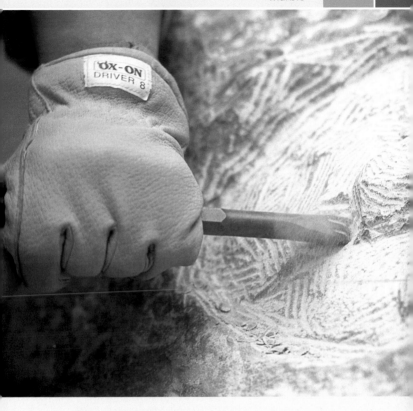

claimed another victim. In the early 20th century lifts and cable cars transported the blocks to a loading ramp. From 1876 to 1891 a 20km/13mi-long railway was built, running over 16 bridges and through 15 tunnels on a hair-raising journey down to the sea. Today large-scale modern technology is employed everywhere in the marble quarries; heavy steam shovels lift blocks weighing up to 25t onto large trucks for transport to the harbours in Marina di Carrara, Marina di Massa and Marina di Pietrasanta. From there the marble is exported to all parts of the world. However, the route to the coast is still full of bends and narrow, with a gradient of 20% in places. One unguarded moment, and the heavy load can quickly become a mortal danger.

The souvenir shops in Carrara and along the serpentine road to the quarries offer every imaginable item in marble, from the much-copied *David* to tabletops to chess sets and ashtrays. The quarries can be visited without special permission but caution is advised when on the premises. To learn about the history of marble, methods of quarrying and the use of marble, two museums are recommended: Walter Danesi's outdoor museum in Fantiscritti and the marble museum in Carrara (Viale XX Septembre).

The centre of Carrara is also characterized by marble.

on a small square above Piazza Alberica. Its Pisan façade is divided in the lower part by early Romanesque blind arcades, while a rose window dominates the upper part. The **four-storey campanile** was built around 1280 and imitates Ligurian models. A look inside is worthwhile if only for the unified Romanesque impression given by the open roof and small upper windows which let in hardly any light. The decorated capitals, mostly from the 12th century, stand out, as does the 16th-century marble pulpit with steps made from a single block of marble. In the right-hand aisle is the 15th-century grave of the city's patron saint, St Ceccardo. Francesco Bergamini created the main altar, and the cross (14th century) in the choir is probably by Angelo Puccinelli. In the left-hand aisle the remains of the former marble top of the main altar can be admired. The reliefs on the predella (1464) were made by Andrea Guardi.

Accademia di Belle Arti Anyone interested in meeting young artists will most likely find them here: the academy of art has had its seat in Via Roma in the historic centre, in an old city palace since 1805. It was founded in 1769 by Maria Theresia Cybo Malaspina.

South-west of the city centre on the road to Marina di Carrara, the ✳
five departments of the **city marble museum** provide information on **Museo Civico**
quarrying techniques since antiquity, local geology and the use of **del Marmo**
marble into the present (Viale XX Settembre; hours: daily except ⏰
Sun, July and Aug 10am–8pm, May, June and Sept until 6pm, Oct to
April 8.30am–1.30pm).

Around Carrara

A four-lane road connects Carrara with Marina di Carrara, which is **Marina di**
both the world's largest shipping harbour for marble and a modern **Carrara**
seaside resort with streets on a grid system and a newly renovated,
somewhat sterile city square (Piazza Menconi). The road from Carrara leads straight to the yacht harbour, which forms something like
a buffer between the marble harbour in the south and the stabili-
menti, the bathing facilities, which unfortunately completely block
the view of the beach.

South of Marina di Carrara lies the somewhat more charming Mari- **Marina di**
na di Massa, Massa's seaside resort. In the centre, i.e. on Lungomare **Massa**
and in the streets behind it as well as Piazza Betti, old **villas with lush**
gardens, palms and yellow-flowered jasmine bushes with their wonderful scent set the scene. Swimming is possible at the beach of fine-
grained sand (which is not very broad).

A **winding road** leads to Campo Cecina, a 1,300m/4,265ft peak north ✳ ✳
of Colonnata, which offers the most spectacular view of the marble **Campo Cecina**
quarries of Carrara. Campo Cecina is signposted from the SS 446. At
the top the forest clears and there is a free view down the mountain
where the quarries have already cut deep »wounds«. From this angle
the transport roads that zigzag up the steep slopes look like ant trails,
the heavy trucks like miniatures.

Do not miss a drive up into the quarries. At present there are still a **Marble quarries**
few hundred around Carrara. Of the quarries that are still in use ✳
today, Cave di Fantiscritti at 450m/1,476ft and the quarries at ◄ Cave dei
Colonnata at 532m/1,745ft are the largest and most interesting. Both Fantiscritti
are accessible by car or bus. At the north-east city limits of Carrara
follow the signs toward Colonnata as far as Miseglia. Just beyond the
town a well-marked road leads into the mountains to Fantiscritti.
The approaching trucks loaded with huge blocks of marble and
the fine white dust that floats everywhere actually show the way already.

The danger and difficulty of **life in a marble quarry** can be seen best **Cava Museo**
in Cava Museo, a somewhat bizarre open-air museum that has been
established in the middle of the quarrying area of Fantiscritti. The
techniques of marble quarrying are explained precisely here. There is

even a completely furnished workers' hut in the museum. The dedicated initiator and manager of the private museum is **Walter Danesi**, who is there most of the time and is always happy to talk to interested visitors about the quarries and his life's work (free admission; hours: Easter to Nov, 9am–7pm, tel. 058 57 09 81).

Colonnata

On the way back from Fantiscritti to Carrara a very winding narrow road branches off high up to the **workers' village** of Colonnata, where marble was quarried as early as Roman times. Not only the processing of marble but also the anarchist movement has a long tradition in this village, and today people still love to talk about the old times and revolutionary ideas. Colonnata is visited today above all for its culinary specialty, **lardo**.

! **Baedeker TIP**

Lardo di Colonnata
The fine white bacon is stored according to an old tradition for six months in marble containers before it can be served in paper-thin slices. It tastes best in layers on unsalted Tuscan bread with a glass of Tuscan wine. Try the former »poor man's meal« locally in one of the friendly trattorias. An especially pretty location is the small, green terrace of Lardarium (Via Fossacava 9) in Colonnata.

What to See in Massa

Piazza Aranci

The most beautiful thing about Massa is the **orange trees**. They stand in two rows around Piazza Aranci in the heart of the old city designed by Alberico I in the 16th century. In the middle of the square a fountain obelisk commemorates the unification of Italy in 1860. The entire south side of the square is taken up by the extravagant Palazzo Cybo-Malaspina, today seat of the prefettura. The inner courtyard with loggia was built in 1665 by Giovanni Francesco Bergamini, who extended an existing 15th-century villa for this purpose. The richly decorated façade was provided by Alessandro Bergamini around 1701.

Duomo, Museo d'Arte Sacra

Only a few steps to the north-east at the end of Via Dante stands the late Gothic cathedral that was begun in 1389, then remodelled in Renaissance and Baroque style and gained a classical façade of Carrara marble in 1936. The Cappella del Santissimo Sacramento to the right of the altar, the funeral chapel of the Malaspina, holds fragmen-

Lessons in the quarry: a school class visits the marble quarries in Fantiscritti.

tary remains of a **Madonna fresco by Pinturicchio** (late 15th century). The Madonna triptych next to it (around 1460) presumably comes from Bernardino del Castelletto. Devotional objects of the 17th and 18th century are displayed in the adjoining cathedral museum.

The castle of the Malaspina (La Rocca), one of the most imposing fortresses in all of Tuscany, rises high above the city. A defensive tower already stood here in the 11th century and was fortified with a ring wall in the 13th century. The Counts of Malaspina built the L-shaped Renaissance palace with fine marble decorations in the 15th and 16th centuries. At the end of the 16th century the Puntone and Cavaliere bastions were added on the north side, in the 17th century the artillery positions on the west side. There is a wonderful view over the city to the sea from the fortifications.

✴ **Castello Malaspina**

✴ Excursion to the Lunigiana

From the Tyrrhenian Sea to the foothills of the Apennines, the varied landscape of the Lunigiana stretches across the extreme north-west of Tuscany and includes the Magra valley and its side valleys. The region gets its name from the city of Luni, which was founded by the Romans. Numerous castles, most of which were built by the Counts of Malaspina, are a characteristic of the area.

✴ **Magra Valley**

**Fosdinovo,
Castello
Malaspina**

The first defensive measures for Fosdinovo's imposing castle (10km/
6mi north of Carrara) on Monte Grosso were built in the early
Middle Ages in order to control the old road that connected the inland valleys of the Lunigiana with the coast. In the 13th century the
Malaspina family had the existing fortress reinforced – in 1306 Dante
is supposed to have stayed here after he was driven out of Florence.
In 1340 the fiefdom passed to Spinetta Malaspina, who had the cylin-
drical towers with battlements built.

In the 16th and 17th centuries imposing residential additions in Renaissance style were made to the property, which is still owned by the
Marchese Torreggiani-Malaspina (viewing for groups of at least six
people Wed–Mon 10am, 11am, 4pm and 5pm).

**Aulla, Fortezza
della Brunella**

The massive Brunella castle of Aulla, about 15km/9mi to the north,
guards the confluence of the Aulla and Magra. The fortress was begun in the late 13th century and expanded at the beginning of the
16th century, presumably to plans by Giovanni dalle Bande Nere.
It holds a museum on the natural history of the Lunigiana (hours:
June–Sept Tue–Sun 9am–noon, 4–7pm, Oct–May 9am–noon and
3–6pm), while the adjacent botanical garden is an inviting place for
a restful stroll.

Equi Terme

On the northern slopes of the Apuan Alps lies Equi Terme (16km/
10mi south-east), which is known for its Palaeolithic finds and its
sulphur springs. The mineral springs are used to treat bronchial illnesses, allergies, skin diseases and rheumatism. Along with a visit to
the thermal spa, take a look at the limestone caves with bizarre stalactites, stalagmites and an underground lake.

**Fivizzano,
Castello della
Verrucola**

The commission for the castle of Verrucola in Fivizzano (16km/10mi
east of Aulla) was given by Marchese Spinetta Malaspina around
1300. The castle had its present dimensions by the middle of the
14th century – except for the church of Santa Margherita, which was
added in the 15th century with a beautiful Renaissance loggia. Today
it belongs to the sculptor Pietro Cascella.

Casola Lunigiana

In Casola Lunigiana (6km/3.5mi south-east) the Museo del Territor-
io dell'Alta Valle Aullela shows archaeological finds from the area
from the Palaeolithic period to the late Middle Ages. It also has information on the Canto del Maggio (May singing), a kind of ancient
folk theatre, and religious art from the region.

**Villafranca,
Castello di Mal-
grate**

About 10km/6mi north of Aulla lies the sleepy village of Villafranca.
The fortress Malgrate underwent continual changes over a period of
more than five centuries. It is privately owned today. The central element is the medieval main tower (13th century). Conversion to a
residence for the Malaspina began in the middle of the 14th century.
In the course of the 15th century a new outer wall was built; in 1641

the Marchesi Ariberti from Cremona took over the fiefdom and enlarged the castle to its present size.

The local museum in a former mill explains old crafts such as basket weaving, carving, smith and stonemason work, traditional forms of agriculture (including the use of chestnuts) as well as old customs (hours: summer Tue–Sun 9am–noon, 4–7pm; winter 9am–noon, 3–6pm). ◄ Museo Etnografico ⏱

In the late 10th century the foundation stone for the castle of the Castiglione family in Bagnone (2km/1.2mi eastwards) was laid. In 1351 the fiefdom passed to Marchese Franceschino Malaspina, who converted the eastern wing and had the round defensive tower built. From 1451 the castle was the main seat for Florentine domination of the Magra valley for almost three hundred years. Bagnone, Castiglione del Terziere

Pontremoli, a pleasant town, is the centre of the Lunigiana and lies 13km/8mi to the north-west. The **Museo delle Statue-Stele Lunigianesi** in Piagnaro castle (16th–19th centuries), which has been rebuilt several times, holds a collection of all the stele found in the Lunigiani either as a copy or an original. Pontremoli

The approximately 60 female and male sandstone figures, some of which are quite odd, were made in the 2nd and 1st millennium BC. by the first inhabitants of the valley to honour their gods and heroes (hours: summer Tue–Sun 9am–noon, 3–6pm; winter 9am–noon, 2–5pm). ⏱

Certaldo

H 9

Province: Florence/Firenze (FI)
Population : 16,000
Altitude: 130m/426ft above sea level

About 40km/25mi south-west of ►Florence, the town of Certaldo lies in hilly country between wheat fields and olive groves . The upper town, Certaldo Alto, also called »Castello«, where the poet Boccaccio (►Famous People) lived at the end of his life, is small but extremely charming.

✳ ## Certaldo Alto

Its position high up on the hill, its complete, mostly intact town wall and red brick houses give the upper part of Certaldo an impressively harmonious appearance but also an almost **fortress-like character**. It does not take much time to see it. Only a few paces from the cable car station is the pretty inner courtyard of the hotel restaurant Il Castello. Apart from the Castello there is another restaurant in the upper town, the Osteria del Vicario near the Palazzo Pretorio. A Appearance cobbled main street named Via Boccaccio after the town's most famous son leads straight up to the highest point of Certaldo Alto, which is crowned by Palazzo Pretorio.

Casa del Boccaccio, Museo del Arte Sacra

Below Palazzo Pretorio, in Casa del Boccaccio (house no. 18), the great Renaissance poet is supposed to have lived. A museum with a library attached has information on Boccaccio, who is buried in the former monastery church Chiesa dei Santi Jacopo e Filippo nearby. The gravestone is inscribed with four verses by Boccaccio (hours: daily 10am–4.30pm, in summer until 7pm). A few steps further uphill in the former monastery is the Museo del Arte Sacra, a collection of altar panels, sculptures and liturgical items from the churches in and around Certaldo (hours: April–Sept 10am–7pm, Oct–March 10.30am–4.30pm).

✶ Palazzo Pretorio

Via Boccaccio terminates impressively at the massive medieval palace with its rich decoration of coats of arms on the façade. The Counts Alberti, and later administrators from Florence, lived in the building, which dates from the late 12th century. From 1530 court judgments and new laws were proclaimed from the front loggia. Visitors first enter the beautiful inner courtyard, which is also decorated with

▶ VISITING CERTALDO

INFORMATION

Viale Fabiani 5
Tel. and fax 05 71 65 67 21

EVENTS

»Mercantia« is the most important event, a mixture of theatre and music festival, and medieval market. The old walls of Certaldo are a wonderful setting for the annual spectacle (3rd week in July).

WHERE TO EAT

▶ Expensive
Osteria Vicario
Certaldo Alto
Via Rivellino 3
Tel. and Fax 05 71 66 82 28
www.osteriadelvicario.it
Very stylish restaurant in a former monastery. The small, covered terrace with a wide view of the hilly landscape is especially charming. Equally pretty:

the guestrooms. Reservations a must in the evening!

WHERE TO STAY

▶ Budget
La Rocca
Tavarnelle (17km/10.5mi to the east)
Tel./fax 05 58 05 01 06
www.laroccachianti.it
Claudia and Angelo Rizzone run the small, but comfortable bed & breakfast with much devotion. It is quiet but Florence and Siena are not far away.

CABLE CAR OR ON FOOT

The narrow street up to Certaldo Alto is closed to all but local traffic. An alternative to the steep steps is a cable car that runs up every 15 minutes. It leaves from the central piazza in the lower town.

*Seat of the Florentine governor and court:
Palazzo Pretorio in Certaldo*

coats of arms, Renaissance frescoes and a small well. In the former offices, which are used for exhibitions today, there are several frescoes to admire, including a pietà (1484) that is attributed to Pier Francesco Fiorentino as well as a fresco *Doubting Thomas* (1490), thought to be a work of Benozzo Gozzoli. On the walls of the 13th-century St Thomas chapel fresco fragments depict the 24 Florentine podestà. After a look at the old prison cells – where the prisoners' writing on the walls can still be read – be sure not to miss the view of enchanting scenery from the tower (hours: April–Sept daily 9.30am to 1pm, 2–7.30pm, Oct–March 10.30am–12.30pm and 2–5pm).

Around Certaldo

10km/6mi north-west in the Elsa Valley lies Castelfiorentino, which goes back to a Roman settlement and was known in the Middle Ages

Castelfiorentino

under the name of Castel Timignano and owned by the Counts Alberti di Vernio. In the 12th century the city was renamed Castelfiorentino (»Florentine castle«) and expanded as a bulwark against the Sienese. However, hardly anything remains from those warlike

✳
Museo
Comunale ▶

days. A visit to the city museum in Via Tilli 27 is worthwhile for the important frescoes by **Benozzo Gozzoli** that are exhibited here. The fresco cycle was created between 1484 and 1490 and comes from the oratory of the Madonna della Tosse nearby. It shows the Madonna with saints, the burial and assumption of the Virgin with the sacred belt as a symbol of the virgin birth of Christ. The fresco cycle which Gozzoli painted in 1466/1467 for the Capella della Visitazione also

🕐

has scenes from Mary's life and from the life of St Joachim (hours: Tue–Sun 9am–noon and 2–7pm).

Right next to the church of Santa Verdiana is a museum with exhibits including art treasures from the church sanctuary.

✳
Barberino
Val d'Elsa

Almost 15km/9mi east of Certaldo, the town of Barberino lies in the middle of broad vine-covered slopes on the old Roman road Via Cassio: it is not visited nearly as often as the neighbouring towns in ▶ Chianti. Yet Barberino Val d'Elsa is still a **pretty medieval town**. The fortress walls served the Florentines in battles against Siena. The two city gates, the impressive Porta Romana and the Porta Fiorentina, date from the 14th century, as does the pilgrims' hospice built by Cecco Barberino in 1365 at the end of Via Francesco da Barberino. Palazzo Pretorio on the central Piazza Barberini is decorated with numerous coats of arms, the oldest from the 15th century. Next to it is the parish church San Bartolomeo with fresco remnants from the 14th–15th centuries (Annunciation).

✳ ✳ Chianti

G – I 10 – 12

Provinces: Florence/Firenze (FI),
Siena (SI)

Everyone who has seen Florence or Siena, done the full programme of culture and longs for a rural scene should go to Chianti, which welcomes visitors with gently rolling hills, olive groves, forests and vineyards.

The Via Chiantigiana runs 70km/45mi through the **famous wine region**, past vineyards, farms and majestic castles and through pretty little towns and medieval villages. Every detour to the left or right of the main route in the »land of the gallo nero« (▶ Baedeker Special p.114) makes the countryside more enjoyable. Chianti Classico is offered for direct sale from many wine estates (»vendita diretta«), including a wine tasting and tour of the fattoria.

First Stage: From Florence to Castellina in Chianti

The south-east road out of Florence (city side of the river) towards Pontassieve leads straight to the feeder road for the Bologna/Roma autostrada. Just before the autostrada approach ramp (A 1), turn off towards Grassina, the first town on the Chiantigiana (SS 222). Follow the SS 222 almost 10km/6mi to Pitigliolo, where there is a turn-off toward Impruneta (5km/3mi).

★
Impruneta

The town, which is enchantingly sited amongst vineyards, is a **centre of pottery**. Here the traditional handmade terracotta is still popular. The roof tiles for Florence cathedral were fired in the terracotta ovens of Impruneta.

Framed in cypresses, Castello Vicchiomaggio occupies a hill commanding a wonderful view just about 4km/2.5mi before Greve. Its oldest parts – tower and enclosure wall – date from the 13th century. It is said that Leonardo da Vinci once stayed in the carefully restored villa, which today holds a wine farm with apartments and restaurant – the castle is at least mentioned in one of his writings.

★
Castello
Vicchiomaggio

Surrounded by vineyards and high walls: Montefiorale is a picture book village in Chianti.

▶ VISITING CHIANTI

INFORMATION

Gaiole in Chianti
Via G. Galilei 11
Tel. and fax 05 77 74 94 11
Greve in Chianti
Via Giovanni da Verrazano 59
Tel. 05 58 54 62 87
Fax 05 58 54 42 40

Radda in Chianti
Piazza Ferucci 1
Tel. 05 77 73 84 94

Castellina in Chianti
Via Ferruccio 40
Tel. 05 77 74 13 92
Fax 05 77 74 13 93

WINE FESTIVALS

Of course every town in Chianti has a
wine festival every year in September
or October – the festival in Greve lasts
a week (mid-September). Anyone who
wants to try good wine outside the
season has a large selection of well-
stocked enoteche in Greve.

BICYCLE RENTAL

Along with excellent information
brochures the tourist information in
Castellina in Chianti (address above)
also rents bicycles.

WHERE TO EAT

▶ Expensive
Fattoria Vignale
Radda in Chianti, Via Pianigiani 9
Tel. 05 77 73 80 94
Fax 05 77 73 87 30
This high-class restaurant – like the
enoteca and the tavern – belongs to the
4-star hotel of the same name.

Gallopapa
Castellina in Chianti
Via delle Volte 14 / 16

Tel. 05 77 42 939
www.gallopapa.com
Closed Mon.
Elegant restaurant in rustic vaulted
cellars in the historic centre. Excellent
food and an enormous selection of
wine.

▶ Moderate

Baedeker recommendation

Sausage and nothing but sausage is available
in this shop on the marketplace of Greve.
But what a selection! The aroma that
welcomes you into this sausage paradise
would make anyone hungry. Of course the
Tuscan specialty, salami made from wild
boar, is available but also fennel salami, ham
and many other delicacies (Macelleria Fa-
lorni, Greve in Chianti, Piazza G. Matteotti
71, tel. 055 85 30 29).

Mangiando Mangiando
Greve in Chianti, Piazza Matteotti 80
Tel. 05 58 54 63 72
A typical osteria without frills, but
with a family atmosphere and solid
Tuscan cooking. In the summer guests
sit and eat on the wonderful piazza of
Greve. Closed Mon.

Do you want to get to know Tuscany? Then visit a wine festival!

Borgo Antico
Greve in Chianti, Loc. Lucolena
Tel. 055 85 10 24, closed Tue.
Stylish trattoria in an old farmhouse.
Light Tuscan cuisine.

Albergaccio
Castellina in Chianti
Via Fiorentina 63
Tel. 05 77 74 10 42
www.albergacciocast.com
Sonia Visman and Francesco
Cacciatori produce
creative and excellent local cuisine.

Badia a Coltibuono
Gaiole, Loc. Badia a Coltibuono
(5km/3mi north of Gaiole)
Tel. 05 77 74 90 31
In Badia it is above all the ambience
that counts; tables in the vaulted
rooms of the monastery or in the
summer outside under a shady pergola with a great view.

▶ **Inexpensive**
Oltre il Giardino
Greve in Chianti – Panzano
Piazza Bucciarelli 42
Tel. and fax 05 58 28 28

Closed Thu.
The homemade pasta and the selected
cheeses taste especially good. Seating
on the pleasant terrace in summer.

WHERE TO STAY

▶ **Luxury**
Fattoria Vignale
Via Pianigiani 9
Tel. 05 77 73 83 00
Fax 05 77 73 85 92, 40 rooms
www.vignale.it
One of the best addresses in Chian-
ti – in a historic building of course.
The hotel is also the seat of the wine
consortium Chianti Classico; gour-
mets should try the restaurant.

▶ **Mid-range**
Podere Le Vigne
Radda in Chianti
(1km/0.5mi outside of town)
Tel. and fax 05 77 73 81 24
The old manor of an estate, trans-
formed into quiet accommodation
with rustic charm.

Belvedere di San Leonino
Castellina in Chianti

Loc. San Leonino
Tel. 05 77 74 08 87
Fax 05 77 74 09 24
www.hotelsanleonino.
In the hills, but nevertheless on the route to Siena: a hotel in Tuscan country-house style with beautifully furnished rooms and a well-tended garden with pool.

Residenzia del Sogno
Castellina in Chianti,
Loc. Pietrafitta 50
Tel. 05 77 74 13 94
Fax 05 77 74 20 39
www.residenziadelsogno.com
5 rooms and 3 apartments
Delightful accommodation in a house on the Chiantigiana that was carefully renovated and equipped with modern furnishings. After checking in, guests can enjoy the skilled cooking of Alexandra Nestle – a special treat on the terrace in front of the house with the evening sun.

▶ Budget
Pensione Elio Pistolesi
Radda in Chianti, Via Roma 46
Tel. 05 77 73 81 24
www.lodgingchianti.it
In the middle of Radda. Not always quiet, but very cheap.

La Fonte del Cieco
Gaiole in Chianti
Via Ricasoli 18
Tel. 05 77 74 40 28,
Fax 05 77 74 44 07
Nice little accommodation in the centre of Gaiole. Tasteful rooms.

Castello di Verrazzano

In the nearby Castello di Verrazzano the production of Chianti has a very long history, back to the 12th century. The most famous off-spring of the Verrazzano family was Giovanni (1485–1528), who in 1524 was the first European to see the peninsula of Manhattan. The New York bridge between Brooklyn and Staten Island is named after the explorer. Not only the wine cellars, also the castle and the garden of Verrazzano are open to the public (reservations tel. 055 85 42 43 or online: www.verrazzano.com).

Castello di Uzzano

Back on the SS 222 about 1.5km/1mi before Greve there is another detour eastwards. A steep road leads up between vineyards and olive groves to the medieval castle of Uzzano, where Tuscan cuisine in the restaurant is an opportunity for indulgence. The Capponi family had the castle converted to a villa in the mid-16th century. In 1641 the elegant estate was passed on the Counts Masetti. In the 18th century there were more expansions and today visitors can stroll under the beautiful arches of the two-storey arcade in the courtyard.

Greve in Chianti

The small town of Greve is the wine centre of Chianti. It has a beautiful triangular Piazza Matteotti with a statue of **Giovanni Verrazzano**, whose home is not far away (see above). Comfortable trattorias in houses with flower-decorated loggias, cafés and one of the best sausage shops in all Tuscany (see p.182) line the square, which is transformed into an outdoor enoteca during the one-week wine festival (Rassegna del Chianti Classico) in mid-September. In the parish church of Santa Croce a 15th-century triptych by Bicci di Lorenzo and a 13th-century Madonna by the Master of Greve can be admired.

An excursion absolutely to be recommended (2km/1.2mi above Greve, extreme inclines but a **wonderful panoramic view**) is to the castle village of Montefioralle, where excellent olive oil is produced. Park in the parking lot behind the village (signposted, but with hardly any shade), since only residents may drive into Montefioralle. The amateur painters in the steep streets decorated with flowers show that Montefioralle is no longer an insider's tip. To enjoy the view for a while, choose between the terrace of the local restaurant and the shady square under the Chiesa Santo Stefano, where a rest on a park bench might lead to a conversation with local residents.

★
Montefioralle

A narrow road leads further to Badia a Passignano (6km/3.5mi), which looks like a fortress with its towers and battlements. Apart from the many potholes in the unpaved road the drive is beautiful, and the Gothic monastery can be seen from afar in the shade of tall cypress trees. San Giovanni Gualberto refounded it in 1049 on the site of an older institution dating from 890, and it was thus one of the first to receive the impulses of the monastic reform movement emanating from Vallombrosa (see p.159).The wonderful *Last Supper* in the refectory was painted by Domenico Ghirlandaio in 1476. The abbey, which was dissolved in 1810, revived briefly in the 19th century and has again been occupied by Vallombrosian monks since the 1980s, has been closed for restoration work for some years.

★
Badia a
Passignano

A right turn off the SS 222 to visit the sleepy town of Panzano is an absolute must. Panzano has a medieval castle, which is not open to the public, and a market on Sundays. But right on the main route the Romanesque church Pieve di San Leolino is worth a look. It holds a 13th-century triptych by the Master of Panzano.

Panzano
in Chianti

The closer to Castellina, the more mountainous and forested the country. The first view of the town is disappointing, because a large animal feed factory dominates the scene from the SS 222. Nevertheless, in the main street of the medieval town centre, Via Ferruccio, there are several proud palazzi and many small gourmet and wine shops. A **castle** with an exhibition on the Etruscans crowns the highest point of the village. The lookout platform provides a wonderful view of the Chianti landscape.

★
Castellina
in Chianti

There is a confined feeling by contrast in **Via delle Volte** on the east side of the town wall, which has been completely covered by other buildings. But almost every visitor strolls through the old street, as it has been carefully restored and is filled with chic galleries and shops with original souvenirs. The burial mound from the 7th century BC at the northern exit from the town, formerly the border between Florence and Siena, bears witness to the fact that it was already settled in the Etruscan period. The square burial chamber is vaulted.

From Castellina to Siena

✳
**Radda
in Chianti**

A country road leads from Castellina via Radda (13km/8mi) to the southern slopes of the Chianti hills. In the sunny valleys of the Monti del Chianti the best **DOCG wines** of the region ripen. Before the year 1000 Radda belonged to the Counts Guidi, in 1203 it passed to the Florentine republic, and from 1415 it was the capital of the Chianti Liga. The medieval town gets many visitors and offers beautiful views from the crown of a hill. Park along the old city wall, which is also an observation platform (parking limited to one hour). In the centre, on Via Roma, stands the Palazzo del Podestà (15th century), which is richly decorated with coats of arms and today houses the tourist information office. The palace clock has marked the hours since the Middle Ages. On the opposite side steps pass a fountain on the way

*The dream of every Chianti lover: The delicious wines are stored
in deep vaulted cellars.*

to the parish church of San Nicolò. The Franciscan monastery of S. Maria al Prato (11th to 17th centuries) is being converted to a cultural and wine museum.

Volpaia, one of the prettiest villages in southern Chianti, 5km/3mi north of Radda, has less than 50 residents. The castle was already mentioned in 1172. Its owner, Giovanella Stianti-Mascheroni, is the daughter of a publisher and produces select top-quality wines like Coltassala, which is produced almost exclusively from Sangiovese-Grosso grapes. Every year in September the castle is transformed into an art gallery with exhibitions on the subject of wine and art.

★
Volpaia

The neighbouring town of Gaiole in Chianti (13km/8mi from Volpaia) is surrounded by vineyards famous for their excellent quality, most of which also sell directly (vendita diretta). Gaiole is situated in a valley, rather than on a hill, and has no special charms, not even in the marketplace with renovated houses. The Romanesque parish church Santa Maria e Spaltenna west of the town was built in the first half of the 12th century. The former monastery attached to it is now a luxury hotel.

Gaiole in Chianti

There is a beautiful view about 5km/3mi to the north (signposted) at the Abbey of Coltibuono, which was consecrated in 1049. The monastery building was taken over in 1402 by Benedictine monks from Vallombrosa, who renovated the cloister and refectory. The secularized property was worked as a farm from 1810 to 1842. Today it is possible to visit the Romanesque church and eat afterwards with a beautiful view of the Arno valley.

★
Badia a Coltibuono

Beyond Gaiole there is a choice between two branches of the Via Chiantigiana, both of which can be recommended for the beautiful scenery.
On the western route (no. 408) the small detour to the Chianti Sculpture Park near Pievasciata is worthwhile – the last section of about 4km/2.5mi is unpaved, one of the newest attractions on the Chiantigiana. As in Daniel Spoerri's Giardino near Seggiano (► Monte Amiata) the charm of the park lies above all in the close symbiosis between the landscape and modern sculptures by contemporary artists from all over the world (hours: April–Oct Tue–Sun 10am until sunset, otherwise by appointment; www.chiantisculpturepark .it).

Chianti Sculpture Park

The eastern route of the Chiantigiana is called the **Strada dei Castelli dei Chianti**, (Chianti castle route). The first castle appears about 4km/2.5mi south of Gaiole in Meleto. Round corner towers from the 11th century crown the castle of Meleto, which the Firidolfi family made the strongest fortification of the Chianti Liga during the 13th century. It defied all sieges until 1498.

Castello di Trebbio

✳
Castello di Brolio
A further 8km/5mi south-east, the imposing Castello di Brolio looms on a mountain ridge 530m/1,739ft high. The history of the mighty bastion is connected closely with the Ricasoli family, which ruled the region from the 13th century. This stronghold not far from the border between Florence and Siena was again and again the site of fierce battles.

After repeated destruction, the last in 1529 by the Sienese, it was thoroughly renovated in the 16th century. Bettino Ricasoli (1809–1890), who developed the classical concept of the full-bodied Chianti in 1841 through his blending of grapes, had the castle converted around 1860 in neo-Gothic style. The interior is not open to the public, but the garden, bastions, walkways and chapel, where members of the Ricasoli family are buried, as well as the baron's magnificent wine cellar, can be visited (hours: Mon–Sat 9am–noon, 3–6pm, Sun until 7pm, in winter Mon–Sun 9am–noon and 2.30–5pm, closed Fri; tel. 05 77 73 02 20, www.ricasoli.it).

Fonterutoli, Quercegrossa
On the last part of the Via Chiantigiana between the wine village of Fonterutoli, first mentioned in 998 and now an attractive place to take a break with a pretty piazzetta, and Quercegrossa the charms of the Chianti landscape become more concentrated again: between the forested hills are level vineyards and olive groves, while dark rows of cypress trees mark the way to rural farms and estates. Finally the rust-red houses of ▶Siena slowly appear.

Chiusi

L 14

Province: Siena (SI)	**Altitude:** 375m/1,230ft above sea level
Population: 8,600	

This is the right place for those who are interested in the art and culture of the Etruscans: in Chiusi, a pretty town on a high plateau of tuff stone almost 20km/12mi south-east of ▶ Montepulciano, there is an excellent Etruscan museum. From here it is possible to explore the area to the west of Chiusi around Radicofani. The scenery is in part stark but nonetheless impressive.

In the 6th century BC the settlement – then called Chamars – became an important Etruscan city and a member of the twelve-city federation. Chiusi flourished under King Porsenna, who defied Rome in 520 BC, after the rising republic on the Tiber chased Porsenna's ally Tarquinius Superbus out of the city. The legendary labyrinthine grave of Porsenna, which was mentioned by Pliny, was discovered in 1840 under a 15m/50ft-high tumulus. Under the name of Clusium the city joined the expanding Roman empire in 296 BC. In the Middle Ages

Orvieto, Siena and Florence alternated as rulers before Chiusi was added to the Grand Duchy of Tuscany in 1556.

What to See in Chiusi

The centre of the small town is the **cathedral square**. The Roman forum once occupied this site. The history of the cathedral goes back to the 6th century; the bell tower was built in the 12th century. In its present form the cathedral dates from the 13th century and bears the marks from less-than-successful restorations between 1887 and 1895, when the imitation mosaics inside were also made. The 18 ancient columns inside the church presumably come from Roman buildings in the area.

Etruscan sculpture in the archaeological museum in Chiusi

Next to the cathedral the cathedral museum (Museo della Cattedrale) invites visitors to see, among other treasures, 22 choir books decorated with miniatures (15th century) from the Abbazia di Monte Oliveto Maggiore (hours: June–mid-Oct daily 9.30am–12.45pm and 4–7pm, mid-Oct–May closed afternoons except Sun).

Museo della Cattedrale

► ⏲

From the museum go underground into a system of canals or corridors, the so-called Labirinto di Porsenna, which already existed in Etruscan times and was used until the 1st century – probably as a water-supply system but also as an escape route when it was necessary to leave the town unnoticed. It was connected to a cistern from the 1st century BC that was carved out of tuff stone, right next to the bell tower (to visit the labyrinth register in the cathedral museum).

Labirinto di Porsenna

The Etruscan National Museum building is only a few metres away from the cathedral in Via Porsenna. Its temple façade faces the side of the cathedral and a small, tree-lined square with a fountain and benches. Behind the entrance of the neo-classical building erected in 1870 is one of the oldest Tuscan archaeological collections, with Etruscan, Greek and Roman finds. On display are burial urns – including an urn from the 2nd century BC, whose coloured relief depicts the battle of the sons of Oedipus, Eteocles and Polynices – sarcophagi, frescoes removed from graves and photographs of wall paintings in closed graves, masks of bronze or clay, gravestones, am-

★ Museo Nazionale Etrusco

► VISITING CHIUSI

INFORMATION
Piazza Duomo 1
Tel. and fax 05 78 22 76 67

EVENTS
Palio delle Torri, a festival in honour
of the patron saint San Mustiola on
the 1st Sunday in July or on the last
Sunday in June.

WHERE TO EAT
► Inexpensive
La Solita Zuppa
Via Porsena 21
Tel. 057 82 10 06
www.lasolitazuppa.it
Closed Tue.
As the name hints: soups are the
speciality of the house. The restaurant
is housed in 18th-century vaults.

WHERE TO STAY
► Mid-range
La Fattoria
Viale Paccianese 48
Tel. 05 78 214 07
Fax 05 78 206 44
www.lafattoria.it
Renovated farm with comfortable
rooms near Lago di Chiusi.

Sette Querce (photo)
San Casciano dei Bagni
Tel. 05 78 581 74
Fax 05 78 581 72
www.settequerce.it, 9 rooms
Anyone who loves the brilliant fabrics
of Tricia Guild is just right in this
design hotel. The suites may be small,
but they are decorated with great taste.
With balcony or terrace.

Baedeker recommendation

La Pace
Celle sul Rigo
(between Radicofani and San Casciano dei
Bagni)
Tel. 05 78 537 16, closed Tue.
A picture-book rural restaurant: outwardly
unassuming – hidden in a street of the tiny
hill-top village – and furnished in a rather
spartan manner, but with wonderful local
cuisine. There is no menu, but you can
confidently try the daily menu in all its
variations. There are few foreign guests here,
instead local families and residents.

► Luxury
Frateria di Padre Eligio
Cetona, Via San Francesco 2
Tel. 05 78 23 82 61
Fax 05 78 23 92 20
www.mondox.it, 5 rooms and 2 suites
A unique mixture of
luxury hotel (with a famous restaurant) and monastery hospice. It was
started many years ago by Padre Eligio
in the oldest Franciscan monastery of
Tuscany (1212) as »Project Mondo x«,
where the cleric enabled young drug
addicts to be resocialized.

phorae and Bucchero pottery. The most interesting items include so-called canopic urns of the Villanova culture, terracotta urns in the form of a portrait of the deceased, and Cippi, gravestones decorated with reliefs (hours: daily 9am–8pm).

There are numerous Etruscan graves around Chiusi, some of which, e.g. Tomba della Scimmia, Tomba della Pellegrina and Tomba del Leone, can be viewed by appointment with the Etruscan museum,. The wall paintings, which still had brilliant colours when they were discovered, have unfortunately suffered in recent years from damp-ness and lack of air circulation. Immediately east of the town the Tomba della Colle, a »hill grave« from the early 5th century BC, was discovered. Its wall paintings includes the depiction of a meal and a classical chariot race with elegant two-horse teams.

Etruscan graves

The **Tomba della Scimmia**, the »monkey grave« from the early 5th century, lies on the road to Lago di Chiusi in Poggio Renzo. Its name derives from a detail in the unique wall paintings. In the first burial chamber, which is almost completely covered in decoration, there are scenes of a burial, musicians, athletic competitions and the afore-mentioned monkey. The nearby cross-shaped Tomba della Pelligrina, the »pilgrim woman's grave« (3rd century BC), is more recent and a so-called dromos grave (corridor grave). A little further to the north is the »grand duke's grave«, Tomba del Granduca, containing urns decorated with figures from the second century BC.

✳ From Chiusi to Radicofani

Just about 10km/6mi west of Chiusi, at the foothills of Monte Cetona, is the town of Sarteano (population 4,500). The hot springs of the so-called Bagno Santo were already known in antiquity. They feed water at a temperature of 24°C/75°F into three large pools in the well-organized bathing pool complex »Parco delle Piscine«. Sarteano was first mentioned in AD 776, but its Etruscan history is also interesting, as the many necropolises testify. Important finds from these local necro-polises are exhibited in the town **museum in Palazzo Gabrielli** (hours: April–Oct daily except Mon 10.30am–12.30pm and 4–7pm, in win-ter Tue–Fri by appointment: tel. 05 78 26 92 61). The neo-classical church of San Martino has a painting of the *Annunciation* (1552), a masterpiece by the Sienese painter Domenico Beccafumi. There is an impressive view of the 11th-century fortress (rebuilt 1469), which still stands as a ruin above Sarteano, from Via della Rocca.

Sarteano

It is only 6km/3.5mi south on winding roads to the picturesque town of Cetona (population 3,000). The town wall spirals up to the rocca, the town's highest point. The castle, once a threatening sight, is pri-vately owned today and not open to the public. From the oblong Piaz-za Garibaldi, which is unusually large for a small town, a steep ascent on Via Roma leads up to the historic centre. 200m/220yd along on the

Cetona

Locanda La Palazzina

This accommodation is so delightful that it really should not be passed on, but just this once …. The beautiful and completely quiet location, the old-fashioned but lovingly furnished rooms and the wonderful pool are only three of many points in favour of the 18th-century villa. The breakfast buffet with different homemade tarts, cakes and salads every day outshines every hotel breakfast (Radicofani, Loc. Le Vigne, 4 km/2.5mi from Radicofani towards Celle sul Rigo, www.verdidea.com, tel. 05 78 557 71, fax 05 78 555 85).

left stands the imposing Palazzo Minutelli from the 17th century, which now houses the city hall and the interesting **municipal prehistoric museum of Monte Cetona**. The various phases of human settlement from the second half of the Palaeolithic Age to the end of the Bronze Age are vividly documented (hours: daily except Mon June–Sept 9am–1pm and 5–7pm, Oct–May 9.30am–12.30pm, Sat only 4–6pm). Almost all finds come from the Belvedere area nearby, where the main prehistoric settlements were located. Today some well-preserved caves, hollowed out of travertine stone and well worth seeing, ⊕ are under protection as an **archaeological natural park** (hours: July–Sept daily except Mon 9am–1pm and 4–7pm, Oct–June only by appointment for at least 10 people: tel. 05 78 23 76 32 or 05 78 22 76 67).

✱
San Casciano dei Bagni

Along the slopes of Monte Cetona a beautiful route leads from Sarteano 14km/9mi south to San Casciano dei Bagni, which as the name suggests has healing springs – there are supposed to be about 40 springs, which were known to the Romans. As a main route north from Rome, the Via Cassia, passed just to the east of the site, it was a popular spa in Roman times. Emperor Augustus is reported to have been among the distinguished guests. In the centuries following the fall of the Roman Empire, the healing waters continued to be used, but a new flowering of spa culture came only from the 17th century under the grand dukes of Tuscany. The old town on the peak of the hill has many freshly renovated houses, but is quickly explored. Outside and below the actual old town lies Piazza Matteotti – a kind of observation terrace with a fine view of the southern Tuscan hills. Keen swimmers should go to the modern **Centro Termale Fonteverde** below the town. The extensive complex offers pretty much everything to do with wellness and relaxation, including of course several thermal pools, sauna, steam baths and a cosmetic studio.

About 17km/11mi south-west of Sarteano lies Radicofani. Long
before reaching the unspectacular town, the tower of its rocca is
visible – an excellent point of orientation in the stark but fascinat-
ingly beautiful hilly landscape of southern Tuscany. The castle itself
was destroyed in the 18th century, but the view from its walls is
wonderful! The remains of the fortress harbour a small archaeological museum; in the Romanesque church on the village square (S.
Pietro) there are terracotta figures by Andrea della Robbia to admire.
Below Radicofani on the old Roman road Via Cassia stands Palazzo
La Villa, built in the 16th century as a customs and postal station,
later a hotel where many famous people stayed including Charles
Dickens.

★ Radicofani

★ Colle di Val d'Elsa

Province: Siena (SI)
Population: 17,000

Altitude: 140–250m/459–820ft above
sea level

**In spite of its proximity to San Gimignano (12km/7.5mi north-west)
and Siena (19km/12mi south-east) Colle di Val d'Elsa is not overrun
by tourists. The reason might be that the community is known
above all as the centre of the Italian glass industry, which has settled in the modern lower town Colle Basso. The historic old part of
the city, Colle Alto, which sits on a narrow, long tuff rock, is surprisingly pretty, although or maybe because it has not been especially spruced up.**

Colle Alto consists of two parts: Borgo, which begins right behind
the massive round towers of the Renaissance fortress Porta Nuova,
and Castello, which is connected to Borgo by a bridge. Borgo takes
its character above all from Renaissance palaces – for example Palazzo Renieri (or Palazzo Comunale), which is situated directly opposite
the Pro Loco, or the elegant Palazzo Campana at the bridge of the
same name.

★ Borgo

With its brick houses and narrow, partly vaulted streets, the Castello
quarter still has a medieval feel, with shops for glass, vases, candelabra and other crystal objects in the narrow Via del Castello. Piazza
del Duomo with the cathedral from 1619 is the centre of Castello.
Giuliano da Maiano created the cathedral pulpit in the late 15th century. The archaeological museum is also on the cathedral square in
Palazzo Pretorio. The Museo Civico e Diocesano with sacred art
treasures and exhibits on the town's history is 100m/110yd further
along the main street of the quarter in an old palazzo on the right
side.

★ Castello

⊙ VISITING COLLE DI VAL D'ELSA

INFORMATION
Via Francesco Campana 43
Tel. 0577 92 27 91
Fax 05 77 92 26 21

SHOPPING
Crystal doesn't appeal to everyone, but those who like it are certain to find something to their taste in Colle di Val d'Elsa. There is a good selection in the shops in Via del Castello.

WHERE TO STAY
► **Budget**
Podere il Caggiolino
Castel San Gimignano,
Loc. Picchena

Tel. and fax 05 77 95 31 90, 5 rooms
This house in quiet surroundings in the middle of the country is a very good alternative to the hotels in Colle di Val d'Elsa or San Gimignano. Comfortable rooms and generous breakfast buffet.

WHERE TO EAT
► **Expensive**
Arnolfo
Via XX Settembre 52
Tel. and fax 05 77 92 05 49
Closed Tue and Wed.
Top-class restaurant (2 Michelin stars) in an old palazzo in the old city. Reservations absolutely required!

✶ ✶ Cortona

K 14

Province: Arezzo (AR)	**Altitude:** 500–651m/1,640–2,136ft
Population: 22,500	above sea level

The home town of the famous Renaissance painter Luca Signorelli is certainly one of the prettiest towns in Tuscany – not least because of its location with fine views on the steep slope of Monte San Egidio on the edge of Val di Chiana.

The difference in elevation between the entrance to the town on Piazza Garibaldi (or at Porta Sant'Agostino) and the Medici fortress at the highest point of the town is no less than 150m/492ft. ►Arezzo is not far away (30km/19mi north) and Lago Trasimeno (Umbria, about 15km/9mi) in good weather seems close enough to touch.

History   The site was probably settled by Umbrians. In the 8th century BC the Etruscans conquered the hill and added »Curtuns« to their twelve-city federation. Toward the end of the 4th century BC the city made a treaty with Rome, in 130 BC it received Roman citizenship and later became a Roman colony. Cortona flourished as an independent community in the 12th and 13th centuries. In 1325 it became a bishop's seat. In 1409 King Ladilaus of Naples conquered the city and sold it to Florence in 1411.

⏵ VISITING CORTONA

INFORMATION
Via Nazionale 42
Tel. 05 75 63 03 52, fax 05 75 63 06 56

EVENTS
The festival on 14–15 August leaves only vegetarians cold, for the steaks at the Sagra della Bistecca come from the famous Chianina cattle.

WHERE TO EAT
▶ Moderate
② *Osteria del Teatro*
Via Maffei 2
Tel. 05 75 63 05 56
www.osteria-del-teatro.it
Closed Wed.
Comfortable osteria, very popular among Tuscans as well. Our tip: ravioli with stuffed zucchini flowers.

▶ Inexpensive
① *Trattoria La Grotta*
Piazza Baldelli 3
Tel. and fax 05 75 63 02 71
Closed Tuesdays.
In the summer the most beautiful place in this trattoria is outside on the tiny Piazza Baldelli at the end of Via

Nazionale, a little away from the busy part of town. The pappardelle with wild boar sauce followed by a semifreddo all'amaretto are especially tasty.

WHERE TO STAY
▶ Luxury
① *Relais Il Falconiere*
Località San Martino
Tel. 05 75 61 26 16
Fax 05 75 61 29 27, 19 rooms
Lovers of an old-world atmosphere will like this stylishly furnished old country house. The two rooms in the former chapel San Girolamo are particularly nice. Seven larger rooms are in the new building opened in 2002.

▶ Budget
② *Athens*
Via Antonio 12
Tel. 05 75 63 05 08
Fax 05 75 60 44 57
Opened from March until October. Reasonably priced hotel in a good location in the old city. The rooms are simple, but spacious.

What to See in Cortona

Approaching Cortona on the SS 71 from the valley, the Renaissance church Madonna del Calccinaio (1485) can be seen on the slope below the town. The church was built because a miracle-working Madonna image was found here. Near the church are a few simple graves from the Etruscan era. The best known is the Tanella di Pitagora.

Outside the town

A well-preserved wall encloses the old town, which is built on a slope. A possible point to start touring Cortona is the Porta Sant'Agostino (large parking lot). The way up on Via Guelfa to the centre, Piazza della Repubblica, is steep. The Palazzo Comunale, which dominates the west side of the piazza, was recorded in 1241,

✶
Piazza della Repubblica

Cortona Plan

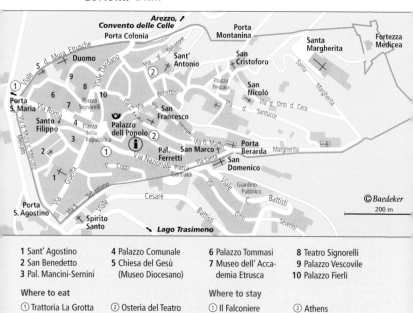

1 Sant' Agostino
2 San Benedetto
3 Pal. Mancini-Sernini

4 Palazzo Comunale
5 Chiesa del Gesù
(Museo Diocesano)

6 Palazzo Tommasi
7 Museo dell' Accademia Etrusca

8 Teatro Signorelli
9 Palazzo Vescovile
10 Palazzo Fierli

Where to eat
① Trattoria La Grotta

② Osteria del Teatro

Where to stay
① Il Falconiere

② Athens

enlarged in the 16th century and restored not very skilfully in 1896. The clock tower (1509) is the main feature on the front of the palace; the outdoor stair also dates from the 16th century. The painting on the ceiling beams in the large council chamber also dates from this period. The east side of the square is taken up by the Palazzo del Popolo (14th–16th centuries).

Porte del Morto The death doors (Porte del Morto), narrow, high doors right next to the main entrance of a medieval house, are a regional curiosity. They were used only to transport the dead out of the house. A fine example of a death door can be seen in Palazzo Cinaglia in Via Roma, not far from the Palazzo Comunale.

Palazzo Casali A few paces along the narrow street next to the steps of the Palazzo Comunale is Piazza Signorelli, which is bordered by Palazzo Fierli, the Teatro Signorelli and Palazzo Casali. The last-named was built in the 13th century by the Casali family, which lived there until 1409. The façade (reconstructed in 1608) and the walls of the inner courtyard are decorated with **coats of arms** of the Florentine town governors and the stone coats of arms with the Golden Fleece of Francesco dei Medici, who was governor in 1570. At the beginning of the

16th century the painter Luca Signorelli had his workshop in the palace. Since the mid-18th century the Etruscan academy has had its seat here.

★
Museo dell' Accademia Etrusca

The Etruscan museum in Palazzo Casali is worth a visit, as some of its pieces are very rare, though they could be arranged more attractively.
The highlights include the large Etruscan **wheel lamp** from the second half of the 5th century BC. The bronze oil lamp with 16 decorated wick openings has the head of Medusa on the bottom, surrounded by an ocean wreath that dolphins jump over and 16 winged harpies. The artistic skill of the Etruscans can be admired in the **bronze statuettes** (including Zeus hurling a thunderbolt and a winged goddess, both from the 7th–6th century BC). The burial urns for ashes made of alabaster and terracotta (6th–5th century BC) date from the Hellenistic period. Egyptian and Roman finds as well as works by Gino Severini complete the collection (hours: April–Oct Tue–Sun 10am–7pm, Nov–March Tue–Sun 10am–5pm).

Duomo Santa Maria

Past the bishop's palace (Palazzo Vescovile), whose appearance goes back to the late 19th century, is Piazza del Duomo. The Renaissance cathedral was built over a Romanesque church and in its present form it is mainly the work of Giuliano da Sangallo (1445–1516). The Baroque high altar (1664) is by the Cortonese Francesco Mazzuoli. Some of the paintings in the choir are attributed to pupils of Luca Signorelli.

Chiesa del Gesù

★ ★
◄ Museo Diocesano

The church was built between 1498 and 1505 directly opposite the cathedral. A second storey was added in 1543, when it was changed to plans by Giorgio Vasari.
The upper church nave with its side rooms is used as the diocesan museum today and has a rich and important collection. The most important work is the colourful *Annunciation* **by Fra Angelico**. The painting, which was executed in 1433 or 1434 for San Domenico, has naturalistic elements and foreshadows the Renaissance in its feeling for form. Fra Angelico also created the triptych with scenes from the life of St Dominic on the predella. In the *Visitation* with views of Lake Trasimeno and the town of Castiglione del Lago the artist was obviously inspired by the surroundings of Cortona. Pietro Lorenzetti's *Madonna with Child and Four Angels* and a *Madonna* attributed to the school of Duccio di Buoninsegna, as well as Luca Signorelli's and Sassetta's painted altar panels are further highlights of the museum. The so-called Vagnucci reliquary (1457) of gilded bronze, silver and gems is also worthy of note. Giorgio Vasari painted frescoes on the vaulted ceiling in the lower church nave. The twelve biblical figures there are by Christoforo Gerardi (16th century), also called Doceno (hours: April until Oct Tue–Sun 10am–7pm, Nov–March 10am–5pm).

On the Piazza della Repubblica

San Francesco

The building of the church of San Francesco, east above Piazza della Repubblica, started in 1245. That makes it the second-oldest Franciscan church after Assisi. The exterior of the church is without decoration; the interior was remodelled in early Baroque style in 1526. The most important treasure of San Francesco was brought back from Constantinople by Brother Elijah in the 13th century: a relic of the cross, which was framed in the 16th century with a Byzantine ivory tablet. The founder of the church, Fra Elia da Cortona, is buried in the choir. Luca Signorelli is also supposed to have been buried here in 1523.

Via Nazionale, Piazza Garibaldi, San Domenico

Via Nazionale with many shops and even more bars and cafés begins at Piazza della Repubblica. Piazza Garibaldi, a popular meeting point for young people, is at the end of the main street in the centre of Cortona. From here it is only a few steps to the church of San Domenico outside the town walls to the south. The church was once part of a Dominican monastery, where the famous painter **Fra Angelico** (around 1400–1455) lived for a while.

It was built in the early 15th century in the plain style of the mendicant orders; it has a beautiful triptych by Lorenzo Gherini (15th century), which shows the *Coronation of the Virgin* in the centre. On the wall of the presbytery there is an *Assumption of the Virgin* by Bartolomeo della Gatta (also 15th century); the lunette is decorated by a *Madonna with Saints* by Fra Angelico. A good place to take a break after this full sightseeing programme is the adjoining Giardino Pubblico.

The small, simple 15th-century church about halfway between Piazza Repubblica and the Medici fortress is worth a look – because of the processional standard that was painted on both sides by Luca Signorelli and now serves as an altar painting.

San Nicolò

Via Santa Margherita leads east up the hill to the pilgrimage church of Santa Margherita, a Byzantine-style building that was dedicated in 1897. Even though St Margaret of Cortona (1247-1297), whose mortal remains rest here in a tomb (1362) inside a silver reliquary (1646), had an unhappy marriage, the church is very popular for weddings today. There is a beautiful view from the front of the church over the ►Val di Chiana.

Santuario di Santa Margherita

The fortress of the Medici rises high above the town centre and constitutes the north-eastern corner of the town wall. It was rebuilt in 1556 on old foundations and is open to the public in the summer months (from Easter to the end of Oct).

Fortezza Medicea

The Franciscan convent just about 4km/2.5mi north-east on the flank of Monte Sant'Egidio is a **collection of monk's cells**, of which the first were established 1211–1221 by Francis of Assisi. The small church from 1573 and a few cells, including that of St Francis, are open to the public. There is a beautiful view of Cortona from the convent.

★
Convento delle Celle

◄ ✶ Elba / Isola d'Elba

M/N 3 – 5

Province: Livorno
Population: 30,000

Area: 223.5 sq km/86 sq mi

Elba is the largest and best-known island in the Tuscan archipelago. With numerous yacht harbours, wonderful beaches for swimming, a fascinating, diverse interior and an excellent infrastructure for tourism, it is not surprising that the island is a popular Italian holiday venue.

Most holiday-makers use the ferry between the port and industrial city Piombino and Portoferraio to get to Elba. The car ferries of Toremar and Moby Lines both take about one hour. In the high season they run between 6am and 22.30pm. There are also connections

Arrival

▶ VISITING ELBA

INFORMATION
Portoferraio, Calata Italia 26
Tel. 05 65 91 46 71, fax 05 65 91 63 50
www.arcipelago.turismo.toscana.it

FERRY CONNECTIONS
see p.199, Arrival

WHERE TO EAT

► Inexpensive
Lo Zodiaco
Procchio
Via del Mare 21
Tel. 05 65 90 76 30
Simple restaurant close to the sea, good home cooking.

► Moderate
Emanuele
Portoferraio, Località Enfola
Tel. 05 65 93 90 03
For seafood-lovers! Grilled fish and seafood are served outdoors under an old fig tree with a view of the sea.

WHERE TO STAY

► Luxury
Hermitage
Portoferraio – Biodola
Via Biodola
Tel. 05 65 97 48 11
Fax 05 65 96 99 84
www.elba4star.it, 130 rooms
Luxury hotel in the most exclusive bay of the island. The holiday bungalows nestle harmoniously in the landscape of this large complex between beach and cliffs right on the sea.

► Mid-range
Belmare
Porto Azzurro
Banchina IV Novembre 21
Tel. 05 65 950 12
Fax 05 65 92 10 77
www.elba-hotelmare.it
The little holiday hotel is on the beach promenade of Porto Azzuro. Some of the rooms have a wonderful view of the sea. The owner organizes mountain-bike tours.

► Budget
Residence Da Pilade
Capoliveri, Loc. Mola
Tel. 05 65 96 86 35
Fax 05 65 96 89 26
www.hoteldapilade.it, 18 rooms and apartments
Open all year, family-run apartment hotel. Generous breakfast; in the summer half board as well.

from Piombino to Cavo (40 minutes) and Porto Azzurro (via Rio Marina, 1 hour 20 minutes). From Piombino hydrofoils (aliscafo) cross to Portoferraio (30 minutes) and Cavo (15 minutes).

In the high season (Pentecost, July/August) reservations are absolutely recommended. There are special rates in the low seasons. From ►Livorno too there are regular car ferries to Portoferraio on the island (direct connection 3 hours). Information online at: www.traghetti.com.

From Pisa there is also a direct flight to the little airfield at Marina di Campo.

The island, which is rich in mineral resources, was already occupied in the Bronze Age. The Etruscans established their dominance in Italy by exploiting the ore deposits, and the Romans also worked the mines for centuries after founding several colonies on Elba around 246 BC. In the Middle Ages Elba was raided by Saracen pirates many times, and in the 11th century the Republic of Pisa took control. The Medici (1546–1559) were followed until 1799 by the Spanish Habsburgs and finally France. In May 1814 the island became the home of the exiled **Napoleon**, who had full sovereignty – he stayed until 26 February 1815. Pig iron was produced on Elba well into the 20th century; the last plant closed only in 1982.

History

The name Piombino comes from the Italian word »piombo« for lead, which indicates the most important industry of the city, the metal industry. In the nearby ►Populonia Elban ore was already smelted in ancient times. Blast furnaces and rolling mills are still features of the industrial city, whose steelworks are an important economic factor in Tuscany.

Ferry port Piombino

The view from the harbour promenade across to Elba and the old harbour, where yachts lie at anchor today, has a certain charm. Apart from that Piombino has few buildings worth seeing. At the central Piazza Guiseppe Verdi the massive torrione, a defensive tower from 1212, and a city gate dated 1447 are reminders of the former fortifications. Corso Vittorio Emanuele, the main street of the old city, leads from here to the Palazzo Comunale, which was originally built in the 12th century and later renovated several times. The adjacent clock tower dates from 1598. At Piazza Curzio Desideri is the small abbey church of Sant'Antimo, which was built in the late 14th century for Pietro Gambacorti. Inside is a marble baptismal font (1470) by Andrea Guardi; a second was made out of an ancient column.

✱ Portoferraio and surroundings

On a rocky spit of land with a natural harbour along the north coast lies the pretty town of Portoferraio (population 12,000), the capital of Elba and the entire archipelago. Its name comes from Latin and means »iron harbour«. The ferries land at Ponte Massimo in the new city. The tourism office is in the tall building across from the landing. Right next to it is the bus terminal.

Capital of the archipelago

The old town on a **rocky spur** jutting into the sea was once cut off from the island by a water channel which was only filled up in 1919. As a reminder of the drawbridge between the old town and the main island the area around the broad Viale Manzoni is called »Ponticell« (little bridge). From 1548 Cosimo I de Medici fortified the town, creating a masterpiece of Renaissance military architecture. Begin a tour of the town at the old fishing harbour Darsena, today a yacht harbour. This is a very busy place in the summer. The gate at the harbour basin, Porta a Mare or Porta Medicea, was built as part of the

On Elba there are sand, gravel and stone beaches: something for every taste.

Medici fortifications. Walk straight into the town from the gate across the long Piazza Cavour to get to Piazza della Repubblica with the cathedral on its short side (begun in 1549). On the opposite short side, in front of the Municipio built in 1559, turn off into the narrow stepped street Via Garibaldi.

Chiesa della Misericordia, Pinacoteca Foresiana ✴

On the right side of Via Garibaldi is the small church Chiesa della Misericordia, in which a mass is read for Napoleon every year on 5 May. It has a picture of the Madonna which is attributed to Tino da Camaino (1285–1337) and a bronze copy of **Napoleon's death mask**. Since 1991 the former Franciscan monastery opposite the church has been the cultural centre Comte de Laugier with the Pinacoteca Foresiana, which exhibits historical paintings and furniture of the Foresi family (hours: Mon–Sat 9.30am–12.30pm and 4–7pm).

Forte Falcone, Forte Stella

From here it is only a few steps to the highest point of the city, Piazza Napoleone, and a wonderful panorama. To the west the view includes the »falcon fortress« (Forte Falcone); eastwards, above the lighthouse built in 1788, stands the star-shaped Forte Stella, where Napoleon's guard was quartered.

Between the two fortresses Napoleon had the simple Villa dei Mulini built in 1814 as his town residence. Since the original furnishings have almost all been lost, the villa was refurnished with furniture from Palazzo Pitti. In the bedroom is one of the few pieces of original furniture: **Napoleon's baronial bed**. His personal library comprised about 2,000 volumes, which came from Fontainebleau. On the upper floor the apartment of his sister Pauline Borghese can be viewed. The shady garden high above the rocky coast has a wonderful view of Forte Stella and the mainland coast (hours: Mon–Sat 9am–7pm, Sun 9am–1pm, in winter 9am–4.30pm).

Villa dei Mulini

The museum at Darsena harbour with its interesting design is well worth seeing – more than just an alternative for bad weather. It shows finds from prehistoric and ancient times, which come in part from sunken wrecks off the coast (hours: mid-June–mid-Sept daily 9.30am–2.30pm and 5pm–midnight, otherwise daily except Tue 10.30am–1.30pm and 4–8pm).

Museo Archeologico

About 6km/3.5mi west of Portoferraio towards Porto Azzurro in the tiny village of Le Grotte, the ruins of a **Roman villa** from the 1st century were excavated in 1960. The nobleman's residence even had a heated swimming pool. It was surrounded by a water channel through which hot water circulated.

Surroundings, Villa Romana delle Grotte

About 6km/3.5mi south-west of Portoferraio on the slopes of the forested Monte San Martino stands the neo-classical manor house of the Russian Duke Anatolio Demidoff, built in 1852. Demidoff collected a large amount of Napoleonic memorabilia here, which was auctioned off after his death. To the left of Demidoff's palace a path leads up to the emperor's summer residence, which is outwardly and inwardly modest compared to the villa. On the second floor eight rooms are open to visitors. Only the **dining room in Egyptian style** is ostentatious. Its decorations glorify Napoleonic victories (hours: in summer Mon–Sat 9am–7pm, Sun 9am–1pm, otherwise Mon–Sat 9am–4pm).

Villa Demidoff, Villa San Martino

✱ Tour of the Island of Elba

18km/11mi to the west of Portoferraio lies the pretty harbour town of Marciana Marina. The road passes the inviting cove of Procchio with one of the most beautiful beaches for swimming on the island. The so-called Saracen tower, which was built in the time of Pisan rule, rises over the town.

Procchio, Marciana Marina

A winding and steep road leads 8km/5mi inland to the centre of Elba's wine production in the middle of beautiful chestnut woods. The charming village of Marciana has narrow streets and the remains of a Pisan fortress, which was extended by the Appiani family around

Marciana (Alto)

1450. Park the car outside the village if possible! Below the fortress the Archaeological Museum in Via del Pretorio displays Etruscan and Roman excavation finds. A paved path passes twelve chapels on its way up to the oldest pilgrimage chapel on Elba, Madonna del Monte, with a picture of the Virgin Mary (15th century). The ascent takes about 40 minutes.

◄ Madonna del Monte

✳ Monte Capanne

The highest point on the island is the 1,018m/3,340ft-high Monte Capanne, which can also be reached by cable car. An undersea flow of magma created this stone panettone. From the granite peak there is a wonderful panorama of the entire archipelago on clear days. Hiking shoes are recommended!

✳ Beaches of Cavoli, Seccheto and Fetovaia

The drive continues via Poggio, Sant'Ilario in Campo and San Piero in Campo down to Cavoli. The resort has a beach of fine-grained sand with crystal-clear water, which attracts many bathers in the summer – not least because they can drive to the beach and park there (parking fee). From Cavoli boats go to the nearby Grotta Azzurra. Two kilometres (1.3mi) further on lies Seccheto. The beach there, which can be reached via two flights of steps, is a little smaller and the sand coarser, but as a result it is much quieter than the cove of Cavoli. Some consider the beach of Fetovaia in a wonderful cove to be the most beautiful because of its white sand.

! Baedeker TIP

Natural bathtubs

A path leads down to the sea between Fetovaia and Seccheto. In the course of time natural seawater pools formed there in the granite – today a wonderful place for swimming.

✳ Marina di Campo

The main attraction of the southern coast is the popular seaside resort Marina di Campo (population 4,200) with the **largest sandy beach on Elba**. Water-sport lovers find sailing, surfing and diving schools; nighthawks enjoy the busy bars and restaurants of the former fishing village. The so-called Medici tower is an 11th-century Pisan fortification. About 2km/1.3mi outside Marina di Campo towards Lacona in the Località La Foce, the aquarium of Elba with its many varieties of fish is worth a visit (L'Aquario dell'Elba; hours: March–May and Oct–Nov 9am–7.30pm, June–Sept until 11pm).

✳✳ Capoliveri

The Gulf of Lacona and Golfo Stella further east also have beautiful beaches. Lacona belongs to the commune of Capoliveri on the south-eastern peninsula Calamita. The **picturesque village**, once a mining town and today one of the most popular holiday addresses on Elba, possesses romantic streets and old houses, of which many have been carefully restored in the last years.

✳ Porto Azzurro

The second-largest harbour on Elba is in the charming village of Porto Azzurro on the east coast, which Spain fortified in the 17th century. Fort Longone, the star-shaped fortress built by King Philip II of Spain, which has served as a prison since 1858, rises impressively above the »azure-blue harbour«. Day trips by boat to the nearby islands leave from here.

The next stop on the north-east coast of the island, Rio Marina, is the former shipping port for ore. The rust-red façades of the buildings along the main street lined by plane trees shows the high content of iron oxide in the nearby mines. Rock collectors find information in the city hall museum on existing find sites and ore mines that are still open (hours: May–Sept Mon–Sat 9am–noon and 3–6pm, Sun 9am–12.30pm).

Rio Marina

Wine production on Elba is on a small scale but excellent in quality. The best comes from the estate La Chiusa. Its »Elba Rosso« is pressed from Sangiovese grapes, »Elba Bianco« from Procanico grapes. The top-quality estate lies almost directly by the sea on the road to Magazzini/Bagnaia in the middle of vineyards. Wines can be tasted and bought directly.

La Chiusa

Before arriving back in Portoferraio, the **medieval mountain castle** Volterraio, which crowns a 394m/1,293ft-high mountaintop like an eagle's nest, can be seen from a distance. This former place of refuge was built by the Pisan Gherardu Rau around 1284. In the 17th century the outer bulwark was improved. Enemy ships could be seen quickly from up here. The car can be parked near an abandoned sheep barn. From here a difficult path (about 40 minutes, hiking shoes a must) leads to the castle on the summit. The wonderful view rewards the effort!

★ ★
Volterraio

Isola Pianosa and Isola di Montecristo

Only 8 sea miles separate Elba from the former prison island of Pianosa. Only 280 people live on the flat, 10 sq km/3.8 sq mi island today. Ten years ago there were about twice as many. The Romans called it Planasia. In the Middle Ages the island was ruled by Pisa, later Genoa and the Appiani family, before North African pirates carried the inhabitants off into slavery in the mid-16th century. From 1835 until 1997 Pianosa was a prison colony. Since the last prisoners were moved to the mainland there have been long discussions on the future of the former prison island. As the tiny natural paradise belongs in its entirety to the Tuscan Archipelago National Park, no new buildings can be built. For those who want to visit the island, there are daily boat trips from Elba (limited number of participants; information at tel. 05 65 97 93 11, 05 65 91 94 11 or www.islepark.it).

Isola Pianosa

The granite island Montecristo, which has a size of almost 11 sq km/4 sq mi and the 645m/2,116ft Monte Fortezza as its highest point,

★
Isola di Montecristo

lies 32 sea miles south of Elba. In 1971 the island was declared a nature reserve because of its unique flora and fauna and since 1996 has been part of the **Parco Nazionale dell'Arcipelago Toscano**. At present the island can only be visited with special permission for a one-day tour, but there are rumours that Montecristo will be opened further for tourism. The island owes its name to St Maximilian, who took refuge here around 450 and renamed it from Mons Jovis to Mons Christi. At the end of the 19th century artists and members of high society met in the newly restored Villa Reale for exclusive hunting parties; after that the Prince of Naples and later king of Italy, Vittorio Emanuele, took over the lease of the Cala Maestra. Date palms, eucalyptus trees and magnolias flourish in the botanical garden behind the villa. The legend of a fabulous treasure buried by Camaldolese monks on Montecristo gave the idea for one of the most successful adventure novels of world literature: Alexandre Dumas' bestseller published in 1846, *The Count of Monte Christo*.

✴ Fiesole

G 10

Province: Florence/Firenze (FI) **Altitude:** 295m/968ft above sea level
Population: 15,000

When the summer gets hot and humid in Florence, the Florentines like to get away to Fiesole, where the wealthy have built their baronial villas. The pretty town is only 8km/5mi away, nestled between two hills above the city on the Arno.

What to See in Fiesole

Piazza Mino da Fiesole
The centre of this likeable town is the broad Piazza Mino da Fiesole, named after the sculptor Mino da Fiesole (around 1430–1484). The monument unveiled on the piazza in 1906 is named »Incontro di Teano«. The two bronze equestrian figures represent King Vittorio Emanuelle II and Garibaldi. In the many street cafés the motto is »see and be seen«. The north-west side of Piazza Mino da Fiesole is occupied by the seminario (1697) and the 11th-century bishop's palace (Palazzo Vescovile).

On the south-west side of the square are the 14th-century Palazzo Pretorio – its portico and loggia were added in the 15th century – and the adjacent medieval oratory Santa Maria Primerana with a portico dating from the 16th century.

Duomo San Romolo
On the north side of the square is the cathedral, which was begun in 1024, expanded in the 13th and 14th centuries and remodelled in the 19th century. The bell tower, completed in 1213, stands 42m/138ft high and is fortified with battlements. It tower majestically over

the whole town. The church contains several notable works of art. The terracotta statue of its patron saint San Romolo is by Giovanni della Robbia.

Adjacent to the cathedral in the north is the Museo Bandini, devoted to works of sacred art collected in the 18th century by Canon Angiolo Maria Bandini, scientist and librarian of the Biblioteca Medicea Laurenziana in Florence (hours: May–Oct daily 10am–7pm, otherwise daily except Tue 9am–5pm).

Museo Bandini

Behind the cathedral to the north-east is the excavation site, Zona Archeologica, dominated by a **Roman theatre** that was rediscovered in the early 19th century. It was constructed in the early imperial period (1st century BC) and enlarged under emperors Claudius and Septimius Severus. The semicircle has a diameter of 34m/37yd and seats about 3,000 spectators in 24 rows. In the summer months the theatre is used for classical theatre and pop music concerts (hours: May–Oct daily 9.30am–7pm, Nov–April daily except Tue until 5pm).

Zona Archeologica

> ! **Baedeker TIP**
>
> ### Take the bus!
>
> To enjoy the view of Florence from the panoramic road to Fiesole at leisure, take bus no. 7, which commutes between Florence and Fiesole every 15 minutes (departure from the main railway station, cathedral square and Piazza San Marco).

Not far from the theatre are the ruins of **Roman baths**, which were also built during the imperial period and expanded under Emperor Hadrian. Even though the arches, which were carried by massive columns, were always visible, the site was recognized as a bath and excavated only at the end of the 19th century.

In the eastern part the water was heated by means of furnaces and hypocausts; the three central rooms were for cold baths (frigidarium), lukewarm baths (tepidarium) and warm baths (caldarium); the larger pools in the western part served as swimming pools and reservoirs. In the north-west corner of the excavation site are the remains of a Roman and an Etruscan temple (1st and 3rd century BC respectively). Towards the north the site is bordered by a section of the massive Etruscan city wall from the 3rd century BC.

Fiesole was founded by the Etruscans in the 7th/6th century BC; the Roman settlement named Faesulae followed in the 1st century BC. The small archaeological museum to the south and above the Roman theatre exhibits finds from the Etruscan and Roman periods, including remains of a marble frieze for the stage decoration of the Roman theatre, a grave stele (470–460 BC; with funeral banquet, dance and animal battle), a copy of the head of Emperor Claudius (41–54) and a Dionysius statue (Roman copy of a Greek original).

Museo Archeologico

▶ VISITING FIESOLE

INFORMATION
Via Portigiani 3-5
Tel. 05 55 98 720
Fax 05 55 98 822
www.comune.fiesole.fi.it

WHERE TO EAT

▶ Moderate
La Panacea
Olmo – Via Bosconi 58/a
Tel. 05 55 48 972
www.la-panacea.it
Closed Mon.
Tuscan home cooking and fish spe-
cialties. In good weather the food is
served on the terrace.

▶ Inexpensive
Pizzeria Etrusca
Piazza Mino da Fiesole 2
Tel. 05 55 99 484

Apart from pizza they also serve pasta
at acceptable prices.

WHERE TO STAY

▶ Mid-range
Bencista
Via Benedetto da Maiano 4
Tel. and fax 05 55 91 63
42 rooms
Pleasantly located country inn in the
middle of olive groves.

▶ Budget
Le Canelli
Via Gramsci 52
Tel. 05 55 97 83 36
Fax 05 55 97 82 92, 4 rooms
Charming inn near the central
piazza.

Antiquarium Costantini

Not far to the east of the entrance to the Zona Archeologica is the
Antiquarium Costantini; the admission ticket for the excavation site
is also valid for this collection of Greek, Etruscan and Italian ceramics.

Museo Primo Conti

North-west of the excavation site in Via Dupré 18 is the foundation
and a small museum for the Tuscan painter Primo Conti
(1900–1988). Conti first painted in Futurist and Cubist styles but
after World War II he developed his own style with wild colours. In
addition to works by Conti, documents on Italian Futurism are also
exhibited (hours: Tue–Sat 10am–1pm).

Sant'Alessandro, observation platform

Between the bishop's palace and the seminar building a path leads
steeply uphill to two small churches and a tree-shaded observation
platform, from which there is an outstanding view of Florence. In
the small park a monument honours the soldiers who fell in World
War I; another one honours three carabinieri who were killed by the
SS in 1944.

San Francesco, Giardini Pubblici

Diagonally opposite is the monastery church of San Francesco, established by Augustinian monks in 1330. In 1407 it passed to the Fran-

ciscan order, was later remodelled and in 1905 renovated extensively. The main altar is particularly worthy of note: The *Annunciation* is by Raffaellino del Garbo, the *Adoration of the Magi* by Cosimo Rosselli. The mission museum and the idyllic cloisters are also worth seeing. In front of the monastery a path leads to the municipal park, and through it to the centre of town.

Villa Medici

Via Vecchia Fiesolana, which runs south-west down from Fiesole, leads to Villa Medici, which the architect Michelozzo built in 1458–1461 for Cosimo the Elder. The Pazzi conspirators at first planned to murder the brothers Lorenzo and Giuliano de Medici here in 1478, before they decided that the Duomo Santa Maria del Fiore in Florence would be a better site. The villa can be visited only as part of an organized tour; inquire at tourist information. Keen walkers can return to Florence from the Villa Medici on foot. Just follow Via Vecchia Fiesolana, which runs from Villa Medici to the monastery San Domenico – unfortunately the road is open to cars as well. The entire descent should take less than two hours.

★
San Domenico di Fiesole

A good 1km/0.5mi to the south-west of Fiesole and right on the Florence city limits (panoramic view) lies a group of houses called San Domenico di Fiesole. The church of San Domenico here is worth viewing. It was built between 1406 and 1435 for Barnaba degli Agli and extended in the 17th century, and it is richly decorated inside. On the altar in the first chapel on the left notice the beautiful **triptych** (around 1430) by Fra Angelico, who also painted the *Crucifixion* and an image of the Virgin in the chapter house of the monastery. The son of a wealthy farmer from the Mugello Valley, he entered the Dominican monastery at the age of twenty.

His reputation as an outstanding painter spread quickly and when the Dominican monastery of San Marco in Florence was remodelled in 1436, Fra Angelico received the commission to paint the cells with themes from the passion of Christ. Fra Angelico's realism had in part a curious effect: it is said that his fellow monks fainted at the sight of his crucifixion scene because of the amount of blood depicted.

Badia Fiesolana

North-west below San Domenico lies Badia Fiesolana at 123m/403ft elevation. The cathedral church of Fiesole stood here until 1028, on the supposed site of the martyrdom of St Romulus, when it was replaced by the duomo. After Camaldolese monks had rebuilt the church with a monastery (badia = abbey), it was handed over to the Benedictine order.

During the Renaissance the monastery and church were remodelled again; Romanesque parts from the 12th century are preserved on the façade. In 1778 the church and monastery were dissolved. Since 1976 Badia Fiesolana has housed the international institute Università Europea, a renowned centre for doctoral and post-doctoral research in the social sciences.

★ Florence / Firenze

Capital of Regione Toscana
Province: Florence/Firenze (FI)

Altitude: 50m/164ft above sea level
Population: 374,000

The combination of dolce vita and cultural pleasures is probably nowhere more charming than in Florence. The city on the Arno is the cradle of the Renaissance. Brunelleschi, Michelangelo, Donatello, Leonardo da Vinci, Boccaccio, Dante, Petrarch, Galileo and the mighty Medici were active here; it was the cradle of written form of the Italian language and the centre of Italian literature.

Since the Middle Ages the Florentines have known how to keep and multiply their wealth as industrious craftsmen, able businessmen and competent administrators. Florentine banks controlled Europe's money market at times, and its bankers influenced European politics decisively. The city became rich through weaving and dying, tailoring and trading in silk; the clothing industry is still an important source of income.

City of the Medici

The Etruscan and Roman settlement on the Arno had little importance. Not until the early 13th century did the city begin to flourish through the fortunes of war and industrious trading, and became the most respected city in central Italy. The guilds gradually grew stronger and took control of the government in 1282. From 1434 **the Medici, a wealthy merchant family,** controlled local politics. The most important members of the family, Cosimo (1434–1464) and Lorenzo (1469–1492), led the republic to its greatest prosperity and made it a centre of the arts and sciences. In 1494 the Medici were driven out. The short-lived **theocracy under the penitential preacher Girolamo Savonarola** ended in 1498 with his execution and led to a new republic.

In 1512 the Medici were brought back by Spanish troops, but driven out again in 1527. In 1530 finally, after the city was taken by Charles V, Alessandro de Medici was installed as Duke of Florence. After his murder in 1537, Cosimo I ruled as Grand Duke of Tuscany from 1569. When the Medici line died out in 1737, Tuscany passed to the house of Habsburg-Lorraine, which ruled until 1860 except for the Napoleonic period. When Tuscany joined the unified Kingdom of Italy, Florence flourished again as the **temporary capital of the monarchy** (1865–1870). Despite war damage in 1944 and the catastrophic Arno flood in 1966, Florence remains one of the most beautiful cities in Italy.

← *In the heart of Florence:*
Palazzo Vecchio on Piazza della Signoria

Florence Plan

A Piazza della Signoria
B Piazza San Firenze
C Piazza del Duomo
D Piazza San Giovanni
E Piazza della Repubblica
F Piazza Santa Maria Novella
G Piazza Ognissanti

H Piazza dell' Unità Italiana
I Piazza Madonna degli
  Aldobrandini
K Piazza San Marco
L Piazza della
  Santissima Annunziata
M Piazza Santa Croce

1 Loggia dei Lanzi
2 Palazzo Fenzi
3 Palazzo Uguccione
4 Badia Fiorentina
5 Casa di Dante
6 Santa Maria
  Maggiore

7 San Gaetano
8 Mercato Nuovo
9 Palazzo Davanzati
10 Palazzo Spini-Ferro
11 Santi Apostoli
12 Palazzo di Parte G
13 Santo Stefano

Where to eat
① Il Cibreo
② Sostanza
③ Zá Zá
④ Pizzeria Antica Porta
⑤ Trattoria Mario
⑥ Il Latini

Where to stay
① Brunelleschi
② Il Guelfo Bianco
③ Beacci Tornabuoni
④ Villa Mangiacane
⑤ Alessandra

▶ VISITING FLORENCE

INFORMATION

Via Manzoni 16
Tel. 05 52 33 20, fax 05 52 34 62 86
Via Cavour 1
Tel. 055 29 08 32, fax 05 52 76 03 83
www.firenze.turismo.toscana.it

DRIVING INTO THE CITY

The centre has little motor traffic by
Italian standards; only local residents
and delivery vehicles are allowed to
enter. Hotel guests may park only to
unload their luggage; illegal parking is
very expensive! Leave the car outside,
ideally on a guarded parking lot or in
a parking garage at the edge of the city
centre. Ask about discounts for hotel
guests!

The parking garage at the main railway station is centrally located but at
€2 per hour in the upper price
bracket. Our tip: Parterre parking
garage above Piazza della Libertà
(about €15 per day), On Saturdays a
free shuttle bus runs into the city
centre.

CITY BUSES

Buses run regularly in the entire city.
Tickets at the railway station, in bars
and at kiosks, but not on the bus!
Recommended: tourist ticket for 1, 2
or 3 days or 1 week. Schedules from
the APT office.

*Things are generally not this rough in Florence. But in the Calcio in Costume,
a kind of Italian rugby, the rules are not too strict …*

EVENTS

The main church festivals are celebrated in Florence, like everywhere else in the country, with the typical Italian sense of drama. In Florence don't miss the Scioppio del Carro on Easter Sunday, when a rocket in the form of a dove is ignited at the cathedral altar. It then »flies« on a rope through the church to the square and there sets off an oxcart full of fireworks. »Calcio in Costume« is much more profane but no less enthusiastic. On a sanded square (Piazza Santa Croce) two teams in historical costumes and with pretty rough manners fight to get a ball into a net. The final game generally takes place on 24 June during the Festa di San Giovanni. All events of the current month are in the city magazine *Firenze Spettacolo.*

SHOPPING

Florence is a mecca for fashion, leather goods, fabrics, gourmet foods and jewellery, but prices can be exorbitant. The main shopping streets are Via Calzaiuoli between the cathedral and Piazza della Signoria. The heart of the fashion world beats on Via Tornabuoni and in the adjoining streets, where all big names from Armani to Dolce & Gabbana can be found. The best place for shoes is Borgo San Lorenzo or Via Cerretani, for jewellery the Ponte Vecchio, for antiques Borgo Ognissanti, Via Maggio and Via Fossi. To see a lively market, go to the Mercato San Lorenzo in Via dell'Ariento or the Mercato Centrale.

WHERE TO EAT

▶ Expensive

① *Cibreo*
Via Andrea Verocchio 80
Tel. 055 234 11 00
Closed Sun and Mon
Reservations are required for this gourmet restaurant near the Sant'Ambrogio market.

▶ Moderate

② *Sostanza*
Via del Porcellana 25
Tel. 055 21 26 91, closed Tue
Traditional Florentine restaurant where Chagall and Steinbeck once ate; recommendation: bistecca alla fiorentina.

③ *Zà Zà*
Piazza del Mercato Centrale 26
Tel. 055 21 54 11
Closed Tue and Sun, except for the last Sunday of the month. Popular restaurant with creative Florentine cuisine. Local people come here above all; reservations a must!

▶ Inexpensive/Moderate

④ *Pizzeria Antica Porta*
Via Senese 23/R
Tel. 055 22 05 27
Closed Mon.
Among Florentines it is no longer a secret that the Pizzeria Antica Porta makes great pizzas.

Baedeker recommendation

▶ Inexpensive

⑤ *Trattoria Mario*
The tiny trattoria near the Mercato Centrale is a typical family restaurant and very popular – where else would you wait on the sidewalk when the restaurant is full until the patrone invites you to come in? Only open from noon to 4pm (Via Rosina 2/R, tel. 055 21 85 50, www.trattoriamario.com).

⑥ *Il Latini*
Via dei Palchetti 6
Tel. 055 21 09 16, closed Mon.
Hams hang from the ceiling, and

plates are weighed down by the famous bistecca fiorentina, an inch-thick cut from the loin, seasoned only with a splash of olive oil. Lighter dishes are also served.

WHERE TO STAY

► Luxury

④ *Villa Mangiacane (Ill.)*
San Casciano, Via Faltignano 4
Tel. 055 829 01 23
Fax 055 829 03 58
www.villamangiacane.it
7 suites and 1 master suite
Villa Mangiacane opened in spring 2004, more luxury accommodation for the demanding visitor to Florence. The completely renovated Renaissance villa sits on the crown of a hill

amidst olive groves and vineyards. The unforgettable view of the city from the wonderful loggia makes it clear that you are only 12km/7.5mi away from Florence.

① *Brunelleschi*
Piazza Sant'Elisabetta 3
Tel. 055 273 70
Fax 055 21 96 53
www.hotelbrunelleschi.it
Come here if you want to live in the heart of Florence in a Byzantine tower. A small private museum tells the history of the house and the man it was named after. Rooftop terrace with a wonderful panorama.

► Mid-range

② *Il Guelfo Bianco*
Via Cavour 29
Tel. 055 28 83 30
Fax 055 29 52 03
www.ilguelfobianco.it
Renovated 18th-century patrician house with pretty rooms in Florentine style.

⑤ *Hotel Alessandra*
Borgo SS. Apostolo 17
Tel. 055 28 34 38
Fax 055 21 06 19
This quiet hotel in a quiet side street between Ponte Vecchio and the church Santa Trinità is very comfortable. The rooms are all bright and nicely furnished, but some have no ensuite bathroom.

► Budget/Mid-Range

③ *Beacci Tornabuoni*
Via de Tornabuoni 3
Tel. 055 21 26 45
Fax 055 28 35 94
www.bthotel.it
Centrally located, well-kept bed & breakfast in the famous shopping street. Breakfast on the roof terrace.

Highlights Florence

Piazza del Duomo
Cathedral, baptistery and campanile: a unique ensemble, since 1982 on the Unesco list of world heritage and a milestone of Florentine architecture!
► page 216

Piazza della Signoria
This majestic square is the heart of Florence.
► page 222

Uffizi Gallery
What the Louvre is to Paris, the Uffizi Gallery is to Florence. One day is not nearly enough for this world-class art collection.
► page 226

Ponte Vecchio
Florence's most famous and oldest bridge
► page 231

Galleria dell' Accademia
Do you want to see Michelangelo's original David? Here he is!
► page 249

Santa Maria Novella and Santa Croce
Anyone who associates mendicant order churches with spartan furnishings will know better after seeing the rich works of art in these two churches.
► page 242, 253

Palazzo Pitti and Giardino di Boboli
Several museums under one roof, and the largest and most beautiful park in the city
► page 231, 235

Museo Nazionale del Bargello
This museum is a must for those interested in Renaissance sculpture and historic craftsmanship.
► page 251

✷ ✷ Battistero (baptismal chapel San Giovanni)

🕐 Opening hours:
Hours: Mon–Sat noon–7pm,
Sun 8.30am–2pm

The oldest building on the cathedral square **Piazza del Duomo** is the baptistery, which was begun in 1059 and completed in 1128. Its octagonal form derives from early Christian baptisteries. The three storeys of the well-proportioned building are differentiated by the varying designs of their marble covering in square and rounded forms. The baptistery owes its fame to the three monumental bronze doors. Between 1330 and 1336 Andrea Pisano created the oldest, southern bronze doors with 28 scenes in relief from the life of John the Baptist framed in Gothic quatrefoils. Pisano's figures, some of which are modelled in high relief or dressed in robes with many folds, move calmly but their gestures are full of suspense. A competition for the north door in 1401 was won by **Lorenzo Ghiberti** against six rivals (including Filippo Brunelleschi and Jacopo della Quercia from Siena). Ghiberti's decorative illusionist style convinced the judges. Between 1403 and 1424 he and his assistants made the double bronze doors with 28 quatrefoil fields depicting 20 scenes from the New Testament as well as the four evangelists and four fathers of the Latin church. Since Ghiberti's style was received well, he also obtained the commission for the eastern doors, which Michelangelo later thought worthy to decorate the gates of paradise – for which reason they are called **Porta del Paradiso**. It took Ghiberti almost 30 more years (1425–1452) to complete them, as the skills of casting bronze and gilding had to be relearned. The doors mounted on the baptistery are copies; the originals are in the cathedral museum. Ghiberti's ten bronze panels with scenes from the Old Testament (starting top left) combined high and low relief to achieve a completely new effect of visual illusion.

Interior

Like the exterior, the inside walls are clad with thin marble panels in geometric patterns. The two-storey interior with its powerful granite columns and pilasters receives little light from outside; an eight-sided, double-skinned dome construction gives it added height. The vaults are decorated with wonderful 13th-century mosaics. From the middle of the dome, six concentric rings show first plant ornamentation, then the heavenly host, followed by the story of the creation, the legend of Joseph, scenes from the life of Christ and the life story of John the Baptist. It is also worth noting the tomb (1425–1427) of the antipope John XXIII, by both Donatello and Michelozzo, and the marble floor.

✶ ✶ Duomo Santa Maria del Fiore

With its area of 8,300 sq m/9,930 sq yd, Santa Maria del Fiore is the third-largest church in Italy after St Peter's in Rome and the cathedral of Milan. It holds about 25,000 people. Even though it was begun during the Gothic period in 1294, the cathedral does not have such typical Gothic elements as flying buttresses, tracery and distinct architectural sculptures. Like the baptistery, the cathedral is richly panelled in marble of various colours. The side doorways are also late medieval, while the richly decorated main façade was carried out only in 1875–1886, to plans by Augusto Conti in the neo-Gothic style. The first cathedral architect was **Arnolfo di Cambio**. After his death around 1310 nothing hap-

A milestone in bronze art: Lorenzo Ghiberti's reliefs (copies) on the Porta del Paradiso of the Battistero

🕐
Opening hours:
Mon–Wed, Fri
10am–5pm,
Thu, Sat
10am–3.30pm,
Sun 1.30–4.45pm,
Dome
Mon–Fri
8.30am–6.20pm,
Sat 8.30am–3.40pm

pened for a long time, until in 1330 the guild of wool weavers took charge of the cathedral office of works and made Giotto its supervisor in 1334. However, Giotto essentially worked only on the campanile. The plans for the nave were changed repeatedly until 1368, when a small trial church was built to scale and heavy fines imposed for any deviation from this model. According to the final building plan, the nave, the walls for the choir and the drum for the dome were completed by the early 15th century. In 1436 Pope Eugene IV dedicated the cathedral, which was complete except for the façade.

The interior of the cathedral has the form of a pillared basilica. The broad nave seems cool, hall-like, monumental. Hardly anything recalls the filigree, ascending forms of Gothic architecture in France and other countries. The inside of the façade with three round windows designed by Ghiberti is decorated by a mosaic of the coronation of the Virgin (around 1300) and the wall tomb of Bishop Antonio d'Orso by Tino di Camaino. The clock face of the painted 24-hour clock (1443) with heads of four prophets or evangelists is by Paolo Uccello. At the beginning of the right-hand aisle a bust commemorates Filippo Brunelleschi, the architect of the cathedral dome, whose grave is in the crypt. Only a few steps further is the tondo-shaped monument (1490) to Giotto, painter, sculptor and architect of the campanile. The adjacent marble statue (around 1409) depicts Daniel and is considered to be an **early work of Donatello**. To the right above the side entrance is

a bust set up in 1521 for the philosopher Marsilio Ficino (1433 until 1499), head of the Platonic academy founded by Cosimo de Medici in 1459.

Leaving the aisle for the crossing, look up at the **dome fresco of the Last Judgement** (1572–1579) by Giorgio Vasari and Frederico Zuccari. The main altar in the crossing and the marble balustrade are mainly the work of Baccio Bandinelli (around 1555). The middle chapel of the choir houses the bronze shrine (1432–1442) of St Zenobius, Bishop of Florence and patron of the city, by Ghiberti, while the angel bearing a candelabra on the altar was made around 1450 by Luca della Robbia.

In the left transept is the **Old Sacristy** with a bronze door (1446–1467) by Michelozzo and Luca della Robbia portraying the church patron Mary and the evangelists and church fathers. In the lunette is a white and blue faience *Resurrection of Christ* (1442–1445) by Luca della Robbia. In 1478 Lorenzo de Medici took refuge during

Piazza del Duomo Plan

1 Porta del Paradiso	A Portale Maggiore	F Santa Reparata
2 North portal (entrance)	B Porta dei Cornacchini	(crypt)
3 South portal	C Porta della Mandorla	G Old Sacristy
4 Main altar	D Porta del Campanile	H New Sacristy
	E Porta dei Canonici	

mass in the cathedral behind the heavy sacristy doors, when his brother Giuliano was murdered in the so-called Pazzi conspiracy. In the left aisle at the fourth pillar a painted panel (1465) by Domenico di Michelino commemorates Dante Alighieri, who is portrayed with his main work, the *Divine Comedy*, with the silhouette of Florence in the background.

Two **equestrian portraits** on the aisle wall are especially impressive. Giovanni Acuto, an English mercenary leader whose real name was John Hawkwood and who first fought in the wars against France in the service of Edward III, was recruited by the Florentines in 1377 to fight against the pope. In 1394 the city government decided to erect a monument for him, which was only carried out in 1436 when Paolo Uccello painted the portrait using newly discovered perspective techniques. The equestrian portrait of Niccoló da Tolentino, the victor of the battle of San Romano (1432), which was painted twenty years later by Andrea del Castagno, is striking for its illusionistic manner.

✱ Campanile

The 82m/270ft-high bell tower was built between 1334 and 1384 to plans by Giotto di Bondone. Apart from the marble relief carvings, the lower walls are decorated with **reliefs by Andrea Pisano** including the seven planets, the seven virtues, the seven liberal arts and the seven sacraments. In the niches above are statues of the prophets, sibyls and patriarchs, some of which were done by Donatello in the years 1420–1435. All reliefs and statues are in the cathedral museum: copies adorn the bell tower. An unforgettable view is the reward for climbing the many steps.

Opening hours: daily 8.30am–7.30pm

414 steps are not easy, but the climb is worth it: view from the campanile to the great dome of the cathedral constructed by Filippo Brunelleschi.

✳ ✳ Museo dell'Opera del Duomo

🕐
Opening hours:
Mon–Sat
9am–7.30pm
Sun 9am–1.40pm

Since 1891 many of the decorations from the cathedral, campanile and baptistery have been in the cathedral museum, which has become one of the leading collections of sculpture in the world.

On the ground floor, the so-called hall of the **cathedral façade** contains statues that once decorated the outside of the façade and were removed before it was torn down in 1587, as well as a drawing of the old façade of the cathedral from the second half of the 16th century. The most important works include a seated figure of St Luke (1412) by Nanni di Banco, a statue of the evangelist John (1415) by Donatello and a seated figure of St Matthew by Bernardo Ciuffagni as well as a statue of Pope Boniface VIII (around 1300) by Arnolfo di Cambio. In the so-called Little Room are missals and valuable reliquaries as well as other gold and silver work from the **cathedral treasury**. The Brunelleschi memorial room with the death mask of the builder of the cathedral dome, the original wooden model for the lantern in the dome as well as tools, pulleys and ropes from the construction, is also worth seeing. In the mezzanine stands one of the most famous sculptures in western art: the *Pietà* by Michelangelo, which stood in the cathedral choir from 1722 until 1891. The artist created a pietà at the age of 23 for the church of St Peter in Rome, a perfect work in the traditional devotional style. At the age of 80 he again created a Pietà, which in combining the themes of the man of sorrows, the deposition of Jesus and mourning was very different from his first work. Michelangelo left the group incomplete and even broke it apart, but was at the same time so fascinated by the work that he wanted to be buried beneath it.

In the large hall on the second floor are two marble choir lofts – the left one by Lucca della Robbia, the right one by Donatello – which served as organ balustrades until they were removed in 1688. Donatello's monumental niche figures for the cathedral and his late *St Mary Magdalene* are epochal works of the early Renais-

✔ DON'T MISS

- the original wooden model of the dome lantern by Brunelleschi
- the *Pietà* by Michelangelo
- niche figures from the cathedral by Donatello
- reliefs from the paradise doors by Ghiberti

sance. In another room the reliefs of the campanile and the restored relief panels of Ghiberti's paradise doors from the baptistery are exhibited. The greatest Gothic and Renaissance treasures in the so-called altar hall are the silk and gold embroideries and the silver altar from the baptistery.

From Piazza del Duomo to Piazza della Signoria

Several routes lead from the cathedral square to Piazza della Signoria: the elegant Via Calzaiuoli or the narrow streets that run parallel, such as Via dei Cerchi, where tiny shops and excellent gourmet food shops are tempting places to linger.

Between the cathedral square and Piazza della Signoria the bulk of Orsanmichele catches the eye. This palace-like building (1337–1350) on Via dell'Arte della Lana was once both the city's grain warehouse and an oratory. The outer arcades of the lower storey, which used to house a market, were added in Gothic tracery decades after the building was built. At the end of the 14th century the guilds took on responsibility for decorating the building and hired sculptors to do the work. Thus most of the figures (in part replaced by copies) in the 14 outer niches date from the early 15th century, including important examples of Renaissance sculpture. In Via Calzaiuoli, beginning on the left: the first figure is a bronze statue (1414) of John the Baptist by Lorenzo Ghiberti, made in a transitional style between Gothic and Renaissance for the guild of cloth traders. The bronze group of Christ and Doubting Thomas (1465–1483) by Andrea del Verrocchio is a work of the high Renaissance for the niche of the court of commercial law. The next two niches contain the evangelist Luke (1597–1603) by Giambologna for the guild of the judges and notaries and the apostle Peter (around 1420) by associates of Donatello for the butchers. For the next two niches Nanni di Banco cre-

※ **Orsanmichele**

◄ Figures in niches

ated St Philip (1410–1412), a robed figure for the tanners' guild that still appears flat despite its contraposto, and four crowned saints (1414–1417) for the guild of stonemasons and carpenters, representing a group of four early Christian sculptors who were martyred under Diocletian (with a relief around the pedestal). Donatello carved St George (around 1416) as a holy knight for the niche of the armour makers (the original is in the Bargello; this is a bronze copy). Even though the figure stands in a niche, the path of development to free-standing sculpture is already apparent. The bronze figure of the evangelist Matthew (1424) by Lorenzo Ghiberti for the money-changers' guild shows more confidence in the physical form than that of St John. Instead of facing forward as in the traditional representation, it now faces slightly to one side. Two more niches show St Stephen (1427–1428) by Ghiberti for the traders in woollen cloth and the tall, slender St Eligius (around 1420) by Nanni di Banco for the blacksmiths' guild. The next evangelist, Mark (1411–1415), was made by Donatello for the guild of linen drapers. In the next niches are St James (after 1422) by Niccolò di Pietro Lamberti for the furriers and fur traders, the Madonna della Rosa (1399), attributed to Giovanni di Piero Tedesco, for the doctors and pharmacists, and the evangelist John (1515) by Baccio da Montelupo for the guild of silk weavers and goldsmiths. Inside Orsanmichele, a two-aisled Gothic hall, there is a marble tabernacle (1359) by Andrea Orcagna with scenes from the life of the Virgin and a panel painting of the Virgin (1347) by Bernardo Daddi to replace a miraculous votive image that was destroyed by fire.

Interior ▶

✶ ✶ Piazza della Signoria

Piazza della Signoria has been the political centre of the city since the 14th century, when houses of Ghibelline families had to make way for the square. Today visitors from all over the world populate the inviting cafés around the broad square. The showpiece of the piazza is the **fountain of Neptune**, which the Florentines mockingly call »biancone« (big white one). It was intended for the wedding of Francesco de Medici, the son of Cosimo I, and Princess Johanna of Austria in 1565, but was only completed in 1578 by Bartolomeo Ammanati. A granite plaque in the ground not far from the fountain of Neptune commemorates the execution and burning of Savonarola and his fellow monks Buonvicini and Maruffi in 1498. The equestrian figure (1594) by Giambologna depicts Grand Duke Cosimo I de Medici.

✶ ✶ Palazzo Vecchio

On the south-west corner of Piazza della Signoria, the Palazzo Vecchio still radiates the self-confidence of the city state of Florence. From the beginning of the 14th century and as long as the city was

©Baedeker

copy of Michelangelo's famous »David« stands in front of the Palazzo Vecchio. The original is in the Accademia (see p.249).

On the first floor is the »Hall of the Five Hundred« (Sala dei Cinquecento), which was intended to be used for the council meetings which Savonarola instituted. Its present appearance goes back to a major reconstruction by Vasari and his school in the second half of the 16th century. The coffered ceiling with allegorical paintings on the history of Florence and the Medici, and the famous marble statue »Victory« by Michelangelo are especially noteworthy.

The Uffizi meet Piaz
della Signoria in
elongated U shap
The famous museu
was built as a
administrati
building for t
ministries of t
grand duch

Equestrian monument of Grand Duke Cosimo I de Medici by Giambologna

1453 in the early Renaissance style. On the upper parts of the wall are 18 large city panoramas from the Habsburg empire, which were painted for the wedding of Francesco de Medici and Johanna of Austria (1565).

Palace rooms

Palazzo Vecchio is truly a treasure chamber. Among its many rooms the **Chamber of the Five Hundred** (Sala dei Cinquecento), a work of Cronaca (1495), stands out. The ceiling has 39 richly decorated fields with allegorical depictions of the history of Florence and the Medici, while the long side walls are decorated with giant battle scenes by Vasari. The famous marble statue of *Victory* (1532–1534) by Michelangelo is on the southern end wall. The

✳ Grand Duke Francesco's study ►

small but sumptuous study of Grand Duke Francesco I (Studiolo di Francesco I) was designed by Giorgio Vasari 1570–1575 and decorated by important painters and sculptors of his time. It is a gem of Florentine Mannerism. The **Room of the Lilies** (Sala dei Gigli) on the third floor with frescoes by Ghirlandaio and his studio (1482–1484) holds the expressive bronze group *Judith and Holofernes* (around 1460) by Donatello. The private rooms of Eleonora of Toledo (Quartiere di Eleonora di Toledo), wife of Cosimo I, who died in 1562, are decorated with ceiling frescoes in the Mannerist style. The **private chapel of Eleonora** is notable for the paintings of the story of Moses (between 1540 and 1545) by Agnolo Bronzino.

✳ ✳ Loggia dei Lanzi

Next to the Palazzo Vecchio is the Loggia della Signoria. This open Gothic columned structure was named Loggia dei Lanzi after the mercenary foot soldiers who served there from the 16th century as guards of the Medici rulers. Before that the loggia, which was built between 1374 and 1381, was used for official ceremonies of the republic: ambassadors and princes were received here, the priori and gonfalonieri were installed in office here. Above the arches outside are small seated figures in niches, allegories of the virtues (1383–1391). On a tour of the hall clockwise, the first work is the bronze statue of *Perseus with the Head of Medusa* (1545–1554), a masterpiece by Benvenuto Cellini commissioned by Duke Cosimo I. In a gesture of triumph the ancient hero holds up the severed head of the Medusa, a monster that Perseus killed with the help of the gods. Under the arcade on the far right Giambologna's *Rape of the Sabine Women* (1579–1582) is another example of Mannerism.

✳ ✳ Galleria degli Uffizi

Entrance Loggiato degli Uffizi 6

A few steps further between Palazzo Vecchio and Loggia dei Lanzi lies one of the richest museum collections in the world, the Uffizi Gallery, built originally between 1560 and 1580 for the administrative offices (uffizi) of the duchy. A corridor connected it with Pal-

ruled as a republic by a nine-man college, the Signoria, it was the **seat of communal government**. The Signoria consisted of eight priori (principals) and the gonfaloniere della giustizia (banner bearer of justice). They were chosen by the citizens, who were organized into guilds, in a complicated process of election, drawing lots and rotation. In 1540 Cosimo I de Medici took over the palace. When the Medici moved into the newly built Palazzo Pitti, Palazzo Vecchio became less important and was called from then on the »old palace«. It became city hall and seat of the communal government again only in 1872.

Opening hours:
Mon–Wed, Fri–Sat
9am–7pm
Thu 9am–2pm
Sun 8am–1pm

The exterior of Palazzo Vecchio with its slender towers is much like a medieval fortress. Decades of running battles between the city's leading families ended in the late 13th century. The building of the communal palace between 1299 and 1314 was the expression of the newly won communal independence and the government's need for security. Numerous statues were erected in front of the palace, **symbols of the commune's desire for liberty**, including the lion bearing the city coat of arms (copy after Donatello, around 1420), the bronze group *Judith and Holofernes* (copy after Donatello, around 1460), *David* (copy after Michelangelo, around 1504) and the *Hercules and Cacus* marble group (1533) by Bandinelli. The medieval inner courtyard where a fountain with figures of a putto and dolphin (copy after Verrocchio, around 1475) splashes, was remodelled by Michelozzo in

Building history and façade

Massive piers support the Ponte Vecchio, the oldest bridge in Florence, which crosses the Arno at its narrowest point.

PIAZZA DELLA SIGNORIA

✶ ✶ The impressive square where public assemblies used to take place is dominated by the massive tower of the Palazzo Vecchio. The best place to enjoy the life of the piazza is one of the street cafés facing the palazzo.

① Palazzo Vecchio
The Palazzo dei Priori was built between 1299 and 1314; it was renamed Palazzo Vecchio when the Medici residence was named Palazzo Pitti.

② Tower
Seat of the city administration to this day

③ Loggia dei Lanzi
The open three-bay arcade houses such famous sculptures as *Perseus with the Head of Medusa* by Benvenuto Cellini. Under the right-hand arcade stands the marble group *Rape of the Sabine Women* by Giambologna.

④ Fountain of Neptune
This fountain is also called »Il Biancone« (the big white one) because of the giant marble figure of the sea god Neptune.

Not far from the fountain a bronze plaque in the ground commemorates the burning of the Dominican monk Savonarola in 1498 on the Piazza della Signoria.

Galleria degli Uffizi Plan

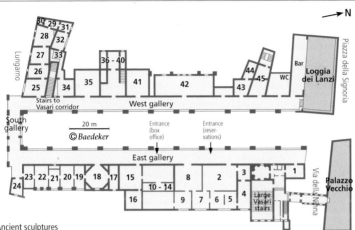

Ancient sculptures
Tuscan painters of the
13th century, including
Cimabue, Giotto
Sienese painters of the
14th century
Florentine painters
of the 14th century
Gothic painting
Tuscan painters
(Early Renaissance)
Filippo Lippi
Botticelli, Pollaiolo
Botticelli, van der Goes
Periguni, da Vinci a. o.

16 Maps
17 Hermaphrodite
   room
18 Tribune: Greek
   sculptures
   Paintings by Vasari,
   Bronzino, Pontormo
19 Perugino, Signorelli
20 Dürer, Cranach
21 Bellini, Giorgione,
   Carpaccio a. o.
22 Holbein, David,
   Altdorfer, Memling

22 Correggio, Mantegna
23 Miniatures of the
   15th – 18th century
24 Michelangelo
25 Fra Bartolomeo
26 Sarto, Raffael
27 Pontormo, Rosso
   Fiorentino
28 Tizian
29 Parmigianino, Dossi
30 Artists of the 16th
   century from the Emilia
31 Veronese

32 Tintoretto, Bassano,
33 Vasari, Bronzino
34 Lotto, Moroni
35 Barocci and the Tuscan
   Counterreformation
36-40 Archaeological rooms
41 Rubens, van Dyck
42 Niobe room
43 Caravaggio
44 Dutch painting
   of the 17th century
45 Works of the
   18th century

azzo Vecchio and Palazzo Pitti. The world-famous collection of the Uffizi with masterpieces of European painting and ancient sculptures developed from a private gallery of the Medici, which was left to the city of Florence by the last Medici heiress. Room 1 holds **archaeological exhibits** from ancient Rome. The tour begins on the first floor in room 2 with Tuscan painting of the period around 1300. From here the paintings are arranged chronologically up to room 16 and then according to schools, regions and countries until 1700.

🕐
Opening hours:
Tue–Sun
8.30am–6.50pm
www.musei.uffizi.
firenze.it

In room 2 three large-scale Madonna panels stand out: *Santa Trinita Madonna* (around 1275) by Cimabue, a *Maestà* (1285) by Duccio and a *Maestà* (around 1310) by Giotto. They show the transition from Byzantine painting depicting the Virgin as an incorporeal queen of heaven to a portrait of a woman based on observation. In

**Rooms 2 to 9
Tuscan art:
13th century to
early Renais-
sance**

room 3 is Simone Martini's *Annunciation* (around 1333), a painting of great delicacy and elegance; in rooms 5–6 the international Gothic style is represented by works including the extravagantly composed *Adoration of the Magi* (1423) by Gentile da Fabriano. The early Renaissance works in room 7 are important for the first use of central perspective including *Madonna and Child with Saint Anne* (around 1420) by Masaccio, *The Battle of San Romano* (around 1456) by Paolo Uccello, the *Enthroned Madonna with Saints* (around 1445) by Domenico Veneziano, which is flooded with natural sunlight, and the **Portrait of the Duke and Duchess of Urbino** (around 1465), in stark profiles in the style of ancient medallions, by Piero della Francesca. In room 8 Filippo Lippi's maidenlike *Madonna and Child with Two Angels* (around 1465) radiates cheer and grace. The small figures by the brothers Antonio and Piero Pollaiuolo in room 9 are expressions of intensive anatomical studies.

! **Baedeker** TIP

Book ahead instead of waiting
Nothing is more frustrating than using valuable holiday time waiting in long lines – for instance at the ticket office of the Uffizi. In order to avoid this, order tickets in advance at tel. 055 29 48 83 (but at least 2 days ahead).

Rooms 10 to 14
Botticelli

At the age of about thirty (around 1475), Sandro Botticelli painted the altarpiece *Adoration of the Magi*, in which he inserted numerous portraits of contemporaries. The **Birth of Venus** and **Primavera** followed, works commissioned by Lorenzo di Pierfrancesco de Medici, a cousin of Lorenzo il Magnifico. The *Birth of Venus* probably dates from around 1482–1483. In it Botticelli combined ancient and Christian ideas. Thus he painted a female nude modelled on an ancient statue of Venus, the goddess of love, and indirectly referred to the model of a Christian baptismal painting. The same room contains the famous **Portinari Altar**, a commissioned work which was painted a short time before the *Birth of Venus* for Tommaso Portinari, the head of the Medici bank in Bruges, by Hugo van der Goes. The naturalism and realism of the altar are impressive, but all in all painting north of the Alps remained strongly influenced by mysticism and religion.

Rooms 15, 16
Verrocchio,
Leonardo

Leonardo da Vinci was a pupil of Andrea del Verrocchio, with whom he painted the **Baptism of Christ in the Jordan** (around 1470–1472). His *Annunciation* (around 1470–1475) in an extremely wide format stands out for its atmospheric treatment of landscape and the emotion expressed in the figures. In the *Adoration of the Magi* (begun 1481) Leonardo subtly captured the developing mood of crisis of his time. His Madonna and Child are surrounded by people who react to the birth of the Son of God with a mixture of amazement and horror. While the story of Christmas was depicted as a fairy tale or folk tale until then, Leonardo's version has a new dimension of salvation for the world.

Stand and stare – enjoying art at the Uffizi

German Renaissance painting in room 20 is represented by master-pieces by Lucas Cranach: portraits of Martin Luther and his wife Katharina von Bora, a self-portrait, an impressive portrait of Melanchthon and *Adam and Eve* in slightly erotic poses. Albrecht Dürer's works include *Madonna and Child* (1526), *The Artist's Father* (1490) and *Adoration of the Magi* (1504), painted shortly before his second trip to Italy.

Room 20 German Renaissance painting

Venetian Renaissance painting, which is characterized by soft colour tones and balanced light as well as harmonious landscape and quiet portrayals of figures, is represented by the *Christian Allegory* (around 1485) by **Giovanni Bellini** and two scenes (*Judgement of Solomon*, *Moses Undergoes Trial by Fire*) and a portrait of a Maltese knight by Giorgione.

Room 21 Venetian Renaissance painting

Michelangelo's *Holy Family* (1503–1504) in round format is without any religious pathos. The picture, which was painted for the wedding of Agnolo Doni with Maddalena Strozzi, shows Michelangelo's unmistakeably strong interest in sculpture, as the family appears to be carved out of a block of stone. Three important works by Raphael can be admired in room 26: a self-portrait (around 1506) which shows him at the age of twenty-three, his charming *Madonna of the Goldfinch*, an effective triangular composition, and finally the portrait *Pope Leo X with two Cardinals*.

Rooms 25 and 26 Michelangelo, Raphael

Room 27
Rosso Fiorentino

Rosso Fiorentino was one of the early Mannerists. His preference for composing bodies with plane surfaces and cool colours can be seen in the painting *Moses Defends Jethro's Daughters* (1523), which refers to the Old Testament story in which Moses drove the shepherds away from the well and allowed the herds of the seven daughters of Jethro to drink.

Room 28
Titian

Titian's paintings *Venus of Urbino* (1538), the adjacent *Ludovico Beccadelli* (1552), *Venus and Cupid* (1560), *Eleonora Gonzaga della Rovere*, *Francesco Maria, Duke of Urbino* and *La Flora*, one of his most beautiful portraits of a woman, are shown here. The *Venus of Urbino*, painted for the Duke of Urbino, stands out especially because of its colour composition. The red tones tie together the separate parts of the picture in their spatial perspective and diagonal positions.

DON'T MISS

- Room 2: Madonna panels by Cimabue, Giotto and Duccio.
- Room 7: portraits of the Duke and Duchess of Urbino by Piero della Francesca
- Room 10: *Birth of Venus* by Botticelli
- Room 15: *Annunciation* by Leonardo da Vinci
- Room 25: *Holy Family* by Michelangelo
- Room 26: *Madonna of the Goldfinch* by Raphael

In room 31 Paolo Veronese's *Holy Family with St Barbara and the Infant St John* and *Annunciation* can be seen. In room 32 *Leda and the Swan*, *Venetian Admiral* and portraits by Tintoretto as well as *The Concert* and *Two Dogs* by Jacopo Bassano are worthy of note. Corridor 33 has small works by such Mannerist painters as Alessandro Allori and Giorgio Vasari. The highlights of room 34 are portraits by Giovanni Battista Moroni and the *Holy Family with St Jerome and St Anne* (1534) by Lorenzo Lotto.

Rooms 41 to 44

Dutch art of the »golden« 17th century is also represented in the Uffizi, including works by Peter Paul Rubens: portraits of Emperor Charles V and the artist's first wife Isabella Brant. In a room decorated in the classical style in 1779–1780 (no. 42) the Niobe Group, a Roman copy of Greek originals which is the most valuable ancient sculpture in Florence apart from the Medici Venus, has found a worthy place.

Room 45

In the last room the exhibition returns to Italian painting. In the 18th century the Venetians took the lead again – especially with the famous **city views by Canaletto** and Guardi, some of which are exhibited here.

Museo di Storia della Scienza

Behind the Uffizi Gallery on Piazza dei Guidici, just before the river Arno, the museum of the history of science in Palazzo Castellani is well worth seeing. Certainly less overcrowded than the Uffizi, but with a very interesting collection of scientific precision instruments from the time of the Medici and Habsburg-Lorraine rulers. A fascinating room holds **Galileo Galilei's original instruments**, including the telescope with which he discovered the moons of Jupiter (hours: daily except Sun 9.30am–5pm, Tue only until 1pm).

After so much art, a stroll to the jewellery shops on the picturesque Ponte Vecchio is a welcome change. The »old bridge«, which crosses the river at its narrowest point, may even go back to the **Etruscan period**. It is certain that the Roman consular road Via Cassia crossed the Arno here on a wooden bridge. After repairing it in the 13th century the city government allowed shops and apartments to be built here. Since the increasing noise and bad odours bothered the grand duke on his way to Palazzo Pitti, a law was passed in 1593 that allowed only the **goldsmiths** to open shops on the bridge. Since 1900 a bust of the most famous Florentine goldsmith, Benvenuto Cellini, has adorned the middle of the bridge.

★ ★
Ponte Vecchio
◀ (photo p. 223)

Palazzo Pitti and the South Bank of the Arno

From Ponte Vecchio walk south to the broad Piazza dei Pitti, which is like a palace forecourt before the monumental Pitti Palace. The Pitti were a **respected Florentine merchant family** who competed with the Medici in pride and ambition. For this reason Luca Pitti planned a large city palace on the left bank of the Arno a short distance outside the city. The architect Luca Fancelli was in charge of the first construction work (1457–1466), possibly following a design by Brunelleschi. Eleonora of Toledo, Cosimo I's wife, acquired the palazzo in 1549 and had it completely renovated and enlarged between 1558 und 1570. The new owners, especially Grand Duke Cosimo III, bought valuable pictures to decorate the rooms – the basis of the famous Galleria Palatina. Ancient and contemporary statues were added. Today several museums are housed in the palace.

★ ★
Palazzo Pitti

From the inner courtyard take the stairs on the right to the Galleria Palatina, the art gallery on the second floor. The pictures are not organized chronologically but on decorative criteria in order to display the state rooms and their valuable furnishings according to the tastes of the Medici rulers. From the stairs the tour passes through the vestibule, the Sala degli Staffieri, the Galleria delle Statue and the Galleria delle Nicchie to the Sala di Venere, where the first paintings are to be seen.
The *Italic Venus* (1810) by Antonio Canova stands in the middle of the room. It was commissioned by Napoleon. Four paintings show the development of the Venetian painter Titian: *The Concert*, *Portrait of a Lady*, portraits of Pope Julius II and Pietro Aretino. *Venus, Amor and Vulcan* comes from Tintoretto's early period. The important works in the adjacent Venus room include the *Return of the Hunters* (by Susterman), *The Return of the Farmers from Work* and *Odysseus*

Galleria Palatina (Galleria Pitti)

🕐
Opening hours:
Tue–Sun
8.15am–7.50pm

◀ Sala di Venere

Palazzo Pitti Plan

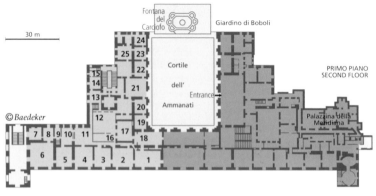

Fontana del Carciofo

Giardino di Boboli

30 m

Cortile dell' Ammannati

Entrance

PRIMO PIANO
SECOND FLOOR

© Baedeker

Palazzina della Meridiana

☐ Galleria Palatina   ☐ Apartamenti Monumentali

1 Sala di Venere
  Tizian, Tintoretto
2 Sala di Apollo
  Van Dyck, Rubens,
  Reni, del Sarto,
  Tizian, Tintoretto
3 Sala di Marte
  Tintoretto, Reni,
  Tizian, Rubens,
  Murillo, Veronese
4 Sala di Giove
  Raffael, Bordone,
  Rubens, del Sarto,
  Perugino, Guercino
5 Sala di Saturno
  Raffael, Perugino,
  Ghirlandaio

6 Sala dell'Iliade
  Velázquez, Raffael
7 Sala della Stufa
  Frescos by Roselli,
  P.da Cortona
8 Sala dell'Educa-
  zione di Giove
  Caravaggio, Allori
9 Bagno di Napoleone
10 Sala di Ulisse
  Raffael, Reni, Lippi
11 Sala di Prometeo
  Signorelli, Lippi,
  Botticelli, Reni
12 Corridoio d. Colonne
13 Sala della Giustizia
  Veronese, Tizian

14 Sala di Flora
  Canova, Bronzino
15 Sala dei Putti
  Jordaens, Rubens
16 Galleria Poccetti
  Pontormo, Rubens,
  Ribera, Dughet
17 Sala della Musica
18 Sala Castagnoli
19 Sala delle Allegorie
20 Sala delle Belle Arti
21 Salone d'Ercole
22 Sala dell'Aurora
23 Sala di Berenice
24 Sala di Psiche
25 Sala della Fama

with the *Phaeacians* (by Rubens) as well as the *Seascape at Sunset* by Salvatore Rosa.

Sala di Apollo ► Of the works of the 16th and 17th centuries in the Apollo room, the following deserve special mention: *Mary Magdalene* (around 1531) and *Portrait of Ippolito Riminaldi* (around 1540–1545), both by Titian. The double portrait of King Charles I of England and his wife Henrietta of France (after 1623) is by van Dyck. Around 1520 Rosso Fiorentino painted the monumental *Sacra Conversazione*, also called *Pala Dei*, for the chapel of the Dei family in Santo Spirito.

Sala di Marte ► The ceiling paintings in the Mars room are by Pietro da Cortona and show war in allegorical scenes. Rubens' large-scale work ***The Consequences of War*** corresponds to the theme of the ceiling painting. It shows how Venus tries in vain to keep Mars from going to war. Rubens created the work in 1638 under the impression of the Thirty Years' War.

The Jupiter room is also decorated with ceiling paintings by Pietro da Cortona. They make reference to the fact that this was the throne room of the grand dukes. The most important works of art here include *The Three Ages of Mankind* (around 1510–1520), which is attributed to **Giorgione**, *Madonna with the Little Swallow* by Guercino, *John the Baptist* (around 1520) by Andrea del Sarto and *The Entombment of Christ* (around 1511–1512) by Fra Bartolomeo. *La Velata* (around 1516), also called *La Fornarina*, is one of Raphael's most beautiful portraits of a woman.

◄ Sala di Giove

Pictures by Raphael and his contemporaries Perugino, Fra Bartolomeo and Andrea del Sarto hang in the Saturn room.

◄ Sala di Saturno

The Iliad room was redecorated between 1819 and 1825. Luigi Sabatelli did the ceiling painting on the subject of *Olympus* and the lunettes with scenes from Homer's Iliad. Two large-scale pictures by Andrea del Sarto from 1526 and 1530, both of which glorify the assumption of the Virgin into heaven, hang opposite each other. *Philip IV of Spain* by Velázquez, Raphael's *Pregnant Woman* and the *Portrait of Count Waldemar Christian* by Sustermans are further works to detain art lovers in this room.

Sala dell'Iliade

The small »stove room« was first decorated in 1627 by the Florentine artist Matteo Rosselli. The paintings for this room are by Pietro Cortona (1637 and 1640–1641). The subjects are the four eras: gold, silver, copper and bronze.

◄ Sala della Stufa

The ceiling of the Ulysses room is decorated with the return of the heroes of Troy, a reference to the return of Ferdinand III of Lorraine to Florence (1815). The showpiece, however, is Raphael's *Madonna dell'Impannata* (around 1512).

◄ Sala di Ulisse

Almost all of the tondi (round pictures) that belong to the Galleria Palatina can be admired in the Prometheus room. Like the other paintings in this room they are works of the 15th and 16th century. Works by Filippo Lippi, Sandro Botticelli as well as Pontormo's *Martyrdom of the Ten Thousand* (1529–1530) are exhibited. The adjacent columned corridor is mainly dedicated to Flemish and Dutch landscape painters of the 17th century.

◄ Sala di Prometeo

The hall of justice displays Venetian painting of the 16th century, including Titian's *Portrait of Tommaso Mosti*, Tintoretto's *Venus, Vulcan and Cupid* as well as Veronese's *Baptism of Christ* (1576).

◄ Sala della Giustizia

The room is named after the artist Giuseppe Castagnoli, who did the ceiling painting after 1815. Two colossal marble statues from the Villa Medici in Rome adorn the walls. The table of the muses in the centre of the room was made in the Florentine workshop for stone intarsia work.

Sala Castagnoli

The series of rooms that begins with the Sala delle Allegorie was the winter apartment of the grand duchess in the Medici period. Only the decorations from the first room come from the time of Medici rule; the other rooms were renovated after 1815.

◄ Quartiere del Volterrano

Appartamenti ex Reali ▶
The former rooms of the kings of Italy, where Vittorio Emanuele II, Umberto I, Queen Margherita and Vittorio Emanuele III lived, are furnished with valuable furniture, paintings, statues and tapestries.

Galleria d'Arte Moderna
The gallery of modern art on the third floor of Palazzo Pitti gives a good overview of Tuscan painting in the 19th and 20th centuries, as well as other Italian schools, including interesting works of the »Macchiaioli«. Representatives of this Tuscan school (including Giovanni Faltori, Silvestro Lega, Telemaco Signorini) got their name from their anti-academic handling of the brush. The exhibition concludes with a collection of works by classic modern Italian masters such as Severini, De Chirico and Morandi that is equally worth seeing (hours: daily 8.15am–1.50pm, closed first and third Monday as well as second and fourth Sunday of the month).

Museo degli Argenti
On the ground floor and mezzanine of Palazzo Pitti (entrance from the inner courtyard of the palace left) the silver collection is housed in the rooms where the Medici lived during the summer months. Silver and gold jewellery, gemstones, ivory work and porcelain are displayed here.

Extravagant setting for a valuable art collection: Palazzo Pitti and Galleria Palatina

The coach museum is also housed on the ground floor of Palazzo Pitti. State coaches, chaises and wagons of all kinds which were used by the rulers in the 18th and 19th centuries, including the coaches of the Duke of Modena, Francesco II and King Ferdinand of Naples can be seen.

Museo delle Carrozze

The costume gallery in the adjacent Palazzina della Meridiana shows men's and women's clothing from 1700 until 1920 (hours as the Galleria d'Arte Moderna).

Galleria del Costume

On the slope behind Palazzo Pitti the Boboli Garden, a **wonderful park** for taking long walks, covers an area of 45,000 sq m/49,000 sq yd. After Duke Cosimo I bought Palazzo Pitti in 1549, the adjacent land, which had in part belonged to the Boboli or Bobolini family – hence the name – was also bought. Niccolò Pericoli began to redesign the park between 1550 and 1560. Bernardo Buontalenti continued the work, and Alfonso Parigi the Younger completed it by 1658.

★ Giardino di Boboli

The park's attractions include, at the entrance to the left of Palazzo Pitti, the Fontana del Bacco (after 1560), a fountain with the figure of Cosimo I's court dwarf riding on a turtle; and the Grotta del Buontalenti (1583–1588) with figures of shepherds and sheep carved from stalactites and plaster reliefs of Michelangelo's *Prisoners*. There is also an **amphitheatre for court festivals** with Egyptian obelisks and Roman granite basins, as well as a fountain of Neptune (1565), a colossal statue representing Abbondanza (1636–1637), the terrace garden Giardino del Cavaliere with a monkey fountain and, in the 18th-century Palazzina del Cavaliere, the porcelain museum with Italian, French and German ware (Jan, Feb, Nov, Dec and Mar daily 8.15am–5.30pm, April, May, Sept and Oct 8.15am–6.30pm, June, July and Aug 8.15am–7.30pm; closed first and last Mon of the month).

> ! **Baedeker TIP**
>
> **Coffee break**
> For a real espresso, a creamy cappuccino or a glass of good wine, take a walk to the 200-year-old coffee house in a rococo pavilion shaped like a water tower in the Boboli Gardens. Along with the coffee there is a magnificent view of Florence at no extra charge!

For a visit to something a little more unusual after seeing so many artistic treasures, the neighbouring Museo Zoologico is just right. The quality and beauty of the 18th-century anatomical wax figures are unique. They are exact copies from nature – a bit creepy and not suitable for people with a weak stomach! (Via Romana 17, to the right next to Palazzo Pitti; hours: daily 9am–1pm except Wed and Sun).

Museo Zoologico »La Specola«

North-west of Palazzo Pitti on Piazza Santo Spirito is an **important Renaissance church by Brunelleschi**. Although the building is out-

★ ★ Santo Spirito

🕐
Opening hours:
Mon–Fri
10am–noon
4–5.30pm
Sat and Sun
4–5.30pm
Closed
Wed afternoon

wardly unassuming, the interior is a masterpiece of Renaissance architecture. The church of the Holy Spirit is a converted and renovated Augustinian church. The work was begun by Brunelleschi in 1434 but only completed 35 years after the master's death in 1481, after several alterations in the plans. The austere composition and symmetry of the interior come as a surprise. The church is a basilica, in which columns separate the nave from the aisles and the dimensions of the square crossing serve as a basic unit of measurement for the rest of the plan. The determining elements of the building imitate Roman antiquity: the columns with their bases and Corinthian capitals, and the entablature resting on them. The rose window in the façade was designed by Perugino. The left aisle leads to a beautiful vestibule built by Cronaca (1494) and from there into the sacristy, an octagonal Renaissance structure on a central plan by Giuliano da Sangallo (1495–1496). The tabernacle altar (1709) by Caccini with stone inlays stands in the crossing. The impressive altarpiece *Madonna with Child, Saints and Donors* (1490) by Filippino Lippi is in the right transept.

Santa Maria del Carmine

Follow Via Sant'Agostino and Via Santa Monaca to Piazza del Carmine in a busy and traditional quarter of the city. The Carmelite church on the piazza was begun in 1268, but not finished until 1476. It was redesigned in the 16th and 17th centuries, but a fire in 1771 caused so much damage that the church had to be completely reconstructed in the years to 1782. Inside, the **Baroque-style Cappella Corsini** by Pierfrancesco Silvani at the head of the left transept is impressive; its dome fresco was painted by Luca Giordano in 1682. The graves of Neri and Piero Corsini with three marble reliefs are in the chapel.

✱
Cappella Brancacci

Access to the Cappella Brancacci is to the right of the church via a cloister added in the early 17th century that Felice Brancacci, a rich Florentine merchant, had decorated with frescoes by **Masaccio and Masolino** between 1424 and 1428. The painters used linear perspective for the first time and created one of the earliest nude paintings, of Adam and Eve.

The unfinished frescoes on the lower part of the long wall were completed in 1483–1485 by Filippino Lippi. After the latest restorations the enormous depth of the figures and landscapes and the subtle colouring can again be seen clearly. Hours: Mon, Wed–Sat 10am–5pm, Sun 1–5pm.

Ponte Santa Trinità

Return to the banks of the Arno and stroll along Lungarno Giucciardini to Palazzo Frescobaldi, a medieval family residence that was altered in the 17th century. The Ponte Santa Trinitá (1567–1570), which was destroyed in in the Second World War but rebuilt to plans by Ammanati, is the connection to the city quarters on the north bank of the Arno.

Western Old City

Walk a few steps to Piazza Santa Trinità, where since 1995 the Gothic Palazzo Spini-Feroni has housed a shoe museum with about 10,000 designs by **Salvatore Ferragamo**. Greta Garbo, Audrey Hepburn and Marilyn Monroe all wore shoes by the Italian designer. He opened his first shoe store in Hollywood at the age of 18 (hours: Mon–Fri 9am–1pm, 2–6pm).

Palazzo Spini-Feroni

✷

◄ Shoe museum

The Gothic church of the Holy Trinity was built in the 14th century, its early Baroque façade in the late 16th century. The Sassetti chapel inside (second to the right of the altar) has a jewel of Renaissance art, a painting by Domenico Ghirlandaio. From 1479 until 1485 he produced the altarpiece of the *Adoration of the Christ Child* and wall frescoes with scenes of the *Legend of St Francis*. A fresco cycle in the fourth chapel to the right on the long side (1420–1425) with scenes from the *Life of the Virgin* by Lorenzo Monaco is also worth seeing.

✷

Santa Trinità

Along Via del Tornabuoni with its luxury shops walk north to Palazzo Strozzi (see below). Just after Palazzo Bartolini turn into Via Porta Rossa. From here it is a short distance to Palazzo Davanzati.

✷

Via Tornabuoni

The simple façade of Palazzo Davanzati is divided at the bottom by three massive portals, closed off at the top by a loggia and decorated in the middle by a magnificent Davanzati coat of arms. The Davizzi first built a city house here around 1300 – a family offspring was gonfaloniere of the republic in 1294. At the beginning of the 16th century the palace passed to the Bartolinis, in 1578 to the Davanzatis. In 1906 the art dealer Elia Volpi bought the building and restored it in its original style. Since 1956 the palace has been a museum showing **a middle-class Florentine residence**. On three storeys furniture, drawings, sculptures, carpets, ceramics, fabric and household utensils from the Middle Ages, Renaissance and Baroque are displayed. A remarkable feature is the »parrot's hall« on the second floor, which gets its name from wall paintings that simulated tapestries adorned with the figures of parrots. The ceiling is made of painted wood (closed for renovation).

✷

Palazzo Davanzati, Museo dell'Antica (Casa Fiorentina)

For the many cafés alone it is worth stopping on Piazza della Repubblica, which was once the site of **Roman forum**. Literature fans should drink their cappuccino in the former artists' and literary café Giubbe Rosse (»Red Vests«), which the Futurists and writers of the 1920s frequented. Today it still has a larger selection of daily newspapers than any other café in the city. Until 1888, when the stalls had to make way for a monumental triumphal arch (1895) and a row of administrative buildings, a market was held on the Mercato Vecchio, which is dominated by Donatello's statue of *Abbondanza* (today a copy).

✷

Piazza della Repubblica

The Medici coat of arms: below the ducal crown is the most remarkable part of the coat of arms – the field with the six spheres.

CULTURE AND COMMERCE

The name Medici stands for Renaissance art and patronage, but also for immeasurable wealth and high finance. Unlike other upper-class Florentine families, the Medici did not gain wealth and influence long before the year 1400. They rose to eminence within one century: the quattrocento, the golden age of Florence.

Giovanni di Bicci de Medici (died 1429) laid the foundation for the family fortune by making generous loans to the pope in Rome during the church schism of 1378. When Rome was rebuilt and beautified as the residence of the popes after the end of the schism, the Medici already had the position of papal bankers and the young Cosimo, later called the Elder, continued to do profitable business. The Roman branch of the banking house accounted for 50–60% of all Medici banking profits. The Medici needed little equity for this, because the Curia deposited so much money with them that they could make profits of up to 20% by making loans. They had branches in many cities: in Venice mainly for oriental trade, in Bruges for trade in northern Europe, in Geneva for trade in central Europe, in London for the English court and the wool trade, as well as in Milan and Naples as important seats of nobles and bishops. They also had the monopoly on alum, traded in wool and silk and sold other luxury goods.

Banking business

The account books of 1397 to 1420 show an increase in net profits of 5,000 gold florins annually – multiply by 130 to estimate the value of gold florins in US dollars today. When **Cosimo the Elder** took over the business he accrued over 8,000 gold florins annually up to the year 1434, later no less than 13,000 gold florins annually. Cosimo was generous in giving but cautious in lending. He paid attention to his clients' credit-worthiness and generally did business with the Curia or noble houses, thus

Lorenzo the Magnificent

increasing the political influence of the Medici as well. He chose only excellent bankers to be branch directors, and reinvested most of the profits. By contrast his grandson **Lorenzo il Magnifico** had little interest in business and enjoyed living beyond his means, so that the family business was almost bankrupt when he died in 1492. However, the international connections of the Medici made them so dominant that, despite a short exile after 1513, they could continue to rule the city with the pope's support and were elevated to the status of dukes.

Patronage

Wealthy Florentine citizens gave considerable amounts of money as donations. Thus Giovanni Tornabuoni, director of the Medici bank in Rome, »as an act of respect and love for God as well as to praise his house and his family«, had Domenico Ghirlandaio decorate the main choir chapel of Santa Maria Novella with beautiful frescoes. Other motives for patronage can be found in the memoirs of Giovanni Rucellai (1403–1481), a merchant engaged in long-distance trade who financed the church façade: »I believe that I have earned more honour by spending money than by making money.«

The extent of this type of public-relations work can be seen in the records of Lorenzo the Magnificent, who after examining the Medici accounts of 1434 to 1471 figured that his family had spent 664,000 gold florins on alms, donations and taxes. Of this, 8,000 gold florins went to decorate the Franciscan church of Santa Croce, 40,000 gold florins to building the monastery of San Marco, 60,000 gold florins to building the parish church of San Lorenzo by Filippo Brunelleschi and 60,000 gold florins to building the Palazzo Medici. This meant an annual expense of about 18,000 gold florins, which were not covered by the annual profit of about 13,000 gold florins, though possibly by land ownership.

The Medici funerary chapel by Michelangelo in San Lorenzo

But why these enormous expenditures? On the one hand it eased the conscience, since credit banking was considered to be immoral and was banned by the church. But pious donations meant that the church benefited from the business and indirectly gave its blessing by accepting the donations. The choice of objects and artists that the patricians supported showed at the same time their education, virtuous intentions and cultured use of the wealth they had accumulated.Last but not least, generosity served political purposes, for the numerous large private commissions created jobs, were visible proof of the families' economic potential and brought them votes for communal offices. Furthermore the donors realized that the works of art they donated would probably outlive them and increase the family's fame.

The subtlety with which piety on the one hand and wealth and political power on the other hand could be depicted in works of art can be seen in the Sassetti chapel in the church of Santa Trinitá. Francesco Sassetti had achieved wealth as the director of and later partner in the Medici bank in Lyon and from 1469 was adviser to the young Lorenzo de Medici. He had his social rise and close contacts with the Medici family depicted in the side choir chapel of Santa Trinità. The *Confirmation of the Franciscan Order by Pope Honorius III in 1223* has been transplanted to contemporary Florence. In the foreground the Sassetti and Medici families appear as observers. Close to the papal throne the bald Francesco Sassetti stands on the right with his son Frederigo, who was already a cleric as a boy. Next to him are the dark-haired Lorenzo de Medici and the grey-haired Antonio Pucci, a Sassetti relative and Medici partisan. On the left opposite are Sassetti's three sons Teodoro I, Cosimo and Galeazzo. The children of Lorenzo the Magnificent are shown climbing stairs led by their tutor Angelo Poliziano: first little Giuliano, then Piero (Lorenzo's successor), and finally Giovanni (the later Pope Leo X), followed by the teacher Matteo Franco and the poet Luigi Pulci. It is interesting that the setting is not the cathedral but the political centre of Florence, a clear sign that

Sassetti was more interested in a demonstration of power than a depiction of Francis of Assisi.

Rise to Noble Status

The *Procession of the Magi* in the private chapel of the Medici palace, painted by Benozzo Gozzoli in 1459–1460, shows that the Medici had already been ennobled around the mid-15th century, in that the family are portrayed as kings. The monumental wall painting refers to three prestigious events in Florence, in which the Medici took a leading role: the council on the unification of the eastern and western churches in 1439; the great feast for Pope Pius II and the Galeazzo Sforza, Duke of Milan in 1459; and the processions of the Brotherhood of the Magi, in which the Medici took part every year.

Further proof of the Medici's aristocratic and royal claims can be found in the altar panel of the *Adoration of the Magi* (around 1475) in the Uffizi, in which Sandro Botticelli immortalized the Florentine upper class. Even though the kings, portraits of Cosimo the Elder with his sons Giovanni and Piero, were subordinated to the Holy Family, they are still at the centre of the picture. The younger Medici, Cosimo's grandchildren, appear at the sides, Lorenzo dressed in dark clothing and his vivacious brother **Giuliano**, who was murdered in the Pazzi conspiracy in 1478, dressed in bright clothing. The actual subject of the picture recedes into the background and is used as an excuse for a grandiose representation of the Medici and their followers.

Palazzo Strozzi

Walk through the triumphal arch along Via del Strozzi to the largest and most impressive Florentine city palace of the Renaissance, which has three free-standing façades. Fifteen medieval houses were torn down in 1489 in order to build it, probably to plans by Giuliano da Sangallo the Elder. It was completed only in 1536. The Strozzi family, rivals of the Medici, had been banished from Florence for many years. Filippo di Matteo Strozzi, who commissioned the palace, asked Lorenzo the Magnificent specifically for permission to build the palace, which has an elegant rusticated façade.

Palazzo Rucellai

Museo di Storia della Fotografia ►

Turn left onto Via della Vigna Nuova to reach Palazzo Rucellai. The architect Bernardo Rossellino built the palace, one of the most important city houses of the Renaissance in Florence, between 1446 and 1451 to plans by Leon Battista Alberti. It was commissioned by Giovanni di Paolo Rucellai, a rich merchant whose coat of arms, a wind-filled sail, can be seen on the frieze around the building. The Museum Fratelli Alinari on the history of photography was installed on the ground floor in 1985 (hours: Tue–Sun 10am–7.30pm).

Loggia dei Rucellai

Opposite is an arched hall that was built in 1460, also by Alberti, for representational purposes for the Rucellai. The loggia is glassed in today and used for exhibitions.

Museo Marino Marini

🕐 Opening hours: Mon, Wed–Sat 10am–5pm, June, July and Aug closed Sat

Behind the block of Palazzo Rucellai, the former church of San Pancrazio (14th–15th century) was converted to a museum in 1988 for the Tuscan sculptor, painter and graphic artist Marino Marini (1901–1980). 176 sculptures, paintings, drawings and graphics by Marini are on display. They are from all his creative periods, beginning with the painting *The Virgins* of 1916. Horse and rider are one of the sculptor's central themes. Marini's preferred female figure is Pomona, a voluminous goddess of fertility. He also created numerous figures of women dancers and street artists.

Palazzo Antinori, Enoteca

Not far to the north-east the busy Via Tornabuoni leads to Piazza Antinori. Here stands the 15th-century palace of the Antinori family with a pretty fountain courtyard. For many generations the Antinori have devoted themselves to the cultivation and sale of excellent wines, which can be tasted in the enoteca along with Tuscan specialties. Especially recommended: a glass of Chianti Classico Villa Antinori Riserva.

✱ ✱ Santa Maria Novella

🕐 Opening hours: daily 9.30am–5pm Fri, Sun 1–5pm

Only a few hundred yards further to the west is the expansive Piazza Santa Maria Novella, where penitential processions took place in the Middle Ages. Between 1246 and 1300 the large Dominican church Santa Maria Novella was built here on the site of an oratory. The bell tower and sacristy date from the first half of the 14th century, and the façade was built from 1458 until 1470 by **Leon Battista Alberti**. He received this prestigious commission from Giovanni Rucellai, whose sail emblem can be seen in the centre. Alberti used the traditional building style of a baptistery, but added the innovation of an attic storey with a pediment, the mark of an ancient temple rather than a conventional Christian building.

? DID YOU KNOW …?

■ … what the obelisks on Piazza Santa Maria Novella are for? They recall the time when the Medici dukes held horse races here – they served as half-way marks.

Interior

The columned basilica, which is almost 100m/110yd long, contains some **outstanding works of art**: a wonderful crucifix by Giotto, at the second column on the left a marble pulpit designed by Brunelleschi in 1445 and a mural of the *Trinity* (1425–1427) by Masaccio, for which the artist was the first since ancient times to use linear perspective. Nardo di Cione painted the frescoes in the elevated Cappella Strozzi around 1357 with subjects from Dante's *Divine Comedy*. The altarpiece *Redeemer and Saints* (1357) by Andrea Orcagna can also be seen here. On the right in the Cappella Gaddi the painting over the altar *Jesus Awakens the Daughter of Jairus* (1571–1572) by Bronzino catches the eye. In the next chapel Cappella Gondi is the **famous wooden crucifix by Brunelleschi** (1421–1425), the first depiction of Christ without a loincloth.

◄ Main choir chapel and right transept

The main chapel of the choir was completely painted by Domenico Ghirlandaio and assistants 1486–1490 with scenes from the lives of Mary and John the Baptist. It also has numerous portraits of famous contemporaries, scenes from cultured middle-class homes, panoramic landscapes and great banquets. To the right of the main choir chapel is the Cappella di Filippo Strozzi, with **frescoes by Filippino Lippi** (1497–1502) that have scenes from the lives of the apostle Philip and John as their subject. The tomb of Filippo Strozzi was made by Benedetto da Maiano 1491–1493. In Cappella Rucellai notice the bronze tomb cover (around 1423) for a provincial of the Dominican order named Dati by Lorenzo Ghiberti and the marble statue *Madonna and Child* (around 1345–1350) by Nino Pisano.

★ Museo di Santa Maria Novella

Opening hours: daily except Fri 9am–5pm, Sun 9am–2pm

Through the entrance to the left of the church façade a walkway leads to the museum of Santa Maria Novella and first into the »green cloister«, which got its name from the green colour of the frescoes by Paolo Uccello. The story begins with the creation of the animals and the fall of man (around 1430); the dramatic depiction of the flood was painted 20 years later. The liturgical vessels and robes in the refectory date from the 14th to 17th centuries. Do not fail to see the **paintings in the Cappella degli Spagnoli** (Spanish Chapel), which was built after 1340 by Jacopo Talenti as the chapter house of the Dominican monastery and turned over to Eleonora of Toledo, the wife of Cosimo I, as a place of worship for her Spanish attendants. Andrea (di Bonaiuto) da Firenze created from 1365 a wonderful visual representation of the programme of Dominican theology, which shows the way to salvation for mankind.

✴ ✴ San Lorenzo and Surroundings

Building history
🕐
Opening hours:
Mon–Sat
10am–5pm

Follow Via Martelli to the north from the cathedral square and turn left into the first side street to reach the church of San Lorenzo. The market stands with clothing and souvenirs in front of the incomplete façade make a colourful picture – with a bit of luck you might even find a bargain, but it is absolutely essential to barter! In the middle of it all stands the monument created by Baccio Bandinelli in 1540 for Giovanni delle Bande Nere (1360–1429), the father of Cosimo I and founding father of the Medici dynasty. The church is said to have been dedicated as early as 393 by St Ambrose, then outside the city walls. San Lorenzo was the parish church of the Medici, who commissioned the Renaissance architect Filippo Brunelleschi to give it its present appearance after 1419. The work was completed after his death by Antonio Manetti (1460). Michelangelo drew up plans for the façade, which were never used however.

The façade of Santa Maria Novella combines traditional elements with details of ancient architecture such as the pediment.

The interior of San Lorenzo is a daring synthesis of early Christian basilica and elements of ancient architecture. Among the highlights is the altar painting in the second chapel in the right-hand aisle, the ***Marriage of the Virgin*** (1523) by Rosso Fiorentino, whose Mannerism is expressed in a complex composition and variations in colour. In the floor a round memorial tablet made of precious materials commemorates Cosimo de Medici the Elder (1389–1464), whose remains rest together with those of the sculptor Donatello (around 1386–1466), whom he greatly admired, in the crypt below it.

In the nave just before the crossing are two bronze pulpits by Donatello, powerfully expressive masterpieces which were completed after his death by his pupils. In the left-hand aisle Agnolo Bronzino's fresco of the *Martyrdom of St Lawrence* (1565–1569) is a **principal work of Mannerism** with extreme contor-

Interior

> ! **Baedeker TIP**
>
> ### A snack between sights
> Sightseers need regular snacks! There are good chances of finding them in the Mercato Centrale near San Lorenzo. In the covered market there is fish, meat and cheese on the ground floor, and fruit, vegetables and snack stands on the upper floor. If you like tripe, try »panino con lampredotto« – a Florentine specialty!

tions of the figures and pale colours. In the first chapel in the eastern wall of the left transept is a striking altarpiece by Fra Filippo Lippi, the *Annunciation* (around 1440).

The entrance to the Old Sacristy is in the left transept. Its donor Giovanni di Averardo, known as Bicci de Medici (1360–1429) and clan father of the non-noble branch of the Medici, intended it to be a burial chapel but it was used as a sacristy. With its domed central plan, it is considered to be the first epoch-making work of Brunelleschi (1418–1428). Donatello produced the furnishings between 1437 und 1443. In the middle of the sacristy is the marble sarcophagus of Giovanni di Bicci de Medici and his wife Piccarda di Odoardo Bueri. In the wall of the transept is the double funerary monument (1472) for Cosimo's sons Giovanni and Piero by Andrea del Verrocchio.

Sagrestia Vecchia

A door in the left wall leads to the pleasant cloister, from which there are stairs to the Biblioteca Laurenziana. Construction was begun in 1524 to plans by Michelangelo in order to accommodate the valuable book and manuscript collection of the Medici, but the library could only be used from 1571. The reading room has a flat ceiling and was furnished with benches and lecterns designed by Michelangelo. Today codices, manuscripts and missals from the 6th to the 16th century are displayed here.

★★ Biblioteca Medicea Laurenziana
🕐
Opening hours:
Daily
8.30am–1.30pm

The Medici chapels are annexed to San Lorenzo, but are a museum with a separate entrance (Piazza Madonna degli Aldobrandini). The entrance leads first to a crypt with tombs of the Medici family, then

★★ Cappelle Medicee

🕐
Opening hours:
daily
8.15am–4.30pm;
except 2nd and 4th
Sun, 1st and 3rd
Mon of the month

into the **monumental burial chapel of the famous Medici rulers** and finally into the New Sacristy. The planning of the gigantic mausoleum, which is 59m/194ft in height, goes back to Grand Duke Cosimo I. Construction was delayed until 1605, and the elaborate interior design with stone inlays was under construction until well into the 20th century.

★ ★
Sagrestia Nuova

From the Medici chapel descend to the New Sacristy, which is actually a burial chapel. It was built and decorated by **Michelangelo** from 1520 until 1534 with interruptions, and was never completed. Lorenzo the Magnificent and his brother Giuliano, who fell victim to the Pazzi conspiracy in 1478, are buried at the entrance wall. To the right and left in wall niches are the graves of Giuliano, Duke of Nemour, a son of Lorenzo the Magnificent who gave Michelangelo the commission for the tombs, and Lorenzo, Duke of Urbino, a grandson of Lorenzo the Magnificent. Seated and dressed in the armour of a Roman commander, Giuliano de Medici turns his head sideways as he looks attentively at the Madonna and the two patron saints of the Medici, Cosmas and Damian. Under Giuliano the figures of night, with half moon and stars in its hair, and day lie on the slanted lid of the sarcophagus. Both sarcophagus figures were modelled on ancient statues. Opposite them another niche figure depicts Lorenzo de Medici, whose head rests pensively in his hand. On the sarcophagus lid below are the two allegorical figures of evening or dusk (left) and morning or dawn (right). The masculine figure of dusk stands for mental exhaustion, the lethargic mass of the body going to sleep, while the feminine figure shows awakening and the slowly developing power of the body and spirit. In this chapel Michelangelo aimed to create through a **combination of architecture, sculpture and painting** a philosophical work of art reflecting the path of life from matter (river gods, sarcophagus) via incarnation (day and night as life and death, statue of Giuliano) to eternal life (resurrection fresco).

★
Palazzo Medici-Riccardi

🕐
Opening hours:
daily except Wed
9am–7pm

Between 1444 and 1464 Michelozzo created in the Palazzo Medici the **prototype of a Florentine city palace** for Cosimo the Elder, with a fortress-like front reminiscent of the Palazzo Vecchio. The non-noble branch of the Medici and the Medici rulers, whose coat of arms with five spheres (the so-called »palle«) and a lily decorate the palace, lived here until Cosimo I moved to the Palazzo Vecchio in 1540. In 1659 the Riccardi family acquired it, enlarged it and lengthened the palace front. In 1818 it passed to the Grand Dukes of Tuscany. The arched entrance leads first into a square courtyard with twelve marble medallions over the rounded columned arch and a statue of Bacchus by Baccio Bandinelli. Behind it is a small garden courtyard.

★
Frescoes by Benozzo Gozzoli ►

From the main courtyard stairs lead to the second floor to the palace chapel. Its walls are decorated by a monumental historical pageant

The Arno divides Florence into two parts, which are connected again by several bridges – the Ponte Vecchio is in the foreground.

by Benozzo Gozzoli, *The Procession of the Magi to Bethlehem* (1459–1460), on which countless contemporaries were immortalized, including the Milanese Duke Cosimo the Elder, Patriarch Josephus of Constantinople as the oldest king, followed by the Byzantine emperor John VII and Lorenzo de Medici as the youngest king.

Around Piazza San Marco

The church of San Marco, built from 1299 to 1310 by the Benedictine order of St Sylvester, was given to the Dominicans of ▶Fiesole together with the monastery in the year the cathedral was dedicated (1436) by Pope Eugene IV. Cosimo the Elder made a renovation of the church and construction of the monastery possible through a generous donation. The architect Michelozzo was commissioned to complete the work between 1437 and 1452. Giambologna added the side altars and the chapel of St Antoninus as well as the Salviati chapel (1588). In 1678 Pier Francesco Silvani remodelled the church and in 1777–1780 the façade was altered.

✳
San Marco

Interior ▶ The outstanding work in the aisle-less church is a crucifix from the school of Giotto. On the left is the burial chapel of St Antoninus, the archbishop and Dominican prior who was elevated to sainthood in 1526. It is **the major architectural work by Giambologna** (1578–1589), who also provided the decoration: six life-size niche statues and six bronze reliefs from the life of St Antoninus. On the way back to the entrance, three treasures are to be seen on the right: a Baroque marble door that leads to the sacristy, a Byzantine mosaic of the *Madonna at Prayer* (705–707) which came from Rome and Fra Bartolomeo della Porta's painting *Madonna and Child* (1509) with a canopy motif.

★ ★
Museo di
San Marco

The monastery of San Marco (the entrance is to the right of the church) was built by Michelozzo in the Renaissance style; its decorations are an impressive example of late medieval piety. In the pilgrims' hospice are several panel paintings by the Dominican monk Fra Angelico, including **the famous altar of the linen weavers** (1433) and further panels with scenes from the life of Jesus (1450), the *Deposition from the Cross* (1435) and the *Last Judgement* (1430). Directly opposite the entrance on the other side is a representation of *St Dominic at the Foot of the Cross*; diagonally opposite the entrance an *Ecce Homo* can be seen in the lunette. Both works are frescoes by Fra Angelico. The works in the large refectory include Fra Bartolomeo's fresco *Last Judgement*. In the Sala dei Lavabo there is also a large and impressive panel by Fra Bartolomeo, the *Madonna with St Anne and Other Saints* (1510). In the chapter house the *Crucifixion* fresco by Fra Angelico fills an entire wall; the small refectory holds a famous depiction of the *Last Supper* (after 1480) by Ghirlandaio (hours: Mon–Fri 8.15am to 1.50pm, Sat, Sun 8.15am–7.50pm; closed 2nd and 4th Monday and 1st and 3rd Sunday of the month).

> ### Baedeker TIP
>
> **Highlights in the background**
> Florence does not lack attractions. On the contrary, with all of its top-quality cultural facilities some highlights get pushed aside. For that reason the following places deserve special mention: the Stibbert Museum (p.257), the Museum for the History of Science (p.230), the museum devoted to the Tuscan artist Mario Marini (p.242) and the wax museum La Specola (p.235).

Monks' cells ▶ On the second floor are more than 40 cells which Fra Angelico decorated with frescoes, alone or with the help of his students. Look out for the intimate depiction of the *Annunciation* opposite the stairs. The prior's apartment is a reminder of Girolamo Savonarola, prior of San Marco from 1491, who was executed as a heretic and schismatic in 1498.

Library ▶ The large hall of the library with valuable manuscripts, missals and bibles was designed in an imposing and austere style by Michelozzo (1444).

The east side of Piazza San Marco is bordered by the university building. Right next to it is the gallery of the academy of art, which emerged from the first academy of 1562 and was revived by Grand Duke Pietro Leopoldo I in 1784. The greatest treasures of the collection are outstanding sculptures by Michelangelo and paintings of the Middle Ages and Renaissance. In the Galleria del David are four incomplete figures of prisoners out of the total of six that Michelangelo created for the grave of Pope Julius II in Rome (1519–1536). After Michelangelo's death they were set up to decorate the grotto in the Giardino di Boboli and in 1909 were transferred to the academy. The figure of the apostle Matthew, which Michelangelo sculpted in 1505–1506, also remained incomplete.

★ ★
Galleria dell'Accademia

⏱
Opening hours:
Tue–Sun
8.15am–7.50pm

Michelangelo's world famous *David* was removed in 1873 from Piazza della Signoria, where it had suffered greatly from the rain and wind, and placed in the rotunda of the academy. At the age of 26 Michelangelo had taken over a giant block of marble that was considered to be misshapen and unusable because of its unfortunate proportions (more than 4m/13ft high, but with little depth) and in the years 1501–1504 created a figure of youthful power and beauty: *David*, a shepherd who according to the Bible won an apparently hopeless battle for the people of Israel against the giant Goliath. The Renaissance figure became a symbol of the Florentine desire for liberty. In the first of the three Florentine rooms is the so-called Adimari chest, an oblong clothes chest with a 15th-century wedding procession on the front.

Shopping in the colonnades of Piazza della Repubblica

There are also works by Filippo Lippi, Fra Bartolomeo and Perugino here. The Byzantine rooms contain the oldest works of the academy's collection from the second half of the 13th century and the 14th century.

Around Piazza Santissima Annunziata

※
Piazza Santissima Annunziata

Follow Via Cesare Battisti south-east to the beautiful Piazza Santissima Annunziata. The square is large and – compared to Piazza della Signoria – not nearly so overrun, an inviting place for a rest. On the north side is the church Santissima Annunziata, on the east side the orphanage and on the south side Palazzo Grifoni (16th century), the imposing seat of the regional administration today.

※ ※
Santissima Annunziata

🕐
Opening hours:
daily 7am–12.30pm
4–6.30pm

The Church of the Annunciation, built around 1250 as an oratory of the Servite order, was thoroughly altered between 1444 and 1481 by Michelozzo. The centre door of the seven-arched portico gives access to the Chiostrino dei Voti, a forecourt named after the votive offerings displayed there, with an important cycle of early 16th-century frescoes which begins on the right wall with the *Assumption of the Virgin* (Rosso Fiorentino). It is followed by the *Visitation* (Pontormo), *Betrothal of the Virgin* (Franciabigio), *Birth of the Virgin* (Andrea del Sarto), the *Three Magi* (Andrea del Sarto), the *Nativity* (Alessio Baldovinetti) and scenes from the *Life of St Filippo Benizzi* (Cosimo Rosselli, Andrea del Sarto).

The aisle-less interior of the church, remodelled in the 17th and 18th centuries, is flanked by chapels on both sides; the choir has the shape of a rotunda. A tour of the church begins on the left with the Cappella Feroni and the fresco *The Redeemer and St Julian* (1455) by Andrea del Castagno. The *Holy Trinity* in the next chapel is by the same artist. The rotunda was begun by Michelozzo (1444) and finished by Leon Battista Alberti to a different design.

The painting by Agnolo Bronzino of the *Resurrection* (1550) in the fourth chapel on the left and the Cappella della Madonna del Soccorso, a work of Giambologna (1594–1598), are also impressive. Giambologna designed the chapel with beautiful frescoes, statues and reliefs to be his own tomb. The dome of the choir rotunda is decorated by a fresco of the *Coronation of the Virgin* by Volterrano (1681–1683).

※
Spedale degli Innocenti

The foundling hospital, which was begun in 1419 by Filippo Brunelleschi, is the first modern secular building with a columned portico like an ancient temple instead of medieval pillars. The architecture is complemented by frescoes in the arcades and lunettes above the entrances as well as by ten coloured **terracotta medallions** in the outer corners of the arches with depictions of swaddled babies (around 1463), which Andrea della Robbia made using a weather-proof tin glaze. The commission for the new building came from the wealthy silk merchants' guild, which had the house built for abandoned new-born babies (innocenti). This institution is still the city's orphanage – until 1875 babies could be left here by their mothers in a revolving wooden cylinder on the left-hand wall of the portico.

Pictures, sculptures, miniatures and furniture from the 14th to the 18th century are displayed in the gallery. They include works by Giovanni del Biondo, Rossellino, Benedetto da Maiano, and above all by Domenico Ghirlandaio and Andrea del Sarto as well as a terracotta Madonna by Luca della Robbia (hours: daily except Wed 8.30am–2pm).

Galleria dello Spedale degli Innocenti

Behind the orphanage, Palazzo della Crocetta on Via della Colonna, which was founded in 1870, holds the most important archaeological museum of northern Italy. The topographical department includes valuable finds from Etruria which give an exact picture of the highly civilized Etruscans.

★ **Museo Archeologico Centrale dell'Etruria**

Items especially worthy of note include the coloured sarcophagus of Larthia Seianti (between 217 and 147 BC) from Martinella near Chiusi. In the garden are reconstructions of Etruscan graves and grave monuments. The Etruscan-Greek-Roman department comprises Etruscan urns and sarcophagi, including the painted marble sarcophagus of Ramtha Hucznai from Tarquinia, as well as Etruscan, Greek and Roman bronzes like *Idolino*, the Greek statue of a young *Ephebos* (5th century BC) or the *Standing Orator* (Aulus Metellus, 3rd century BC). Statues, busts, ceramics, reliefs, sarcophagi, mummies, pictures and utensils document the various Egyptian dynasties, including a well-preserved wooden wagon from the time of Ramses I. The museum also has a collections of coins from the Etruscan and modern periods, a jewel collection with gemstones, glasses, cameos, gold and silver items and a vase collection with the famous Françoise Vase from the 6th century BC.

⏲ Opening hours:
Mon 2–7pm, Tue and Thu 8.30am–7pm
Wed, Fri–Sun 8.30am–2pm

★ ## Museo Nazionale del Bargello

From Piazza della Signoria (see p.222) follow Via Gondi along the left side of Palazzo Vecchio to Piazza San Firenze then to Via del Proconsolo and Palazzo del Bargello, a monumental building erected in 1250 by the citizens of Florence as a sign of their victory over the nobility. After 1261 the building was the seat of the podestà, from 1502 a court with prison and from 1574 the seat of the president of the police, who was called the »bargello«. In 1859 it was made into a museum of sculpture and is among the most important in Italy today.

⏲ Opening hours:
daily 8.30am–1.50pm, closed Mon

The first room to the right of the entrance contains **major works by**

✔ **DON'T MISS**

- Giambologna's *Mercury*
  Donatello's *David*
  the museum's little-known artisan collection

Studying sculpture in the Palazzo Bargello

Michelangelo, including the expressive early *Drunken Bacchus* (1496 / 1497). In its depiction of the Virgin as a seer, the round relief of the *Madonna* (1504–1505) for Bartolomeo Pitti is a precursor of his sibyls in the Sistine Chapel. Michelangelo's marble bust of *Brutus* (around 1540) alludes to the murder of the cruel Duke Alessandro de Medici by his cousin Lorenzino in 1537, but remained unfinished.

Second floor　In the loggia of the second floor, the highlights are bronzes by Giambologna: the fountain figure of *Mercury* (1580), a virtuoso piece that appears to break the laws of structural engineering, as well as the classical coolness of the *Allegory of Architecture.* Masterpieces by the great Renaissance sculptor Donatello are in the room named after him, including the marble *David* (1410–1416), his earliest monumental statue, as well as a statue and relief of *St George* (1415–1417), which show his dramatic conception of figures. The marble lion called *Marzoccox* (1418–1420) is also a masterpiece, as is the softly modelled, youthful bronze figure of *David* (around 1435), the first nude figure since antiquity. It is also interesting to compare the styles of Ghiberti and Brunelleschi, whose competing reliefs for the second door of the baptistery depicting the *Sacrifice of Isaac* (1401–1402) have been preserved. Among the coloured ceramics the *Enthroned Madonna* (around 1460) by Luca della Robbia is outstanding. Along with these exhibits the following can also be seen on the second floor: frescoes of paradise and hell as well as legends of saints (around 1330–1340) in the chapel of the podestà, ivory works, majolica, enamel and goldsmith work as well as furniture and glass.

Third floor　Andrea del Verrocchio, Leonardo da Vinci's teacher, made a finely modelled, naturalistic figure of a shepherd boy in his bronze *David* (before 1476). Further outstanding works are the highly realistic portrait bust of *Pietro Melini* by Benedetto da Maiano (1474), the marble bust of *Matteo Palmieri* (1468) by Antonio Rossellino and the ceramic bust of a *Young Warrior* (1479–1480) by Antonio Pollaiuolo with a Hercules and Hydra relief on the breastplate. Pollaiuolo modelled the bronze group of *Hercules and Antaeus*, also around 1480. In other rooms the **Medici medallion collection** is displayed, a weapons collection, valuable textiles as well as numerous high-quality small bronze figures and works in glazed terracotta by Andrea della Robbia.

Santa Croce and Surroundings

From the Bargello walk along Via Ghibellina to Via Isola delle Stinche, where a stop in the ice-cream shop Vivoli – one of the best in Florence – is an absolute must, before arriving at the magnificent Piazza Santa Croce further to the east. In June the popular Calcio Storico takes place here (► Events). Ball games were held on this square as early as the 16th century.

Piazza
Santa Croce

With its many **graves and monuments** as well as numerous **important paintings** – including impressive works by the famous Giotto – the church is one of the finest in Italy. Its imposing dimensions (115m/125yd long and 38m/41yd wide) make it the largest Franciscan church. Building began in 1294, presumably under Arnolfo di Cambio. It was completed in 1385 except for the façade, which dates from the 19th century.

✶ ✶
Santa Croce
🕑
Opening hours:
daily 9.30–5.30pm,
Sun 1–5.30pm

The tour begins in the left aisle. Opposite the first pillar is the 18th-century monument to Galileo Galilei with allegories of geometry and astronomy. Near the fifth pillar the **tombplate of Lorenzo Ghiberti**, the creator of the paradise doors, is set in the floor. The chapel at the front of the left aisle holds the wooden crucifix (around 1421) by Donatello. Brunelleschi criticized it with the words that his friend had nailed a farmer to the cross, and then himself created a noble-looking crucified Christ for the church of Santa Maria Novella. On the right opposite is the Cappella Bardi di Vernio with frescoes (1340) on the *Life of St Sylvester* by Maso di Banco. The paintings in the adjacent Cappella Pulci shows the *Martyrdom of the Archdeacons Lawrence and Stephen* by Bernardo Daddi (around 1330).

◄ Left aisle

The large **main chapel of the choir** is decorated with wall frescoes (around 1380) on the *Legend of the Holy Cross* by Agnolo Daddi. The adjacent **Cappella Bardi** on the right, which has a fresco cycle (around 1320) with important stations from the legend of St Francis, has been attributed to Giotto. The revolutionary nature of his compositions is made clear in comparison to the altarpiece from around 1270 with small individual scenes and the large, flat-looking figure of St Francis.

Next is the Cappella Peruzzi with some of **Giotto's main works**: frescoes with scenes from the life of John the Evangelist and John the Baptist, made around 1320. The Cappella Baroncelli is at the end of the transept. Taddeo Gaddi, a pupil of Giotto, painted the frescoes

✶ ✶
◄ Wall paintings
by Giotto

(1332–1337) of the prophets and the life of Mary, including the *Annunciation to the Shepherds*, a rare night scene in medieval painting. The frescoes in the adjacent Cappella Castellani were painted by Agnolo Gaddi and his pupils around 1383.

Sacristy An elaborate door to a corridor (Corridoio della Sagrestia) designed by Michelozzo leads to the sacristy. It contains valuable cabinets from the Renaissance and a *Crucifixion* by Taddeo Gaddi. Behind the sacristy is the 14th-century Cappella Rinuccini with frescoes by Giovanni da Milano showing scenes from the lives of the Virgin and Mary Magdalene. At the end of the sacristy corridor is the novitiate chapel built by Michelozzo for Cosimo de Medici between 1434 and Scuola del Cuoio ► 1445. The corridor also leads to the leather school, where handmade bags and leather articles are sold.

Right-hand aisle Return to the right-hand aisle to see the funerary monument of the composer Gioacchino Rossini as well as the tomb of the Florentine scholar and chancellor of the republic, Leonardo Bruni, in which Bernardo Rossellino created the **prototype of the Florentine Renaissance tomb** around 1450. A few steps further is a graceful relief by Donatello of the *Annunciation* (1435). About in the middle of the aisle is the wall tomb (1787) with an allegory of diplomacy for the political philosopher Niccolò Machiavelli. At the next pillar is the marble Renaissance pulpit (around 1480) by Benedetto da Maiano. Vittorio Alfieri (†1803), a poet and forerunner of the Risorgimento, rests in a classical grave by Antonio Canova in the opposite wall. Next is the monumental cenotaph (1829) for Dante Alighieri, who died in Ravenna in 1321 and is buried there. Vasari designed the **tomb of Michelangelo** with personifications of sculpture, painting and architecture.

Monastery, cloisters, Santa Croce Museum To the right of the church is the entrance to the monastery of Santa Croce. In the first cloister is the Cappella dei Pazzi built by Brunelleschi from 1430 and commissioned by Andrea de Pazzi. This early example of central-plan Renaissance architecture with terracotta reliefs by Andrea della Robbia served as family chapel and as chapter house for the Franciscan monks. A passageway leads from the first cloister to the large two-storey cloister built around 1452 by Bernardo Rossellino to plans by Brunelleschi. The museum is housed in the refectory and adjacent rooms. Its main works include the 120 sq m/ 1,300 sq ft *Last Supper* (1330–1340) by Taddeo Gaddi; a large crucifix (after 1270) by Cimabue, a masterpiece that was unfortunately severely damaged by the Arno flood in 1966; a bronze statue by Donatello, *St Louis* (1423); as well as *Stigmata*, a terracotta group by Andrea della Robbia (hours: daily except Wed 10am–6pm).

★ Casa Buonarroti Via dei Pepi runs past the Santa Croce façade on the left-hand side to Via Ghibellina, where Michelangelo Buonarroti bought house

Villas with extensive gardens are also a feature of Florence.

number 70 for his nephew Leonardo. Michelangelo himself never lived there. Today it is a place of memorial to the world-famous artist, housing the powerful and dynamic *Battle of the Centaurs*, a marble relief which Michelangelo sculpted when he was 17 years old, and the flat marble relief which he created a little earlier, *Madonna with Child* (also called *Madonna della Scala* because of the steps). It is full of melancholy since Mary's eyes seem to look knowingly into the future at the death of Jesus. Further notable works here are a wooden crucifix (1494) for Santo Spirito, which shows Christ not as a man of sorrows but as a gentle youth, and a wooden model of the unfinished façade of the church of San Lorenzo.

🕐
Opening hours:
Mon, Wed–Sun
9.30am–2pm

Outside the Old City

A short path leads from Piazzale Michelangelo to the monastery San Miniato al Monte, which is built over the grave of St Minias, who was martyred in Florence in the year 250. It was founded by Cluniac monks around 1018. Building work probably began between 1050 and 1060. The church was largely complete by the early 13th century. It was converted into a fortress in the 16th century, used as a hospital, paupers' and old people's home in the 17th century and restored in the 19th and early 20th centuries. The monastery was turned over to Olivet monks in 1924. To the left of the church lies **an atmospheric**

✶
San Miniato al Monte
🕐
Opening hours:
daily in summer
8am–7.30pm, in
winter 8am–noon
and 3–6pm

cemetery, to the right the 14th-century summer palace of the bishops of Florence, part of the monastery since 1534. The two-storey white and green façade is covered with thin marble panels. The mosaic from the second half of the 13th century on the upper floor depicts Christ between Mary and San Miniato. The gable is crowned by a gilded eagle with a bunch of wool in its talons. It is the figure from the coat of arms of the textile merchants' guild, which financed the construction and maintenance of San Miniato for a long time. The campanile collapsed in 1499 and was left incomplete.

Interior ► The impressive interior takes up the late antique, early Christian form of the columned basilica: a long church consisting of a nave and two aisles, with an exposed roof structure and without a transept. The choir, which was traditionally built over a martyr's grave, originally gave the pilgrim entering the church a view of the hall crypt (11th century) and the remains of St Miniato. Michelozzo's barrel-vaulted **marble ciborium** with white and light-blue terracotta cassettes by Luca della Robbia in the nave was created in 1448 and commissioned by Piero de Medici. The back is an altarpiece by Agnolo Gaddi (around 1396) with scenes of the martyrdom of St Miniato.

Cappella del Cardinale di Portogallo ► The funeral chapel of the Portuguese cardinal was commissioned by King Alfonso V of Portugal and built by Manetti between 1461 and 1466. As a space with a central plan it is strongly oriented to Brunelleschi's Old Sacristy in San Lorenzo. The interior decoration combines Christian and ancient ideas. Thus Antonio Rossellino's conception of the sarcophagus is reminiscent of Roman models; a Mithras sacrifice as well as putti decorate the tomb niche. The reclining figure of the deceased faces an empty judge's seat as a reminder of the Last Judgement. The terracotta figures are by Luca della Robbia.

Crypt ► To the left and right of the marble ciborium, steps lead down to the crypt with frescoes (14th century) by Taddeo Gaddi.

Presbytery and apse ► The decoratively sculptured marble screens and the marble pulpit from the second half of the 12th century are among the most valuable late Romanesque decorations of the church. The apse is decorated with a mosaic *Christ with Mary and San Miniato*, in which Byzantine influence is recognizable. It was originally made in 1297 but restored several times later and in the second half of the 19th century almost completely renewed.

Sacristy ► From the apse go right into the sacristy, where Spinello Aretino created his masterpiece, the *Legends of St Benedict*, in 1387, then through to the cloister with frescoes by Andrea del Castagno and Paolo Uccello.

Cascine Cascine, a park with swimming pool and racetrack, is a popular picnic site for Florentines on weekends. It covers more than 3 sq km/ 1.2 sq mi on the north bank of the Arno in the western part of the city. The land used to be farmland belonging to the Medici, later the Lorena; the park has been open to the public since the 18th century.

The English officer Frederick Stibbert, a well-travelled and wealthy man, collected weapons, art, but also religious items, clothing and utensils all over the world. In his villa in the hills above Florence this gigantic collection fills 60 (!) rooms today. For adults the furnishings alone – ostentatious and educational at one and the same time – of this »modest« residence and its expansive garden would justify a visit, but the attractive presentation of the museum makes it an experience for children as well (Via Federico Stibbert 26, northern city limits; hours: Mon–Wed 10am–2pm, Fri–Sun 10am–6pm, closed Thu).

★ Museo Stibbert

Around Florence

The former Carthusian monastery 5km/3mi south of the city centre lies on the road to Siena at the outskirts of Galluzzo (bus route 37). Niccolò Acciaiuoli, a Florentine statesman and friend of Petrarch, had the fortress-like Carthusian monastery built in 1341. The complex was later expanded several times and is used by Benedictine monks today. In the monastery church of San Lorenzo is the famous grave of Cardinal Agnolo II Acciaiuoli, which is attributed to Francesco da Sangallo. The monastery picture gallery includes lunette frescoes by Pontormo to designs by Albrecht Dürer and a *Madonna with Child* by Lucas Cranach.

★ Certosa del Galluzzo

Not easy to find because not signposted, Villa la Petraia (Via della Petraia 40) lies on the right above the Florence – Sesto road. Ferdinando de Medici acquired the estate in 1575 and had it converted by Buontalenti, but the defensive tower was preserved. In the 19th century the estate served as the summer residence of the Italian kings. It is still owned by the state and open to the public.
The charming park offers a good view all the way to Florence (hours: Tue–Sun 8.15am–7.30pm, in winter until 4.30pm, in spring until 5.30pm, in fall until 6.30pm; the villa closes a half hour earlier).

★ ★ Medici villas
★ ◄ Villa la Petraia

Only a few hundred metres to the west of Villa la Petraia lies Villa Medicea di Castello (Via Castello 47), which dates from the 16th century in its present form. The villa is the seat of the Accademia della Crusca and not open to the public, but the extensive park with its elaborate waterworks, grottoes and statues is. In the sculptural group on the central fountain Hercules battles against the giant Antaeus (hours: Tue–Sun 8.15am–7.30pm, in winter until 4.30pm, spring / fall until 5.30pm or 6.30pm respectively).

Villa di Castello

North of the Florence city centre in Careggi is another Medici villa (Viale Pieraccini 17). Cosimo the Elder commissioned Michelozzo to convert it to a country estate in 1433. Lorenzo the Magnificent died in this villa on 8 April 1492. It can only be viewed upon request (tel. 05 54 27 97 55).

Villa di Careggi

Villa di Pratolino   On Via Bolognese, before the town of Pratolino, lies the park of the Villa Demidoff. The formerly magnificent villa, which Buontalenti built in 1575 for Francesco I de Medici, was torn down in the 19th century. The park, which was also laid out in the 16th century, was preserved and is a popular place for recreation in the summer. Its main attraction is the 10m/33ft-high *Colossus* statue by Giambologna (1579–1589), one of the most important examples of Florentine Mannerism (hours of the park: April–Sept Thu–Sun 10am–8pm, March and Oct only Sun).

Other Medici villas   The two Medici villas west of Florence, Poggio a Caiano and Artimino, can be found under ▶Prato, Surroundings.

✷ ✷ Giglio / Isola del Giglio

Province: Grosseto (GR)   **Area:** 21 sq km/8 sq mi
Population: 1,600

The second-largest island of the Tuscan archipelago lies in the Tyrrhenian Sea, 11 nautical miles west of Monte Argentario. It is no longer a secret that the green and mountainous Giglio is a small paradise for holidaymakers and divers looking for peace and quiet.

Beautiful beaches, diving area   Giglio has a few small but not unattractive sandy coves, which are suitable for **swimming and snorkelling**. North of the little peninsula Lazzaretto lie Arenella beach and Caletta cove, to the south are the beaches Cala delle Canelle and Cala degli Alberi. The biggest beach is Campese Bay; most of the others can only be reached on foot. The underwater world off the coast of Giglio with a sandy or sea-grass bottom offers lots of variety for divers.

Giglio Porto   The ferries from the mainland arrive at the harbour of Giglio Porto on the east side of the island – this makes the town lively and busy. In the old houses that cluster around the quay on a narrow coastal strip, restaurants, bars and shops await customers. The massive Torre del Porto was built in 1596 by Grand Duke Ferdinand I.

✷ Giglio Castello   A steep winding road leads up to the main part of town and the administrative centre of the island, Giglio Castello, which lies at an elevation of 400m/1,312ft. The fortress, which was begun under Pisan rule and later strenghtened by the Genoese and the Medici grand dukes, gave the village its name. Within the enclosing wall **tiny streets** and typically narrow outside steps give the picturesque town its character.

▶ VISITING GIGLIO

INFORMATION

Pro Loco
Via Umberto I
Giglio Porto (at the harbour)
Tel./fax 05 64 80 94 00
www.isoladelgiglioufficioturistico.
com

FERRIES

Ferries to Giglio depart from Porto
Santo Stefano. Information at Mar-
egiglio ferry line
Tel. 05 64 81 29 20

WHERE TO EAT

▶ Moderate
Da Maria
Via della Casamatta
Giglio Castello
Tel. 05 64 80 60 62
Restaurant with family tradition.
Fresh fish daily – as you would expect
on this island.

WHERE TO STAY

All accommodation on Giglio fills up
quickly in the high season! It is
essential to reserve early.

▶ Mid-range
Castello Monticello
Via Provinciale, Giglio Porto

Tel. 05 64 80 92 52
Fax 05 64 80 94 73
Open Easter to the end of September.
Comfortable hotel above Giglio Porto
with its own restaurant.

▶ Mid-range to budget
Arenella
Giglio Porto
Tel. 05 64 80 93 40
Fax 05 64 80 94 43
www.albergoarenella.it
Family-friendly (27 rooms), good
food. There is a large terrace for
sunbathing, but the beach is only a
few minutes' walk from the house.

CAMPING

▶ Budget
Baia del Sole
Near Campese
Tel. 05 64 80 40 36
Fax 05 64 80 41 01
The only campground on Giglio;
with just about 50 pitches and a
few bungalows it fills up quickly.
The places right on the sea are
especially popular. It has a rocky
beach for swimming. No dogs
allowed!

Campese

The attractions of this modern town in a bay on the north-west coast
are its location and its long sand beach. The former fishing village
has long since become a holiday resort with a considerable tourist
infrastructure (including diving schools).

Surroundings, Isola di Giannutri

The island of Giannutri lies about 15 nautical miles south-east of Giglio. It has the shape of a half moon and an area of 2.6 sq km/1 sq
mi. Car and pedestrian ferries connect it to Porto Santo Stefano (►
Monte Argentario; information see above). This southernmost island
of the Arcipelago Toscano is comparatively flat and has a mostly

An island for holiday-makers who want to be close to the sea and to nature: Giglio

rocky coast; the only beaches are in the north-west and north-east. Giannutri is therefore above all a tip for keen **divers**. On the north-west side of the island above Cala Maestra cove are the remains of a Roman settlement from the 1st and 2nd centuries, including baths and the stately villa of the patrician family of Domizi Aenobarbi.

★ Grosseto

Province: Grosseto (GR)
Population: 72,500

Altitude: 10m/33ft above sea level

It is actually unfair that Grosseto is off the tourist path. The provincial capital lies just over 10km/6mi from the seaside and does not seem very attractive at first glance, but has a charming and neat old town and an impressive city wall. The bicycle-friendly city also offers interesting collections, such as that of the archaeological museum and the Museo d'Arte della Maremma.

History   Grosseto grew in the Middle Ages from a small castle which guarded the Via Aurelia, the old Roman road that connected Pisa and Rome.

After the Etruscan town of Rusellae was destroyed in the year 935 by the Saracens, Pope Innocent II moved the bishop's seat to Grosseto in 1138. The Medici had the fortifications strengthened from 1574 and new irrigation canals built. The grand dukes of Tuscany also made improvements which brought modest prosperity to the town. Only after 1930 when the ►Maremma was finally completely drained did the town grow to be a wealthy centre of agriculture with some industry.

What to See in Grosseto

The historic city centre is surrounded by an irregular six-sided wall with six bastions, which was begun by Baldassare Lanci in 1574 under orders from the Grand Duke Francesco I and completed in 1593 under Ferdinand I. In 1835 Leopold II had the fortifications converted into a **public wall garden**. A half-hour walk on the wall gives a first impression of the old town, which has an amazing re-semblance to the old city of Lucca.

✱
Medici fortifications

The main square of the old city is Piazza Dante Alighieri, which was restored in 2001 and has a monument to Leopold II (1797–1870), the last Habsburg hereditary grand duke of Tuscany. Even though it is obvious that it was restored, the square has found acceptance among residents and visitors as a meeting place. The north side is marked by the red-and-white marble façade of the cathedral of San Lorenzo, which was restored in 1840–1845. Of the original building, which Sozzo di Rustichino built from 1294 to 1302 on the founda-tions of an older church, only the south doorway remains, its archi-trave adorned with figures of Christ and the evangelists. The interior has been restored several times. In the left transept is an *Assumption of the Virgin* (1474) by Matteo di Giovanni.

✱
Piazza Dante Alighieri, Duomo

▶ VISITING GROSSETO

INFORMATION
Viale Monterosa 206
Tel. 05 64 46 26 11, fax 05 64 45 46 06

EVENTS
International jazz festival in July

WHERE TO EAT
▶ **Moderate**
① *La Buca di San Lorenzo*
Viale Manetti 1
Tel. 056 42 51 42, closed Mon.
Luciano Nonnini's gourmet restau-rant in the medieval fortress wall serves creative regional cuisine.

WHERE TO STAY
▶ **Mid-range**
① *Maremma*
Via F. Paolucci de Calboli 11
Tel. 056 42 22 93, fax 056 42 20 51
www.hotelmaremma.it, 30 rooms
This classic hotel with its own parking lot is in the middle of the pedestrian zone. Most of the rooms have air conditioning.

Grosseto *Plan*

A Piazza Dante Alighieri
B Piazza del Duomo
C Piazza Baccarini
D Piazza dell'Indipendenza
E Piazza del Popolo
F Piazza Frateli Rosselli
G Piazza Palma
H Piazza del Mercato
J Piazza De Maria
K Piazza Esperanto
1 Prefettura
2 San Francesco
3 Museo Archeologico
  e d'Arte della Maremma
4 Municipio

Where to eat
① La Buca di San Lorenzo

Where to stay
① Maremma

© Baedeker

250 m

Museo Archeologico e d'Arte della Maremma

★ North of the cathedral on Piazza Baccarini (no. 3) a visit to the museum of archaeology and art is recommended. It holds finds from prehistoric, Etruscan and Roman times as well as a collection of medieval art.

The excavations of Roselle (see below) and its more and more complex city infrastructure, types of houses and wall techniques are documented clearly on the ground floor and second floor. The exhibits include Etruscan black ceramic vases, terracottas and ceramics of the Hellenistic period as well as imperial Roman statues. **Finds from the Villanova culture from Vetulonia**, the frieze of a woman's head from (▶Maremma), a bronze statue of a woman and two golden earrings decorated with semi-precious stones as well as ossuaries from ▶Pitigliano can also be seen. The third floor is reserved for the art museum with works from the 13th to the 19th century, including Sassetta's masterly *Madonna delle Ciligie* (1450), majolicas and a collection of coins from the Middle Ages and Renaissance.

Opening hours:
Nov–April Tue–Sun
9am–1pm and
4.30–7pm,
May–Oct daily
10am–1pm and
5–8pm

San Francesco

The church of San Francesco on Piazza dell'Indipendenza was founded in the 13th century by Benedictines and later taken over by Franciscan monks. The fine panel cross from the 13th century is attributed to Duccio di Buoninsegna.

★ ★ Parco Archeologico di Roselle

Remains of the Etruscan city Rusellae

A must for everyone with an interest in ancient times lies on the hill flank of Poggio di Moscona, 9km/5.5mi north-east of Grosseto: the remains of the Etruscan city of Rusellae, a member of the twelve-city

The main square of Grosseto: cathedral on the left, town hall on the right.

league. In ancient times it was separated from Vetulonia by a lake, while a trade road secured the connection to northern and southern Etruria.

According to Livy, Rusellae was conquered by the Romans in 294 BC and expanded under Augustus. The city declined after the fall of the western Roman Empire. Parts of the 3km/1.8mi-long wall made of limestone blocks 2m/6.5ft high, which presumably enclosed the two hills of the city from the 7th century BC, have been preserved. The oldest part of the settlement is the northern area **with Etruscan houses** made of unfired brick, which go back to the 7th century BC. The regularly ordered rows of stones on the western side date from the 2nd century BC.

The quarters of the craftsmen were sited on the southern hill from the Hellenistic period until the end of the 2nd century BC. Several wells and cisterns ensured the water supply, and a **sewer system** disposed of waste water. Excavations have exposed three city gates, and the existence of four more is supposed because of the access roads. Along these roads remains of graves from archaic and Hellenistic-Roman times can be seen. Within the walls Roman buildings were excavated, including an amphitheatre on the northern hill and an imperial forum in the valley between the two city hills, as well as remains of a villa from imperial times and a Roman road paved with flagstones.

✴ Vetulonia

The picturesque town, which goes back to one of the oldest and most flourishing cities founded in northern Etruria, lies a good 20km/12mi north-west of Grosseto above the delta plain of the Ombrone, which is criss-crossed with canals.

Etruscan stronghold Vetluna

The stronghold called Vetluna or Vatluna was a member of the twelve-city Etruscan league. Gold, silver and ore made the city rich in the 7th and 6th centuries BC. The graves contained gold jewellery which can be admired today in the Museo Archeologico of ▶ Florence. The reasons for and time of the decline of Vetulonia are not known. Most of the grave finds belongs to museums in Grosseto and Florence; only a very few pieces can be seen in the Antiquarium of Vetulonia.

✳
Etruscan necropolises

The Etruscan graves are on the slopes in the north-east and west of the ancient city (hours: sunrise to sunset). The characteristic graves of Vetulonia are the so-called **circoli**, stones set in a circle with a burial chamber covered by an earth mound. Along Via dei Sepolcri – the »grave route« which runs toward Grilli – lies first the Tomba del Belvedere, a chamber grave with a short passage.

Tomba della Pietrera ▶

The two-storey Tomba della Pietrera is an architecturally interesting grave dating from the second half of the 7th century BC to the north-east of the settlement. The tomb looks like the domed graves of Mycene in Greece. It is an artificial hill bordered by a circular base with a diameter of more than 60m/65yd. The grave is 14m/46ft high and the entry is 22m/24yd long. A pillar in the middle of the lower chamber supported the limestone ceiling. When it caved in, presumably already during construction, the grave was mounded up and a more stable sand-lime structure was used in order to make the upper chamber with the artificial dome.

The square chamber of the Tomba del Diavolino, further to the north and 15m/50ft high, dates from the same period. It also has an artificial tumulus, which is bordered by a circular base. The base of the central pillar in the middle of the burial chamber has been preserved. The dome grave got its name from a bronze statuette of Charon, the god of death, which was found here and was first thought to be a devil (Museo Archeologico, Florence).

Livorno

H 4/5

Province: Livorno (LI)	**Altitude:** Sea level
Population: 162,000	

The provincial capital 20km/13mi south of ▶ Pisa is the most important harbour of Tuscany – both for passenger and freight shipping. No wonder then that the modern container harbour, ferry traffic and fishing industry dominate life in the second-largest Tuscan city.

Old town, youthful looks

In view of the industrial complexes and modern buildings it is easy to forget that Livorno is a city rich in tradition. It was Pisa's harbour for a long time, but after the defeat of the Pisans was taken over in

Livorno *Plan*

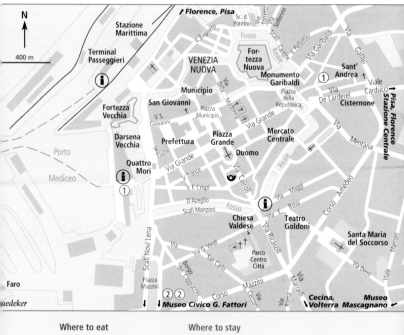

Where to eat
① Il Sottomarino
② La Perla

Where to stay
① Gran Duca
② Villa Tramonto

1405 by Genoa, which then sold Livorno to Florence in 1421 for 100,000 gold florins.

The Medici founded a new harbour in 1571 and at the same time built a **city on a five-sided plan**, which they surrounded with a water channel, the Fosso Reale. This pentagon is the centre of Livorno today. Under Medici rule, as a free port in which religious tolerance was practised, Livorno attracted a cosmopolitan community of Armenian, Jewish, Greek, Dutch and English merchants, and by the end of the 18th century Livorno was the second-largest city in Tuscany after Florence. In World War II the industrial centre was bombed heavily.

The buildings, mostly **post-war** but resembling 1930s architecture in the choice of materials and their monumental structure, e.g. the Palazzo del Governo which is faced with natural stone, and the strictly right-angled street grid are of interest to students of 20th-century architecture, but otherwise the scene is not very inviting. The main axis of the centre is Via Grande, which is bordered by tall arcades.

⏵ VISITING LIVORNO

INFORMATION
Piazza Cavour 6
Tel. 05 86 89 81 11, fax 05 86 89 61 73
www.livorno.turismo.toscana.it
www.costadeglietruschi.it

FERRIES
From Porto Mediceo ferries run back
and forth to Elba and to the islands of
the Arcipelago Toscano (Isola di Gorgona, Isola di Capraia). The ferries to
Sardinia and Corsica start from the
neighbouring Porto Mercantile.

WHERE TO EAT
▶ **Moderate**
① *Il Sottomarino*
Via Terrazzini 48
Tel. 058 61 88 70 25
Closed Thu and Sun evenings.
Friendly trattoria where everything
revolves around seafood. Try the
famous Livornese fish soup cacciucco.

② *La Perla*
San Vincenzo, Riviera degli Etruschi
Via della Meloria 9
Tel. 05 65 70 21 13
Restaurant right at the beach with a
sophisticated, creative fish cuisine. Our
tip: »tonno rosso alle erbe e riso
basmati con pesto di sedano e mandorle«.

WHERE TO STAY
▶ **Mid-range**
① *Gran Duca*
Piazza Micheli 16
Tel. 05 86 89 10 24, fax 05 86 89 11 53
www.granduca.it
This full-service hotel lies opposite the
harbour in an ideal location. The
perfect starting point for visits to the
islands.

② *Villa Tramonto*
San Vincenzo, Riviera degli Etruschi
Via Sirena 16
Tel. 05 65 70 18 58, fax 05 65 70 69 00
www.hotelvillatramonto.com,
12 rooms
The absolutely beautiful location right
on the sea and with its own beach
makes this small family hotel a top
address for seaside holidays. All of the
rooms have recently been renovated.
Lounges and sunshades are included
with the room. The only small disadvantage: the breakfast is authentically Italian, i.e. a bit small.

What to See in Livorno

Piazza della Repubblica From the main railway station go to the centre via the oval Piazza della Repubblica, which covers part of the Fosso Reale. Statues of Grand Dukes Ferdinand III and Leopold II, both from the 19th century, face each other on the large historic square.

Via Grande, Piazza Grande, Duomo The modern Via Grande, Livorno's main shopping street, begins at Piazza della Repubblica. At the intersection with Via Cairoli, where the cathedral stands, it broadens into Piazza Grande. The cathedral was built between 1594 and 1606, and rebuilt exactly like the original after being destroyed in 1943.

On Piazza Micheli, which opens up to the harbour, stands Grand Duke Ferdinand I (1587–1609), represented as the liberator of the seas and successful fighter against piracy. This is shown by the four slaves who writhe in their chains at the foot of the monument – for this reason it is also called the »Moors' monument«. The old harbour is called the Porto Mediceo after its founders.

Quattro Mori, Porto Mediceo

At the northern end of the old harbour stands the Old Fort, built in 1521–1523 by Antonio da Sangallo on orders from Cardinal Giulio de Medici. The complex has a high tower, a survival from an older fortification of the 11th century (viewing upon appointment). Between the Old Fort and the New Fort on the northern edge of the old city the merchants' quarter Venezia Nuova grew after 1629. The **quarter is characterized by canals and bridges** and is one of the prettiest parts of Livorno. The oil warehouse Bottini dell'Olio, built in 1705, is now a hand some venue for exhibitions. In the church of Santa Caterina a *Coronation of the Virgin* by Giorgio Vasari is the artistic highlight. Follow Fosso Reale eastwards to get to the New Fort, a fortification surrounded by water channels that was built in 1590 and is a park today.

Fortezza Vecchia
✸
Venezia Nuova, Fortezza Nuova

Livorno has several museums. Villa Maria lies in the south-eastern part of the old city surrounded by a park. It is of most interest for opera fans, because the museum housed here is dedicated to the life and work of the composer Pietro Mascagnano, who was born in 1863 in Livorno (closed temporarily). The **Museo Civico** has been in Villa Mimbelli on Via San Jacopo in Aquaviva since 1997. It exhibits work of the Macchiaioli group of artists around Giovanni Fattori (1825–1908). The Macchiaioli cast off the academic style and oriented themselves to the upcoming Impressionist movement. Amadeo Modigliani (► Famous People), who came from Livorno, studied with the Macchiaioli before he went to Paris (hours: Tue–-Sun 10am–1pm). The nearby Villa Henderson from the 18th century houses the **museum of natural science** (hours: Tue–Sun 9am–1pm and 3–7pm). At Terrazza Mascagni the city aquarium presents the wonders of the Mediterranean underwater world and has a research institute for marine biology.

Museums

> **?** **DID YOU KNOW …?**
>
> ■ The »Macchiaioli« were in their time the most progressive artists in Tuscany. But they were not taken seriously in the established art circles, as you can easily see by their name: they were called »spot painters«.

The city's most pleasant side is south of the harbour area, where it is greener and there are more and more views of the sea. Along Viale Italia, which follows the coast to the south, there is a succession of green areas, art nouveau villas with imaginative towers and small beaches.

✸
Viale Italia

Livorno is no beauty, but the city has its charms – like here on Piazza dell Repubblica.

✳ Riviera degli Etruschi

Coast south of Livorno

The broad Viale Italia turns into a coastal road that runs right along the sea south of Livorno. The Riviera degli Etruschi (Etruscan coast) begins south of Livorno and extends to ►Piombino and then continues as the coast of the ►Maremma up to the border to Latium. The Riviera degli Etruschi is popular among beach lovers as several beautiful stretches of coastline here are well suited for swimming and water sports. The section up to Rossignano Marittimo has the most interesting scenery, since the mountains come right up to the coast here. South of Rossignano the mountains retreat and the coast becomes flat. Here the beaches are wider and bordered by pine forests.

✳ **Quercianella**

After Calafuria the coastal road passes Quercianella, a likeable beach resort with many private holiday homes under shady pines and a stony beach which can be reached over steep steps.

✳ **Castiglioncello**

About 8km/5mi further is the pretty and very leafy seaside resort Castiglioncello, where the wealthy took their holidays in the 19th century. The continuing popularity of Castiglioncello can be seen not least in the **wide selection of hotels and bed & breakfasts** and the comparatively high prices. In Castello Pasquini with its attractive 19th-century park above the through road there are Italian language schools.

But Castiglioncello is not the place to seek solitude, as bathing areas are lined up along the small sandy bay.

The old mountain village of **Rosignano Marittimo** is beautifully situated below a castle on the top of a hill about 3km/2mi inland. From here it can easily be seen how the landscape gets flatter and the hills withdraw into the interior. Further to the south the towns become less attractive, the beaches broader and there are more camp grounds. The pines of the »Pineta«, which is a protected nature reserve, grow all the way to the fine-grained sandy beach and stretch from Cecina to Marina di Bibbona near Bolgheri. Sun worshippers can be found above all at Vada, as this town has one of the most beautiful beaches on the Etruscan Riviera.

! *Baedeker* TIP

Picnic with a view
About 10km/6mi south of Livorno the coast road suddenly starts to climb and leads around the rocky cape called Calafuria. Park your car along the road and go to the moderately steep coast to climb around on the red rocks, sunbathe or have a wonderful picnic.

✱
◀ Vada beach

The town itself attracts less attention than the bathing resort Marina di Cecina right next to it, where holiday-makers swim in the sea or the Aquapark and have a choice from a wide range of accommodation, including six camp grounds. Anyone interested in Etruscan culture should visit the museum in Cecina, where excavation finds from the Etruscan necropolis are preserved (info at www.comune.cecina.li.it).

Cecina,
Marina di Cecina

◀ Museo Etrusco-Romano

It takes just about a half hour to get from Marina di Cecina to Bolgheri. It is worth it! The **cypress-lined road**, straight as an arrow between twin rows of tall, proud trees, runs 5km/3mi from San Guido to Bolgheri and can be seen from far off. The poet and Nobel laureate Giosué Carducci described the avenue in his ode *Davanti a San Guido* and thus immortalized this pretty old village.

Bolgheri

San Vincenzo, just 30km/19mi south of Cecina, is famous for wide, white sandy beaches (those south of the town are accessible to the public) and a dense pine forest that runs right up to the beach. The well-known holiday village Riviera degli Etruschi is also here.

✱
San Vincenzo

For an alternative to the beach, drive inland to the archaeological park between San Vincenzo and the picturesque hill town of Campiglia Marittima (turn off about 5km/3mi after San Vincenzo). The extensive park was established in 1996 and is still being developed – also great for a walk, by the way. It documents the long **history of metal mining** in this region, which goes back to Etruscan times. The exhibition in the visitor centre introduces the subject, which becomes even clearer upon touring the ruins of the medieval miners' town of Rocca San Silvestro with a partially preserved town wall and a guided tour of the Miniera del Temperino, a 360m/390yd-long shaft that is part of the mining museum.

✱
Parco Archeologico Mineraio di San Silvestro

Campiglia Marittima The admission ticket to the park is also valid for the archaeological museum in the Palazzo Pretorio in Campiglia Marittima (hours: from Pentecost daily except Mon, otherwise only Sat, Sun and holidays and upon appointment, tel. 05 65 83 86 80).

✳ Populonia and San Cerbone

Necropolis of an Etruscan city Populonia was one of the twelve cities of the Etruscan league. It became wealthy through its production of iron ore and had a population of about 25,000 at its zenith. The necropolis of Populonia, San Cerbone, is one of the best-preserved Etruscan excavation sites and thus a popular attraction on the Etruscan Riviera – from which the residents of modern Populonia also profit.

The town is on an elevation above the Bay of Baratti about 15km/9mi north of Piombino (▶ Elba). In the 14th and 15th centuries it was fortified with a castle whose towers offer an **excellent view of the bay**. Grave offerings, statuettes and vases as well as other finds from the necropolis of the Etruscan city can be seen in the small private Etruscan museum in Villa Gasparri (Via di Sotto).

✳ San Cerbone Earliest traces of Etruscan **Pupluna** go back to the 9th century BC. In Portus Falesia the Etruscans smelted the copper ore of the Colline Metallifere and the iron ore of the island of Elba at an early date. The wealthy iron industry brought prosperity to the harbour; its ships sailed to Greece and Asia Minor. Rome, which became an ally of Populonia around 300 BC, also profited from the iron smelting until the city was destroyed in the confusion of the civil war between Sulla and Marius in the 1st century BC. Populonia's necropolis, San Cerbone, lay outside of the city to the east. It was in use from the 9th until the 2nd century BC. Until the beginning of the 20th century the burial site was covered with slag from the smelting ovens of Populonia – and so was well preserved. From 1908 the slag was smelted to extract ore again and the grave sites were exposed. Most of the finds went to the archaeological museum in Florence, but the graves can still be viewed locally. There are three types of grave: the oldest are chamber graves which were carved out of tuff stone and the so-called tumuli, burial mounds that are covered with grass today and have a »false« vault made of overhanging stones. Aedicula graves are newer. These constructions of ashlar stone with saddle roofs made of flagstones look like small free-standing houses or temples.

Islands

Isola di Gorgona Gorgona, only a little more than 2 sq km/0.7 sq mi in size, is the northernmost and smallest of the islands of the Tuscan archipelago. It lies a good 20 nautical miles off the coast of Livorno and can be reached from the harbour by car ferry in about 1 hour and 20 minutes. Since it is still used as a prison colony only organized guided tours are allowed on the island (information and reservations in Livorno in the Ufficio Turismo, tel. 05 86 89 81 11 or through the Cooperativa Parco Naturale Isola di Gorgona, tel. 05 86 88 45 22).

Capraia, 35 nautical miles from Livorno, was also a prison colony until 1987. Now the 19 sq km/7.3 sq mi island is in the hands of water sports fans, especially **divers and snorkellers**. The infrastructure is still being developed, but the fact that the island is part of a nature reserve means that the development will, fortunately, be limited. Ferries of the Torema shipping company sail on the route Livorno – Gorgona – Capraia – Elba (to Capraia about 3 hours), and in the summer numerous private yachts sail to the island.

Isola di Capraia

Monte Castello is its highest peak at 447m/1,467ft. The only town on the island is Capraia on the northern coast above the harbour. Its fortress San Giorgio was carved out of the cliff in the Pisan era and strengthened in the 14th century by the Genoese. South-east on Monte Campanile common buzzards and kestrels can be seen, while sea birds like the common shag and the herring gull nest in the steep cliffs of the unapproachable west coast.

Islands ahead: the ferries run from Livorno to Corsica, Elba and the smaller islands of the Tuscan archipelago.

✳ Lucca

Province: Lucca (LU)
Population: 85,000

Altitude: 19m/62ft above sea level

For many people Lucca is the definitive Tuscan city – open, lively, but still with an agreeable atmosphere. The romantic old city streets are an attractive ambience for browsing in traditional shops. Lucca is a city for lovers of good pastries. The delicacies are produced according to old recipes; castagnaccio, for example, a sweet chestnut cake, or buccellato, a yeast cake with aniseed and raisins, best eaten warm from the oven.

The name of the city is thought to derive from the Etruscans, who called a swamp between the tributaries of the Serchio River »luk«. The name was passed on to the Roman colony Colonia Luca, where Julius Caesar, Gnaeus Pompeius and Marcus Licinius Crassus met in 56 BC to form their triumvirate. The Holy Roman emperors favoured Lucca, so that it was the largest community in Tuscany into the high Middle Ages, more important even than Florence and Pisa. The **production of soap and brocade** as well as gold leaf brought wealth. The self-confident Lucchese fought and won their independence as early as 1117. Under the rule of condottieri (mercenary leaders), Lucca temporarily regained its independence from Emperor Charles IV in 1369.

History

From Porta Vittorio Emanuele to Piazza San Michele

Walkers and cyclists have a beautiful recreation area on the park-like city fortifications with a wonderful view of the old city and the silhouette of the Apennines. The first wall with four gates of massive limestone blocks already stood in Roman times. When the settlement spread to the north-east the new parts were also enclosed in a wall in the 12th–13th centuries. In the 14th century on the order of Castruccio Castracani another fortification, the Augusta, was built within the city walls. Today the old city is surrounded by a 4.2km/2.6mi long **wall with eleven bastions** (baluardi) and six gates. This fortification, 12m/40ft high with foundations 30m/100ft thick, was built between 1504 and 1645 by Flemish engineers and defended with 126 large cannons. The massive wall did not protect the city from attacks but from the floods of the Serchio River. Maria Luisa of Bourbon, Duchess of Parma, had the broad wall planted from 1823 to 1832 and a tree-lined avenue built. Thus the fortification became a **park for strollers and cyclists**.

★★
A walk on the
city wall

← *Lighting creates atmosphere in the streets of Lucca*

⏵ VISITING LUCCA

INFORMATION

Piazza Guidiccioni 2
Tel. 05 83 49 14 05, fax 05 83 49 07 66
www.lucca.tourist.it
Offices also on the Piazzale Verdi and
at Porta Elisa.

SHOPPING

Lucca is a city for people who like to
shop in traditional shops. Of course
there are boutiques with modern
fashions, but Lucca's specialty is family-run businesses which have existed
for generations. Most of them are in
Via Fillungo.

Vineria Marsili Costantin
Piazza San Michele
Shop for spirits and gourmet foods
with an absolutely enticing selection.

Pasticceria Taddeucci
Piazza San Michele (Nr. 34)
Wonderful, old-fashioned pasticceria
founded in 1881.

Carli
Via Fillungo 95
A little paradise for lovers of old
jewellery and fine table silver.

Lucca Plan

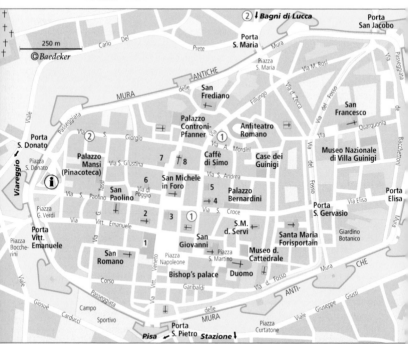

1 Palazzo della Provincia	3 Palazzo Pretorio	Where to eat	Where to stay
2 Sant' Alessandro	4 San Cristoforo	① Antica Locanda dell' Angelo	① La Luna
		② Da Giulio in Pelleria	② San Marco

Caffè Casali
Piazza San Michele
Here are authentic Toscani cigars made in Lucca – by hand of course. The display is a feast for the eyes even for non-smokers.

Cerri
Via Fillungo 178
Lucca has a long tradition of producing fabric. Dressing in good-quality cloth is here – as in Florence – a matter of courtesy. A special service of this cultured shirt shop: have shirts monogrammed – within a few minutes, your own shirts as well.

WHERE TO EAT
▶ **Moderate**
Antico Caffè di Simo: see p.279

① *Antica Locanda dell'Angelo*
Via Pescheria 21
Tel. 058 34 77 11
www.locandadellangelo.it
Closed Sun evenings and Mon
Food has been cooked and eaten here since 1414. Family-run business where mama creates classic dishes as if by magic.

▶ **Inexpensive**
② *Da Giulio in Pelleria*
Via delle Conce 45
Tel. 058 35 59 48
Closed Sun
Popular trattoria with cheerful staff where you will be inducted into the secrets of Lucchese cuisine at well-scrubbed tables. The spelt soup is irresistible.

WHERE TO STAY
▶ **Mid-range**
① *La Luna*
Via Fillungo, Corte Compagni 12
Tel. 05 83 49 36 34, fax 05 83 49 00 21
30 rooms, 2 suites
www.hotellaluna.com
The hotel is right in the middle of Lucca; only a stone's throw from Piazza Anfiteatro.

② *San Marco*
Via San Marco, tel. 05 83 49 50
Fax 05 83 49 05 13, 42 rooms
Located near the city wall; San Marco was once a factory, later a church and then a cinema. Today it is a fully air-conditioned hotel with a garden in a quiet location!

The following walking tour begins on the west side of the old city behind Porta Vittorio Emanuele. Just a few steps to the north of this large city gate is the tourist information with hotel reservation service and a place to leave luggage. Walk through Via San Paolino where some shops are open Sundays towards the centre of the city.

Porta Vittorio Emanuele

About 100m/110yd to the north of the intersection of Via San Paolino and Via Galli Tassi is Palazzo Mansi (no. 43). The outwardly simple 16th-century palazzo was altered in the 18th century in ornate Baroque; today it is the home of the state picture gallery. The collection, which is well worth seeing, has Venetian, Flemish and Florentine painting as its focus. Most of the paintings were a gift of Grand Duke Leopold II to the city on its incorporation in the Grand Duchy of Tuscany in 1847. The highlights include works by Fra Bartolommeo (*God the Father with Mary Magdalene and St Catherine*), Dome-

Pinacoteca Nazionale e …
… Museo di Palazzo Mansi

nico Beccafumi (*Abstinence of Scipio*, 1520–1530) and the Mannerist Pontormo (*Portrait of the Young Alessandro Medici*, 1525), as well as *Peter the Hermit before the Doge* by Paolo Veronese, Andrea del Sarto's *St Anne with Mary and Jesus* and paintings by Bronzino, among which are several portraits of rulers (hours: Tue–Sat 8.30am–7pm Sun 8.30am–1pm).

San Paolino, Piazza Cittadella

Continue on Via San Paolino to the only Renaissance church in Lucca, which probably occupies the site of a Roman temple and was built between 1522 and 1539. In the presbytery an early Christian sarcophagus in which St Paulinus is interred bears a depiction of the Good Shepherd. Both of the choir lofts are works of Nicolà and Vincenzo Civitali. A few steps further on the left is the little Piazza Cittadella. Here the ice-cream parlour Gelateria Santini and Café Cittadella are tempting places to take a break and watch the life of Lucca go by before arriving at Piazza San Michele.

Around Piazza San Michele

Piazza San Michele, Palazzo Pretorio

✷ The heart of Lucca beats at Piazza San Michele. The square, surrounded by restored medieval merchants' houses and dominated by the white façade of the church of San Michele, is the **centre of the city**. Here, too, visitors who appreciate good shops and café life are spoilt for choice. The recommended addresses are Vineria Marsili Costantin on the east side of the square (see p.274) and the famous Pasticceria Taddeucci. The most striking building next to the church is Palazzo Pretorio on the south side of the square, which was begun in 1492 to designs by Matteo Civitali and completed in 1588 in the Renaissance style by Vincenzo Civitali. Its loggia on the ground floor is adorned by a statue of the architect.

San Michele in Foro

✷ In 800 there was already a chapel on the site of the former Roman forum. A new building, in the form of a columned basilica, was begun in the 12th century but only finished in the 14th century. The wonderful five-storey west façade was conceived for a larger building, which was never built. The top storeys have dwarf galleries whose columns are clad with stone of different colours; a larger-than-life-size statue of the archangel Michael crowns the gable. The Romanesque character of the building remained until 1512, when a vault roof replaced the flat wooden ceiling.

The large crucifix created by local artists around 1200 shows the body of Christ in stucco without a wound in his side, in a triumphant posture surrounded by painted scenes such as the entombment and a fine ornamental border. The white and blue terracotta figure (*Madonna with Child*) on the first side altar on the right is by Andrea della Robbia, while a panel from around 1480–1500 *St Roch, St Sebastian, St Jerome and St Helen* by Filippino Lippi adorns the east wall of the right transept.

In a side street south-west of Piazza San Michele, the church of Sant'Alessandro stands on the piazza of the same name. It is thought to date from the mid-11th century. The relief of Pope Alexander was not added until the 13th century. Blind arches from the 12th century decorate the apse; the baldachin portal in the side aisle is from the late 15th century. The columns and capitals of the austere interior are partly Roman spolia.

Sant'Alessandro

The birthplace of the celebrated composer Giacomo Puccini (► Famous People) is only a few paces west of Piazza San Michele in Corte San Lorenzo 9 off Via de Poggio. He was born here on 22 December 1858. A small museum with personal memorabilia tells the story of his life (hours: June–Sept daily 10am–6pm, Oct–May Tue–Sun 10am–1pm and 3–6pm).

Casa di Puccini

Northern Old City and Via Fillungo

From Piazza San Michele Via Calderia runs north to Piazza San Salvatore with a beautiful classical fountain from the year 1842. Here is also the church of San Salvatore, with its simple façade. It goes back to the 12th century and is framed by a residential tower, also from the 12th century. At the right side door is a richly decorated architrave with a miracle of St Nicholas by the master Biduino (1180).

Piazza San Salvatore

Buccellato, panforte or chestnut cake? In Lucca's pasticcerias you will be spoiled for choice.

Santa Maria Corteorlandini, Palazzo Orsetti

The church of Santa Maria Corteorlandini (entrance on Via del Loreto) was built at the end of the 12th century in place of the medieval courtyard building Corte Rolandinga. It is also called Santa Maria Nera because a copy of the Madonna of Loreto is revered here. A side portal with inscribed architrave, the bell tower and two choir apses remain from the Romanesque building, whose interior was given a Baroque facelift around 1719 with frescoes and stucco, column-framed altars and an **ornate organ loft**. Opposite the church lies the office of the mayor, Palazzo Orsetti, a Renaissance building from the early 16th century with two beautiful round-arched entrances.

✳ Palazzo Controni-Pfanner

The special feature of this palazzo, which was built around 1667 near the northern fortification belt, is its ornate staircase and pretty Baroque garden with statues and fountains. In the state rooms on the second floor a costume museum displays fashion and accessories from the 18th and 19th centuries (hours: March until 15 Nov, Tue–Sun 10am–6pm, otherwise upon request).

✳ San Frediano

Basilica San Frediano, which is dedicated to an Irish pilgrim monk and later bishop of Lucca who died in 588, was built between 1112 and 1147 in place of a 6th-century church. The fact that the church faces west is unusual and remarkable. The reason is that when the building was extended in the 13th century, and the existing baptismal chapel and Cappella della Santa Croce were integrated, the city walls already stood in the place where the church entrance would have been. The entrance was therefore placed on the east side and the apse with the altar on the west. A **gold mosaic** with Christ in an aureole dominates the façade, flanked by two angels with the twelve apostles in a row underneath. The design, which was heavily restored in the 19th century, is attributed to Berlinghiero Berlinghieri (around 1230). The tall, crenellated bell tower makes a charming contrast to the broad church façade.

Interior ►

In the Romanesque interior the unusually high nave with a flat ceiling stands out first. In the first chapel of the right-hand aisle there is an especially beautiful **Romanesque baptismal font** from the mid-12th century. The round lower basin has reliefs of the life of Moses around the outside. The depiction of Christ as the Good Shepherd with apostles or prophets shows Byzantine influences. The upper basin is shaped like a small temple. The fourth chapel of the left aisle, the so-called Cappella Trenta (1413), contains a rich Gothic marble polyptych with bas-reliefs by Jacopo della Quercia (*Madonna with Child and Saints*, 1422). The same artist made the memorial for the merchant Lorenzo Trenta and his wife. A Roman sarcophagus from the 3rd century contains the remains of the Anglo-Saxon King Richard, who died in Lucca in 729 while on a pilgrimage. The frescoes in the chapel of St Augustine include a depiction of how the revered Byzantine cross is transported from the harbour of Luni to the cathedral of Lucca.

The oval shape is not a coincidence but was defined by the former Roman theatre on which the beautiful Piazza del Anfiteatro was built.

From San Frediano it is not far to Piazza del Anfiteatro, which gains its atmosphere from the perimeter houses with bright façades and the typical green shutters. From the 2nd century the **Roman amphitheatre** stood here – hence the oval shape. In the Middle Ages houses were built over the walls of the arena, and their entrances or passages made use of the arches of the ancient spectators' stands. Until the beginning of the 19th century the square was completely covered by buildings. Only in 1830–1839 were the houses inside the oval torn down to create the square.

★

Piazza del
Anfiteatro

Fine old façades line Via Fillungo which runs north to south. Its many traditional shops, some of them extremely elegant, make it the main shopping street of Lucca. There are plenty of cafés here, too – as everywhere in Lucca.

★ ★

Via Fillungo

Among the most beautiful is the Antico Caffè di Simo (no. 58), which was Giacomo Puccini's favourite café. Later such illustrious guests as the poet Salvatore Quasimodo (1901–1968), Nobel laureate of 1959, came here. To this day the café is a popular meeting place with an old-time atmosphere.

★

◄ Antico Caffè
de Simo

A short detour from Via Fillungo leads east to Via S. Andrea, where a 44m/144ft-high tower with holm oaks growing from the top catches the eye. It is part of the Case and Torre Guinigi group of

★

Case and
Torre Guinigi

buildings, city houses of the noble family under whose rule Lucca flourished peacefully in the early 15th century. The two palaces which face each other were built in the 14th and 15th centuries and later rebuilt. The Loggia dei Guinigi on Via Sant' Andrea was once the centre of family festivities, but is walled up today (hours: March 9.30am–5pm, April 9am–8pm, May–Sept 9am–midnight, Oct–Feb 10am–4.30pm).

Eastern Old City

Via Santa Croce, Santa Maria Forisportam

Via Santa Croce, which is called Via San Paolino in the west, is the main axis at right angles to Via Fillungo. Follow it a short distance eastwards to the broad, three-storey Palazzo Bernardini, which was built around an elegant inner courtyard in the early 16th century. The ground floor has flat pilasters, the upper floors round-arched windows. On the next piazza is the 13th-century church of Santa Maria Forisportam. The name Forisportam means »in front of the gate«–the church was built outside the city gate and Roman walls. The **façade is Pisan Romanesque** and was never finished, but possesses three beautiful portals with decorations in an antique style. The early Christian sarcophagus inside the church is now used as a baptismal font (with depictions of the Good Shepherd and Daniel in the lions' den). The right aisle has a Baroque ciborium as well as two 17th-century altar panels, *St Lucia* and *Assunta* by Guercino.

Porta Santi Gervasio e Protasio

A few yards north-east of the church on Via del Fosso stands Porta Santi Gervasio e Protasio, also called Portone dell'Annunziata, next to the former city moat. The massive gate with two round towers was part of the 13th-century inner city wall which has all but disappeared now.

✶ ✶
Museo Nazionale di Villa Guinigi

⊙
Opening hours:
Tue–Sat
8.30am–7pm
Sun
8.30am–1.30pm

It is undoubtedly worth paying a visit to Villa Guinigi, about 300m/ 330yd north of the botanical garden. It was built in 1420 for the Lucchese patrician Paolo Guinigi and houses the national museum today (enter from Via Quarquonia). The interesting collection has everything from Etruscan grave finds to Roman mosaics, architectural fragments and medieval stonework, from woodcarving to altars and paintings. The **medieval art treasures** are especially impressive: e.g. the coloured marble relief *Madonna with Child* by the Lucchese sculptor Matteo Civitali (around 1470), part of the seating from Lucca cathedral and the choir screens from Santa Maria Forisportam. The showpieces include three superb crucifixes: a panel cross from around 1150 from the Servite church of Lucca, a famous cross signed by Berlinghiero Berlinghieri which was probably created after 1220 and a cross from the Convento di San Cerbone which is dated 1288 and signed. Among the paintings Fra Bartolomeo's Lucchese works stand out, especially the monumental *Appearance of God the Father to Mary Magdalene and Catherine of Siena* from the year 1509.

The Franciscan church opposite Villa Guinigi shows how quickly the **San Francesco** Franciscan movement spread in Italy: in the year that Francis was canonized (1228), just two years after his death, the construction of a Franciscan church was begun in Lucca. Today its interior shows above all work of the 14th and 17th centuries.

Via del Fosso, which runs along a canal, leads back to the southern **◄ Via del Fosso** part of the old city.

✳ Duomo San Martino

It is likely that as early as the 6th century Bishop Frediano of Lucca **History** established the church that became the cathedral in the 8th century. Bishop Anselmo da Baggio, later Pope Alexander II (1061–1073), had the church rebuilt. Now dedicated to St Martin, it was completely renovated from the 13th to the 15th century. The exterior has mainly Romanesque, the interior numerous Gothic elements.

The richly decorated Romanesque façade is the work of the Lombard **Façade** architect Guidetto da Como – an inscription in the first dwarf gallery bears the date of completion: 1204. The portico is the dominant feature of the ground floor. Above it are three floors with dwarf galleries which were probably intended to be crowned by a gable. Due to the campanile, the right side of the façade has two fewer arcade arches

The façade of the cathedral of Lucca is a wonderful sight at night, too, when it is illuminated.

DUOMO SAN MARTINO

✳ ✳ In the cathedral are some unique masterpieces: the grave of Ilaria del Carretto, a marble sculpture so finely carved that it seems to be made of porcelain; Tintoretto's *Last Supper*, painted in 1592, and the wooden crucifix Volto Santo which St Nicodemus is said to have carved out of cedar wood with the help of angels.

① Portico
In the mid-13th century Lombard sculptors decorated the portico with reliefs.

② St Martin on horseback
The sculpture was made around 1300 and shows the patron saint of the Franks, to whom the church was dedicated after Charlemagne conquered the Lombards in 774.

③ Interior
Inside coloured marble and several high-quality works of art await the visitor; they include Alessandro Allori's *Portrait of the Virgin in the Temple* in the right aisle (see foldout).

④ Sacristy
In the sacristy in the right aisle is the sarcophagus of Ilaria del Carretto, Marchesi di Savona, the wife of Paolo Guinigi who died in 1405, as well as

Domenico Ghirlandaio's brightly coloured altarpiece *Sacra Conversazione*.

⑤ Important altar paintings
Federico Zuccari's *Adoration of the Kings* (1595) and Tintoretto's *Last Supper* (1592) are above the second and third altars respectively on the right.

⑥ Grave of Pietro da Noceto
Considered to be Matteo Civitali's first work, completed in the late 15th century on the model of the Florentine tombs of Santa Croce.

The highlight of the year is the festival of light on 13 September. Every building in the historic centre is lit with candles and at 9pm a procession goes from the cathedral of San Martino through the old city.

FLORENTINVS CRISTOFORI FIL · PINGEBAT

The cathedral façade is an elaborate construction of white and green marble with three galleries, one above the other.

© Baedeker

Tomb of Ilaria del Caretto (around 1406): the dog at her feet is the »symbol of marital fidelity« (Giorgio Vasari).

The main attraction of the cathedral is undoubtedly the tempietto containing the Volto Santo, a small marble temple which holds a wooden crucifix carved by St Nicodemus, which according to legend was found in the Orient in the 8th century and brought to Lucca.

than the left. The slender six-storey bell tower, which is 69m/226ft tall, is made of brown stone at the bottom and light travertine at the top, and crenellated. The portico was decorated in the mid-13th century by Lombard artists with high-quality **sculptural decoration**. Four reliefs with scenes from the life of the church patron adorn the main portal. The right-hand portal shows *St Regulus with the Apostle's Creed, Disputing with the Arians*; his beheading is depicted in the tympanum. On the lintel of the left portal are the *Annunciation, Nativity,* and *Adoration of the Magi.* In the tympanum the *Deposition from the Cross* can be seen, excellent works from the period around 1260–1270; the last two are attributed to Nicola Pisano.

Interior The interior, which largely acquired its present form in the 14th and 15th centuries, holds several important works. The famous sculpture group of St Martin and the Beggar, dated about 1300, was originally on the west façade but is now on the inside wall. The statue of a rider, which is almost a free-standing figure, exemplifies the transition from Romanesque to Gothic style. In the right transept is the tomb of Pietro da Noceto, the secretary of Pope Nicholas V (1447–1455); it faces the grave of the patron Domenico Bertini. Both are by Matteo Civitali and are important examples of 15th-century funerary sculpture. To the right of the apse is the large tomb altar of St Regulus (1484) with a reclining figure in Renaissance style.

★ ★
Tomb of Ilaria del Carretto ▶ The free-standing marble tomb of Ilaria del Carretto, second wife of Paolo Guinigi, is by Jacopo della Quercia of Siena. It is a major work of the early Renaissance and stands in the sacristy. Ilaria died young in 1405 and is portrayed lying with a peaceful expression, as if she were only sleeping. Even though the robe is artistically draped in folds, her delicate form beneath can be recognized – a clear break with the »bodiless« Gothic rendering of figures. At her head is the coat of arms shared by the powerful Guinigi and Carretto; at her feet a dog watches as the symbol of marital fidelity.

★ ★
Volto Santo ▶ The most important religious and artistic work in the cathedral is the Volto Santo (Holy Face). The crucifix stands in a small eight-sided marble temple that was especially made for it in 1484 by Matteo Civitali. The miraculous image probably dates from the 13th century.

According to legend it was carved by Nicodemus from the wood of a cedar of Lebanon and had an adventurous journey to Lucca. It is still carried through the streets of Lucca every year on 13 September.

Museo della Cattedrale
🕒 In the cathedral museum, which has stood opposite the cathedral since 1994, the cathedral treasure, various altars and sculpted decorations are on display there (hours: Nov–March Mon–Fri 10am–2pm, Sat and Sun 10am–6pm, April–Oct 10am–6pm).

The bishop's palace on the west, which despite several restorations clearly shows the form of the 13th century, stands next to the cathedral campanile. It was also used temporarily as the cathedral office of building works.

Bishop's palace

Around Piazza Napoleone

The little Mannerist-style Palazzo Micheletti on the west side of the cathedral square was built around 1556 for the Bernardi family. A few steps further is the Basilica San Giovanni, which to be exact consists of two churches, Santa Reparata and the baptistery San Giovanni. The façade of Santa Reparata, a 12th-century construction, was completely rebuilt in the 16th century – only the middle door and part of the south façade were preserved. In the right transept of the church the funerary monument of Countess Matilda of Tuscany (1046–1115) can be seen. Emperor Henry IV and Pope Gregory VII met in 1077 in her castle of Canossa to resolve their dispute, the so-called investiture controversy about the powers of church and state; the penance of the emperor before Gregory VII was a high water mark of the influence of the papacy. The left transept gives access to the domed baptistery, which was renovated in the 14th century. Interesting discoveries were made under the floor of the double church. The remains of walls and floors testify to a house from Roman times and to several churches as well as a square baptistery from late antiquity.

Palazzo Micheletti, San Giovanni

A few steps further to the west the street opens into Piazza del Giglio with the classical theatre on the south side. The square merges almost without a break into the expansive tree-lined Piazza Napoleone, which was laid out in the early 19th century. It is closed to cars, to the benefit of the ambience and cafés there. In the middle is a **monument for Maria-Luisa of Bourbon-Parma**, who was very popular among the citizens of Lucca.

★
Piazza Napoleone

The entire west side of Piazza Napoleone is taken up by the stately façade of Palazzo della Provincia. It was built from 1578 to plans by the Florentine Bartolomeo Ammanati; from 1805 Napoleon's sister Elisa Baciocchi lived here. The Museo del Risorgimento on Cortile degli Svizzeri (no. 6) documents the Italian unification movement between 1815 and 1870.

Palazzo della Provincia

Around Lucca

Lucca lies both close to the sea (► Versilia) and close to the mountains of Garfagnana, where there are beautiful hiking trails and the once-famous hot springs Bagni di Lucca (►Alpi Apuane and Garfagnana). The route from Lucca towards Pistoia or Florence passes almost directly by the patrician villas and the Pinocchio Park in Collodi described below.

Sea and Mountains

In Parco di Pinocchio everything revolves around the famous long-nosed puppet.

Villa Reale

Villa Reale, also called Villa Orsetti or Villa Pecci-Blunt, lies about 6km/3.5mi west of Lucca in Marlia. The decorative residence was built at the beginning of the 18th century for the Orsetti family and expanded in the course of the century. In 1806 Napoleon's sister **Elisa Baciocchi** acquired it and had it decorated in the style of her time. The illustrious guests included not only Prince Metternich but also the virtuoso Paganini. The wonderful park was originally modelled after the Baroque garden of Versailles but was transformed into an English park in the 19th century.

✳ **Villa Mansi**

Villa Mansi is 14km/9mi north of Lucca, at the upper town limits of Segromigno in Monte (turn off from SS 435, then follow the signs through the town). The Mansi family from Lucca bought the villa in the early 18th century, remodelled it in Baroque style and had an English park laid out around. The **extensive garden with some very old trees** is the biggest attraction of Villa Mansi today, but the interior is disappointing. It can be rented for private parties but is also open for viewing – for a comparatively high admission charge!

✳ **Villa Torrigiani**

Villa Torrigiani is also surrounded by a wonderful old park; it lies a few miles to the east in Camigliano (signposted). Like Villa Mansi it originated as a country residence in the 16th century and was later given a Baroque appearance. The façade is charming with its figures of tuff stone, sandstone and marble. The furnishings, stucco work and ceiling frescoes from the 18th century can only be viewed as part of a guided tour, which lasts about 20 minutes (in English and Italian). Admission is also charged for the park (hours: March–Sept daily except Tue 10am–12.30pm, 3–6.30pm). ☉

About 5km/3mi further on the SS 435 toward Pistoia is the pretty mountain village of Collodi. Here, in his mother's birthplace and under the pseudonym Carlo Collodi (►Famous People), Carlo Lorenzi wrote in 1878 the *Story of a Mannikin*, later known as the *Adventures of Pinocchio* (Avventure di Pinocchio). Collodi's book is not only Italy's most famous children's book, but has also become an international bestseller.

Collodi, Parco di Pinocchio

The main attraction in Collodi is the amusement park below it, in which everything revolves around Pinocchio. A stroll through this amusing **outdoor museum with 21 bronze figures** feels like a walk through a living fairy tale. Visitors meet Pinocchio, old Geppetto, the forgiving fairy with the blue hair, the falcon who freed Pinocchio when he hung in the oak tree, the talking cricket and the giant shark, while the two murderers tomcat and fox wait in the woods, hidden in coal sacks with large pistols sticking out. Children can play in the maze explore the pirates' grotto or climb on the corsairs' ship (hours: daily 8.30am–6.30pm).

Above Collodi the »villa with a hundred windows« is worth a visit. The manor was built from 1652 by Count Romano Garzoni. The frescoes in the villa were executed by the school of Carracci. The wonderful park gives one of the most beautiful examples of 18th-century Italian garden architecture with a maze of boxwood hedges, a Baroque garden, waterworks and outdoor theatre. Unfortunately the villa is closed for renovations, but the garden is open (hours: ☉ 9am until sunset).

★ Villa Garzoni and park

★ Maremma

M 5–P 13

Province: Grosseto

The southern part of the Tuscan coast between Piombino and ► Monte Argentario is called Maremma, which means »belonging to the sea, by the sea«. In fact in prehistoric times the area was part of the sea – as were the coasts to the south and north – before lagoons and fertile alluvial land gradually formed and finally a swampy plain developed. This area, once notorious for malaria, is now a nature reserve and homet to the Maremma cattle and their »cowboys«.

▶ VISITING MAREMMA

INFORMATION
Castiglione della Pescaia
Piazza Garibaldi 6
Tel. 05 64 93 36 78
Fax 05 64 93 39 54
www.castiglionepescaia.com

WHERE TO EAT
▶ **Moderate**
Pierbacco
Piazza della Repubblica 24
Tel. 05 64 93 35 22, www.pierbacco.it
Excellent fish restaurant with a pleasant atmosphere in the centre of

Castiglione della Pescaia. Closed Wed, Mon and Sun afternoon.

WHERE TO STAY
▶ **Mid-range**
Hotel L'Approdo
Castiglione della Pescaia
Via Ponte Giorgini 29
Tel. 05 64 93 34 66
www.hotellapprodo.com
Modern hotel right on the canal harbour. Almost all rooms have a balcony and sea view, 5-minute walk to the beach.

The characteristic features of the flat plains, which are bordered by the hills of the Colle Metallifere and the slopes of Monte Amiata to the east, are drainage canals, swamps, sand dunes, pine groves and pastureland. In order to preserve the typical Maremma landscape an area of about 70 sq km/44 sq mi south of Grosseto was set aside as a nature reserve – the Parco Naturale della Maremma. Long beaches of fine-grained sand, edged with dense pine forests and Mediterranean macchia, crystal-clear water, lonely coves and well-equipped campsites constitute the charms of this coastal region. There are particularly beautiful beaches on the southern Gulf of Follonica around the luxury holiday resort **Punta Ala** and the fishing village **Castiglione della Pescaia**. The sparsely populated, varied hinterland is perfect for cycling or hiking. There are pretty old mining villages like such as ►Massa Marittima and Etruscan cities like Populonia to see.

> ## ! *Baedeker* TIP
>
> **Cowboys up close**
>
> The mounted cattle drovers of the Maremma are known as »butteri«. They tend the free-ranging cattle and drive them over rough territory. Anyone who wants to watch can make a date to visit at Azienda Agricola di Alberese under tel. 05 64 40 71 80.

What to See in the Maremma

Golfo di Follonica Sun worshippers are attracted to the broad beaches of the Golfo di Follonica. Follonica was already known in antiquity for iron smelting, a sign of the early industrialization of the area. In the 16th century the Appiani ruled here; in the 18th century the grand dukes of Tuscany promoted the foundry Fonderia di Ghisa at the eastern edge of town.

In the mid-19th century Carlo Reishammer designed the typical iron architecture of the plant, which is used today as a library, archaeological museum and for an exhibition on the early industrial age.

This picturesque town 22km/14mi west of Grosseto is the pearl of the coast of the Maremma. The fishing town is popular in the summer and often booked up. The privately owned medieval **Rocca Aragonese**, which dates from the 14th–15th centuries, dominates the town from its mountain spur above the sea. The climb through pretty narrow streets is rewarded with a beautiful view. The area around the canal harbour, where the town grew, is much busier. The fish here is guaranteed to be fresh since fishing, along with tourism, is still an important source of income for the residents of Castiglione. The long, clean sand beaches stretch to the left and right of the mouth of the Bruna River. A little further away the beaches can be used free of charge.

✳
Castiglione della Pescaia

About 15km/9mi further to the north on a tongue of land lies Punta Ala, an elegant bathing resort. This is the exclusive part of the Mar-

Punta Ala

Tourists can enjoy the long sandy beaches at Castiglione della Pescaia.

emma: first-class hotels, orderly campsites, beautiful villas, elegant shops and a large yacht harbour. Sports are important in Punta Ala – from water sports to polo, everything is available. The 18-hole course of the **Punta Ala Golf Club** is among the most beautiful in Italy (►Baedeker Tip p.102).

Marina di Grosseto

This small coastal village lies in a beautiful cove about 12km/7.5mi south of Castiglione della Pescaia. It was originally the local beach for the residents of Grosseto, but thanks to its broad expanse of sand and pine forests it has developed into a popular holiday resort. Unfortunately there has been much construction work recently, as Marina di Grosseto is intended to become the most modern bathing resort in the Maremma.

Principina a Mare

3km/1.8mi south of Marina di Grosseto is Principina a Mare, a small beach and villa resort at the edge of the nature reserve Parco dell'Uccellina with a sloping beach and dense belt of pine trees.

✴ ✴
Parco Naturale della Maremma

The coast between Principina a Mare and Talamone with the parallel mountain range Monti dell'Uccellina was declared a nature reserve in 1975. It is best to come in the spring or fall when the park is open daily between 9am and sunset and visitors can move about freely in the park. Summers are different: since the park can only be visited as part of a guided tour and only a certain number of visitors are allowed in each day, waiting periods can be expected. Moreover the reserve is then open only on weekends and Wednesdays from 9am until one hour before sunset. Private cars are not allowed in the park, except to drive to Marina di Alberese (parking lot). There is a shuttle service from the visitor centre to the starting point for hikes. Information is available in Alberese at the Centro Visite (in Via del Fante, tel. 05 64 40 70 98, fax 05 64 40 72 78).

Hiking trails

Eight beautiful hiking trails of various levels of difficulty (3–6 hours, mid June–Sept only with guide) cross the 100 square kilometres (40 square miles) of the nature reserve, the home of wild boar, red deer, badgers, stone martens, weasels, Maremma horses and the characteristic white Maremma cattle. On the banks of the Ombrone storks, small egrets and cormorants can be seen. One trail leads past ancient oaks to the ruins of San Rabano Abbey (10th century). On the so-called forest trail the most important species of tree and bush are marked. The tower trail passes the olive route and two of the eight old lookouts. There is an interesting variety of landscape features, including wave-eroded cliffs in the south and lonely beaches further to the north. The vegetation here, which can grow in a salty environment, gives way to Mediterranean macchia with garrigue and evergreens further away from the shore.

Natural tunnel: avenues of pines in the Maremma →

Paludi di Trappola ► North of the mouth of the Ombrone in the swampy Paludi di Trappola, little coastal lakes alternate with flat dunes; the inland areas have been drained. The characteristic sight in this area are the half-wild **Maremma cattle** which graze all year on the fertile pastures of the former malaria swamps. In the winter the inland bodies of water harbour countless migrating birds. South of the Ombrone lies a compact area of dunes, interrupted by small marshy low-lying areas and extended groves of shady stone pine.

Monti dell'Uccellina The Monti dell'Uccellina, whose highest peak is the 417m/1,368ft Poggio Lecci, constitute the central and southern part of the park. Dense macchia forests with holm oak, maple, mountain ash and strawberry trees grow on these hills. Only the lower parts of the eastern slopes are used as pasture and olive groves.

Talamone Talamone, a pretty little fishing village on the rocky foothills at the southern end of Monti dell'Uccellina, has a wonderful panoramic view of the wide Gulf of ►Monte Argentario. The coast is not suitable for swimming since it is mostly rocky or has no access to the sea. The Sienese, who ruled Talamone in the Middle Ages, built the castle above the town in the 15th century.

★★ Massa Marittima

L 8

Province: Grosseto (GR) **Altitude:** 380m/1,247ft above sea level
Population: 8,700

Marittima means »on the sea«, and Massa possibly really lay on the coast in earlier times. Today, however, this wonderful town now lies almost 20km/12mi inland at the edge of the ►Maremma on a hill in the southern foothills of the Colline Metallifere. Torre del Candeliere, at the highest point in Massa, commands a fantastic view over the beautiful surroundings.

Mining town The Etruscans and Romans exploited the lead, copper and silver deposits of the Colline Metallifere. Massa's rise to be the main centre of the Maremma began in the 8th century. Around the year 1300 the mining town had about 10,000 residents; in 1310 the first mining law passed in the free town, the Codice Mineraio, determined mining rights, royalties and profit distribution. Under Sienese rule mining stopped from the middle of the 14th century and resumed only in the 19th century. Swamp fever caused a decline in the population and the economic importance of Massa until the 19th century. After the swamps were drained the city enjoyed new prosperity, but mining ceased once again.

▶ VISITING MASSA MARITTIMA

INFORMATION
Via Todini 3 / 5
Tel. 05 66 90 27 56
Fax 05 66 94 00 95

EVENTS
Balestro del Girifalco, the town festival with archery contest in medieval costume, on
20 May or the following Sunday.

WHERE TO EAT
▶ Moderate
Osteria da Tronca
Vicolo Porte 5
(near the cathedral square)
Tel. 05 66 90 19 91
Only open evenings, closed Wed
Comfortable osteria with typical dishes from the Maremma. Try the regional wines here.

Enoteca Balestracci
Via Ximenes 5 (at the cathedral)
Excellent wine shop with selected vintages and light dishes that suit them.

WHERE TO STAY
▶ Mid-range/budget
Duca del Mare
Piazza Dante Alighieri 1 / 2
Tel. 05 66 90 22 84
Fax 05 66 90 19 05
Old house newly renovated, location very central but quiet. There is even a pool in the garden.

Il Girifalco
Via Massetana 25
Tel. and fax 05 66 90 21 77, 30 rooms
ilgirifalco@massamarittima.info
Nice hotel at the edge of Massa Marittima in restful surroundings with garden and pool.

What to See in Massa Marittima

The centre of the old town is the broad, irregular Piazza Garibaldi, a square completely surrounded by medieval buildings that possesses both individuality and charm.

★ ★
Piazza Garibaldi

A broad flight of steps on the south side of the piazza leads to the cathedral, which was begun in 1228 in Romanesque style on the model of Pisa cathedral and completed in 1304 in the Gothic style. Round-arched blind arcades – the lower parts continue on the walls of the church – adorn the façade, which was built in the mid-13th century with the help of Giovanni Pisano. On the lintel of the main portal a carefully worked relief recounts five episodes from the life of the church patron St Cerbone. The church possesses outstanding works of art such as the baptismal font in the right aisle, which was made from a single block of travertine (1380) with reliefs by Giroldo da Como of scenes from the life of John the Baptist. The altar painting *Madonna delle Grazie* in the left choir chapel, which was executed around 1316, is attributed to the workshop of Duccio di Buoninsegna or Simone Martini.

Duomo San Cerbone

Another treasure is behind the high altar: the **sarcophagus of St Cerbone** (493–575), who was born in Africa and later became bishop of Populonia. Eight reliefs carved in 1324 by the Sienese sculptor Goro di Gregorio relate the life of the »Apostle of the Maremma«: Totila, king of the Goths, throws Cerbone into a cage of bears, but they set the saint free; Cerbone reads the mass, is the victim of libellous reports to Pope Virgilius and has to face trial in Rome, where geese prove his innocence; the saint milks a deer for emissaries of the pope and heals the sick.

Palazzo Pretorio

✳

Museo Archeologico ▶

Opposite the cathedral on the south-west corner of Piazza Garibaldi stands Palazzo Pretorio or Palazzo del Podestà (around 1230), which is built entirely of travertine stone. Its façade is decorated with the city coat of arms of Massa and Siena and the arms of the podestà. Today it houses the archaeological museum with finds from the excavation of Etruscan sites in Poggio Castiglione and Lago dell'Accesa.

The painting collection includes the greatest art treasure of Massa, a *Maestà* painted by Ambrogio Lorenzetti around the year 1335 which was discovered in 1867 in this very monastery. The panel painting shows Mary as a loving mother with her child, seated on a throne to which lead steps personified as faith (fides), hope (spes) and love (caritas), while numerous apostles, doctors of the church and angels kneel devoutly at the feet of the mother of God (hours: April–Oct Tue until Sun 10am–12.30pm, 3.30–7pm, Nov–March only until 5pm).

Small town, great place: Piazza Garibaldi in Massa Marittima is one of the most fascinating squares in all of Tuscany.

For the neighbouring travertine palace three Romanesque residential towers of the 13th and 14th centuries were joined together to form an imposing building. The office of the mayor is decorated with 16th-century frescoes.

Palazzo Comunale

The narrow Via Moncini, a street of craft workshops, leads up to the fortezza, fortifications that were strengthened by the Sienese in the 14th century. Its well-preserved remains include the graceful Arco dei Senesi (1337) and the massive Torre del Candeliere (1228), where a visit to the observation platform is an absolute must – even though the steps to the top are extremely narrow and dizzily steep (hours: April–Oct daily except Mon 10am–1pm, 3–6pm, Nov–March daily except Mon 11am–1pm and 2.30–4.30pm).

✦ Fortezza, Torre del Candeliere

Opposite in the 16th-century Renaissance Palazzo delle Armi, the mining museum (Museo dell'Arte e Storia delle Miniere) explains the golden age of iron-ore and mineral mining, with information on mining techniques and the composition of the rock. Hourly tours go to the 700m/765yd-long mine on Via Corridani, now no longer in operation (hours: in summer Tue–Sun 10am–12.30pm and 3.30–7pm, in winter only on appointment, tel. 05 66 90 22 89).

✦ Museo dell'Arte e Storia delle Miniere

Massa Marittima has further museums in store. A few steps east of the mining museum on Corso Diaz is the monastery church Sant'Agostino (1299–1313) in the Romanesque and Gothic styles. Its campanile was added to the cloister in 1627. In mid-2005 the new **city art gallery** opened here. The adjacent Complesso di S. Pietro all'Orto houses the **Collezione Martini**, a contemporary exhibition comprising 750 works. **Traditional olive presses** can be seen in the museum in Via Populonia (Museo Antico Fratoio; hours: April–Oct daily except Mon 10.30am–1pm).

Interested in more museums?

✦ Montalcino

L 11

Province: Siena (SI)
Population: 5,100

Altitude: 564m/1,850ft above sea level

Montalcino can be seen from far off because of its location on the ridge of hills above the rivers Ombrone and Asso. A castle towers over the town, which is surrounded by vineyards where the grapes for the famous Brunello di Montalcino grow. The town must have been surrounded by forests originally – thus the name »holm-oak mountain« (Mons Ilcinus). But the ground and the climate here were especially good for growing grapes, and the best wines from this area are world famous.

▶ VISITING MONTALCINO

INFORMATION
Costa del Municipio 8
Tel. 05 77 84 93 31, fax 05 77 84 93 43,
www.prolocomontalcino.it

EVENTS
The Sagra del Tordo takes place on the
2nd Sunday in August: parade in
historic costumes and archery contest.

WHERE TO EAT
► Moderate
Sciame
Via Ricasoli 9
Tel. 05 77 84 80 17, closed Tue
Cosy trattoria with regional specialties.
The homemade pasta and
spicy ragout of wild boar are recom-
mended.

WHERE TO STAY
► Luxury / Mid-range
Vecchia Oliviera
Porta Cerbaia
Tel. 05 77 84 60 28
Fax 05 77 8460 29
www.vecchiaoliviera.com, 12 rooms

Sleep in style where olives were once
pressed. Ask for a room with a view!
Friendly service, garden with pool.

► Mid-range
Al Brunello di Montalcino
Loc. Bellaria
Tel. 0577 84 93 04
Fax 05 77 84 94 30, 18 rooms
Friendly modern house with garden
and pool, about 1.5km/1mi south of
Montalcino.

Baedeker recommendation

► Budget
Porta Castellana
Via S. Lucia
Tel. and fax 05 77 83 90 01
www.portacastellana.it
This is the place for everyone who likes
unique accommodation. The three double
rooms have been carefully restored, and
Annalisa Mancini personally sees to it that
her guests are comfortable.

Brunello di Montalcino, which is produced only from Sangiovese
Grosso grapes, was developed by the Bondi-Santi family in 1842. 140
years later the garnet-red wine was the first in Italy to receive the
highest classification D.O.C.G. If the vines are younger than ten
years, ruby-red Rosso di Montalcino is pressed from the grapes. This
is the more affordable version of the costly Brunello, which is indis-
putably one of the best wines in Italy.

History A hill settlement already existed here in the Etruscan and Roman periods. The present town was probably founded by refugees from
Roselle in the 11th century. The free town on an ancient road wav-
ered between Florence and Siena in the Middle Ages. After the battle
of Montaperti (1260), when Florence was defeated by Siena and the
Ghibellines, Montalcino submitted to the Sienese, who then built a
fortress on the top of the hill.

What to See in Montalcino

It is best to park at Piazza Fortezza on the parking lot in front of the massive castle that was built in the mid-14th century under Sienese rule. Between 1555 and 1559 it was the refuge of 600 Sienese who had fled from their home city when it was besieged by Emperor Charles V and formed a kind of government in exile here. Today the castle has an excellent **enoteca** with all sorts of Brunello, pecorino cheese, wild boar ham and olive oil.

✱
Fortezza

From the castle follow Via Ricasoli, today the pedestrian zone, into the town centre. On the way be sure to stop in the former Augustinian monastery at Via Ricasoli 31. The former cloister and 12 other rooms of the monastery are an **atmospheric setting** for the sacred art in the city and diocesan museum. The late Gothic altar pictures, painted in sumptuous colours on a gold ground by Sienese masters like Simone Martini, Giovanni di Paolo and Bartolo Fredi, are all the more impressive for their simple and modest presentation. The museum's wood carvings from the 12th to 17th centuries are of high quality, as are two volumes of a 12th-century »Biblia Atlantica« from the neighbouring monastery Sant'Antimo and the terracottas from

✱
Museo Civico e Diocesano

Line up for the historic parade: every year for Sagra del Tordo Montalcino reverts to the Middle Ages.

⊙ the della Robbia atelier (hours: April–Oct daily except Mon 10am–6pm, Nov–Dec daily except Mon 10am–1pm and 2–6pm, Jan–March daily except Mon 10am–1pm and 2–5pm).

✴ **Piazza del Popolo**

The two squares Piazza Garibaldi and Piazza del Popolo a little further down, both on a slope, are the centre of the walled town. The slender high tower of the Palazzo Comunale, which is decorated with coats of arms, dominates Piazza del Popolo. Today it is the seat of the local administration and the Brunello and Rosso di Montalcino consortium. **Caffè Fiaschetteria** with its small marble tables, bentwood chairs and two large mirrors on the wall, has been a popular meeting place on this square since it opened in 1888.

City walls

For a view over the town take a walk on the medieval city walls. They are well preserved and were fortified with six gates and originally 19 towers.

Around Montalcino

✴✴ **Abbazia Sant'Antimo**

⊙ Opening hours: daily 10.30am–12.30pm, 3–6.30pm, Sun 11am mass with Gregorian chant

The former Benedictine abbey Sant'Antimo and its church, a jewel of Romanesque architecture, stand among meadows and olive groves in the gentle Starcia valley, 10km/6mi south of Montalcino. According to legend Charlemagne had the foundation stone of the monastery laid in 781 – out of gratitude for the end of a plague epidemic. Numerous donations enlarged the lands of the abbey to a princely fief and made Sant'Antimo one of the **wealthiest and most powerful monasteries in Tuscany** in the high Middle Ages. After the demise of the Staufer imperial dynasty, but presumably also because of the high costs of building the church, the monastery lands diminished towards the end of the 13th century, the convent declined and in 1462 was dissolved by Pope Pius II, who gave the ruins to the newly founded diocese of Montalcino. At the beginning of the 20th century the architect Giuseppe Partini initiated the restoration of the monastery, of which only the church, part of the chapter house and the refectory remained. Since 1979 Augustinian monks have occupied Sant'Antimo and it is open to the public.

The abbey was begun in 1118 and was constructed entirely of travertine stone. The architecture clearly exemplifies the **style of the Romanesque period**. Construction of the church stopped in 1260, leaving it without a transept. The aisles continue into and around the choir with its radiating chapels reminiscent of French churches. The shortened campanile stands to the north of the church; it was added in the 12th century. To the south stands the Carolingian chapel which is now used as the sacristy. The side doors are adorned by fine **reliefs with Lombard leaf ornament and animal motifs**. Columns and compound piers divide the interior of the 42m/138ft-long basilica into three aisles. The rich ornamentation of Burgundy-influenced Romanesque is uniquely evident in the capitals: eagles, griffons,

Its wonderful location at the end of a valley is part of the charm of Sant'Antimo.

sheep, rams and other animal motifs alternate with chequer and braided patterns. The depiction of Daniel in the lions' den (second column on the right), which is attributed to the Maître de Cambestany, is especially worthy of note.

Buonconvento

Almost 11km/7mi north of Montalcino is the romantic brick-built town of Buonconvento. It rose in the 14th century over the remains of the Roman fort Percenna on the Via Cassia and was surrounded by a wall modelled on that of Siena. On 24 August 1313, Emperor Henry VII died here on the way from Rome to Pisa; he is buried in the cathedral of ►Pisa.

★
Brick-built town

There is not much to see in Buonconvento, but a walk through the pedestrianized main street Via Soccini is nevertheless recommended. Near the old town hall, which can be recognized by its clock tower and the ornate floral decoration on the façade, is the Museo dell'Arte

Attractions

Sacra (museum of religious art; house no. 18). Along with liturgical items and clerical robes the little museum presents in carefully renovated art nouveau rooms a few panel and altar paintings of the Sienese school, including a *Madonna* by Duccio di Buoninsegna (hours: March–Oct Tue–Sun 10.30am–1pm and 3–7pm, Nov–Feb only Sat and Sun 10am–1pm and 3–5pm).

✱ ✱ Monte Oliveto Maggiore

Main seat of the Olivetans

On a wooded rise at the southern edge of the Sienese Crete landscape, just 10km/6mi north-east of Buonconvento, behind high cypress trees and a little away from the road to Asciano, lies the Abbazia di Monte Oliveto Maggiore, the mother house of the Olivetan congregation of Benedictines. Die »Abbey of the Great Mount of Olives« is visited particularly for its famous fresco cycle on the life of St Benedict of Nursia, a masterpiece of Italian mural art.

In 1313 the Sienese nobleman Bernardo Tolomei bid the world farewell and withdrew to this place with two friends in order to live an ascetic life according to a strict interpretation of the rule of St Benedict. In 1320 the foundation stone for the monastery was laid. It soon flourished and developed into a centre of spiritual and cultural life. Bernardo Tolomei died in a plague epidemic in August 1348 while nursing the sick along with 80 of his brothers in the order (hours: in winter 9.15am–noon and 3.15–5pm, in summer until 6pm; no admission charge).

Monastery and church

A shady avenue of cypresses leads to the entrance of the monastery complex, which is guarded by a crenellated gate tower (around 1393). Above each side of the monastery gate is a terracotta sculpture by Luca della Robbia. The monastery buildings were built of red brick between 1387 and 1514. The early 15th-century church was given a Baroque make-over in 1772. It has choir stalls decorated with early 16th-century intarsia and a large lectern that was designed by a member of the order in 1520. In the refectory, which dates from 1387–1390, are 17th-century frescoes by the lay brother Paolo da Alfidena. The monastery also has a library, pharmacy, chapter house, working quarters and living quarters, which can only be seen as part of a guided tour.

✱ ✱ Fresco cycle of St Benedict

The large two-storey cloister, built between 1426 and 1443, is the main attraction of the monastery. Abbot Domenico Airoldi of Lecco commissioned the murals, which were executed by the famous Renaissance painter **Luca Signorelli** after 1495 and the Piedmontese Giovanni Antonio Bazzi, better known as Sodoma, after 1505. The cycle consists of 35 scenes, episodes from the life of the founder of the order, St Benedict (around 480–547). Numbers 1–19 and 30–35 were painted by Sodoma, numbers 21–29 by Signorelli and his assistants.

The 35 episodes from the life of St Benedict begin on the east side of the cloister. First his childhood in Nursia is shown, and his taking leave of his family in order to study in Rome (1). Hedonistic and epicurean teachings do not convince Benedict, so he leaves the school in Rome (depicted in the background as Castel Sant'Angelo and Tiber River), in order to leave an ascetic life (2). In the following scene Benedict prays in the village of Affile and a broken wooden trough is mended miraculously (3) – the young man on the right of the spectators is a self-portrait of Sodoma. In the hermitage in Subiaco Benedict gets the robes for his order from the monk Romanus (4), who also supplies him with bread in his hermit's cave (5) despite all attempts of the devil to hinder this. At Easter Christ appears to a diocesan priest, who then brings his feast-day meal to the fasting Benedict (6). In front of his cave Benedict teaches the farmers of the area about God (7). When the spirit of unchastity haunts the isolated monk in a paradise-like landscape with erotic visions, Benedict castigates himself in a thorn bush (9). At the request of several hermits Benedict becomes their abbot, but his strict teachings find little response and the monks plan to kill him (10). When he crosses himself over the poisoned cup it breaks. Finally Benedict leaves the monastery (11). The saint now has 12 monasteries built to honour God.

Detail of the frescoes by Sodoma in the large monastery cloister

Frescoes on the south side Sodoma's fresco depicts the meeting between Benedict and two Roman boys, Maurus and Placidus, in a colourful and lively manner (12). Benedict liberates a possessed brother in the faith by physical castigation (13). He invokes a spring on a mountain top to supply three monasteries with water (14) and causes the axe-sheath of a fellow monk that had fallen into a lake to return miraculously to its place (15). When the monk Placidus falls while fetching water Benedict has the boy Maurus walk across the water to save him from drowning (16). Benedict tells a messenger who gave him only two jugs of wine and intended to keep the third one for himself that the jug would be transformed into a snake (17). In order to kill his opponents the jealous priest Florentius sends Benedict a poisoned loaf of bread, which is then taken away by a tame crow (18). The attempt to seduce the monks with seven pretty courtesans also fails – the monks remain chaste (19). The following fresco (1540), where Benedict sends the monks Maurus to France and Placidus to Sicily (20), is by Sodoma's son-in-law Bartolomeo Neroni, called Riccio, who is supposed to have depicted himself as the king of France in the painting to the left of Maurus. On the first of Signorelli's pictures a monk tells of God's just punishment: Benedict's opponent Florentius was killed by the collapsing walls of his palace (21). Benedict moves on to Monte Cassino and preaches the gospel to the residents – on the right of the picture monks take down a pagan statue of Apollo (22); he also removes idols and

Cloister of M. Oliveto Maggiore

drives Satan out of a stone (23). When the devil causes a monk to fall from a wall during the construction of the new monastery, Benedict brings the dead man back to life (24). Against the rules of the order two monks eat outside the monastery in an inn with two pretty maids, whereupon Benedict confronts them (25). He also reprimands the brother of the monk Valerianus for not keeping the fast (26). The king of the Goths Totila, too, cannot deceive the pious man: when Totila sends his shield bearer Riggo in shiny armour to Benedict, the saint orders the servant to take off the robes that he is not entitled to (27). In the background Riggo reports to the king. The magnificent clothing of the courtiers and knights is especially remarkable. Then Totila comes himself in order to pay his respects to the saint (28). Benedict also stands up to honour the king.

The following frescoes are by Sodoma. The first picture shows how Benedict prophesies to the noble Theoprobus the destruction of Monte Cassino by the Lombards, which is depicted in the foreground (29). Benedict feeds his monks with flour supplies that were multiplied miraculously – the fish on the table symbolize Christ's miracle of the loaves and fish in the New Testament (30). The saint appears to two monks in a dream and tells them to build a monastery in Terracina (31).

Frescoes on the north side

The monk with the plumb line is probably a self-portrait of the Olivetan Fra Giovanni da Verona, who designed the choir stalls in Monte Oliveto Maggiore. Two noble women who cannot find peace for their souls after death and rise out of the grave to attend a mass for the dead are redeemed by Benedict's alms (32). A young monk who has died cannot find peace in the grave until Benedict lays a consecrated host on him (33). When a monk wants to leave the monastery he meets a horrible monster just outside the walls; he sees this as a sign from heaven and returns penitently (34). With just a glance Benedict frees a chained farmer in the last scene from the hands of the thieving Goth Zalla (35).

✷ Monte Amiata

M 12

Province: Siena (SI) and Grosseto (GR)　　**Altitude:** 1,738m/5,738ft above sea level

Between the river valleys of the Orcia, Fiora and Paglia, the massif of Monte Amiata rises above the hills of southern Tuscany. Chestnut, oak and beech forests cover the slopes, where there are trails for long hikes. With a little luck mushrooms and chestnuts can be found in the fall; in the winter skiers populate the slopes. At the foothills of the extinct volcano, in Saturnia, Bagno Vignoni and Bagni San Filippo, there are opportunities to bathe in warm springs (25–52°C/77–125°F).

The peaks of Amiata are circled by a ring road which is quite steep in places, but is a rewarding drive. From the southern section a road runs up to the peak (Vetta Amiata) with restaurants and shelters, a radio tower and a cross of steel mesh (1910). This popular excursion site has a wonderful panoramic view.

✷
Vetta Amiata

What to See around Monte Amiata

State road no. 2 in the Formone valley passes Bagni San Filippo. The tiny village blessed with hot springs has a spa hotel. Despite appearances it has been renovated. Non-residents may often use the thermal baths.

Bagni San Filippo

Fosso Bianco ▶

A valuable and impressive alternative lies outside the village in the wooded valley: the waterfall »Fosso Bianco«, so called because of its white limestone sediments. The water in the natural basin below the waterfall is so warm that bathing is possible even in cool weather! For centuries the Tuscans have used the plentiful thermal springs not just here but all around the volcano Monte Amiata.

Abbadia San Salvatore

The former mining town lies on the eastern flank of Monte Amiata, at the edge of the Paglia valley between chestnut forests and pine groves. In the 8th century the Lombards built a Benedictine monastery here. Its church has survived and is the town's main attraction. In the newer part of the town mines and chimneys, now closed, are a reminder of the time when generations of miners excavated valuable mercury in Abbadia. From the abbey (see below) walk through the northern gate (Porta del Castello or Porta della Badia) to the historic town centre, which has preserved its medieval character quite well. Near Porta del Torrione are **the remains of a fort** which was passed in 1347 from the counts of Santa Fiora to the city of Siena and from them to the Medici. At the upper edge of the town on Viale Hamman the Museo Mineraio on the huge former mine compound has information on mining.

Abbazia di San Salvatore

The »Abbey of the Holy Redeemer« is one of the oldest monasteries in Tuscany. Historians still dispute over the actual age of the monastery: according to a charter of donation from the 8th century the foundation stone was laid in 743 by the Lombard king Rachis. Another version claims that the founder and first abbot was Erfo, a Lombard from Friuli who came here in 762. In the year 800 an epidemic presumably forced Charlemagne's troops to rest here while on the way to Rome to his coronation. As thanks for the healing qual-

ities of their herbs, the monks received generous privileges and lands a short while later. In the 11th and 12th centuries the monastic properties extended to Monte Cetona and from the Orcia River to Monte Argentario. The high point of their power was achieved under Abbot Winizzone who built a new church, dedicated in 1036. In 1228 the abbey passed to the Cistercians, and finally to Siena. The monastery was closed in 1782, but since 1939 it has belonged to the Cistercian order again.

A gently rolling landscape with meadows and forests in the foothills of Monte Amiata near Radicofani

The fact that the abbey church was built in the Romanesque style can still be seen clearly despite several reconstructions. In the aisleless interior of the upper church **17th-century frescoes** tell the legend of King Rachis. Next to it four Latin inscriptions describe a hunting trip of the king to Monte Amiata, where the Redeemer is supposed to have appeared to him – Rachis then took the vows of a monk and founded the abbey. The late 12th-century wooden crucifix to the right of the entrance, which is similar to the cross of the abbey of ►Sant'Antimo, was presumably made in Siena and based on Burgundian models. There is an impressive crypt with five aisles from pre-Romanesque times, whose vaults are supported by 28 trachyte columns with richly decorated capitals.

◄ Church

From Abbadia San Salvatore it is about 16km/10mi (via Piancastagnaio and Pietralunga) to the charming village of Santa Fiora (population 3,000), which occupies a 687m/2,254ft-high bluff south-west of Monte Amiata. The main square, Piazza Garibaldi, was built over the remains of an Aldobrandeschi castle. In the church of Santa Fiora e Lucilla **many beautiful terracotta works**, attributed to Andrea della Robbia, are to be seen. Below the village at the source of the Fiora River, Count Sforza had a walled-in fish pond built in his park where trout still swim today.

✳
Santa Fiora

▶ VISITING MONTE AMIATA

INFORMATION
APT Amiata
Via Adua 25, Abbadia San Salvatore
Tel. 05 77 77 58 11, fax 05 77 77 58 77
www.amiataturismo.it

WHERE TO EAT
▶ **Moderate**
Ainole
Arcidosso, Loc. Aiuole
Tel. 05 64 96 73 00
This restaurant lies between Arcidosso
and Monte Amiata in Bivio Aiuole.
Mother Bargali and her son Ugo run it
on the turn-off to Ainole. They spoil
their guests with local delicacies. It also

has accommodation. Closed Mon (and
in winter).

WHERE TO STAY
▶ **Budget**
Kappa Due – K2
Via del Laghetto 15
Abbadia San Salvatore
Tel. 05 77 77 86 09
www.hotelk2.net
Small family hotel 500m/550yd out-
side town in a chestnut forest. Res-
taurant in the house, regional cuisine.
The meat is grilled in the open
fireplace.

Arcidosso ✳

On the western slope of Amiata at 660m/2,165ft lies the romantic
mountain village of Arcidosso with a castle of the Aldobrandeschi
family, which was occupied in 1331 by the Sienese under their
commander Guidoriccio from Fo-
gliano and handed over to the
Medici in 1559. In the mid-19th
century the charismatic waggoner
David Lazzaretti (1834–1878) lived
in the village. In 1872 he founded
a brotherhood with about 80 poor
farmer and shepherd families in
order to »make the kingdom of
God real«. Since the »prophet of
Amiata« was a thorn in the flesh of
both the church and owners of lat-
ifundia, he was shot on 18 August
1878 by carabinieri during a peaceful procession. His grave is in the
cemetery of Santa Fiora.

! *Baedeker* TIP

Howl with the wolves

Not only children enjoy this attraction: Parco
Faunistico dell'Amiata south of Arcidosso,
where along with many other animals wolves
can be seen up close. In complete safety, of
course, since the path to the observation deck
in the middle of the wolf compound is protected
by a high mesh fence (tel. 05 64 96 68 67,
fax 05 64 96 77 20, www.parcofaunistico.it;
open daily except Mon from 7.15am until
sunset).

Giardino di Daniel Spoerri ✳

About 10km/6mi to the north, just outside the little hamlet of Seggiano (signposted), Daniel Spoerri, an active pioneer of experimental
art, created a small paradise with his »art garden« on a 15ha/37-acre
property on the slopes of Monte Amiata. More than 50 sculptures,
many by internationally known artists who are friends of Spoerri, are
spread over a wide area so that landscape and sculptures form a sym-

biosis. In the woods, for example, he hid a hotel room cast in bronze with all its furnishings and personal props (*Chambre no. 13 de l'Hotel Carcassonne Paris*); on the grassy parking lot in front of the actual entrance Susanne Runge's *Escalator Bench* stands as if by chance.

Because he was fascinated by the varied plant life of this region Spoerri, who claims that he knew nothing about plants until he came here, constructed an interesting botanical nature trail, a wonderful complement to the works of art. The art park is open all year round upon request. Information from tel. 05 64 95 04 57, fax 05 64 95 00 26 or www.ilgiardinodidanielspoerri.it.

⏰ Opening hours:
Easter –June Sat/
Sun 4–8pm,
July–Oct Tue–Sun
4–8pm

Monte Argentario

P 9/10

Province: Grosseto (GR)

Macchia-covered hills, gorges and grottoes, rugged bluffs and between them coves with small beaches, some of which are difficult to reach, characterize the landscape of Monte Argentario, the peninsula that extends into the Tyrrhenian Sea 35km/22mi south of ► Grosseto. Three small spits of land connect the mainland with the »silver mountain«, whose yacht harbour and palatial summer residences show that wealthy holidaymakers have created a high-class hideaway here. Susanna Agnelli, the granddaughter of the founder of Fiat and mayor, saw to it that no mass tourism developed here.

In prehistoric times the Promontorio dell'Argentario was an island off the coast. A spit 4km/2.5mi long and 500–600m (550–660yd) wide developed when the channel sanded up in the place where the town of Orbetello is situated today. Later the two outer sandbanks, the Tombolo di Feniglia in the south and the Tombolo di Giannella in the north, were formed and with them the Orbetello lagoon, which covers an area of 26 sq km/10 sq mi.

What to See on Monte Argentario

The real heart of Monte Argentario is the bustling Porto Santo Stefano to the north-west. The town has a spectacular location in a hollow which opens up towards the sea. Just a few decades ago it was a small fishing village. Today it is a bathing resort where luxury yachts anchor next to fishing boats in the harbour. Ferries depart from here to the islands of ►Giglio and Giannutri. In the 17th century the harbour was an important base for the Spanish merchant fleet for the middle and northern Tyrrhenian Sea. The fortress on higher ground dates from this period and commands a beautiful view of the holiday resort.

Porto Santo Stefano

Monte Telegrafo The highest elevation of Monte Argentario is Monte Telegrafo (635m/2,083ft), 17km/10.5mi to the south-east, which can be climbed from Porto Santo Stefano. On the cul-de-sac that turns off south from SS 440 (towards Orbetello), at a height of 275m/902ft, lies the Conventi dei Padri Passionisti (Passionist monastery), the mother house of the order founded in 1720 by Paolo Francesco Danei (St Paul of the Cross).

The road ends just before the peak where there is a transmitting station with a large antenna complex. On a clear day the view extends seawards all the way to Corsica and landwards to ▶Monte Amiata.

▶ VISITING MONTE ARGENTARIO

INFORMATION
Porto Santo Stefano
Corso Umberto 55
Tel. 05 64 81 42 08
Fax 05 64 81 40 52

WHERE TO EAT
▶ Moderate
Il Cantinone
Capalbio, Piazza Porticina 4
Tel. 05 64 89 60 73,
Closed Mon (not from July–Sept).
Elegant restaurant in Capalbio castle vaults. Regional cuisine of excellent quality is served here. In the summer there are tables on a terrace with a wonderful view.

Il Gambero Rosso
Porto Ercole, Lungomare Doria 62
Tel. 05 64 83 26 50, fax 05 64 83 70 49
This stylish fish restaurant is considered to be the best place in town. In summer food is served on the terrace with a view of the harbour (closed Wed).

WHERE TO STAY
▶ Luxury
Il Pellicano
Porto Ercole
Tel. 05 64 858 11
Fax 05 64 83 34 18
www.pellicanohotel.it

This exclusive hotel (32 rooms, 4 apartments) near Porto Ercole is one of the best in the Maremma. The villa is covered with wild grapevines and nestles into the steep cliffs of Monte Argentario. Antique furniture and paintings of the 18th and 19th century give the rooms a personal touch. There is a small private beach for sun-seekers.

▶ Mid-range
La Palma
Capalbio, Loc. Marina
Via di Chiarone 5
Tel. / fax 05 64 89 03 41
www.albergolapalma.com
Well-kept hotel and apartment complex with pool and whirlpool. 800m/875yd from the fine sandy beach Chiarone. Starting point for trips into the Maremma.

Vecchia Maremma
Orbetello, Statale 1 – Aurelia km 146, Quattrostrade
Tel. 05 64 86 21 47
Fax 05 64 86 23 47
www.vecchiamaremma.it
This comfortable house in the middle of the Maremma has a nice family atmosphere. Pool and garden on premises.

The main settlement on the east coast is the former fishing village Port'Ercole, which goes back to ancient Portus Herculis. The holiday resort has a picturesque location **on a small cove** bordered in the south by a mountain spur with an old fortress which, like Orbetello, was built by the Spanish around 1600. The small parish church in the pretty old town holds the grave of the painter Michelangelo da Caravaggio, who died of his wounds here on 18 July 1610.

Port'Ercole

The spit of land reaching out from the mainland, on which the town of Orbetello (population 15,000) is situated, was presumably already **settled by the Etruscans** in the 8th century BC. The city changed hands often during the Middle Ages. At first the Aldobrandeschi ruled, then the Orsini family before Siena took over in the period 1414–1455. From the mid-16th century the Spanish temporarily ruled Monte Argentario and made Orbetello the capital of their little »Stato dei Presidi«. In 1815 the peninsula was annexed to the Grand Duchy of Tuscany; in 1842 the spit was extended to Monte Argentario by means of a dyke and the lagoon was divided.

Orbetello

Orbetello has considerable remains of the Etruscan sea wall from the 4th century BC as well as the fortress begun in 1557 under King Philip II of Spain and completed in 1620 under Philip III. The cathedral was built in 1376 and enlarged in the 17th century with two aisles. The Gothic travertine façade is decorated with a beautiful portal and a bust of St Benedict. Opposite the cathedral, in the former Ursuline convent, a terracotta frieze of an Etruscan temple, which was found near Talamone, is on display (hours: daily Oct–March 9am–12.30pm and 4–7pm, April–Sept 9.30am–1pm and 4–7pm, July–Aug 9.30am–1pm and 4–8pm).

◀ Attractions

Around Monte Argentario

The ruins of the ancient city of Cosa lie about 7km/4.5mi south-east of Orbetello above the residential town Ansedonia at 113m/370ft elevation. Cosa was founded in 273 BC by the Romans, and around 130 BC was granted rights of Roman citizenship. However, as early as the 1st century AD many had left the town again – probably because of malaria. For a long time the remains of Cosa were thought to be Etruscan until an excavation by American archaeologists showed that the city was founded by Rome and was used as a defence against the Etruscans. The 1.5km/1mi-long **enclosing wall from the 3rd to 1st centuries BC**, which has a polygonal form and is fortified by 18 crenellated towers and three gates, in part still visible, is impressive. The Porta Romana in the north-east is best preserved. It is the entrance to the ancient quarters, which are spread over two hills. Outside the old city is the forum with a basilica, two temples and the walled acropolis on higher ground (upper city) with the 2nd-century capitol. Despite the unevenness of the terrain, the streets in the city centre are laid out in a grid. In a small museum ex-

★
Ruins of Ansedonia-Cosa

An idyllic bay: Cala Grande

cavation finds are on display, including two torsi from the Julian-Claudian era, parts of friezes and mosaics, amphora, dishes, bronze and silver coins.

Tagliata Etrusca Walk downhill past the massive Torre San Biagio built by the Saracens to the so-called Tagliata Etrusca (Etruscan cut), a drain cut into the tuff stone. The name is misleading: the drain was dug by the Romans who, however, largely owe their knowledge of waterway construction to the Etruscans. The channel, which is 2–2.5m/6-8ft wide, not only prevented the ancient harbour from silting, but also drained the low-lying interior and kept the small lake Burano from becoming swampy. Since 1980 it has been a riserva naturale, where the typical fauna of the Maremma and countless varieties of water fowl can be seen (guided tours only in the winter months, Sept–April Sun 10am–2pm).

✳ Capalbio About 18km/11mi east of Ansedonia lies Capalbio, a picturesque town with a well-preserved wall that can be walked on. The Castello dei Collacchioni can be viewed by giving advance notification at the town hall.

✳ ✳ Giardino dei Tarocchi On the coast road (Via Aurelia) about 20km/12.5mi south of Orbetello, just before the border to the province of Lazio, follow the sign »pescaia fiorentina« into the interior. The fantasy figures of the artist

Niki de Saint Phalle, who died in May 2002 at the age of 72, can be seen from far away. She fulfilled her lifelong dream in a former quarry in the village Garavicchio. Giant mythical creatures, winged monsters and shining towers rise up out of the olive grove where the sculptress worked from 1979 to 1997 to create her unique fantasy landscape. Niki de Saint Phalle began the tarot garden with her life partner Jean Tinguely. Tinguely built skeletons of steel mesh based on his wife's models, which were then covered with a 15cm/6in-thick layer of cement and decorated with glittering mirror fragments, colourful Murano glass and ceramic tiles. Every tile had to be formed and baked individually for the larger sculptures. The model for the 22 colourful figures was the ancient game of fortune-telling, tarock or tarot, whose cards can be used for both astrological and cabbala explorations of destiny. The strict symbolism of tarot is supplemented here with personal associations and symbols from other cultures.

🕐
Opening hours:
May–Oct
Mon–Sat
2.30–7.30pm

✴ Montecatini Terme

F 7

Province: Pistoia (PT)
Population: 20,500

Altitude: 27m/88ft above sea level

Montecatini is the largest and most elegant spa in Tuscany and one of the most famous thermal spas in Europe. In the magnificent facilities many members of European royal families, world-famous writers and Hollywood stars have sought remedies for their aches and pains. Montecatini has plenty to offer the 800,000 annual guests – most of them from the older generation. The attractions include horse races (on the local sulky track), fashion shows and conventions, high quality concerts and exhibitions.

The healing springs were known already in antiquity, as finds of Roman devotional offerings from the 1st century prove. In his book on Italian baths the doctor Ugolino Simoni mentions three bathhouses in the town and the efficacy of the water for curing liver disease in 1417. The water was drunk under the Medici, the owners of Montecatini after 1583, but the importance of the spa was only rediscovered in the 18th century. At the initiative of Grand Duke Leopold I the town was modernized and adorned with the glamorous establishments Regina, Terme Leopoldine, Tettuccio and Palazzina Regia after 1773.

When European spas became the meeting place for high society at the turn of the 19th to 20th century, **illustrious guests** came to Montecatini. Verdi completed his opera *Otello* here, and Puccini composed *La Bohème* in Montecatini in 1895.

▶ VISITING MONTECATINI TERME

INFORMATION
Viale Verdi 66
Tel. 05 72 77 22 44
Fax 05 27 01 09
www.montecatini.turismo.it

WHERE TO EAT
▶ Moderate
① *Pier Angelo*
Viale IV Novembre 99
Tel. 05 72 77 15 52
Closed Sun and Mon afternoon.
In a beautiful art nouveau villa on the edge of the spa park, Pier Angelo Barontini spoils his guests with modern, out-of-the-ordinary regional cuisine.

② *La Torre*
Montecatini Alto
Piazza Giusti 8 / 9
Tel. 05 72 706 50
Fax 05 72 732 08
Closed Tue.

As the name already says, this restaurant is in a tower in the upper part of Montecatini, right on the main square of the atmospheric little borgo.

WHERE TO STAY
▶ Luxury
② *Tettucio*
Viale Verdi 74
Tel. 057 27 80 51
Fax 057 27 57 11
Elegant house from the turn of the century (70 rooms) directly opposite the Excelsior Therme.

▶ Mid-range
① *Golf Hotel Corallo*
Viale Cavallotti 116
Tel. 05 72 78 288
www.golfhotelcorallo.it
A comfortable house with very helpful staff and an excellent restaurant.

What to See in Montecatini Terme

✱
Spa district

If Montecatini Terme has anything at all like a centre, then this is the expansive spa park and with it Viale Verdi, the main axis around which everything revolves. The tourist information office and the finest hotels are here; people stroll, watch, sit on benches and in cafés, chat and of course shop. Befitting a spa there are many pharmacies and perfumeries, stylish shoe and clothes shops as well as art galleries. To entertain younger guests the amusement park Parco Giochi Termeland (Viale Biechierai) is open at no charge.

✱
Spas

The fact that a cure in Montecatini is a rather exclusive pleasure can be seen in, among other things, the architecture of the baths. Impressive buildings on Viale Verdi include the **Stabilimento Excelsior**, which was expanded in 1968 with an eccentric but insensitive annex, and the **Terme Leopoldine** in the classical style, which was opened in 1775. The neo-Baroque **Terme Tettuccio** dating from 1927 at the end of a tree-lined avenue decorated with flowerbeds is also imposing. Even visitors who are not here for treatment should take a look inside this elegant facility. Beyond the colonnades there are wonderful pump rooms where the guests pick up their daily water ration. The monumental architecture opens up to a beautiful park behind the baths.

Take either the funicular railway or the winding road (past Terme Tettuccio) up to Montecatini Alto. The lower station of the funicular is at the north-east corner of the spa park. The funicular runs March, April and October 10am–7.30pm, May–Sept until midnight, on the half and full hour. The old town on the 290m/951ft high hill above the spa has a **wonderful view of the plain**. The centre is closed to cars, and the centrally located, somewhat sloping Piazza Giuseppe Giusti has been almost completely taken over by welcoming cafés and restaurants, although a small theatre from the period around 1900 has hung on. For a view of the surroundings instead of the bustle on the square, go to the terrace of Gran Caffe Il Giardino. There are beautiful views higher up, too, at the church.

★
Montecatini Alto
◄ Funicolare

Neo-Baroque ambience is part of the treatment:
in the Tettuccio spa the healing waters flow out of luxurious taps.

Montecatini Terme Plan

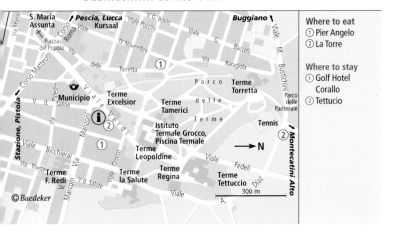

Where to eat
① Pier Angelo
② La Torre

Where to stay
① Golf Hotel
  Corallo
② Tettuccio

© Baedeker

Around Montecatini Terme

Monsummano Terme

An old city on the hill and spas below it are also the attractions of Monsummano Terme, about 5km/3mi to the east. The large Giusti dripstone cave with an underground lake was discovered here in 1849. The water temperature in the connected grottoes is as high as 34°C/93°F and creates highly effective atmosphere for sulphurous and alkaline steam baths, which are especially good for arthritis, metabolic disorders and bronchial illnesses. The attached thermal centre with an elegant four-star hotel offers balneo, fango and inhalation therapy. The grotto was named after the satirist Giuseppe Giusti, born in 1809 in Monsummano, who helped to prepare the way for the Risorgimento.

Grotta Giusti Terme ▶

Buggiano

Between Montecatini Terme and Pescia (see below) a steep road leads up to the fortified mountain village Buggiano. Of the medieval buildings the 13th-century Palazzo Pretorio is most noteworthy; its façade is decorated with coats of arms from the 15th and 16th centuries. The Romanesque parish church was established in 1038 for a Benedictine abbey and in part renovated in the 13th to 16th centuries. Inside the church, columns with ancient capitals on the right and pillars on the left support the arcades that separate the nave from the two aisles.

Villa di Bellavista

A few kilometres to the south-west is the magnificent patrician palace Villa Bellavista. The Florentine Antonio Maria Ferri was commissioned by the wealthy merchant Francesco Feroni, who had bought the estate from the Medici in 1671, to design the three-storey villa with four corner towers. The late 17th-century **ceiling frescoes** by Pier Dandini represent the triumph of faith, the love of virtue and the heroic deeds of the military commander Fabio Feroni. Giovanni Battista Ciceri decorated the twin alcoves in the west wing with beautiful white-gold stucco. The villa has been under restoration for some years and only parts can be viewed (only with advance notification, information at tel. 05 72 335 53).

? DID YOU KNOW …?

- … that Ivo Livi was born in 1921 in Montesummano Terme? He is better known under the name Yves Montand. The family had to flee to Marseilles from the Fascists when the future actor was three years old. In 1944 Montand went to Paris and began his career as a singer and »king of the French chansons«.

Pescia

About 10km/6mi north-west of Montecatini Terme on the SS 435 towards Lucca, the town of Pescia is situated in Valdinievole on both banks of the Pescia River, which supported the town's paper mills, silk weaving and leather tanning industry for centuries. Today asparagus fields, olive trees and flowers characterize the surroundings of Pescia.

Provincial town on the river

The river divides Pescia into two different parts. The bustling centre of the west bank is the oblong Piazza Mazzini, where there is a market every Saturday. The northern end of the square is dominated by the Palazzo del Vicario, embellished with coats of arms (13th–14th century) and used as a town hall today. At the nearby Piazza Santo Stefano the city museum in Palazzo Galeotti displays examples of Tuscan painting of the 14th–16th centuries. Nearby in the Palazzo della Podestà at Piazza del Palagio 7, about 230 works of the sculptor Libero Andreotti (1875–1933) are displayed, above all plaster busts and figures.

West bank

The cathedral attracts the eye on the east side of the river. The people who live on this side call themselves »Domaioli« after it. The Baroque church was built in the late 17th century on Romanesque foundations and became the seat of a bishop in 1726. The façade dates from the late 19th century, the massive campanile possibly from the previous Romanesque building. For art lovers the simple **Franciscan church** is far more interesting. It holds a famous panel from 1235 by Bonaventura Berlinghieri from Lucca with a depiction of St Francis and six scenes from his life. This painting of a man who had lived only shortly before and was canonized soon after his death – the figure in the centre surrounded by scenes from his life story – employed a pictorial composition that had previously been reserved for Christ and the Virgin.

East bank

◀ Duomo

◀ San Francesco

5km/3mi north of Pescia in the little town of Pietrabuona there is an interesting **paper museum**. The importance and the long tradition of the paper industry in the Pescia valley is documented clearly here. Visits only with advance notification (tel. 05 72 47 80 77).

Surroundings, Pietrabuona

Montepulciano

★ ★

L 13

Province: Siena (SI)
Population: 14,000

Altitude: 605m/1,985ft above sea level

A steep tuffstone hill between ►Val di Chiana and Val d'Orcia is the site of a charming architectural gem: stately Renaissance palaces and well-maintained medieval brick houses in a labyrinth of narrow streets make Montepulciano one of the best-preserved historic towns in Tuscany. Music lovers come here for the festival every summer, wine lovers for the many enoteche and the Vino Nobile di Montepulciano, one of the best-known Italian wines.

History

According to legend Montepulciano was founded by the Etruscan king Porsenna. It is probably closer to historical truth that Montepulciano owes its existence to the Roman dynasty of the Publicii. Today the residents of Montepulciano still call themselves **Poliziani** – from Mons Politianus, the Roman name for the town. In the Middle Ages this independent community was allied with Siena and Florence in alternation until 1511, when it submitted finally to Florence.

What to See in Montepulciano

Orientation

Montepulciano is closed to cars and visitor friendly – as can be seen by the many parking lots around the town. Tourism has made its mark on the town in other ways too: no rundown houses, but restored streets; few normal shops, but rather almost exclusively souvenir, gourmet or craft shops as well as restaurants and cafés.

Sant'Agnese

The church of Sant'Agnese lies outside the town wall opposite Poggifanti public park. Survivals from the first church are the Gothic doorway and the fresco of the Madonna from the school of Simone Martini in the first chapel on the right. The marble reliquary of St Agnes is at the main altar.

Enter the old city through the **Porta al Prato** which bears Tuscan coats of arms and the Florentine lion. It was built in the 14th century and incorporated into the new Medici fortification by Antonio da Sangallo the Elder around 1520. From here the slightly winding corso leads through the city to the south-east gate, the 14th-century Porta delle Farine.

! Baedeker TIP

Caffè Poliziano
The stylish old café treats guests to a wonderful selection of baked goods. The few seats on the balconies offer a wonderful view of the landscape around Montepulciano (Via do Voltaia 27 – 29).

A few yards along, Piazza Savonarola appears with the Baroque church of San Bernardo and Palazzo Avignonesi (no. 91), whose design is attributed to Giacomo da Vignola. The late Renaissance façade, in the lower part made of so-called cushion masonry, was designed with a row of windows, each with alternating triangular and segmented pediments, on the two upper floors.

Piazza Savonarola

 VISITING MONTEPULCIANO

INFORMATION
Piazza Don Minzoni 1
Tel. 05 78 75 73 41

SHOPPING
Consorzio del Vino Nobile di Montepulciano
Piazza Grande 7
Tel. 05 78 75 78 12
54 wines from producers in the region can be tasted, and some can be also bought here.

EVENTS
Bravio delle botte
is the name of the Montepulciano city festival on 29 August, when wine barrels weighing 80kg/176lb are rolled through the city.

Cantiere Internazionale d'Arte
At the annual music festival, classical and modern music is performed (end of July / beginning of August).

WHERE TO EAT
► **Moderate**
① **Le Logge de Vignola**
Via delle Erbe 6
Tel. and fax 05 78 71 72 90
In a former bakery in the middle of Montepulciano three friends opened this stylish restaurant. The tourist menu at noon is worthwhile; candlelight atmosphere in the evenings.

② **Osteria Borgo Buio**
Via di Borgo Buio 10

Tel. 05 78 71 74 97
Closed Thu
In a medieval vaulted cellar typical Tuscan dishes are served in a congenial atmosphere.

Baedeker recommendation

Frattoia Bartolomei Elena
Chianciano Terme, Strada Cavine e Valli 34 (below Chianciano Terme)
Tel. 05 78 303 77
Don't let the sober atmosphere put you off: Dora Forzioni and her team produce an excellent olive oil!

WHERE TO STAY
► **Mid-range**
① **Il Borghetto**
Borgo Buio 7
Tel. 05 78 75 75 35
Fax 057 81 75 73 54, 11 rooms
Centrally located small hotel in a 15th-century house with a wonderful view of the old city.

② **Il Marzocco**
Piazza Savonarola 18
Tel. 05 78 75 72 62
Fax 05 78 75 75 30, 16 rooms
Traditional family business in a 16th-century palazzo. The rooms are simple but tastefully furnished, some with balcony.

Montepulciano Plan

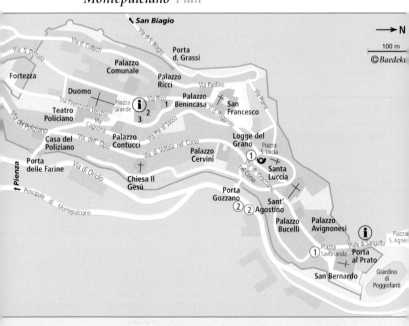

1 Museo Civico
2 Palazzo del Capitano
del Popolo

3 Palazzo Tarugi

Where to eat
① Le Logge del Vignola
② Osteria Borgo Buio

Where to stay
① Il Borghetto
② Il Marzocco

Palazzo Bucelli   Palazzo Bucelli, further along on the right side, deserves a close look. Etruscan urns with mythical creatures are set in the wall, as are Etruscan and Latin inscriptions.

Sant'Agostino, Torre di Pulcinella   The showpiece of Piazza Michelozzo a few steps further uphill is the elegant façade of the church of Sant'Agostino. Michelozzo di Bartolomeo designed it in 1427, skilfully combining Gothic forms with early Renaissance elements. The terracotta relief in the tympanum over the portal depicts the Virgin, John the Baptist and St Augustine. Inside the aisle-less church, which was reconstructed in the late 18th century, are a 15th-century wooden crucifix and paintings by Alessandro Allori and Federico Barocci from the 16th and 17th centuries. A curiosity can be seen on the clock tower opposite, the 16th-century Torre di Pulcinella: a masked **Pulcinella** figure dressed in white, which a monk is said to have brought back from Naples, strikes the hours.

The Baroque church of Santa Lucia, which was completed in 1653 to designs by Flaminio del Turcos, stands in Via Saffi. In the Ceppari chapel there is a *Madonna della Misericordia* by Luca Signorelli.

Santa Lucia

Follow Via del Poggiolo to the travertine-clad Palazzo Benincasa and the church of San Francesco, which owes its present appearance to a reconstruction in the 18th century. The terrace next to the church offers a wonderful view of the surroundings and of Chiesa San Biagio.

Palazzo Benincasa, San Francesco

Palazzo Neri Orselli (Via Ricci 10) in late Gothic-Sienese style houses the city museum; its collection goes back to a donation by Francesco Crociani in 1859. The exhibits from the 15th–18th centuries include several terracottas by Andrea della Robbia, Madonna paintings by Jacopo di Mino del Pelliccaio and Raffaelino del Garbo, Filippo Lippi's *Crucifixion* as well as works by Carlo Cignani and Antonio Coli. The second and third floor also have some Etruscan urns from ►Chiusi and San Casciano (hours: summer Tue–Sun 10am–1pm, 3–7pm).

★
Museo Civico

🕐

At the highest point of the walled old city is the centre of Montepulciano: Piazza Grande – officially Piazza Vittorio Emanuele – surrounded by dignified Renaissance palaces. At the corner of Via Ricci stands the 14th-century Palazzo del Capitano del Popolo, one of the few remaining examples of Gothic architecture in Montepulciano. Palazzo Tarugi, set back a little, is attributed to the architect **Antonio da Sangallo the Elder**, although the upper storeys were probably executed by Baldassare Peruzzi. However, there are also reasons to attribute it to Giacomo da Vignola. The open loggia of the ground floor corresponds to a similar one on the second floor which is walled up today. The fountain in front of the palace with the two griffins and two lions holding the Medici coat of arms was built in 1520 using two Etruscan columns.

★★
Piazza Grande

Palazzo Contucci, like many other buildings in Montepulciano a work of Antonio da Sangallo the Elder, stands on the east side of the square. It was commissioned in 1519 by Cardinal Giovanni Maria del Monte, the later Pope Julius III. When Sangallo died in 1534, Baldassarre Peruzzi took over the construction of the piano nobile; the upper mezzanine storey was only added in 1690 by the Contucci family. The main hall has frescoes by the Baroque painter Andrea Pozzo.

★
Palazzo Contucci

The first thing about this building to catch the eye is that it is incomplete: the front is made of brick; there is no façade. The cathedral was built when the bishop of Chiusi moved his seat to Montepulciano in 1561 because the Chiana valley was becoming swampy. It is in early Baroque style and was built to plans by Ippolito Scalza 1592–1630 on the south side of the square on the site of an earlier

★
Duomo

parish church. The lower storeys of the campanile come from the previous 15th-century building. Inside the church to the left of the main portal is the reclining figure of Bartolomeo Aragazzi, a secretary of Pope Martin V (1417–1431). The tomb, created in 1437 and later dismantled, is an early Renaissance work by Michelozzo di Bartolomeo. Other parts of the tomb are displayed elsewhere in the cathedral: on the first two piers in the nave are reliefs of the Virgin and members of the Aragazzi family; on the south-east pier of the crossing is a statue of St Bartholomew, and the base of the tomb is the slab of the high altar. The late Gothic triptych over the high altar was painted by the Sienese master Taddeo di Bartolo in 1401.

Palazzo Comunale The west side of Piazza Grande is bordered by the massive Palazzo Comunale. Its tower offers a **wonderful panorama** over the city and as far as ▶Monte Amiata. The palace was begun at the end of the 14th century; it got its present form in 1424 to plans by the Florentine Renaissance architect Michelozzo, as the architect's plans which were discovered in 1965 show. The simple façade with crenellations and the tower with a crown are reminiscent of the Palazzo Vecchio in ▶Florence.

The old town of Montepulciano occupies a narrow ridge. Rust-red roof tiles and undressed natural stone give the town its appearance.

From the cathedral follow Via S. Donato southwards past the fortress rebuilt around 1880 in historicizing style to the church of Santa Maria dei Servi with its Gothic façade outside the city walls. The foundation stone for the church was laid in the 14th century, the aisle-less interior was then converted to Baroque in the late 17th century by the Jesuit Andrea Pozzo. The panel painting on the third altar to the left by a pupil of Duccio di Buoninsegna is worth noting.

Via S. Donato, Santa Maria dei Servi

Follow Via del Poliziano, which is called Via dell'Opio further along, to the eastern part of the old city. Via dell'Opio no. 5, built around 1400, is the birthplace of the poet **Poliziano** (1454–1494), whose real name was Agnolo Ambrogini. After his father was murdered the 15-year-old Agnolo left his home town for Florence, where he later became a friend of Lorenzo de Medici. A little further – the street is now called Via di Voltaia – is the Church of Jesus built between 1702 and 1714 by Andrea Pozzo.

Via dell'Opio

In Via di Voltaia there are many shops selling ceramics and wine, as well as the city's traditional café, Caffè Poliziano (no. 27 – 29). Palazzo Cervini, no. 21, is occupied by the Banca Populare dell'Etruria. The massive three-wing palace was commissioned by Cardinal Marcello Cervini, later Pope Marcellus II, and built by Antonio da Sangallo the Elder between 1518 and 1534, but was never completed. On Piazza delle Erbe the Logge del Grano (or Logge del Mercato) by Vignola are worth seeing.

★
Via di Voltaia, Palazzo Cervini

Around Montepulciano

About 1km/0.5mi north of Piazza S. Agnese is the church of Santa Maria delle Grazie, built in the 16th century to plans by Ippolito Scalza. It holds a valuable organ, which was probably donated to the church at Christmas 1600 by the patrician Vincenzo Salimbeni. The organ has pipes made of cypress wood and the variety of tone characteristic of Italian Renaissance organs.

Santa Maria delle Grazie

Travellers coming from Chianciano Terme (see below) or ► Pienza see one of the most significant late Renaissance buildings in Tuscany 2km/1.2mi south-west of Montepulciano: the impressive church of San Biagio at the end of a avenue of cypresses. It was built to designs by Antonio da Sangallo the Elder between 1518 and 1545 as a **pilgrimage church for a picture of the Madonna**. The ground plan has the shape of a Greek cross. A high tambour dome rises above the central crossing. Of the two free-standing towers planned by Giuliano di Baccio, only one was completed. The building, which was conceived in the tradition of Bramante and built of yellow-gold travertine, is not only interesting on the outside: the frescoes in the presbytery are probably 16th-century works of the Zuccari brothers, and

★
San Biagio

the marble altar retable (1584) behind the main altar is attributed to Lisandro and Giannozzo Albertini. The carefully restored 18th-century organ includes parts of its predecessor.

San Albino, Thermal springs

About 4km/2.5mi out on the road to Chianciano Terme lies the little spa of San Albino. Its two carbonated springs were already known in antiquity and are used in a modern thermal spa today.

✷

Chianciano Terme

Chianciano is for southern Tuscany what Montecatini Terme is for the north – the **most popular thermal spa**. The modern spa, which is known for its hot mineral springs, lies nestled in the forested hills of south-eastern Tuscany on the western edge of ► Val di Chiana, about 10km/6mi south of Montepulciano. Numerous graves in the Chianciano area show that it was already settled by the Etruscans. The water was so prized in the Middle Ages that Orvieto, Siena and Montepulciano fought over the location.

Chianciano was developed into a thermal spa only in 1915 with the founding of the Società delle Terme di Chianciano. Two beautiful parks, which charge admission, are the heart of the town: Parco Acqua Santa with spa facilities and east of Viale delle Terme the much larger Parco di Fucoli with a roller-skating rink, tennis courts and boccia. Admission tickets for Acqua Santa Park are also valid in Fucoli Park. The Bagni di Sillene are a short distance to the west, while Parco Sorgente Sant'Elena, which has a mini-golf course, is at the northern end of the spa.

✷

Centro storico ►

Chianciano also has a pretty little historic town centre with old houses and romantic arcades – about 3km/2mi north of the spa district. Halfway up Via Solferino is the 13th-century Palazzo del Podestà with a façade embellished by coats of arms. Next door is a small museum with religious art, including a *Crucifixion* from the school of Duccio.

✷

La Foce

5km/3mi west of Chianciano Terme, in enchanting scenery directly on the road to Bagno Vignoni (►San Quirico d'Orcia), lies the old estate La Foce. The pretty gardens of La Foce are an absolute must. The former owners Antonio and **Iris Origo** had them designed by an English landscape gardener in the 1920s. Iris Origo wrote an impressive diary (► Baedeker Tip p.41) about her time in La Foce during World War II. The tour begins in a clearly structured geometrical garden with narrow gravel walks between boxwood hedges, pomegranate trees, lavender beds and lemon trees in terracotta pots. From there a few steps lead to the rose garden on the slope, which is crossed by a **pergola with wisteria**. Further away from the manor house the garden becomes more »natural«, until it reaches the edge of the woods. The small belvedere offers a wonderful view of the cypress avenue, which winds down from La Foce into the valley and up the hill on the opposite side (open for viewing only on Wed 3–6pm as part of a tour every hour, in the winter until 5pm).

★ Pienza

Province: Siena (SI)   **Altitude:** 491m/1,611ft above sea level
Population: 2,300

Corsignano was conceived as a model Renaissance city by its builder, Enea Silvio Piccolomini (1405–1464), the later Pope Pius II. Work
on the papal residence began in 1459 and was so far advanced
three years later that Pius II elevated the place to a city and seat
of a bishop and named it after himself, »city of Pius«. He died before his project was complete, but what remained is a unique ensemble of urban architecture and one of the most popular tourist
attractions in southern Tuscany.

✱ Piazza Pio II

The heart of Pienza is the trapezoid piazza, which – how could it be   **Heart of town**
otherwise – is called Pio II and is framed by important buildings: cathedral, Palazzo Comunale, Palazzo Borgia and Palazzo Piccolomini. Since
the tourist information office is here, too, the square is seldom empty.

The cathedral of the Assumption of the Virgin, built 1459 until 1462   ★
to plans by Rossellino over a Romanesque church dedicated to Mary,   **Duomo Santa**
occupies the south side of the square. Pillars and blind arcades struc-   **Maria Assunta**
ture its travertine façade. The gable bears the **papal coat of arms of**
Pius II: the crown and the crossed
keys of St Peter, and the shield with
coat of arms of the Piccolomini
family. The church was influenced
by Gothic architecture. It is a hall
church, a relatively rare type in
Italy. Because of the sloping
ground, elaborate supporting constructions were necessary for the
apse; the soft ground still causes
problems today. The light interior

> ! **Baedeker TIP**
>
> **For cheese lovers**
> Pienza pecorino is considered the best in all of
> Italy. It is available in all of the city's gourmet
> shops. Even better: come here on the first
> Sunday in September for the cheese fair.

comes as a surprise. It contains several beautiful Madonnas, including the *Madonna with Saints* by Matteo di Giovanni on the left wall
and the *Assumption of the Virgin* by Vecchietta in the chapel on the
left of the choir.

Cardinal Rodrigo Lanzol Borgia, the later Pope Alexander VI and pro-   **Palazzo Borgia**
totype of the clever and unscrupulous Renaissance politician, was
known for his excessive lifestyle. He commissioned the bishop's palace
on the west side of the square at the end of the 15th century. For this
reason the Borgia coat of arms with a bull was placed above the portal.

Museo Diocesano

In the Renaissance palace next to Palazzo Borgia, where once the canons of the cathedral chapter lived, the diocesan museum shows its treasures, including 14th-century painted panels from the school of Bartolo di Fredis and 16th-century Flemish needlepoint. The beautiful Madonna picture from the neighbouring Montichiello by Pietro Lorenzetti is on display here, having been stolen twice from its original location. Pienza is also especially proud of the gold-embroidered vestments of Pius II, English work dating from the 14th century, which were given to the pope by Thomas Palaiologos, the brother of the last Byzantine emperor (hours: April–Oct daily except Tue 10am–1pm and 3–6pm; Nov–March Fri, Sat and Sun 10am–1pm and 3–6pm).

City wall, panorama

Between the cathedral and Museo Diocesano a path leads to the Pienza city wall. The broad wall, which can be walked on, is a wonderful place to view the Val d'Orcia.

Palazzo Comunale

The travertine façade of the city hall gains lightness from its loggia and seems almost delicate in comparison to the cathedral opposite. The 14th-century building got its tower in the 17th century. A fresco of the Madonna from the Sienese school of the 15th century decorates the council hall. Palazzo Ammannati opposite was never finished.

VISITING PIENZA

INFORMATION
Corso Rosselino 59
Tel. 05 78 74 90 71

SHOPPING
Gourmets and art lovers will love Pienza: everywhere, but especially on Via Rossellino, there are small artisan shops and wonderful delicatessens with fresh pasta (especially the pici noodles), sausage specialties and tasty cheeses.

WHERE TO EAT
▶ **Budget**
Latte di Luna
Via San Carlo 2/4
Tel. 05 78 74 86 06
Closed Tue
Trattoria with very pretty seating outdoors. Try the fried pork!

WHERE TO STAY
▶ **Luxury to mid-range**
Il Chiostro di Pienza
Corso Rossellino 26
Tel. 05 78 74 84 00
Fax 05 78 74 84 40, 37 rooms, 6 suites
A 15th-century monastery was converted to this tasteful hotel in the old town of Pienza.

Baedeker recommendation

▶ **Budget**
Il Giardino Segreto
Via Roma 44
Tel. 05 02 90 00, fax 05 02 52 18, 21 rooms
Family hotel only a few paces from the botanical gardens and about 250m/275yd from the cathedral square. Simple, clean and quiet (request a room facing the back!).

To the right of the cathedral stands the three-storey Palazzo Piccolomini, a major work of Rossellino **modelled on the Florentine Palazzo Rucellai**. The façade is made of carefully worked sandstone and travertine. Pilasters and horizontal string courses with windows in between are the main features of its composition. Rossellino also designed the well Pozzo dei Cani (1462). The interior courtyard with its arcades – the two top floors only as tromp l'oeil – are worth a look, as is the garden front on the south side with three loggias one above the other, from which there was a view of the »hanging gardens«.

Piazza Pio II is definitive Renaissance architecture.

The rooms on the first floor – including a dining room, armoury and library – are open to the public (hours: Tue–Sun 10am–12.30pm and 3–6pm. Closed from 15 Nov to 6 Dec and 20 Feb to 7 March).

✶ Palazzo Piccolomini

The simple church behind Palazzo Piccolomini goes back to the 13th century. The adjacent former monastery with 15th-century cloister now accommodates hotel guests.

San Francesco

Around Pienza

About 5km/3mi south-east of Pienza, on a hilltop and surrounded by defensive walls, stands the medieval village of Monticchiello. Drink your cappuccino on the wall right next to the entrance in the summer. Walk through the medieval gate into the picturesque village, which is lavishly decorated with flowers and has beautifully restored houses. The walk to the top leads past the façade of the Chiesa dei Santi Leonardo e Cristoforo, a simple 13th-century church which surprises visitors with beautiful medieval frescoes. Every year at the end of July and the beginning of August street theatre »teatro povero« is held in Monticchiello – by the residents themselves, who began this tradition in the 1970s.

✶ Monticchiello

Bernardo Tolomei founded the Olivetan monastery Sant'Anna in 1324 about 7km/4.5mi north of Pienza. Its refectory contains beautiful frescoes (1503–1507), the first works by the Piedmontese Sodoma which have certain dates. They depict the *Entombment of Christ, Madonna with St Anne and Two Monks, The Bishop of Arezzo Blessing the Congregation* and the *Feeding of the 10,000* set in charming landscape.

Sant'Anna in Camprena

★ ★ Pisa

Province: Pisa (PI)
Population: 92,000

Elevation: 4m/13ft above sea level

Probably no other city has become as famous as Pisa through a construction error. The Leaning Tower should never have been built here because the ground that it stands on is too soft for such a building. The capital city of the province of Pisa once stood on a lagoon and today lies on the banks of the Arno only 10km/6mi from the Versilia coast. Visitors who leave the surroundings of the cathedral, to which the leaning campanile belongs, discover a pretty, extremely lively university city with beautiful palaces, interesting museums and above all many excellent shops.

Once a harbour, now a university city

Pisa was probably founded by Greeks in the 7th or 6th century BC. Etruscans later settled on the lagoon. The name Pisa comes from the Etruscan word for mouth and refers to the delta region of the Serchio and Arno rivers. The Romans built a harbour in Pisa at the time when it lay right on the sea. The victory over the Saracens by Messina and Palermo in 1063 initiated the rise of the city to be the preeminent commercial power of the western Mediterranean. The maritime republic had become rich through **trade with the Orient** and dominated the coastal regions of the Near East, Greece, North Africa, Sicily, Sardinia and the Balearic Islands in the 12th century. However, from the late 12th century Pisa got competition from other cities, including Lucca and Florence, but also from the coastal cities Amalfi and Genoa.

Highlights Pisa

Cathedral and baptistery
Two highlights of Romanesque architecture in Tuscany
▶ page 333, 334

Leaning Tower
Despite or maybe because of its leaning tendencies the famous tower is worth climbing.
▶ page 329

Camposanto
Cemetery with excellent fresco decorations
▶ page 335

Museo Nazionale di San Matteo
One of the great museums of Tuscany
▶ page 340

Borgo Stretto
A narrow alley, but Pisa's prettiest shopping street.
▶ page 337

Piazza Vettovaglie
The Pisans buy their fruit and vegetables on this atmospheric square.
▶ page 337

VISITING PISA

INFORMATION

– Via Pietro Nenni 24
Tel. 050 92 97 77, fax 050 92 97 64
– Piazza del Duomo
Tel. 050 56 04 64
– in the railway station (stazione ferroviaria)
Tel. 050 422 91,
www.pisa.turismo.toscana.it

ARRIVAL

Pisa airport is a destination for cheap flights. San Giusto airport is also very close to the centre (bus ticket to the railway station costs about 1 euro).

PARKING

Pisa has many one-way streets and few parking spaces. The large parking lot by the cathedral square is easiest to find.

COMBINATION TICKETS

are available for a visit to the cathedral, baptistery, Camposanto and Museo dell'Opera dell'Duomo.

EVENTS

Regatta di San Ranieri

The four city districts compete in rowing races on 17 June.

WHERE TO EAT

► Expensive / moderate

③ *Al Ristoro dei Vecchi Macelli*
Via Volturno 49, tel. 05 02 04 24
Closed Sun afternoon and Wed
The cosy restaurant in the former meatpacking district serves excellent food.

► Moderate

① *La Mescita*
Via Cavalca 2, tel. 050 54 42 94
Closed Sat and Sun
Fresh vegetables and herbs feature in the imaginative cuisine in this stylish trattoria on the picturesque market-place Vettovaglie.
Well-chosen wine list.

► Inexpensive / moderate

② *Osteria dei Cavalieri*
Via San Frediano 16
Tel. 050 58 08 58
Tasteful restaurant in the university quarter. Typical Pisan dishes such as tripe and tagliata with porcini (closed Sat and Sun).

WHERE TO STAY

► Mid-range

② *Royal Victoria*
Lungarno Pacinotti 12
Tel. 050 94 01 11
Fax 050 94 01 80
www.royalvictoria.it
An old palace right on the Arno with a grand staircase and luxurious marble floors, impressive for its old-fashioned charm, personal service and understatement.

③ *San Francesco*
Via Santa Maria 129
Tel. 050 55 41 09
Fax 050 55 61 45
Pleasant little hotel in the old city with breakfast terrace.

► Budget

① *Amalfitana*
Via Roma 44
Tel. 050 290 00
Fax 050 25 218
www.hotelamalfitana.it
Family hotel only a few steps from the botanical gardens and about 250m/ 275yd from the cathedral square. Simple, clean and quiet (request a room facing the back!). Good value.

Pisa Plan

Where to eat

① La Mescita
② Osteria dei Cavalieri
③ Al Ristoro dei Vecchi Macelli

Where to stay

① Amalfitana
② Royal Victoria
③ San Francesco

The city engaged in many wars with its rivals: in 1003 Pisa fought the first Italian communal war to gain its independence from Lucca, and in later years did battle with Venice in the Adriatic and Genoa for the control of French trade. The **defeat of the Pisan fleet by the Genoese on 6 August 1284** sealed the fate of the Tuscan sea power. Pisa had to give up occupied territory, came under the control of the Milanese Visconti and was taken over by Florence in 1406. The Medici promoted major construction plans in the city, such as the regulating of the Arno and Serchio as well as the building of bridges and canals. From the 16th century to the unification of Italy in 1859 Pisa was part of the grand duchy of Tuscany.

Tips for sightseeing

The fame of the cathedral and Leaning Tower make it is easy to forget the rest of the city. This is undeserved, since Pisa's old quarter has not been dressed up for foreign guests – or at least only at a few places – and is an opportunity to discover everyday life in a university city. In the streets and squares between Via Santa Maria and Borgo Stretto there are markets, attractive little shops, new and secondhand bookshops and pleasant student cafés to discover. Above all Borgo Stretto and its extension to the south, Corso Italia (on the opposite side of the Arno), are good shopping areas. Corso Italia is closed to car traffic on Saturday evening.

✱ Piazza del Duomo

Pisa's »Miracle Square«

Pisa's most popular attractions – the cathedral and the Leaning Tower (► Baedeker Special p.330), the baptistery and Camposanto – are all sited on the cathedral square, an expansive area on the north-western edge of the old town by the city wall, also called the Campo dei Miracoli, «Miracle Square». The monuments were all built of Carrara marble and have been on the UNESCO world heritage list since 1987. To avoid the many souvenir sellers and the crowds on the Campo, go there early in the morning when the city is still asleep.

Hours
🕐

Cathedral: in summer daily 10am–7.40pm, in winter daily 10am–12.45pm, 3–4.45pm. Baptistery: in summer daily 8am–7.40pm, spring/fall 9am–5.40pm, in winter 9am–4.40pm. Camposanto and Museo delle Sinopie: hours as baptistery. Museo dell'Opera del Duomo: in summer daily 8am–7.20pm, spring/fall 9am–5.20pm, in winter 9am–4.20pm.

✱✱ Leaning Tower

Every child has heard of it but no one was able to climb it in the 1990s: the Leaning Tower, Torre Pendente, the city's landmark, was closed for vital restoration work – it was leaning too far. It has been open again since the end of 2001, but only to small groups and children above the age of eight years (advance tickets via internet at www.opapisa.it).

At night the square is especially atmospheric: Il Campo dei Miracoli, the Field of Miracles, is the site of the cathedral, baptistery and Leaning Tower.

THE TILTING MONUMENT

Construction failures do not normally attract tourists. But Pisa is different. Probably the first act of every visitor to Pisa is to marvel at the Leaning Tower, which does present the city with some problems due to its extreme angle of inclination, but at the same time is a landmark that overshadows every other local monument.

As is often the case when the unbelievable happens, there is a legend behind it. This states that the Leaning Tower stood **straight as a ramrod** when it was first completed. When the architect wanted to collect his payment from the city fathers, they tried to cheat him. In his anger, the master builder ordered the tower to follow him. And then, to everyone's dismay, the tower began to lean. The city fathers paid him the agreed amount immediately, but the builder left the town with a leaning tower.

Famous Builders

An inscription to the right of the entrance names the year when the foundation stone was laid: 1173. Pisa had risen to be most powerful naval republic in Italy and could invite the most eminent architects and stonemasons to build the campanile. The cathedral architect Bonannus, together with Guglielmo from Innsbruck, was responsible for the first three storeys. But before it was completed, the tower began to lean southwards.

When counterweights on the north side and supporting walls on the leaning side had no effect, construction was stopped. Almost 100 years passed before another architect dared start on the tower again. Giovanni di Simone added another three storeys to the campanile in 1272 and tried to balance the angle by bending the axis of the tower to the vertical. In 1301 the bells were hung, and between 1350 and 1372 Tommaso Pisano completed the marble tower with an open belfry. Up close the 57m/187ft-high, free-standing bell tower leans even more than expected. The base rests on an artificial bed of gravel and is some 4m/13ft high. Above it on the loggia storeys the thickness of the cylinder walls (inner diameter 7.4m/24ft) is reduced to 3.3m/11ft, still enough to hold the circular stairway inside with 294 steps that lead to the top platform. In the more than eight hundred years of its crooked existence Pisa's trademark had tilted 5 degrees and 22 minutes away from the vertical by 1990, a **deviation of 4.86m/16ft**.

The foundations had sunk 2.25m/7ft 4in towards the south-east. At an estimated movement of 1mm per year the building would have fallen over in the year 2000: that is, when the vertical axis of the cylinder had moved through the leaning northern edge. When experts discovered that the building was also turning on its own axis, not to mention the unpredictable sudden sinking of the ground, an earthquake or other material fatigue, the tower was closed in November 1990 in order to begin an extensive reconstruction that would keep it from falling over.

The Ground Is Sinking

The reason for the instability of the tower is the soft ground underneath. While the first 10m/30ft of ground was compressed to a stone-like consistency by the weight of 14,450t, the deeper layers consist of clay and sand and are difficult to calculate. The more liquid the clay-sand layer contains, the more it can resist the sinking campanile, which is why the removal of any water in a radius of 1.5km/1mi has been prohibited for over 20 years. When the first recorded attempts at correction were made, little was known about this: in 1839 water was removed to stabilize the ground – with damaging results. When cement injection was invented the Torre Pendente got its »booster shots« in 1934 and 1959 which appeared only to have accelerated the tilting, since the cement attached itself to the foundation like an anchor and pulled it down. The suggestions for solving the problems were as odd as they were imaginative. Someone from Japan suggested building another tower that leaned in the opposite

direction; an Australian proposed a supporting corset. Others even suggested taking the tower down and rebuilding it later. The method of a German company stimulated discussion. The proposal was to push up the building millimetre by millimetre with the help of hydraulic presses. More than 300 buildings have been adjusted like this in German coal-mining regions. In 1992 the decision was made to wrap 18 steel cables around the base at the lowest arcade in order to keep the walls from breaking apart. At the same time a 600t concrete-and-steel plate was anchored on the north side of the foundations to stabilize the ground and compress it. This suggestion also had its critics, as it was not absolutely certain whether the tower would straighten or turn sideways. The good news came in mid-1994: the sinking had stopped. In 1999 the tower was almost as »straight« as 30 years earlier. A final attempt has straightened the tower by another 400mm/16in. But an inclination of almost 4.5m/15ft remains. Now the campanile just **leans but will not fall over**. The reasons why the Pisans do not want to make their Leaning Tower into a completely normal straight tower are clear …

✳ Duomo Santa Maria Assunta

A naval victory over the Saracens in 1063 made it possible: according to an inscription on the façade the building costs of the large cathedral were covered by the freight »of six Saracen ships seized off Sardinia that were loaded with treasures«. The unfinished building was dedicated in 1118 by Pope Gelasius II. The first architect, Buscheto, entered uncharted territory with his plans. There were no precedents in Italy for his double-aisled Romanesque columned basilica with aisles in the transept and a crossing dome. In the mid-12th century the church was extended to the west where Buscheto's successor, Rainaldo, added the façade to the nave.

Building history

The magnificent, clearly structured façade was a **model for Romanesque church architecture in Tuscany**. The ground floor has a unified appearance with blind arcades and three entrances. Above it are four stepped storeys where rows of arches like loggias stand out from the actual walls. The gable over the nave is crowned with a statue of a Madonna, thought to be by Andrea Pisano. The three bronze doors were made in Giambologna's workshop after the massive fire in 1595. The carefully restored Porta di San Ranieri, the former main entrance to the church, is more important than the doors in the main façade. It is in the southern transept on the side facing the Leaning Tower and is named after the patron saint of Pisa. The bronze doors, cast around 1180 by the master Bonannus in one piece each, have four large and 20 small reliefs of the life of Christ and the Virgin. Ivories from Byzantium and Roman bronze doors were models for these doors, which are pioneering works of western sculpture.

✳ ✳
Façade

✳ ✳
◄ Porta di San Ranieri

The interior of the cathedral was largely destroyed in a fire in 1595, but a few outstanding pieces were preserved. The most famous work of art in the cathedral is the pulpit, which was made between 1302 and 1312, a **late work by Giovanni Pisano**. The pulpit itself rests on pillars, of which four are shaped like figures: the archangel Michael, Samson or Hercules (a personification of Christian strength), Christ (with the four evangelists at his feet) as well as Ecclesia (a personification of the church with two infants as the Old and New Testament). At the feet of the evangelist John is Pisano's self-portrait and a portrait of the man who commissioned the work, Burgundio di Tado. The central support of the pulpit is shaped like three women, presumably representing the cardinal virtues faith, love and hope. Reliefs on the pulpit show scenes from the New Testament, for example the birth of John the Baptist, the Annunciation and Assumption of the Virgin, the Nativity etc.

Interior
✳ ✳
◄ Pulpit by Giovanni Pisano

The chandelier from the year 1586 that hangs in the nave is incorrectly said to have drawn Galileo Galilei's attention to the laws of pendulum movement. At the right front pillar in the choir note the depiction of St Agnes by Andrea del Sarto. The apse mosaic has been

The cathedral pulpit by Giovanni Pisano – a late work of the master and a milestone in late medieval statuary.

restored several times and dates from the 13th and 14th centuries. It shows Christ enthroned between Mary and John the Evangelist – a work of the Florentine Cimabue from 1302. In the southern transept is another important piece, the fragmentary grave monument of Holy Roman Emperor Henry VII, who died after a short reign (1308–1313). It was created after 1313 by Tino di Camaino.

✷ ✷ Battistero

West of the cathedral stands **one of the largest baptisteries of Christendom**, which was begun in 1152 under the architect Diotisalvi and continued by others including Nicola Pisano and his son Giovanni. It is not part of the main church, a common arrangement in Italy. Baptisteries with round or octagonal plans derive from separate, early Christian baptismal churches. Since construction took more than two centuries the building combines elements of the **Romanesque and Gothic** styles. It is interesting that the dome-like roof originally had an elliptical shape; in 1358 the exterior was altered to suggest a semi-spherical dome. Most of the **outside figures on the galleries and doors** have been replaced by copies. The originals are in the cathedral museum. The main doorway opposite the entrance to the cathedral is striking for its sculptural decoration that recalls ancient sarcophagus art. The baptistery is flooded with light and has excellent acoustics; it is almost 55m/180ft high. At the centre is the octagonal baptismal font which according to an inscription dates back to 1246. It is a magnificent basin decorated with rosettes and marble inlays by Guido Begarelli from Como.

The marble pulpit made in 1260 by Nicola Pisano is one of the most important works of Romanesque sculpture. It rests on seven columns and is completely free-standing. The lions are interpreted in the tradition of medieval images; they carry the columns and are intended to express the overcoming of evil. The figure of Hercules or Samson as the personification of strength, which supports the six-sided pulpit along with other figures of virtues, is an epoch-making innovation. The reliefs on the facing include expressive images of the Annunciation and Nativity, Adoration of the Shepherds, Adoration of the Magi, Presentation in the Temple, Crucifixion and Last Judgement.

✳ ✳
◄ Pulpit by Nicola Pisano

Pisan tradition has it that Archbishop Ubaldo dei Lanfranchi brought back several shiploads of earth from Golgotha in the fourth crusade so that Pisan citizens could be buried in holy ground. But the construction of the buildings of the Camposanto, the »holy field«, was not carried out until 1278 under Giovanni di Simone. This cemetery on the northern edge of Piazza del Duomo is bordered by monumental arcaded passages with Gothic windows. The gravestones of Pisan patricians are set into the floor of the arcades; ancient sarcophagi stand along the edge including one with the tragic love story of Hippolyte, son of Theseus, who fell in love with his stepmother Phaedra.

✳ ✳
Camposanto

Until World War II frescoes of the 14th and 15th centuries decorated the walls of the arcades. During a bombing raid on 27 July 1944 they were destroyed by molten lead that ran down from the roof. What was not completely destroyed was removed and restored, and is now on display in the rooms of the north wing. There are plans to return the frescoes to their original location. The *Triumph of Death*, a large-scale painting which shows the influence of the Great Plague of 1348, is particularly impressive: at the front left three noble horsemen encounter the open caskets of three kings, above them hermits pray. On the other side a wealthy group holds a carefree celebration in the forest. The grim reaper, half devil and half woman, waits for the people, who will either go to eternal damnation or eternal righteousness at the Last Judgement.

✳ ✳
◄ Frescoes

A visit to the Sinopie Museum is a recommended addition to the Camposanto. The **preliminary sketches for the frescoes** in the Camposanto, which were made with red chalk, are displayed here. The sinopia was the artist's most important contribution because it determined the composition of the work in detail. The actual execution of the frescoes was often done by students and assistants. The museum shows the sinopie of the Camposanto frescoes together with reproductions of the wall paintings.

✳
Museo delle Sinopie

✷
Museo dell'Opera del Duomo

At the eastern end of the cathedral square at Piazza dell'Arcivescovado 6, the Museo dell'Opera del Duomo gives an impression of the office of building works of a medieval cathedral and presents works of art and sculptures from the cathedral and baptistery. **Pisan sculpture** between the 12th and the 15th century is especially well documented with original sculptures from the façade of the baptistery by Nicola and Giovanni Pisano, sculptures from the destroyed grave (1315) of Emperor Henry VII as well as parts of the funerary altar of San Ranieri (1306). The cathedral treasure includes three reliquaries, one made of ivory from Arabia and two of enamel from Limoges, as well as a fragment of the so-called cathedral belt, other reliquaries, vestments and liturgical utensils.

From the Cathedral Square to the Banks of the Arno

✷
Via Santa Maria Orto Botanico

🕐
Opening hours:
Mon–Fri 8am–5pm,
Sat 8am–1pm,
closed Sun / holidays

The city tour begins at the cathedral square and goes first through Via Santa Maria, which is bordered by beautiful old city palaces, down to the Arno River. At Via Luca Ghini 5, a small side street of Via Santa Maria, is the entrance to the botanical gardens of Pisa. It was laid out in 1543 by the physician and botanist Luca Ghini under orders from Grand Duke Cosimo de Medici. It is used today above all for research by the Botanical Institute. Plants from different climate zones, including laurel, bananas, Californian palm trees, gingko trees and rare medicinal herbs flourish in hothouses and outdoors.

Domus Galilaeana

In the house at Via Santa Maria no. 26 Galileo Galilei, the great scientist and mathematician who was born in Pisa in 1564, (▶Famous People) is supposed to have lived – the house where he was born was probably in the eastern part of the city near the church of Sant'Andrea Forisportam. Today the place of memorial, which has a well-stocked library, displays a collection of writings by Galilei and his students.

✷
Museo Nazionale di Palazzo Reale

Palazzo Reale is situated by the Arno and the busy Lungarno Pacinotti. Partially restored magnificent patrician palaces, like Palazzo Reale, show that the street used to be the finest in Pisa. It was begun in 1559 by the Florentine Baccio Bandinelli on behalf of Cosimo I and later reconstructed several times. Today it houses the Museo Nazionale di Palazzo Reale. The main attraction of the museum's 14 rooms is an altar panel by Raphael, which he painted when he was only 17 years old. The collection also contains paintings by Francesco Francia, Bernardo Strozzi, Frans van Francken and Joos van Cleve.

Arno riverbank

Walk from Palazzo Reale eastwards toward Piazza Garibaldi and Borgo Stretto past the Renaissance-style Palazzo alla Giornata, today the seat of the university rector. Notice the 16th-century Agostini palace

(Lungarno Pacinotti 27) with its trefoil windows and terracotta reliefs. Inside is the oldest café in Pisa **Caffè dell'Ussero**, where supporters of the Risorgimento met in the mid-19th century. The adjacent Hotel Royal Victoria (Lungarno no. 12) also dates from the 19th century.

Borgo Stretto and the University

Where Ponte di Mezzo, the oldest bridge over the Arno, crosses the river the promenade opens up into Piazza Garibaldi, which – no sur-

★★
Borgo Stretto

prise here – is decorated with a monument to the national hero Guiseppe Garibaldi. Borgo Stretto which does its name proud (literally: »narrow city quarter«) begins to the right of the arcades of the Casino dei Nobile, which faces the Arno. The pedestrian zone with its atmospheric arcades is the most important shopping street and promenade in Pisa. A few yards along on the right is the church of San Michele in Borgo, which was built almost 1000 years ago, pre-

> ! **Baedeker TIP**
>
> **Pane e vino**
> Caffèteria delle Vettovaglie is the name of a snack bar under the arcades of Piazza Vettovaglie which is equally popular among businesspeople and students, market traders and boutique owners from Borgo Stretto. Sandwiches and a glass of wine – all you need to feel at home here.

sumably over a temple to Mars. It gained its Romanesque-Gothic façade in a renovation in the 14th century. It was severely damaged during a bombing raid in 1944. During the reconstruction afterwards a fresco of St Michael (13th century) was revealed over the left door.

A small covered passage leads from Borgo Stretto into the maze of streets of the old city, first to Piazza Vettovaglie, a square courtyard with arcades where produce is sold every day.

★
Piazza Vettovaglie

From there follow Via di Cavalca west to Piazza Dante Alighieri. In nice weather this **traffic-free square with palm trees in the middle of the university quarter** is a wonderful place to take a break and sit on the lawn or in one of the cafés. About 40,000 students are registered at the renowned University of Pisa. It goes back to a law school in the 12th century, which received the papal privilege of teaching theology, jurisprudence and medicine in 1329 and in 1543 was elevated to the status of University of Tuscany by Cosimo I.

★
Piazza Dante Alighieri, University

To the north-east Piazza Dante Alighieri adjoins the little Piazza San Frediano with the church of the same name. The church, a columned basilica that already existed in 1077, was completed in the 12th century. Blind arcades with rhombi adorn the Romanesque façade; the interior was reworked in contemporary style during a restoration in the 16th and 17th centuries.

San Frediano

✳ Piazza dei Cavalieri

Renaissance square

Via San Frediano connects to the north with Piazza dei Cavalieri, which is surrounded by stately Renaissance buildings. The »knights' square« was the worldly centre of the old city in the Middle Ages and Renaissance period.

✳ ✳ Palazzo dei Cavalieri (della Carovana)

This magnificent palace, which is decorated with coats of arms, sgraffiti and the busts of six Tuscan grand dukes from the Medici dynasty, is a conspicuous feature on the north side of the square. Since the 13th century the palace of the city elders has stood here. In 1562 Giorgio Vasari was commissioned to expand it as the seat of the knights of St Stephen. A year earlier the order of knights, which Cosimo I de Medici founded to commemorate the Florentine victory over Siena on 2 August (St Stephen's day) 1554, had been recognized by the pope.

The »knight's square« got its name from Palazzo dei Cavalieri.

The official duty of the Order of Knights of St Stephen was to defend the Tuscan coast against Saracen raids, but unofficially it also served to stabilize the rule of the Medici dukes over Pisa. Since 1810 the palazzo has been the home of the university college named Scuola Normale Superiore, an elite school founded by Napoleon. In front of the building is a statue of Grand Duke Cosimo I (1596) by Piero Francavilla.

Palazzo dell'Orologio

The palazzo on the north-west side of the square was built in 1607 for the Order of St Stephen. The architect here was also Vasari, who cleverly used this building to connect the prison (Torre delle Sette Vie, after the seven streets that lead to this square) and Palazzetto dei Gualandi (also Torre della Fame, »tower of hunger«). Count Ugolino della Gherardesca is supposed to have died of hunger here in 1288 with his sons. He was accused of abusing his office as Capitano del Popolo of Pisa.

Santo Stefano dei Cavalieri

Giorgio Vasari also designed the church of Santo Stefano, which he built in 1569 for the **order of St Stephen**. In 1606 the building got a marble façade in the late Mannerist style designed by Giovanni de Medici. The two wings were originally changing rooms for knights of the Order of St Stephen who wore the robes of the order for worship. They were not incorporated in the church until the 17th century. The squares of the coffered ceiling, which was added in 1605, depict the history of the order. Paintings on the walls show episodes from the life of St Stephen.

Via Corsica, Piazza Cavallotti

The fact that Pisa is a university city can be seen by walking from Piazza dei Cavalieri towards the cathedral square – above all along Via Corsica, which leaves Piazza dei Cavalieri on the west, and then into Via dei Mille with street traders, internet cafés, new and second-hand bookshops. At the little Piazza Cavallotti, Via Mille emerges into Via Santa Maria, the main connection between the cathedral square and the Arno.

A Walk to Museo Nazionale

San Pierino

Start this walk in Borgo Stretto. A few minutes' walk south-east of the shopping street Via Cavour leads to San Pierino or San Pietro in Vinculis (St Peter in Chains), which was probably built on ancient foundations in 1072–1119. Inside the columned basilica the mosaic floors and some capitals from the Roman period are worth noting, as well as the unusually large crypt, which lies under the whole church.

Palazzo Toscanelli

According to tradition the Toscanelli palace on the riverside street, which is called Lungarno Mediceo here, was built in the 16th century to plans by Michelangelo. In 1821 and 1822 Lord Byron lived here.

Palazzo Medici The origins of the palace on Piazza Mazzini are older than the Medici rule in Pisa. The stately building, today seat of the prefecture, was built in the 13th century and remodelled when the Appiano dynasty ruled Pisa in the 14th century. In the late 15th century Lorenzo de Medici lived here when he was in Pisa.

✳
Museo Nazionale di San Matteo
☺
Opening hours:
Tue–Sat
8.30am–7.30pm,
Sun
8.30am–1.30pm

The national museum is housed in the former Benedictine monastery San Matteo on Lungarno Mediceo. It is one of the **most important art collections in Tuscany**. Among the numerous exhibits are first of all paintings and sculptures of Tuscan schools from the high Middle Ages to the Renaissance. The museum also has valuable textiles, manuscripts and a large collection of ceramics from the 11th to the 15th century.

Painting 12th–13th century ►
Pisan paintings from the 12th and 13th centuries are among the museum's special treasures. Monumental crucifixes painted on wood from the end of the 12th century show the change in depictions of Christ from a divine triumphal interpretation of the Byzantine-Romanesque type to the human, suffering Christ of early Gothic style from the period when the mendicant orders began to preach repentance. Magnificent **panel crosses** by Bonaventura Berlinghiero and Giunta di Capitinio are the highlight of the first half of the 13th century. Along with the Exultet scroll the so-called Maestro di San Martino (possibly Raniero di Ugolino) created the Byzantine-influenced panel painting *Virgin Enthroned with Child*, a masterpiece of the Pisan school from around 1280. *St Catherine of Alexandria* was painted at the same time.

14th–15th century ►
In 14th century painting the 43-part **polyptych by Simone Martini**, which was completed in 1320, takes first place. On a gold background the Madonna and child appear in the centre, to the left the evangelist John, St Dominic and Mary Magdalene, to the right John the Baptist, Peter of Verona and St Catherine of Alexandria. The predella shows Christ as man of sorrows in the middle between the evangelist Mark and the Virgin, surrounded by other saints. Other 14th-century works include panels with the legend of St Galgano (around 1355), a picture of great narrative power from the hand of an unknown master, a charming Madonna depiction by Francesco Traini (around 1350) as well as the *Madonna del Latte* (around 1370) by Barnaba da Modena. Renaissance painting is represented by a panel of *St Paul* (1426) by Masaccio, an *Adoration* by Benozzo Gozzoli and a *Sacra Conversazione* by Domenico Ghirlandaio. Among the Baroque paintings *Divine and Earthly Love*, a work from the first half of the 17th century by Guido Reni stands out.

Sculpture 14th century ►
14th-century sculpture includes the expressive pulpit relief by Tino di Camaino and the marble, colourfully framed *Madonna del Latte*, a figure in a robe with many folds which Nino, the son of Andrea Pisano, carved for the church of Santa Maria della Spina. The nursing mother of God holds her son tenderly in her arm, a strong boy who rests securely on her breast with eyes closed. Further notable works

Pisa is a popular university city – maybe because the bridges are such a nice place to sit and chat?

are parts of a 15th-century Annunciation group by Francesco di Va-lambrino, a bust of Christ attributed to Andrea del Verrocchio and a reliquary bust of St Rossore, a Sardinian martyr from the 3rd century, worked in gilded bronze by Donatello in 1427.

From the Museo Nazionale it is not far to the Giardino Scotto on the south bank of the Arno. The park was laid out in the 19th century and begins right behind the Ponte alla Fortezza. The bridge takes its name from the fortezza (fortress) built by Giuliano da Sangallo in 1512 in the south-east corner of the old city. It was partially destroyed in World War II.

Giardino Scotto, Fortezza

North-Eastern Old City

East of Piazza dei Cavalieri lies the quarter of San Francesco. The small church on the piazza of the same name was documented as early as 1211, while St Francis was still alive. The building was completed in 1270. In the second chapel on the right is the **grave of Count Ugolino della Gherardesca and his sons**, who were starved to death in Palazzo dell'Orologio. The paintings on the legend of St Francis and a 14th-century marble polyptych by Tommaso Pisano, which shows the Virgin with saints, are also worth seeing. Walk through the sacristy to a chapel with frescoes by the Sienese Taddeo di Bartolo (1397).

San Francesco

Santa Caterina Between 1251 and 1310 the Dominican order had a church built over older buildings not far to the north-west of San Francesco on Piazza Santa Caterina. Around 1327 the façade was added and decorated in Pisan style with a tracery rosette and dwarf gallery. A campanile was added later. Inside note the marble Annunciation group (around 1360) by Nino Pisano, and also by him the elaborate marble grave for Archbishop Simone Saltarelli. One of the main works of Pisan 14th-century painting, *The Gloria of St Thomas Aquinas* (around 1342) by Francesco Traini, is on the north wall of the nave.

South-Western Old City

South bank of Arno, Palazzo Gambacorti The few sites on the south bank of the Arno are not as close together as on the northern side. Plan enough time to walk to them or take a car. The starting point is Palazzo Gambacorti which was built in the 14th century opposite the Ponte di Mezzo, today the seat of the city administration (municipio). The former owner Pietro Gambacorti ruled Pisa and was killed in his palace by conspirators in 1393.

Romantic setting: the banks of the Arno at night with its brightly lit palazzi

Nearby are the Logge dei Banchi, the covered cloth market which was built from 1603 to 1605, where an antique market is held every second weekend of the month (except August). The shopping street Corso Italia begins at the Logge and runs directly to the railway station.

Follow the riverside street west for about 400m/440yd to what is probably the most famous of the smaller Pisan churches. Originally intended as an open prayer hall for travellers and bargemen, it was converted to a Gothic oratory in 1332. The reason for the reconstruction was a thorn (spina) from the crown of Christ brought back from the Holy Land, which was to be kept here. The **richly decorated façade** with three gables, tabernacle-like towers and tracery rosettes is striking for such a small church. Behind the Renaissance altar is a group *Madonna with St Peter and John the Baptist* (around 1345) by Andrea Pisano and assistants. Pisano's *Madonna del Latte* is a replica of the original in the Museo Nazionale di San Matteo.

About 300m/330yd south-west not far from the Arno is the church San Paolo a Ripa d'Arno. The church of the apostle Paul, a Romanesque domed church, rare in Tuscany, was built in the 12th century and rebuilt after being destroyed in the war. The influence of the cathedral is obvious on the façade decorated with round arches and dwarf galleries (12th century). The interior of the basilica holds the tomb of the scholar Burgundio (late 12th century), an ancient Roman sarcophagus. Another was set in the wall over the door of the left transept.

The remains of an Etruscan and Roman harbour were found in December 1998 on the grounds of the Pisa-San Rosso railway station, about 500m/550yd west of the cathedral square. During the excavations **several ships and their cargo** – amphorae, ceramics, oriental crafts, Celtic gold jewellery among other things – were found. Some of these finds are now on display in a permanent exhibition in the Arsenali Medicei on the south-west edge of the old city. These warehouses were restored in the mid-16th century by the Medici and then used for the building and maintenance of Pisan ships. In the 18th century the buildings were used as stables. A small fault of the private museum: the texts explaining the exhibits are in Italian only.

From the warehouses it is only a few steps to the old citadel (Citadella Vecchia) with the massive Guelf tower (Torre Guelfa) which reinforced the medieval city wall. Today it is the ideal place for a panoramic view of Pisa.

Around Pisa

About 6km/3.5mi south-west of Pisa, San Piero a Grado is worth a visit. Legend has it that the apostle Peter landed here on his way to

Rome, at a time when this was still a coastal area. From an early date the church said to have been founded by St Peter, »ecclesia ad gradus« (church at the steps), was an important station for pilgrims going to Rome from the north. The basilica was built in the 11th century from tuff and marble. Excavations prove the existence of a previous church from the 6th century. Unusually this church also has an apse in the west. The main decoration of the simple interior is the important **fresco cycle** that covers the walls of the nave. It was probably painted around 1300 by an artist from Lucca, Deodato Orlando. The lower part consists of portraits of popes; the middle part depicts scenes from the life of the apostles Peter and Paul, and the top part shows the heavenly Jerusalem.

★
Parco Naturale di Migliarino

Beautiful pine groves and forests of holm oak extend about 4km/2.5mi west of Pisa as part of the 23,000 ha/57,000-acre Parco Naturale di Migliarino – San Rossore – Massaciuccoli. The park is described in more detail under ►Versilia.

★
Marina di Pisa, Tirrenia

Only about 10km/6mi from downtown Pisa lies the popular seaside resort Marina di Pisa. The former fishing village became popular as a resort at the beginning of the 20th century, as the pretty art nouveau villas show today. There is only one narrow beach but the fish restaurants, which stand on piles in the water, are excellent, and popular not just among the Pisans. A bit further to the south the modern resort Tirrenia has broad beaches of fine sand that are suitable for swimming.

Monte Pisano, San Giuliano Terme

North-east of Pisa lies Monte Pisano, a mountain range that is not very spectacular but very pleasant and not over-run with hikers. A drive of only 6km/3.5mi on the tree-lined SS 12 from Pisa leads to San Giuliano Terme, a small spa at the foot of Monte Pisano. This is not a particularly popular spa: numerous treatments are available but there is no thermal bath in San Giuliano Terme.

Calci
★
Pieve di Sant'Ermolao ►

8km south-east of San Giuliano Terme, Calci lies on the south-west flank of Monte Pisano in Valgraziosa, a valley rich in olive groves. In the middle of the village stands the parish church Sant'Ermolao, which was first mentioned in 823 . The present building dates from the 11th and 12th centuries. The elegant façade has blind arcades in Pisan Romanesque style; the campanile was never finished. The Romanesque baptismal font by an unknown master of the 12th century is the main attraction in the church. The influence of ancient sarcophaguses is clear.

The Carthusian monastery was founded in 1366 about 1km/0.5mi outside Calci on Via Roma, in the middle of olive groves. It is the second-largest Carthusian monastery in Italy after Pavia. The large complex owes its overall appearance today to a Baroque remodelling in the 17th and 18th centuries. Of the two church cloisters, the smaller one was designed by Lorenzo da Settignano in the 15th century, the larger with the monks' cells by Cartoni in the early 17th century. The church was built in pure Baroque forms with a 17th-century dome fresco and the Sala del Granduca in the guesthouse, which was reserved for the grand dukes of Tuscany. The natural science museum of the University of Pisa is also part of the monastery. It displays fossils and minerals, mounted mammals and birds from the various regions of Italy (hours: Tue–Sat 8.30am–6.30pm, Sun until 12.30pm, tours every hour).

★
Certosa di Pisa

What would Italy be without its cult scooter, the Vespa? A fine selection of beautiful old Vespas can be admired in Pontedera, 21km/13mi to the south-east in the Museo Piaggio. The first-ever model, »April 1946 98cc«, is on display here (hours: Wed–Sat 10am–6pm).

Pontedera

◄ Museo Piaggio

★ Pistoia

F 8

Province: Pistoia (PT)   **Altitude:** 65m/213ft above sea level
Population: 85,000

Compared to the neighbouring cities Florence and Pisa, Pistoia, about 35km/21mi north-west of Florence in the fertile Ombrone valley, attracts few tourists. Nevertheless it does not lack buildings and tourist attractions, as the old city has kept its medieval charms very well. This is especially true of the cathedral square and market district, which are among the prettiest in Tuscany.

Pistoia started as a trading settlement on the Roman military road Via Cassia. In the 12th and 13th centuries the city flourished. However, disputes with neighbouring cities had consequences. Pistoia quarrelled with Bologna to the north over control of the Apennine passes; in the west Pisa lay in waiting, and Guelf Florence expanded in the east. A military defeat in 1254 brought on Florentine rule. The razing of the city walls in 1307 meant the submission of Pistoia, which was incorporated into the Tuscan grand duchy in the 16th century.

Old
merchant city

▶ VISITING PISTOIA

INFORMATION

Piazza Duomo
Tel. 057 32 216 22
Fax 05 73 343 27
www.pistoia.turismo.toscana.it

PARKING

The sights in Pistoia lie close together and cars are not allowed in the core of the old city – enough reason to park the car along the southern city wall, in front of the south-east city wall (with bus connection) and also at the railway station.

WHERE TO EAT

▶ Moderate

① San Jacopo
Via Crispi 15
Tel. 057 32 77 86, closed Mon
Small but up-market restaurant directly opposite Hotel La Patria. Popular, so reserve your table!

② Lo Storno
Via del Lastrone 8
Tel. 057 32 61 93, closed Sun
Historic osteria with local cuisine in the heart of the city. Wide selection of traditional primi and secondi.

WHERE TO STAY

▶ Mid-range

① Leon Bianco
Via Panciatichi 2
Tel. 05 73 266 76
Fax 05 73 266 75, 27 rooms
Small, comfortable hotel with modern furnishings in the pedestrian zone near the cathedral square. Parking lot at the hotel.

② Patria
Via Crispi 6/8
Tel. 05 73 251 87
Fax 05 73 36 81 68, 27 rooms
Its charms are already a bit faded but the central location of this traditional hotel makes up for that.

Baedeker recommendation

Giostra del Orso

If the crowds at the Palio in Siena or the Giostra del Saraceno in Arezzo are too much for you, try Pistoia's town festival.
On 25 July the citizens celebrate Giostra del Orso, a festival in honour of St Jacopo – as in Siena and Arezzo with a parade and a contest on Piazza del Duomo, where four teams compete to kill a (symbolic) bear.

What to See in Pistoia

✴ Piazza del Duomo
The surprisingly large cathedral square, centre of the historic quarter, has always presented an appearance of harmonious austerity and – unusual for an Italian city – has neither shops nor street cafés. Clerical and secular power are united peacefully here: the Romanesque cathedral with campanile and baptistery, the bishop's palace, Palazzo del Podestà and Palazzo Comunale, decorated with coats of arms, as well as the medieval residential tower Torre di Catilina.

✴ Duomo San Zeno
The Romanesque cathedral was built in the 12th and 13th centuries in place of a 5th-century building. The **Pisan-Luccan Romanesque**

Pistoia *Plan*

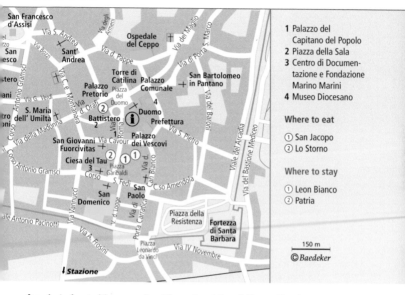

1 Palazzo del
   Capitano del Popolo
2 Piazza della Sala
3 Centro di Documen-
   tazione e Fondazione
   Marino Marini
4 Museo Diocesano

Where to eat

① San Jacopo
② Lo Storno

Where to stay

① Leon Bianco
② Patria

150 m
© Baedeker

façade is fronted by a portico. The colourful majolica coffered vault in front of the main portal is by Andrea della Robbia, as is the terra-cotta relief in the lunette of the door, which shows the Madonna with two angels (1505). The interior of the cathedral was restored to the 13th-century style. Next to the entrance is the grave of Cino da Pistoia with a seated figure of the poet. It is the work of an unknown master, done in 1337. The most important work in the Capella di San Jacopo, which can be entered from the right aisle (extra admission) is the **silver altar of St James**, a masterpiece of Italian gold and silver work created between 1287 and 1456 for a relic of St James, which the bishop of Pistoia obtained in 1144 from the archbishop of Santiago de Compostela in Spain. The 628 figures are made of silver metal, in part gilded and mounted on a core of wood, wax and resin. 15 scenes from the New Testament are depicted (1316) on the front. The right side has nine scenes from the Old Testament (1361–1364); the left side nine scenes from the life of James (1367–1371). The statue of St James enthroned is by Giglio Pisano. The two figures of prophets have been attributed to Brunelleschi.

The campanile next to the cathedral, the emblem of Pistoia, is 66m/217ft high. It is reminiscent of Venetian bell towers. The three upper storeys with delicate arcades and green-and-white striped marble cladding from the 13th century are especially beautiful. The bell storey and the brick-covered tower top are 16th century additions. The climb to the observation platform during the guided tour is a little

★
Campanile

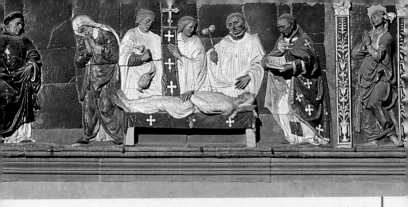

The majolica frieze of the Ospedale del Ceppo is intended to show the viewer the meaning of brotherly love.

⊙ strenuous but the reward is a beautiful view (hours: Sat–Mon 10am–1pm and 2–6pm; reservations at the tourist information on the cathedral square, Palazzo Vescovi).

Palazzo dei Vescovi
Next to the right-hand aisle of the cathedral stands the former bishop's palace, which shows its Romanesque character again after the most recent restoration of the façade. The front is decorated with 14th-century coats of arms. Today the palace is home to the tourist information office and the cathedral chapter museum (hours: Tue, Thu and Fri 10am–1pm and 3–5pm).

✳ Battistero
The baptistery has the characteristic eight-sided ground plan of a baptismal church. The building was begun in 1338 by Cellino di Nese to plans by Andrea Pisano. The outer covering is made of green and white marble. In the tympanum of the Gothic main door there is a Madonna, while the lintel below it bears scenes from the life of John. The interior is surprisingly empty but nevertheless impressive. The baptismal font by Lanfranco da Como dating from 1226 has been preserved.

Palazzo Pretorio
The austere Palazzo del Podestà or Palazzo Pretorio to the right of the baptistery was built in 1367 as the seat of the city ruler (podestà) appointed by Florence. Only the inner courtyard is in its original condition. A restoration between 1844 and 1846 gave the palace its present appearance. Today it holds part of the city court.

✳ ⊙
Opening hours:
Tue–Sat
10am–7pm,
Sun and holidays
9am–12.30pm
Opposite stands the Palazzo Comunale, decorated with coats of arms, which radiates medieval elegance with its street-level arcades and bundled trefoil windows in the upper storeys. The building was begun in 1294 under Guelf government and only finished in 1385 by the Sienese architect Michele di Memmo. In 1637 the bridge-like connection to the cathedral was added.

In the middle is the Medici coat of arms with the papal keys, which refers to Clement VII's intervention in the city history. Today the palace is the seat of a documentation centre on the work of the Pistoian architect Giovanni Michelucci (1891–1990) and the city museum, which includes a large number of panel paintings, frescoes and paintings from the 13th to 18th centuries in its collection.

To the right of the Palazzo Comunale a small street branches off to the palace of the Rospigliosi. Pope Clement IX was the illustrious offspring of this influential family . The palace houses the diocesan museum with its works of sacred art, old choir books and manuscripts from Pistoia and the area (hours: Tue–Sat 10am–1pm and 4–7pm).

Palazzo Rospigliosi, Museo Diocesano ⏲

The hospital, about 250m/275yd north of the cathedral square, was founded in the 13th century as a hospital and pilgrims' hospice. Its nickname is a reference to the offertory box (ceppo) where alms were collected for the needy. At the beginning of the 16th century it was placed under the Ospedale di Santa Maria Nuova, Florence's hospital and foundling home and decorated with a portico like its Florentine model. Artists from the della Robbia workshop created the beautiful polychrome **majolica frieze** of the portico.

Ospedale del Ceppo

The seven works of mercy are depicted here – corresponding to the duties of a hospital: clothing the naked, hosting pilgrims, nursing the sick, caring for prisoners, giving the last rites, feeding the hungry and giving drink to the thirsty. The frieze is considered to be one of the most beautiful works from the workshop of della Robbia. In the ospedale there is a small, unusual museum on the history of surgical instruments, which unfortunately can only be visited on appointment (tel. 05 73 35 22 20).

On the way back to the cathedral square make a detour to this church, which was built from 1159 in a swamp outside the city walls (pantano = swamp). Its façade, which has rounded arches on half columns, is decorated by a beautiful relief architrave above the main portal (1167). It resembles stylistically the reliefs on Roman sarcophaguses. The pulpit is a masterpiece of early Tuscan sculpture by Guido da Como (around 1250).

San Bartolomeo in Pantano

Pistoia is at its prettiest in the small streets between the cathedral square and Piazza della Sala. Here there are still medieval **workshops with stone benches** in front of the windows and wooden shutters on the doors. Since Pistoia has not yet really been discovered by tourists like many other cities in Tuscany, there are »normal« shops here with daily necessities. The **vegetable market** every morning on Piazza della Sala, the square with the well in the middle, is attuned to the needs of the residents of Pistoia. This is just the right place to find seasonal vegetable specialties from the Pistoia area.

★
Piazza della Sala

San Giovanni Fuorcivitas

From the market it is only a few steps to Via Cavour, which runs along the path of the old city wall. Originally outside the city wall (fuor civitas = outside the city), the Benedictine church was begun in 1150 and completed in the 14th century. Its white-green striped northern façade faces the street. On the lintel of the main door there is a **relief of the Last Supper** dating from 1160 by the local sculptor Gruamonte, one of his most beautiful works. In the aisle-less interior the pulpit by Fra Guglielmo da Pisa (around 1270) is worth a look. The basin for holy water is probably the first independent piece by Giovanni Pisano. The figures on the six-sided basin include personifications of the three cardinal virtues faith, love and hope. A further masterpiece of sacred art, a polyptych (1353–1355) by Taddeo Gaddi, is next to the main altar.

Centro di Documentazione e Fondazione Marino Marini

Follow Via Crispi to the southern part of the old city, to the shopping street Corso San Fredi. In the former church of Sant'Antonio dei Frati del Tau on the Corso San Fredi a museum was started for the sculptor Marino Marini, who was born in 1901 in Pistoia and died in 1980, and was known for his archaic human and animal figures (hours: Tue–Sat 9am–1pm and 3–7pm, Sun and holidays 9am–12.30pm).

Shops with workshops like this one are not common in Tuscany any more – except in Pistoia.

The church to the south and opposite was started in 1300 and embodies the simple Gothic style of the mendicant orders. The church was heavily damaged in World War II but still has fresco fragments from the 14th century. Behind the right side altar is the imposing grave of Filippo Lazzari which was made from 1462 to 1468 by Bernardo and Antonio Rossellino.

San Domenico

Also outside the old city but to the west is an unusual church, Pistoia's most important Renaissance building. The central-plan church was begun in 1495 and completed in 1561 by Giorgio Vasari. Vasari also designed the dome, which looks like a miniature version of the cathedral dome in Florence. The octagonal main space is actually much smaller than the broad vestibule suggests. At the main altar is the miraculous Madonna fresco (Giovanni di Bartolomeo Cristiani, around 1370) from the previous building, which was the reason for the new building in 1490.

Madonna dell'Umiltà

The Romanesque church Sant'Andrea, which goes back to the 8th century, is in the north-west part of the old city. Its **beautiful façade** is now constructed exactly like that of San Bartolomeo and the other churches in Pistoia. The capitals and the relief over the main portal (1166) are especially fine work. The pulpit by Giovanni Pisano, one of this artist's major works dating from 1298–1301, is undoubtedly the most valuable piece from an artistic point of view. It is supported by seven red porphyry columns which carry pointed arches. The figures of sibyls and prophets appear on the elaborately decorated capitals. The pulpit relief tells the story of Christ in five panels. Giovanni Pisano also created the wooden crucifix in the chapel on the left side of the church.

★ **Sant'Andrea**

★ ◀ Pulpit by Giovanni Pisano

★ Pitigliano

O 12/13

Province: Grosseto (GR)
Population: 4,200

Altitude: 313m/1,027ft above sea level

A visit to Pitigliano is like a trip into the past – especially if you arrive late in the evening. Even from outside the town, the closely nestled stone houses seem like something from a fairy tale, and this impression becomes even stronger in the dimly lit, labyrinthine alleys. The medieval houses of Pitigliano look as if they grew out of the steep tuffstone cliff, instead of being built on it. The most impressive view of the plateau with the cliff town, which looks like a fortress without a wall, can be seen when coming from Manciano.

VISITING PITIGLIANO

INFORMATION
Piazza Garibaldi 5
Tel. and fax 05 64 61 71 11

WHERE TO EAT

► **Moderate**
Il Tufo Allegro
Vicolo della Costituzione 5
Tel. 05 64 61 61 92, closed Tue
Small restaurant in a tuffstone cave,
super food, great service. Reservations
a must.

WHERE TO STAY

► **Mid-range/luxury**
Hotel della Fortezza/Sorano
Piazza Cairoli
Tel. 05 64 63 20 10
www.fortezzahotel.it

The Fortezza Orsini in Sorano is a
building with a history. In 1998 it was
converted into a hotel (12 rooms) with
loving attention to detail. The stylishly
furnished rooms all have a unique
view. Guests get a friendly reception.

► **Mid-range**
Valle Orientina
Loc. Valle Orientina
Tel. 05 64 61 66 11
Fax 05 64 61 77 28
www.valleorientina.it
Anyone looking for quiet will find it in
this peaceful hotel, 3km/1.8mi outside
Pitigliano in the Orientina valley. A
swimming pool, tennis court and
archery facilities are available for
sports lovers.

History

The Etruscans settled here and the Romans followed them. The Roman Orsini family which was allied with the Guelfs made Pitigliano
the seat of their county in 1293. The town later passed on the Florentine Strozzi family and in 1604 to the Grand Duchy of Tuscany. In
Pitigliano the shops with kosher products stand out. There was a
large Jewish community here into the 20th century; today only a few
Jewish residents remain.

What to See in Pitigliano

✷ Alleys and caves

Narrow streets, tiny flights of stairs and vaulted passageways are just
as typical for Pitigliano as the many caves which were dug into the
soft stone by the first inhabitants of the plateau, initially as graves
and later as storerooms. The Romans already used the cool rooms as
wine cellars, and today the best wines of the region, especially Bianco di Pitigliano, are stored here.

Palazzo Orsini, aqueduct

The palazzo with the crenellated roof recalls the Orsini family from
Rome. It was built in the 14th century and later converted by the
Renaissance architect Giuliano da Sangallo to a palace with a courtyard fountain. Today the Museo Civico is housed here. Gian Francesco Orsini had an aqueduct built on 15 pillars to provide water in
1545.

Piazza Gregorio VII is dominated by the Baroque façade of the cathedral, which was built in the Middle Ages but much altered in the 18th century, and its massive campanile. A travertine column on the square bears the Orsini coat of arms. Their heraldic animal was the bear (Italian orso).

Piazza Gregorio VII

The synagogue, which was built at the end of the 16th century and renovated in the 18th century, is open to the public.

Synagogue

The Vie Cave, Etruscan sunken roads carved out of the tuff, connect Pitigliano with the neighbouring Sorano and Sovana – a unique walking experience. Via Cava di San Giuseppe, which was renovated in 2001, is especially recommended.

Vie Cave

Around Pitigliano

The medieval town of Sorano is also beautifully situated, crowned by an Orsini castle, on the peak of a tuffstone plateau above the Lente gorge. Even though it is only a short distance from Pitigliano (9km/ 5.5mi), Sorano has remained unnoticed to this day and thus still has the charms of an almost unchanged medieval town.

✳
Sorano

The medieval character of Pitigliano is even more visible when illuminated at night than by daylight.

Attractions ▶ Close to Sorano, dark openings in the cliff walls are visible. They hold cave-like, Etruscan-Roman grave chambers from the 2nd and 3rd century BC. In 1293 the city passed from the legendary Aldobrandeschi to the Orsini– the coats of arms of both families are above the gate of the rocca. In the 16th century the fortress, which was expanded several times, played a decisive role as a border defence against the Papal States. It was never conquered and is considered to be a **masterpiece of military architecture**. Today there is a hotel in the fortress and a museum in one of the buildings. Orsini Park adjacent to the fortress is closed temporarily. Masso Leopoldino is worth a visit, not least because of the wonderful view. The tuffstone plateau, which was fortified by Leopold of Lorraine in the 18th century, is an observation platform.

San Quirico/ Vitozza The cave dwellings of Vitozza was built on the edge of San Quirico, a village about 5km/3mi south-east of Sorano, probably around 1000 BC. With about 200 grottoes the settlement is the largest of this kind in Italy. The caves were inhabited into the 20th century.

✳ Sovana Sovana is a picture-book town just like Pitigliano and Sorano and consequently attracts many visitors, but is still worth the trip. It was founded by the Etruscans on a tuffstone hill 8km/5mi north-west of Pitigliano. It flourished in the 11th century. In 1021 it was the birthplace of the monk Hildebrand, who in 1077 as Pope Gregory VII brought the Holy Roman Emperor Henry IV to his knees at Canossa. The entrance to the town is guarded by the fortress of the Aldobrandeschi. It was built in the 11th century on Etruscan foundations. The double-aisled hall crypt of the cathedral is from the same period. Its low Gothic vaulting was added in the 14th century. Lombard and southern French stonemasons created the remarkable **relief scenes on the pillar capitals** in 1100. On Piazza del Pretorio the late Romanesque church of Santa Maria has an excellent example of Lombard-Carolingian stone carving: The high altar is covered by a ciborium from the 9th century with fine ornamentation.

✳ Tomba Ildebranda Around Sovana road signs point out numerous Etruscan necropolises from the 4th to 2nd centuries BC, which include both monumental temple graves as well as underground grave chambers. The Tomba Ildebranda (late 3rd/early 2nd century BC) to the right of the road to San Martino sul Fiora on the Poggio Felceto is undoubtedly the most impressive grave site. It gets its name from Gregory VII, formerly Hildebrand. It is a temple grave carved out of rock. Ribbed columns with profiled bases and beautifully decorated capitals rise above a base with steps at the sides. The imitation temple was originally covered with stucco and had colourfully painted lintels in the upper part, traces of which are still visible. A steep underground dromos leads to the actual, square grave chamber with a stone bench for the dead.

In the high valley of the Albegna river about 25km/16mi west of Pitigliano, the hot springs of Saturnia are situated on a remote travertine rock on the ancient Via Clodia. According to legend the god Saturn sought refuge here – hence the name. The Etruscans called it Aurinia; it became Roman in 280 BC. The most striking survival from the Roman city is the Porta Romana on the west side. In the Middle Ages the Aldobrandeschi took power; in the 13th and 14th centuries the Sienese burned the city repeatedly.

Saturnia

◄ Terme di Saturnia

There is only one reason to go to Saturnia, as the Etruscans and Romans knew – the 37.5°C/99.5°F warm, sulphurous springs, which promise relief from rheumatism,

> ## ! Baedeker TIP
>
> ### Slippery!
> For swimming and exploring the basins of Cascate del Molino, waterproof shoes are essential because the natural stone is in part rough and also very slippery!

bronchial disorders and digestive problems. About 5km/3mi outside Saturnia towards Manciano below the luxurious spa hotel Terme di Saturnia, the thermal water bubbles over the travertine waterfalls Cascate del Molino into natural basins, where free bathing is possible. A parking lot and a bar are nearby; unfortunately there are no showers for washing off the unpleasant smell of sulphur. Anyone who prefers greater comfort should go to the four-star hotel Terme di Saturnia, where the thermal pool is open to non-residents too.

✳ Prato

F 9

Province: Prato (PR)
Population: 174,000

Altitude: 63m/206ft above sea level

Prato lies in the lower Bisenzio valley more or less halfway between Florence and Pistoia. But don't expect pretty countryside between the cities, as the heavily industrialized suburbs of Prato and Florence have almost joined up. Prato is not only the third-largest but also the richest city in Tuscany and has been the centre of the textile industry for a long time – this is the place to hunt for chic bargains! And even though this is a surprise in an industrial city like Prato, the historic centre is completely intact and well worth a visit.

Prato was probably founded on the ruins of an Etruscan-Roman settlement. During the glorious period of the Staufer dynasty, the city was the seat of an imperial viceroy. In the 14th century Prato was acquired by Florence for 17,500 gold florins, and despite occasional revolts the histories of these two cities have been tightly knit ever since.

First »rag city«, now »outlet city«

● VISITING PRATO

INFORMATION
Piazza delle Carceri
Tel. and fax 057 42 41 12
www.prato.turismo.toscana.it

WHERE TO EAT
▶ **Expensive**
② *Il Piraña*
Via Tobia Bertini, tel. 05 74 257 46
Closed Sat midday and Sun
First-class fish restaurant in
post-modern style.

▶ **Moderate**
① *Il Borbottino*
Via Fra Bartolomeo 13
Tel. 057 42 38 10
Closed Sun and Mon
Modern, innovative cuisine

WHERE TO STAY
▶ **Mid-range**
① *Flora*
Via Cairoli 31
Tel. 05 74 335 21
Fax 05 74 402 89
www.pratohotels.it
This spotless three-star hotel lies in the
middle of the old city.
Tastefully decorated rooms. Service is
important here.

▶ **Mid-range and budget**
② *Villa Rucellai*
Loc. Canneto, Via di Cannetto 16
Tel. and fax 05 74 46 03 92
Comfortable holiday hotel (12 rooms)
in a Renaissance villa with medieval
tower.

As in Florence, the **textile industry** developed early in Prato. The industry had its greatest upswing after World War II when Prato collected the rags of war-bombed Europe and turned them into new fabric. This business flourished and the population had tripled by 1975. Asian competition caused economic stagnation in the late 1970s, but further specialization soon led to recovery: today Prato has become »outlet city«. In 1992 it also gained something it had wanted for a long time: administrative independence from Florence and the status of an independent province.

What to See in Prato

Castello dell'Imperatore

⏱ Opening hours:
Summer: daily except Tue
9.30am–12.30pm
and 3.30–7pm,
Winter
8.30am–12.30pm
and 3–5.30pm

The massive fortress of the Staufer emperors on Piazza Santa Maria delle Carceri, built in 1237–1248 **for Holy Roman Emperor Frederick II**, is unique in northern central Italy for its building style and excellent state of preservation. Castello dell'Imperatore (or Fortezza di Santa Barbara) was built as an enlargement of a 10th-century castle of the counts of Prato and is similar to the numerous defensive structures that Frederick II built in his favourite southern Italian provinces. The imperial castles looked like a Roman castrum on the outside and primarily served defensive purposes, but the interiors are very liveable – unfortunately no interiors of Castello dell' Imperatore remain in their original form.

Prato *Plan*

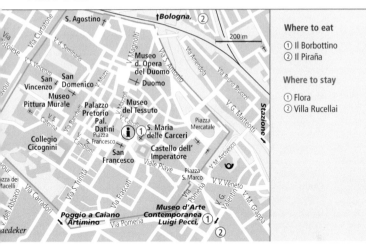

Where to eat

① Il Borbottino
② Il Piraña

Where to stay

① Flora
② Villa Rucellai

The so-called Cassero in the street of the same name has only recently re-opened. It was a medieval enclosed walkway, which led from the castello to the city wall and served as an invisible escape route. Its floor was apparently made so that even the clatter of horses' hooves cannot be heard.

Cassero

Opposite the northern corner of the castle is the imposing Santa Maria delle Carceri, built for a miraculous image of the Virgin which once hung on the wall of a prison (carcere) here. Giuliano da Sangallo designed a Renaissance church of outstanding beauty (1484–1495) on the ground plan of a Greek cross. A restrained dome crowns the crossing, coloured marble covers the façade and inside there are valuable terracotta medallions by Andrea della Robbia.

Santa Maria delle Carceri

Via Cairoli ends on Piazza del Comune, the centre of the city. Here is a statue of the textile merchant and banker Francesco di Marco Datini (1330–1410) who was famous beyond Prato's boundaries. The medieval, completely regular façade of Palazzo Pretorio dominates the square. Capitano del Popolo Fresco de Frescobaldi bought the residence in 1284 and made it into the first office of the city government. The open stair with balcony, crenellations and the bell tower were added in the 16th century. Since the 19th century the

Palazzo Pretorio, Museo Civico

Baedeker TIP

From the factory

Factory outlets are heaven for money-conscious fashion fans. In the textile city of Prato the density of outlets is almost unbeatable. The tourist office in Prato will help you find the right one, with a brochure that lists all the important addresses.

palace has housed the Museo Civico with the city art gallery (Galleria Comunale). The museum has a large collection of works of art of the 14th and 15th centuries, including masterpieces by Fra Filippo Lippi, Filippino Lippi, Bernardo Daddi and Giovanni da Milano (closed for restoration at present).

✳ **Museo del Tessuto**

The Palazzo Comunale opposite, which was built in the 13th century and remodelled in classical style in 1780, is home to the textile museum. The interesting collection contains textile patterns from the 5th century BC until today (hours: daily except Tue 10am–6pm).

✳ **Palazzo Datini**
🕐 Opening hours: Mon–Fri 9am–noon, 4–6pm, Sat only mornings Closed Sun

Francesco di Marco Datini, whose statue adorns Piazza Comunale, lived a few steps from Piazza del Comune in a palace in Via Rinaldesca, built at the end of the 14th century. It is a rare example of late Gothic secular architecture and foreshadows the developments of the 15th century. Only a few fragments of the paintings on the outer façade, which show the family history, can be discerned. The frescoes in the inner courtyard are well preserved. The large Datini archives are fascinating for students of economic history: **business letters, sales contracts, account books,** insurance policies and the voluminous correspondence of the merchant Marco Datini are stored here – a unique documentation of the everyday life of a medieval textile merchant.

✳✳ **Duomo Santo Stefano**

The cathedral is dedicated to St Stephen and John the Baptist and has been the spiritual centre of the city since the 10th century. It acquired its present form between 1385 and 1457. The wealthy city of Prato could afford the best artists, including Giovanni Pisano and Donatello, Michelozzo and Filippo Lippi. The festive, decorative character of the green-and-white stone covering of the façade is augmented considerably by the **outside pulpit**, a joint work of Donatello and Michelozzo 1434–1438 (copy; original in the cathedral museum) for the veneration of the belt of the Virgin, which is shown several times a year including Easter, 15 August and Christmas. The church has retained its Romanesque character. The pulpit in the nave, which is decorated with reliefs, was created by Mino da Fiesole and Antonio Rossellino in 1437.

✳✳ **Frescoes by Filippo Lippi ►**

The painting of the main choir chapel (1452–1466) by the Dominican monk Fra Filippo Lippi – and his assistant Fra Diamante – is one of the most beautiful fresco cycles of the early Renaissance in Italy. The frescoes are being restored at present but can be seen from a scaffold as part of a guided tour (only Sat 10am, 11am, 4pm, 5pm; Sun 10am and 11am; register for a guided tour one week in advance at tel. 057 41 41 12).

The cycle shows scenes from the life of the two patron saints of the church, which the artist interpreted in a relatively undramatic, even playful manner by the standards of the time. This can be seen especially clearly in *Herod's Feast*, painted in a wonderfully light style

The outside pulpit is an eye-catcher on the cathedral of Prato.

with the dancing Salome, for whom Filippo Lippi's mistress is supposed to have been the model. The holy belt of Mary is kept in Cappella del Sacro Cingolo (1385–1395) to the left of the entrance. The frescoes executed by Agnolo Gaddi from 1392 until 1395 tell the legend of the relic: Mary gave the belt to the apostle Thomas when she went to heaven, who gave it to a priest. A merchant from Prato brought the miraculous belt back to Prato on a trip to the Holy Land, where he turned it over to both the clerical and the secular powers. For this reason both the bishop and the mayor have keys to the shrine today.

★
◀ Cappella del
Sacro Cingolo

The treasures of the cathedral museum in the bishop's palace include medieval panel paintings, liturgical utensils, gold work, a *Madonna with the Archangel Michael and Saints Peter and Paul* dated 1262 by Giroldo di Jacopo da Como and Donatello's seven original reliefs for the cathedral outside pulpit (hours: Mon, Wed–Sat 9.30am–12.30pm, 3–6.30pm, Sun 9.30am–12.30pm).

★
**Museo dell'
Opera del Duomo**

🕐

The church not far to the west was built between 1283 and 1322. No one knows why the marble façade remained unfinished. Apart from a polychrome wooden cross (around 1400) the church is decorated in Baroque style.
The religious reformer Fra Girolamo Savonarola lived in the adjacent monastery until he went to Florence. The monastery holds a museum with frescoes and sketches from the local church and offers excellent insights into the technique of mural painting (pittura murale) and its restoration (hours: daily except Tue 10am–6pm, Sun and holidays only mornings).

★
**San Domenico,
Museo di
Pittura Murale**

✳
Centro d'Arte
Contemporanea
Luigi Pecci

⏲

South-east of the city on Viale della Repubblica is a futuristic museum complex for modern art that was opened in 1988, an international forum for contemporary painting, sculpture, design and video art with a programme of temporary exhibitions and teaching rooms. The museum building conceived by Italo Gamberini with an extensive sculpture park (including works by Enzo Cucchi, Barbara Kruger and Mauro Staccioli) symbolizes the public and private wealth of Prato (information under www.centropecci.it; hours: Mon, Wed–Sun 10am–7pm).

Around Prato

Calenzano
Toy soldier
museum ▶

About 15km/9mi south-east of Prato in Calenzano there is a charming Museo del Soldatino e della Figurina Storica, a collection of toy soldiers which was assembled with loving care (hours: Tue–Fri 4–7pm).

Country
villas

The country houses scattered over the gentle hills around Prato are a reminder of the enthusiasm that wealthy city-dwellers of the 15th and 16th centuries developed for rural life – though no one was willing to give up urban luxury for fresh air. While Prato's wealthy sited their country homes in the fertile Bisenzio valley, the Florentine Medici built two of their most beautiful villas south of Prato at the foot of Monte Albano, one near Poggio a Caiano, one near Artimino.

✳ ✳
Poggio a Caiano,
Villa Medicea

One of the most magnificent Medici villas of all stands on the edge of Poggio a Caiano, which can be reached on the road south out of Prato (about 9km/5.5mi, signposted). The villa was built as a summer home for Lorenzo il Magnifico from 1485 by Giuliano da Sangallo. The owner did not live to see it completed; but Leo X, the first Medici pope, enjoyed the rural luxury to the utmost. It possessed residential quarters of considerable size. The ground floor is decorated by arcades; large terraces surround the first floor and a stately loggia with columns and architrave recalls ancient temple and palace architecture. The **painting of the interior** was done by the most famous fresco artists of the 16th century, including Andrea del Sarto, Pontormo and Alessandro Allori. The noble Medici country residence shows a few architectural changes today (for example the outside

Classical interior in
Villa Poggio a Caiano

stairs) after being converted to the royal residence of Emanuele II in the second half of the 19th century. It lies in the middle of a wonderful park with hothouses and exotic decorative gardens. The interior furnishings have unfortunately survived only in part, but the main hall (Salone di Leone X) with frescoes painted by Allori in 1580 is original (hours: June–Aug 9am–4.30pm, April–May and Sept until 5.30pm, March and Oct 8.15am–4.30pm, Nov–Feb 8.15am–3.30pm, closed every 2nd and 3rd Mon).

From Poggio a Caiano a winding country road (about 5km/3mi, signposted) runs to the Medici villa of Artimino, also called La Ferdinanda, which can now be rented for conferences and meetings. From 1587 Buontalenti built this stylish country villa for Ferdinando I, obviously following the model of the nearby Medici villa in Poggio a Caiano. But La Ferdinanda is comparatively modest and suits the landscape much better. It lacks the generous arcades and terrace of its neighbour and the loggia is also much simpler. Decorative roof constructions are missing. Instead chimneys decorate the tiled roof, giving the house its nickname Villa dei Cento Camini. Inside the reserved style of the architecture is continued. The expressly **rural garden** suits it with its beautiful wine and olive plants. La Ferdinanda has a small but interesting archaeological museum with finds from excavations in the immediate area, including valuable Bucchero ceramics and Etruscan urns, bronze vases and iron statues (garden: daily except Wed 9.30am–12.30pm; villa: Tue 9.30am–12.30pm upon request, tel. 05 58 75 14 27).

★
Artimino,
Villa Medicea

★ San Gimignano

19

Province: Siena (SI)
Population: 7,000

Altitude: 334m/1,096ft above sea level

They can be see from afar, rising skywards on a hilltop in the upper Elsa valley: the famous towers of San Gimignano, the »Manhattan of the Middle Ages«. A picture of what urban life must have been like in the Middle Ages can be seen here as in no other place in Tuscany, thanks to careful restoration of the buildings using UNESCO funds.

The hill was already settled by the Etruscans, but the community is first mentioned in the 8th century. An ancient trade route to Rome led right through the town and brought it lucrative business. As in many cities **the rival noble families** of San Gimignano built towers as an expression of their political power – there were 72 at the end of the Middle Ages; today there are only 15.

To each family its own tower

San Gimignano Plan

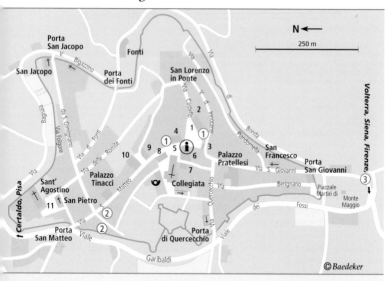

1 Piazza della Cisterna
2 Palazzo Tortoli
3 Arco dei Becci
4 Palazzo del Podestà
5 Piazza del Duomo
6 Palazzo del Popolo

7 Museo d'Arte Sacra,
   Museo Etrusco
8 Torri Salvucci
9 Palazzo Cancelleria
10 Palazzo Pesciolini
11 Piazza Sant' Agostino

Where to eat
① Dorando
② Osteria delle Catene

Where to stay
① La Cisterna
② L'Antico Pozzo
③ Podere Il Caggiolino

Since every family wanted to out-do the others with its tower, the city had to intervene in the end: in 1255 it was decided that the tower of the city hall should be the highest and no other should exceed it. In 1353, after the Great Plague, the formerly free commune was swallowed up by Florence – and from then on there was no more building.

What to See in San Gimignano

Porta
San Giovanni,
San Francesco

Porta San Giovanni is the best-preserved city gate in the medieval wall that dates from around 1300. Past small souvenir shops, cafés and wine shops, walk north along Via San Giovanni about 100m/110yd towards the centre to reach the Romanesque façade of the former parish church San Francesco, today an enoteca with a beautiful view of the valley. Diagonally opposite, the 14th-century Palazzo Pratellesi now holds the public library. In the reading room there is a fresco by Vincenzo Tamagni (1528) depicting the *Mystical Marriage of St Catherine of Alexandria*.

▶ VISITING SAN GIMIGNANO

INFORMATION

Piazza del Duomo 1
Tel. 05 77 94 00 08
Fax 05 77 94 09 03
www.sangimignano.com

PARKING

Do not even think about parking within the city walls; this is not even always possible for hotel guests (ask when making reservations). The parking lots outside the wall fill up quickly too. The largest is below Porta San Giovanni.

EVENTS

Fiera delle Messi

is the name of the festival on the third weekend in June. With a parade and competitions of course.

JOINT TICKET

A joint ticket is available for the most important museums, including Museo Civico, Torre Grossa and Cappella di Santa Fina. Tickets and information at the tourist information (see above).

WHERE TO EAT

▶ Expensive / moderate

① **Dorando**
Vicolo dell'Orto 2, tel. 05 77 94 18 62
Rustic restaurant not far from the cathedral with creative traditional cuisine (member of »Slow Food«). To finish off: panna cotta with strawberry cream (closed Mon).

▶ Budget

② **Osteria delle Catene**
Via Mainardi 18
Tel. 05 77 94 19 66, closed Wed
Beautiful dining room with old vaulted ceilings and tasty regional cuisine.

The pot roast in Chianti is incomparable.

WHERE TO STAY

It has to be seen to be believed: San Gimignano by day and San Gimignano in the evening are two completely different places. An overnight stay within the city walls is worthwhile for this if for no other reason. When the tourist buses leave, the town is yours!

▶ Mid-range

① **La Cisterna**
Piazza della Cisterna 24
Tel. 05 77 94 03 28
Fax 05 77 94 20 80, 50 rooms
The house is a 14th-century palazzo with pretty rooms furnished in the Florentine style. From the dining room there is a view over the Elsa valley.

② **L'Antico Pozzo**
Via San Matteo 87
Tel. 05 77 94 20 14,
Fax 05 77 94 21 17
www.anticopozzo.com
Hotel (18 rooms) in a tastefully restored medieval palazzo with patio in the middle of San Gimignano. Minibuses run between the parking lots outside the city wall and the hotel.

▶ Budget

③ **Podere Il Caggiolino**
Loc. Picchena
Castel San Gimignano
Tel. and fax 05 77 95 31 90
A pleasant and reasonably priced alternative to the hotels in San Gimignano 11km/7mi away. Generous breakfast, 5 rooms.

Piazza della Cisterna
✳

The atmospheric Piazza della Cisterna, the heart of the medieval city, got its name from the well built of travertine stone which was dedicated in 1273. The square was enlarged in 1346 and is bordered by **towers and palaces**. Starting at the arch of the Becci, which marks the path of the oldest city wall from the 11th century, in the south are Casa Razzi (no. 28) with the stump of a tower, Casa Salvestrini (no. 9), formerly Ospedale degli Innocenti and now Hotel La Cisterna, and Palazzo Tortoli with the stump of a tower from the Palazzo del Capitano del Popolo. On the north side of the square stands the Palazzo dei Cortesi with the high »devil's tower«. According to legend its owner returned from a trip to find it higher than it was before he left and thought that the devil was responsible.

> ### ! Baedeker TIP
>
> **There is gelato and then there is gelato**
> Everyone who has a sweet tooth raves about the ice cream in the gelateria at Piazza della Cisterna no. 4. Don't miss out on the delicious chocolate ice cream!

Museo della Tortura

Only a few yards to the east in Via del Castello is the museum of torture (information tel. 05 77 94 22 43). It is interesting but grisly to see the »aids« used by the Inquisition to make its victims talk. The detailed descriptions and comments are in English and Italian).

Collegiata Santa Maria Assunta
✳

A broad outdoor stair leads up to the Romanesque church of the Assumption of the Virgin on the neighbouring Piazza del Duomo. The name is misleading since San Gimignano was never a bishop's seat. In 1456 Giuliano da Maiano enlarged the church, which was dedicated in 1148, but the front, which was reconstructed several times in the course of the centuries, was never given a façade. Inside a fresco (1456) by **Benozzo Gozzoli** shows the martyrdom of St Sebastian. There are also two wooden statues of the Annunciation (around 1421) by the Sienese sculptor Jacopo della Quercia, which were colourfully painted by Martin di Bartolomeo in 1426. The church is mainly worth seeing for its frescoes. The realistically portrayed **scenes of the Last Judgement** (around 1393) on the western wall are by the Sienese Taddeo di Bartolo. In the right aisle Barna da Siena painted a monumental fresco cycle with scenes from the New Testament in the mid-14th century: the first row covers events from the Annunciation to the Flight to Egypt, the second from Jesus in the Temple to the Triumphal Entry into Jerusalem, the third from the Last Supper to Pentecost. As the artist biographer Giorgio Vasari relates, Barna fell from the scaffold while admiring his completed *Crucifixion* and died of his injuries. The frescoes were completed by his nephew and student Giovanni d'Asciano around 1380. In the left aisle there are similarly fine frescoes (around 1356–1367) by Bartolo di Fredi with scenes from the Old Testament. At the end of the right aisle is the Cappella di Santa Fina, built between 1468 and 1475 in

Frescoes ▶
✳ ✳

Cappella di Santa Fina ▶

A bird's eye view of San Gimignano: of the 72 towers that once stood in the town, 15 remain today.

purest Renaissance forms, the work of Giuliano and Benedetto da Maiano. The farmer's daughter Fina is said to have performed miracles and is the patron saint of San Gimignano. The top of the marble altar supports the sarcophagus that held the remains of St Fina until 1738. Domenico Ghirlandaio painted the frescoes *Pope Gregory Announces to St Fina that She Will Die* and *Funeral of the Saint* in 1475. The fresco of the Annunciation in the Loggia del Battistero dated 1476 has also been attributed to Ghirlandaio.

The adjacent museum for sacred art (Piazza Pecori) exhibits paintings and sculptures from the Middle Ages, choir books from the 14th century, an oriental carpet shaped like a Greek cross (16th century) and richly decorated vestments.

Museo d'Arte Sacra

To the left of the Collegiata stands the town hall, also called Palazzo Nuovo del Podestà, which was probably begun in 1288 by Arnolfo di Cambio and expanded in 1323. The town government met here from the 13th century. From the top of the 54m/177ft-high »broad tower«, completed in 1311 as the tallest of all towers in San Gimignano according to a city ordinance, there is a **beautiful panoramic view**. An inner courtyard decorated with coats of arms, a well from 1361 and three frescoes on the judge's loggia connects to a covered flight of steps leading to the city museum. The first hall on the second floor is called Sala Dante, as the poet came here on 8 May 1300 to persuade the city councillors to join the Guelf league. A

✱
Palazzo del Popolo, Torre Grossa

🕐
Opening hours: March–Oct daily 9.30am–7.30pm, otherwise 10am–6pm

wonderful *Maestà* by Lippo Memmi dated 1317 takes up the right wall of the room. The collection of paintings contains excellent Florentine and Sienese works of the 13th to 15th centuries, including a crucifix by Coppo di Marcovaldo (13th century), a *Mother of God with Child and Saints* by Benozzo Gozzoli dated 1466, *Madonna in Glory* by Pinturicchio (1512) as well as an *Annunciation* by Filippino Lippi which consists of two round panels and was commissioned in 1482. In the adjacent Camera del Podestà 14th-century frescoes by Memmo di Filippuccio show scenes of medieval everyday life.

Palazzo del Podestà
Torre Rognosa

Opposite the Collegiata stands the old Palazzo del Podestà, which was built in 1239 on the houses of the Mantellini family, enlarged in 1337 and converted to a theatre in 1537. A 51m/135ft-high tower rises over the building. From 1255 no private citizen was allowed to build a tower higher than that of the city ruler. The final standard was set in 1311 when the new town hall tower was completed at 54m/177ft.

Via San Matteo

Left of the Torre Rognosa at the beginning of Via San Matteo are the 13th-century twin towers of the Salvucci family. The other buildings worthy of note in this street are the 14th-century Casa-Torre Pesciolini (no. 32) with its arched windows and Palazzo Tinacci (no. 60/62) with windows in the style of different periods.

Rocca

Behind the Collegiata a short but steep walk goes up to the castle, which was built in 1353 by the Florentines on the highest point of

The journey is its own reward: Tuscan roads will take you there, slowly but restfully.

the town hill but razed in 1555 on the orders of Cosimo I de Medici. Parts of the wall and the defensive tower are preserved. An unforgettable view is the reward for the climb.

The brick church in the north of the walled city was built between 1280 and 1298 in the austere style of the mendicant orders. Inside the church with its exposed roof beams the Cappella di San Bartolo is on the right. It has an elaborate marble altar by Benedetto da Maiano (1494) where the remains of St Bartolo of San Gimignano rest. The main altar is decorated by a panel of the *Coronation of the Virgin* (1483) by Piero del Pollaiuolo.

Sant'Agostino

The main attraction is the fresco cycle dated 1464–1465 in the central choir chapel, a work by Benozzo Gozzoli. The painter represented the life of St Augustine (354–430) in 17 scenes. The chronological scenes start on the left in the bottom row: Augustine is placed in the care of a schoolmaster by his parents; as a youth he is admitted to the university in Carthage; St Monica prays for her son Augustine; he travels to Italy by ship; Augustine is received on land; he teaches in Rome when he is barely 20; Augustine travels to Milan. In the middle row: audience with the bishop of Milan and Emperor Theodosius; Monica prays for her son's conversion; disputation between Augustine and Ambrose; Augustine reads the epistle of Paul in the garden of his friend Alipius; Augustine is baptized by Ambrose on the following Christmas day and founds his order; Augustine and the boy at the sea; explanation of the rules of the order; death of St Monica. In the top row: Augustine as bishop of Hippo blessing his congregation; conversion of the heretic Fortunatus; vision of St Jerome; death and ascension of St Augustine. The frescoes on the third altar to the left are worth seeing: *St Sebastian* (1524) by Benozzo Gozzoli, Sebastiano Mainardi's *St Bartolo* (1487) as well as *Birth and Assumption of the Virgin* (around 1400) by Bartolo di Fredi in the chapel next to the altar. The sacristy gives access to the adjoining cloister to the south (15th century) with the chapter house.

★ ★
◄ Frescoes by Benozzo Gozzoli

San Giovanni Valdarno

H 12

Province: Arezzo (AR)
Population: 20,000

Altitude: 134m/439ft above sea level

The upper Arno valley (Valdarno) is best crossed on the Autostrada del Sole southwards. On the west the valley is bordered by the hills of ►Chianti, on the east by the higher Pratomagno. The valley itself is heavily industrialized and not very inviting at first glance. However, towns like San Giovanni Valdorno, about halfway between Arezzo and Florence, are worth a stop.

VISITING SAN GIOVANNI VALDARNO

INFORMATION
Piazza Cavour 3
Tel. / fax 055 912 11 23

WHERE TO EAT
▶ **Moderate**
Osteria di Rendola
Loc. Rendola / Montevarchi
Via di Rendola 78 / 81
Tel. 05 59 70 74 91
Fax 05 59 70 74 90
www.osteriadirendola.it
In the middle of the countryside with
a view of Valdarno. Creative seasonal

cuisine is offered here. Food is served
on a beautiful veranda in the summer.

WHERE TO STAY
▶ **Mid-range**
Valdarno
Via Traquandi 13 / 15
Montevarchi
Tel. 05 59 10 34 89
Fax 05 59 10 34 99
Modern hotel near the railway station.
Elegant very comfortable rooms.

Sightseeing — The centre of the town is Piazza Cavour where the Palazzo Pretorio, thought to have been built by Arnolfo di Cambio in the 13th century, attracts the eye with its lavish coats of arms. Behind the Palazzo Pretorio stands the Basilica Santa Maria delle Grazie, which was dedicated in the 15th century and has a classical veranda dating from 1840. Inside the church is a miraculous picture of the Virgin Mary (around 1400). The Oratorio di San Lorenzo from the 14th century also stands on the main square with two naves of different heights. The main altar has a 14th-century triptych by Giovanni del Biondo.

Around San Giovanni Valdarno

Convento di Montecarlo — About 2km/1.3mi south of San Giovanni Valdorno the convent of Montecarlo lies at a higher elevation. It was founded in the 15th century. The monastery church dedicated to San Francesco has a beautiful *Annunciation* by Fra Angelico (around 1440).

Montevarchi — No more than 5km/3mi south of San Giovanni Valdorno lies the medieval town of Montevarchi, which has an impressively harmonious and unspoiled appearance. The Palazzo del Podestà, the church of San Lorenzo on Piazza Varchi and, for those interested in prehistory, the palaeontological museum in the former monastery of San Lodovico are worth seeing.

Loro Ciuffenna — Only about 10km/6mi separate Montevarchi from Loro Ciuffenna on the opposite side of the valley. The town is one of the nicest in Pratomagno and a good place to **start hikes**.

A small artistic jewel is hidden 2km/1.3mi further in Gropina. The **Gropina**
Romanesque parish church of St Peter was built between 1150 and
1220 on Roman and Etruscan foundations. The monolithic columns
and pillars with carefully worked early Romanesque capitals in the
Lombard tradition are a joy to behold. They show a pig with her lit-
ter, a wolf with its prey, an eagle, lions, the battle of the virtues and
vices, riders, leaf ornaments and grape vines. The beautiful pulpit
with reliefs of the evangelists' symbols (lion, angel, eagle) and rich
decorations is from the 12th century.

San Miniato

G 8

Province: Pisa (PI)   **Altitude:** 156m/511ft above sea level
Population: 26,000

**The town lies on three hills about halfway between Florence and
Pisa. In the Middle Ages it was the most important Tuscan base of
the Holy Roman emperors. As a result of this special relationship
to Germany, the town had the words »al tedesco« attached to its
name in World War II.**

Under the Holy Roman emperor Otto I in the 10th century there
was an imperial castle on the hill and a village with increasingly
Guelf sympathies outside the castle walls. The tensions culminated in
1172 in a revolt that ended with the destruction of all houses and
possessions outside the castle walls. Emperor Frederick II had the
fortress renovated in the mid-13th century and his hapless adviser
Pier delle Vigne locked in the tower on the hill. The Germans destroyed this tower in 1944 – and rebuilt it in 1958.

▶ VISITING SAN MINIATO

INFORMATION
Piazza del Popolo
Tel. 057 14 27 45

WHERE TO EAT
▶ Budget
Omero
Piazzale La Pace 4 / a,
Tel. 05 71 40 05 20
Closed Sat
Typical Tuscan trattoria at the foot of
the rocca of San Miniato.

WHERE TO STAY
▶ Mid-range
Miravalle
Piazza del Castello 3
(near the bishop's palace)
Tel. 05 71 41 80 75
Fax 05 71 40 19 68
www.albergomiravalle.com
Pretty little hotel in a quiet location.
Most of the rooms have a beautiful
view of the Arno valley.

What to See in San Miniato

Town with a view
The town lies on one of the highest points in the area. At the top is »Frederick's tower«, a relic of the former imperial castle. It is the landmark of the town now that it has been rebuilt, and commands a fantastic view.

Piazza del Popolo, San Domenico
Piazza del Popolo is a good starting point for a tour, with the church of San Domenico (also called Santi Jacopo e Lucia de Forisportam) with its undressed façade. The aisle-less interior has frescoes on the life of St Dominic (around 1700) and the tomb by Bernardo Rossellino of the respected physician Giovanni Chellini († 1461), who founded the hospital next to the church of Santa Maria a Fortino.

★
Seminario Vescovile
Between 1650 and 1708 the episcopal seminary was built on the valley side of Piazza Santa Maria. The building complex was extended over time by adding smaller houses along the city wall until it formed an uninterrupted, beautifully painted façade.

★
Duomo, Museo Diocesano
A steep stairway leads from here to the »cathedral meadow« (Prato del Duomo) with an excellent view. The church is dedicated to the Virgin and St Genesio, was built in 12th century and later reconstructed several times. In the 15th century a massive tower of the citadel was incorporated into the cathedral as a campanile. It was later remodelled in Baroque style and only the façade was preserved. The little diocesan museum displays religious art including works by the Florentine school of Giotto.

Empoli

Industrial city
The modern town lies in the Arno valley about 8km/5mi north-east of San Miniato and is known for its glass and textile industry. 20 or 30 years ago there was almost no Tuscan family that did not have some item handmade out of green glass from Empoli, be it only a vase or cup. But today the small workshops have almost all fallen victim to industrial production. Despite its industrial character Empoli has a small centre with pleasant pedestrians streets such as Via del Giglio.

Sightseeing
Empoli's centre, Piazza Farinata degli Uberti, is surrounded by arcades and decorated with a fountain with naiads. The square got its name from an illustrious 13th-century member of the Florentine patrician Uberti family. The most noticeable building on the square is the collegiate church of St Andrew with its façade of green and white marble which was added in the late 12th century. Its present appearance comes above all from the later reconstructions. A visit to the collegiate museum on the neighbouring Piazzetta della Propositura is recommended. The **art collection** was reorganized in 1991 and contains Tuscan paintings and sculptures from the late 14th to the 17th century.

Archaeological excavations in the area of Montelupo 10km/6mi east of Empoli uncovered signs of Stone Age settlements of the Villanova culture as well as Etruscan and Roman habitation. Under Florentine rule the fortified town of Montelupo developed in the early Middle Ages to be an important centre for ceramics with coloured glaze, the so-called majolica, from the 13th century. The well-presented archaeological and ceramics museum at Via Bartolomeo Sinibaldi 45 displays both prehistoric finds and many items from ceramics workshops of the 14th to 18th centuries, including beautifully painted vases and coats of arms of such famous Florentine families as the Medici, Strozzi and Machiavelli.

Surroundings, Montelupo

✶

◄ Museo Archeologico e della Ceramica

Vinci

In fertile land about 11km/7mi north of Empoli on the southern slopes of Monte Albano lies the community of Vinci, birthplace of the artist, engineer and natural scientist Leonardo da Vinci (► Famous People).

Birthplace of Leonardo da Vinci

Anyone interested in engineering should visit the elongated medieval castle that dates from the 10th to 13th centuries. The museum here has models built to scale of devices from Leonardo da Vinci's drawings – for example a flying machine, a bicycle and a construction similar to water skis (hours: daily 9.30am–6pm, in summer until 7pm). The attached library possesses reproductions of drawings and manuscripts of the universal genius da Vinci (hours: Tue–Fri 3–7pm).

✶ **Museo Leonardiano**

Precision by Leonardo: a stabilizer

In the large vaulted cellars below the castle (Via Montalbano 2) a further museum has an interesting exhibition of traditional agricultural implements (oil presses, fermentation barrels, ploughs, ceramics etc.), models of utopian machines and drawings by Leonardo, copies of paintings and sculptures by the master, the copy of a bas-relief by Pierino da Vinci, a nephew of Leonardo, as well as fossils and archaeological finds from the area (hours: daily 10am–1pm, 3–7pm).

✶ **Museo Ideale Leonardo da Vinci** ⏰

A final attraction is Leonardo's supposed birthplace in Anchiano 3km/1.8mi away, which has reproductions of designs by Leonardo as well as Tuscan landscapes and a copy of a map of the Arno valley that he drew (hours: daily 9.30am–6pm, in summer until 7pm).

Casa Natale di Leonardo ⏰

✴ San Quirico d'Orcia

L 12

Province: Siena (SI)　　　　　　**Altitude:** 424m/1,391ft above sea level
Population: 2,400

San Quirico d'Orcia is not spectacular, but it is an orderly and pleasant town with instant appeal due to its almost complete town wall. It lies on the old Frankish road through the river valleys of Orcia and Asso, about 45km/28mi south-east of Siena. In 1154 Emperor Frederick Barbarossa received the emissaries of Pope Adrian IV here – an event that is celebrated every year on the third Sunday in June.

Sightseeing

The Romanesque **collegiate church** in the middle of town is easy to find. As early as the 8th century a parish church, pieve di Orsenna, is mentioned at this location. In the 12th century the Romanesque structure was built, to which the transepts were added in the 13th century. The Baroque choir was completed in 1653, the tower added in 1806. The simple façade has an impressive Romanesque west door (around 1080) with a depiction of Pope Damasus II in the lunette. The side door is attributed to the school of Giovanni Pisano (around 1288). Inside note above all the choir stalls, which were decorated with intarsia work in 1502.

The little **park** Horti Leonini next to the medieval city gate Porta Nuova is ideal for a break. Behind a modest entrance lies an Italian-style garden designed by Diamide Leoni in 1540 with pretty flower borders and boxwood hedges.

> **! Baedeker TIP**
>
> **Free bath**
>
> Bathing is free in the natural pools below the town and the old mill, which is being restored. The water flows into the valley in little streams and collects in turquoise-coloured pools. It is easy to miss: on the road to Bagno Vignoni right after the bridge across the Orcia there is an unpaved road. The pools themselves are a short climb but it is worth the effort!

Around San Quirico d'Orcia

✴ Val d'Orcia

The hilly landscape between San Quirico d'Orcia in the west, Sarteano in the east and Radicofani in the south is some of the most beautiful that Tuscany has to offer: forests and fields, small roads that wind through them, picture-perfect cypress avenues, remote hilltop farms, small hidden castles and villages with beautiful views.

✴ Bagno Vignoni

The little spa resort Bagno Vignoni, whose springs were already known in Roman times, is only 4km/2.5mi south of San Quirico d'Orcia. Catherine of Siena and Lorenzo de Medici also valued the

► VISITING SAN QUIRICO D'ORCIA

INFORMATION
Via Dante Alighieri 33
Tel. 05 77 89 72 11
www.comunesanquirico.it

WHERE TO EAT

► Inexpensive / moderate
Osteria del Leone
Via dei Mulini 3, Bagno Vignoni
Tel. 05 77 88 73 00
The owner treats his guests to wonderful Tuscan specialties like pappardelle with wild boar ragout and rabbit roasted on pine nuts.

WHERE TO STAY

► Mid-range / luxury
Posta Marcucci
Via Arca Urcea 43
Bagno Vignoni
Tel. 05 77 88 71 12
Fax 05 77 88 71 19
www.hotelpostamarcucci.it
Traditional hotel below the town centre of Bagno Vignoni with its own thermal pool (also open to the public).

---

healing powers of the spring waters of Bagno Vignoni. It is easy to understand why the Russian director Andrei Tarkovsky chose this place as the setting for his cult film *Nostalghia*: the large pool filled with bubbling spring water at a temperature of 51°C/123°F was built in the 15th century in the middle of the village. Together with the beautiful Renaissance building that now holds the refined Hotel Le Terme, the pool makes a beautiful setting. Bathing is not permitted here but in the modern swimming pool in the hotel named Posta Marucci (open to the public for an admission charge; closed Thu). The pool itself is small but the tree-shaded lawn, sun terrace and the wonderful view of the scenery and Rocca d'Orcia are delightful.

Sansepolcro

outside

Province: Arezzo (AR)
Population: 16,000

Altitude: 330m/1,083ft above sea level

Piero della Francesca, Sansepolcro's most famous son, is the reason to visit this somewhat colourless industrial and commercial town in the upper Tiber valley, 35km/22mi north-east of ►Arezzo, since important works by the outstanding Renaissance painter can be admired in the local art gallery. Sansepolcro is also known for its gold jewellery.

Sansepolcro means »holy grave«. The town got its name according to legend from two pilgrims, Arcano and Egidio, who brought relics of the grave of Christ back from Jerusalem in the 10th century and

▶ VISITING SANSEPOLCRO

INFORMATION
Piazza Garibaldi 2
Tel. 05 75 74 05 36

WHERE TO EAT / WHERE TO STAY

▶ **Moderate / mid-range**
Relais Oroscopo di Paola e Marco
Via Togliatti 68

Pieve Vecchia
Tel. 05 75 73 48 75
Fax 05 75 73 48 75
www.relaisoroscopo.com
Here you can sleep like a king and dine
like a prince. Paola and Marco's
kitchen is known far beyond Sansepolcro. The hotel also has a pool!

built an oratory for them. At first Camaldolese monks devoted
themselves to caring for the holy site and later founded an abbey
here. In later years the rulers of Sansepolcro changed repeatedly until
it was attached to Florence in the mid-15th century.

What to See in Sansepolcro

✷
**Pinacoteca
Comunale**

🕓
Opening hours:
June–Sept
9am–1.30pm and
2.30–7.30pm, Oct–
May 9.30am–1pm
and 2.30–6pm

The municipal art gallery (Via Matteotti no. 10) in the former Palazzo Comunale is not to be missed. It displays paintings from the
14th–16th centuries including works by Luca Signorelli and Santi di
Tito, who was born in Sansepolcro, and terracottas from the della
Robbia workshop. However, the gallery owes its fame primarily to
Piero della Francesca (around 1416–1492), who found work above
all in Umbria and at the courts of Ferrara, Rimini and Urbino. He
was highly honoured in his home town and was interred in the cathedral on 12 October 1492 – the day when Columbus first set foot
in the New World. The use of perspective, strict geometry and a new
spatial style of composition are important elements of his art, which
can be seen in his poetic *Resurrection*, painted in 1463 for the council
chamber of the palace.

Piero's largest independent work was the so-called *Misericordia Altar*
for the lay brotherhood of Sansepolcro. Even though Piero promised
in 1445 to complete the 23 panels within three years, it took him 15
years in the end. The centre picture is dominated by a Madonna of
Mercy with the most important donors of the brotherhood at her
feet.

**Duomo
San Giovanni
Evangelista**

The cathedral also lies on the busy Via Matteotti. It was already part
of the Camaldolese monastery, which was built from 1012 to 1049,
as the abbey church and was altered several times later. Behind the
Romanesque façade with a rose window that was added later is a basilica whose interior already shows the **transition to the Gothic style**.
The church has an altar by Matteo di Giovanni – the original of the

centre panel with the *Baptism of Christ* by Piero della Francesca is in London today. The larger than life-size crucifix (12th century) of walnut wood in the left choir chapel shows the influence of the *Volto Santo* from Lucca. There is also a beautiful terracotta tabernacle from the della Robbia workshop in the presbytery.

To the left of the cathedral stands the **Laudi palace** with an arcaded inner courtyard (today the town hall). It was built from 1591 until 1609 on the threshold between Renaissance and Baroque.

Beyond the Portadella-Pesa gate is **Piazza San Francesco** with the church of the same name. The façade and the bell tower are all that remain of the original 13th-century building; the rest was changed considerably in the late Baroque period.

No one has bathed here for a long time: the thermal pool of Bagno Vignoni.

Fortezza Medicea The Medici fortress was built on older foundations in the early 16th century, when Sansepolcro was already Florentine. The plans might be the work of Giuliano da Sangallo.

Around Sansepolcro

✶ Anghiari This picturesque town 10km/6mi west of Sansepolcro is a labyrinth of narrow alleys. The only attraction is the 14th-century Palazzo Pretorio, which is embellished with coats of arms. Anghiari is famous for the battle on 29 June 1440, when Florentine troops allied to the pope defeated the army of the Duke of Milan and brought about the final victory over eastern Tuscany – a triumph that was commemorated in the Great Hall of the Palazzo Vecchio in Florence by Leonardo da Vinci.

Monterchi The main reason why visitors come to the modest village of Monterchi, about 10km/6mi south of Sansepolcro, is to see a famous work by Piero della Francesca: during restorations to the pilgrimage chapel in 1888 the beautiful *Madonna del Parto* (the Virgin Mary before giving birth, around 1460) by Piero della Francesca came to light. It has been housed in the local school building since 1992.

✶ ◄ Fresco by Piero della Francesca

✴ Siena

Province: Siena (SI)   **Elevation:** 322m/1,056ft above sea level
Population: 54,500

Florence may be the capital and artistic centre of Tuscany, but Siena is considered to be the most beautiful city of the region. Its impressive silhouette with towers and domes can be seen from far away. The characteristic red-brown colour of the buildings is not a coincidence: the clay from this area was once used as a natural pigment by artists – the coveted warm Siena brown. Within the mighty Medici wall, the Gothic city spreads over three ridges which meet in the secular centre at the famous Piazza del Campo, one of the most celebrated squares in Europe and venue of the Palio horse race.

Three hills, three cities or in this case: thirds of a city (terzi). In the south lies the Terzo di Città around the shopping street Via di Città with the Pinacoteca Nazionale and the cathedral at the highest point of the city; in the north the Terzo di Camollia around Via Banchi di Sopra takes its character from the beautiful palaces of wealthy merchants; and in the east lies Terzo di San Martino. | **City on three hills**

The history of Siena goes back to the Roman period. The rivalry between the city, which was loyal to the Holy Roman Emperor, and papal Florence ended in 1235 with a peace treaty that was severe for Siena and simultaneously led to a reform of the city government. From this time the city was governed by a council of 12 noblemen and 12 commoners. The city owes its wealth partly to the **silver mines of Montieri** and the flourishing banking business – Sienese banking houses were among the most profitable in all Europe. Despite the victory over Florence in the battle of Montaperti in 1260, Siena had to submit to Florence again in 1269 and place city government in the hands of the merchants. They established the Council of Nine as the governing body, which gave Siena a period of peace from 1287 to 1355. This in turn allowed **a magnificent flowering of the arts**. In 1348 the Great Plague caused the economy and population to decline. From 1487 until 1512 Pandolfo Petrucci, called »Il Magnifico«, ruled the city. Under his less popular successors Siena was again the object of rival imperial and papal interests. In 1559 in the Peace of Chateau-Cambrésis Siena was given to Duke Cosimo I of Tuscany – the end of the city republic was sealed, the government-in-exile formed of Sienese families in Montalcino powerless to restore the old status. | **History**

← *The Sienese call it simply »Il Campo«: a place to sit and look.*

Siena *Plan*

Viale R. Franci
La Lizza
Viale Cesare Maccari
Florence,
Porta Camollia,
Stazione
Piazza A. Gramsci
Sant' Andrea
Via dei
Fonte Nuova
Via di Pian d'Ovile
Arezzo ③
Osservanza
MURA
San Francesco

Forte di Santa Barbara
(Fortezza Medicea)
①
Viale
Stadio
Stadio Comunale
Via F. Tozzi
Montanini
Via della secca Stufa
Via Vallerozzi
San Donato
Piazza S. Francesco
Orat. di Sa Bern

Viale dei Mille
Via Comunale
Piazza Matteotti
Santa Maria dei Nevi
Palazzo Salimbeni
Piazza Salimbeni
Via d. Rossi
San Pietro Ovile
Santa Maria di Provenzano

Via Curtatone
Via di Paradiso
Via della Sapienza
Palazzo Tantucci
Via dei Termini
Palazzo Spannocchi
Piazza Provenzano Salvani

ℹ
Piazza S. Domenico
V. di Città
Via S.
Via Caterina
Casa di Santa Catarina
Via delle
Palazzo Tolomei
Via Banchi di sopra
San Cristoforo
Caffè Nannini
San Vigilio
Università
Loggia del Papa

San Domenico
Fonte Branda
Via di Fontebranda
Galluzza
Terme
Croce del Travaglio
V. Banchi di sotto
Via di Pantar

Porta Fontebranda
Via Esterna di Fontebranda
Via Diacceto
Loggia d. Mercanzia
Fonte Gaia
ℹ
Palazzo Piccolomini
San Martino
Via S. Martino

Piazza S. Giovanni
Palazzo del Magnifico
Il Campo
Torre d. Mangia
Palazzo Pubblico
④

MURA
Palazzo Arcivesco-vile
②
Duomo
Piazza del Duomo
Museo d. Opera Metropolitana
Via di Città
Casato di sotto
Palazzo Chigi-Saracini
Piazza del Mercato
①
V. di Salicott
Via d. So

San Sebastiano
Via del Fosso di Sant'Ansano
Prefettura
Palazzo delle Papesse
Piazza Postierla
Via di Stalloreggi
Casato di sotto
Dupré

Ospedale di S. Maria della Scala
Pinacoteca Nazionale
④
San Pietro
San Giuseppe
Via di Fontanella

③
V. Stalloreggi
San Quirico
Prato S. Agostino
Sant' Agostino

Pian
Via Paolo Mascagni
Porta Laterina
①
Palazzo Pollini
dei
Via Tommaso Pendola
Via Sarrocchi
Museo di Storia Naturale
Via Per Andrea Mattioli

San Niccolò al Carmine
Mantellini
Santa Lucia
Orto Botanico
Porta Tufi
Monte Oliveto Maggi
Grosseto

100 m
©Baedeker
Porta San Marco
Grosseto

Where to eat
① Trattoria Papei
② Antica Osteria da Divo
③ Antica Botteganova
④ Castelvecchio

Where to stay
① Palazzo Ravizza
② Santa Caterina
③ Hotel Duomo
④ Locanda Garibaldi

⊙ VISITING SIENA

INFORMATION

Piazza del Campo 56
Tel. 05 77 28 05 51, fax 05 77 27 06 76
www.siena.turismo.it

TRAFFIC

Except for a few small streets, Siena is
closed to private cars – which does not
mean that there are no cars in the
city! Buses arrive at Piazza San
Domenico; drivers should follow the
signs and park their cars in one of the
parking lots or garages along the city
wall. The railway station is below the
centre of the old city, about 2km/
1.3mi away.

DON'T MISS!

2 July and 16 August are dates to take
note of – on these two days the
legendary horse race known as the
Palio takes place in Siena, and the
whole city flips out. Be sure to book
tickets in time (see Baedeker Special
p.394)

SHOPPING

Most of the shops are to be found on
Via di Città and Via dei Banchi di
Sopra. This includes the most expensive ones, such as Drogheria Manga-
nelli (Via di Città 71–73), where
cakes, especially the Sienese fruit cake
panforte (see photo), are still made
from old recipes. The café and
pasticceria scene in Siena is dominated by the Nannini family. For this
reason a stop in at least one of their
bars or cafés should be part of every
visit to Siena. True wonders of con-
fectionery can be found in the
Nannini institution Conca d'Oro (Via
Banchi di Sopra 24). Enoteca Italiana
on Piazza Matteotti 30 and Enoteca in
Forte di Santa Barbara are good places
to buy wine.

Pretty accessories, especially by Alessi,
are available at Ditta Muzzi Sergio,
Via dei Termini 97.

JOINT TICKET

Siena offers a combined admission
ticket (biglietto cumulativo) for two
days as well as an expensive and
comprehensive one for seven days.
The tourist information office will
help you choose the right one.

WHERE TO EAT

► Expensive

③ *Antica Botteganova*
Via Chiantigiana 29
Tel. 05 77 28 42 30
Closed Mon.
The restaurant in the north of the
city – outside of the old walls – was
awarded a Michelin star for its out-
standing cuisine.

► Inexpensive/moderate

② *Antica Osteria da Divo*
Via Franciosa 25
Tel. 057 77 28 43 81
This restaurant near the cathedral
stands out for its enchanting vaulted
rooms and excellent Tuscan cooking.
Open daily.

④ *Osteria Castelvecchio*
Via Castelvecchio 65
Tel. 05 77 495 86, closed Mon
Rustic restaurant in the vaulted cellars
of an old palazzo. The menu changes
every day and is written by hand.
The tasting menu is not to be missed.

► Moderate

① *Trattoria Papei*
Piazza del Mercato 6, closed Mon.
Regional cuisine at decent
prices – and right in the middle of
town!

WHERE TO STAY

▶ **Mid-range to luxury**

② *Santa Caterina*
Via E. S. Piccolomini 7
Tel. 05 77 22 11 05
Fax 05 77 27 10 87, 22 rooms
Quality hotel at the edge of the old city (15 min. to Piazza del Campo) with stylishly furnished rooms and a generous breakfast buffet. Be sure to request a room on the garden side!

① *Palazzo Ravizza*
Pian dei Mantellini 34
Tel. 05 77 28 04 62
Fax 05 77 22 15 97
www.palazzoravizza.it
This hotel in an old city palace has been in business since 1924. The rooms with wooden and stucco ceilings have an old-fashioned charm.

▶ **Mid-range**

③ *Hotel Duomo*
Via di Stalloreggi 38
Tel. 05 77 28 90 88, fax 05 77 43 043
www.hotelduomo.it, 23 rooms
Very comfortable three-star hotel near the cathedral.

▶ **Budget**

④ *Locanda Garibaldi*
Via G. Duprè 18
Tel. 05 77 28 42 04, 7 rooms
Reasonably priced hotel right in the centre behind Piazza del Campo. Reserve ahead, since there are only a few rooms!

✳ ✳ Piazza del Campo

Heart of the city Visitors are first drawn to Piazza del Campo, which was built in the 13th and 14th centuries and became Italy's first pedestrian zone in 1956. The harmonious appearance of the piazza, scene of the legendary Palio races twice a year (▶Baedeker Special p.394), makes it one of the most beautiful squares in Europe. The fan-shaped paving, which is divided into nine parts and made of light travertine stone and red brick, slopes toward the elegant Gothic palaces that line the north-west side of the square.

✳
Fonte di Gaia ▶ The middle section is bordered at its higher end by the Fountain of Joy (Fonte di Gaia), once the city's main source of water. The richly decorated well, a **masterpiece by Jacopo della Quercia** dating from 1419, was thoroughly restored in 1868. The original reliefs are in the Palazzo Pubblico.

✳ ✳
Palazzo Pubblico with Museo Civico On the south side of the campo stands the magnificent Palazzo Pubblico, a Gothic communal building erected in 1309 of travertine and brick. Its bulk is relieved by pointed triple windows and roof crenellations. The arches are decorated with the black-and-white arms of Siena, the »Balzana«. In the middle of the first upper storey are arms of the Medici, who ruled as grand dukes of Tuscany from 1570. The façade also bears several depictions of the Capitoline she-wolf – a **reference to the legendary founding of Siena by Senus**, the son of Remus. Today the palazzo houses the Museo Civico, where the wonderful frescoes reflecting the city's self-confidence in the 14th and 15th century should not be missed.

The most famous is the allegory of *Good and Bad Government* (1340), with which Ambrogio Lorenzetti decorated the Sala della Pace (Room of Peace). This fresco is one of the earliest examples of secular pictorial art in Italy. »Buongoverno« is an impressive depiction of virtues like justice, generosity, love of peace and unity, as well as everyday scenes with a veduta of Siena. These are contrasted with »Malgoverno«, which shows the consequences of tyranny, pride, greed, deception, betrayal, malice and mismanagement.

✱ ✱
◄ Frescoes by Lorenzetti

In the Sala del Mappamondo Simone Martini painted the magnificent fresco of the *Maestà* (around 1315), and facing it the portrait of the military commander Guidoriccio da Fogliani (1329), one of the oldest equestrian portraits in Gothic art, stylistically a pioneering work. The explanation for the numerous examples of a *Maestà* (= Madonna enthroned) in Siena lies in the local **veneration of the Virgin**, since the keys to the city were dedicated to her for assistance before the victorious battle of Montaperti in 1260, after which Siena called itself »Civitas Virginis«. Two other large frescoes in this room, by Giovanni di Cristoforo and Francesco d'Andrea (1479), show the victory of the Sienese troops over Florentine forces near Poggio Imperiale. The Sala del Mappamondo takes its name from a lost world map by Ambrogio Lorenzetti dating from 1344. Attached to this

✱ ✱
◄ Sala del Mappamondo

Piazza del Campo spreads like a fan when seen from the observation platform of the Torre del Mangia.

room is the palace chapel with an antechamber (anticappella), which Taddeo di Bartolo decorated with a fresco cycle in 1414. The Sala di Balìa was painted by Spinello Aretino in 1407 with scenes from the life of Pope Alexander III. To end a tour of the Palazzo Pubblico on a high note, enjoy the view of the square and the city from the top floor (loggia dei nove). The original panels of the Fonte Gaia are also here.

Torre del Mangia

To the left of the Palazzo Pubblico is the city hall tower, one of the most daring towers of the Middle Ages. It is 102m/335ft high to the top of the metal bell cage and was built by the brothers Minuccio and Francesco di Rinaldo between 1338 and 1344. It got its name from the sexton Mangiaguadagni (which literally means »the one who eats up the wages«), who regulated working hours by ringing the bell. A spectacular panoramic view of the city and surroundings is the reward for the climb up to the tower platform.

Cappella di Piazza ▶

In front of the palace façade at the base of the tower lies the Cappella di Piazza, which was built in 1352 out of gratitude for salvation from the plague of 1348, and substantially altered in 1463. Its forms, which hark back to ancient architecture, are a striking contrast to the austere façade of the Palazzo Pubblico (tower hours: Nov–mid-March daily 10am–4pm, mid-March–Oct daily 10am–6.15pm).

Palazzo Piccolomini

On the north-east corner of Piazza del Campo, with its main façade facing Via Banchi di Sotto, stands Palazzo Piccolomini, which was built in 1469 for Nanni Todeschini, brother-in-law of the later Pope Pius II. The beautiful Renaissance building today holds the state archives and a little museum with the curious **Tavolette di Biccherna**. These painted wooden panels, which developed into little works of art, were made from the 13th century for the financial administration of Siena, which used them as file covers (hours: Mon–Sat 9am–1pm).

Between Piazza del Campo and the cathedral

★★ Via di Città, Loggia della Mercanzia

From Piazza del Campo it is only a few steps uphill to Via di Città, the main street of the old city. The Loggia della Mercanzia, the old commercial court which was built in 1428, stands here. It is an example of the transitional style from late Gothic to Renaissance; the upper storey was added in the 17th century. On the pillars with richly decorated capitals that support open arcades, statues of St Peter and St Paul, St Victor and St Ansano can be seen.

★ Palazzo Chigi-Saracini

The ground plan of Palazzo Chigi-Saracini has been fitted to the bend in Via di Città; it was completed around 1320 and enlarged in 1787. A massive crenellated tower rises above the façade, which has windows with pointed arches and is one of the most beautiful in the city. The grey stone in the two lower storeys contrasts attractively with the brick on the top floor. The palazzo houses the music academy, which holds master classes, summer concerts and other events. The rooms can be viewed upon request.

On the corner where narrow steps go up to the cathedral stands the residential palace built around 1460 for Caterina Piccolomini, the sister of Pope Pius II. It is also called the »Palace of the Woman Popes«. The plans for this beautiful Renaissance palace in the Florentine style probably derive from Bernardo Rosselli. Today the Centro di Arte Contemporanea holds rotating exhibitions of contemporary art here.

Palazzo Piccolomini delle Papesse

✳ Duomo Santa Maria Assunta

The cathedral stands at the highest point of the city and is one of the most impressive Gothic churches in Italy. It was begun over a previous building, probably around the middle of the 12th century, but the dome was not finished until 1264. In 1284 construction of the west façade began, and from 1316 the choir was extended toward the east. The bell tower, slender and covered with black and white marble, dates from the second half of the 13th century. In 1339 the citizens decided on an **enlargement** of the cathedral to make it the largest building in Italy: the existing structure was to become the transept of a church over 100m/110yd long, whose main axis was to run perpendicular to the present one.

🕐 Opening hours:
Nov–mid-March
daily 7.30am–1pm
and 2.30–5pm,
mid-March until Oct
daily 9am–7.30pm,
Reservations under
tel. 05 77 28 30 48

The project was slowed by lack of funds and mistakes in construction, and after the devastating plague epidemic of 1348 was abandoned.

The unbelievable size of the planned new building can be seen from the parts that were completed in the extension of the right transept: the north-east aisle, which

> ❗ *Baedeker* TIP
>
> **You are in luck …**
> … if you come to Siena in September or the first week of October. The entire cathedral floor is visible then, but covered with wooden boards the rest of the year.

houses the cathedral museum today, the massive »great façade« and three bays of the south-west wall of the nave.

No less an artist than the eminent Giovanni Pisano was brought in from Pisa to design the west façade of the cathedral, which was completed in 1297. Pisano abandoned Romanesque architectural vocabulary in favour of the style of **French cathedral façades**, producing a composition of powerful spatial depth, a lavish programme of sculptures and three doorways set well back into the façade. Except for the storey with the rosette window, all of the sculptural decoration is by Pisano.

✳ ✳ West façade

The interior, which is divided by high arcades, is a marked contrast to the radiant façade. The dark green-and-white striped marble and

Interior

the atmosphere of gloom are reminiscent of Arab architecture, an impression that is underscored by the lack of pews. The middle door is decorated on the inside of the façade with reliefs of the life of the Virgin (1483) and the legend of St Ansano (around 1480). The busts of Christ and 172 popes – from St Peter to Lucius III (†1185) on the prominent cornice below the clerestory are complemented by 36 medallion portraits of Roman emperors (15th–16th centuries) in the spandrels of the arches. The floor of the cathedral is a unique work

✶ ✶
Floor ►

of art. Its many images cut into the marble or made of inlay work are like an open book relating events from early times to the salvation of humankind through Christ. The floor was started in 1369. The 56 pictures took about 200 years to complete, and numerous renowned artists were involved, including Pinturicchio (*Happiness*).

✶
Piccolomini Altar ►

The tour of the cathedral begins with the Piccolomini altar in the third bay of the northern aisle. Andrea Bregno made it in 1485 for the Sienese Cardinal Francesco Piccolomini. It was intended to be decorated with sculptures afterwards, including 15 by Michelangelo. Opinions differ about which sculptures the artist actually made himself. Presumably most were made not by him but from his sketches.

✶ ✶
Libreria
Piccolomini

⏱
Opening hours:
Mid-March–Oct
9am–7.30pm,
Nov–mid-March
10am–1pm and
2.30–5pm

The entrance to the Piccolomini Library is next to the Piccolomini Altar. The entrance wall, a high Renaissance masterpiece, was constructed by Lorenzo di Mariano in 1497; the library itself is one of the most beautiful and best-preserved rooms of its time. The building was begun in 1495 on behalf of Cardinal Francesco Piccolomini, from 1503 Pope Pius III, who wanted to provide a worthy place for the book collection of his uncle, Enea Silvio Piccolomini (Pope Pius II, ►Pienza). The wonderful **frescoes on the ceiling and walls** were painted between 1502 and 1509 by Pinturicchio of Perugia and his pupils. Beginning at the right-hand window, the murals depict the following scenes: Enea Silvio Piccolomini accompanies Cardinal Capranica to the Council of Basle (1432); as emissary of the council Piccolomini appears before the Scottish King James I; Emperor Frederick III crowns Piccolomini as poet; Piccolomini submits to Pope Eugene IV; as archbishop of Siena he brings Frederick III and Eleanor of Aragon together; Pope Calixtus III gives him the cardinal's hat; Piccolomini becomes Pope Pius II; in Mantua Pius II tries to unite the Christian rulers against the Turks; canonization of Catherine of Siena; Pius II arrives in Ancona in order to prepare for the military campaign against the Turks. The display cases on the walls hold valuable manuscripts from the 15th century. The Roman marble group of the three graces, a copy of a Greek original, was found in Rome around 1500.

Cappella di
San Giovanni
Battista,
Cappella Ansano

The next point of the tour is the Renaissance chapel of John the Baptist (1482) with the bronze statue of the Baptist (1457), an expressive late work by Donatello, a statue of St Catherine of Alexandria (1487) by Neroccio and frescoes with scenes from the life

Duomo Santa Maria Assunta *Plan*

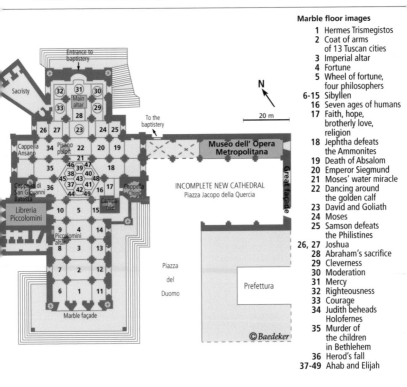

Marble floor images
1. Hermes Trismegistos
2. Coat of arms of 13 Tuscan cities
3. Imperial altar
4. Fortune
5. Wheel of fortune, four philosophers
6-15. Sibyllen
16. Seven ages of humans
17. Faith, hope, brotherly love, religion
18. Jephtha defeats the Ammonites
19. Death of Absalom
20. Emperor Siegmund
21. Moses' water miracle
22. Dancing around the golden calf
23. David and Goliath
24. Moses
25. Samson defeats the Philistines
26, 27. Joshua
28. Abraham's sacrifice
29. Cleverness
30. Moderation
31. Mercy
32. Righteousness
33. Courage
34. Judith beheads Holofernes
35. Murder of the children in Bethlehem
36. Herod's fall
37-49. Ahab and Elijah

of St John by Pinturicchio. In the chapel of St Ansanus, who is supposed to have brought Christianity to Siena and died under Emperor Diocletian, the tomb of Cardinal Riccardo Petroni (1317–1318), an early masterpiece by Tino di Camaino, is notable. Four supporting figures bear the sarcophagus with reliefs and figures of apostles. The bronze graveplate of Bishop Giovanni Pecci, dated 1430, is by Donatello.

★ ★
Pulpit by Nicola Pisano

Among the most important works of art in the cathedral is the pulpit, created in 1266–1268 by Nicola Pisano with the assistance of his son Giovanni and Arnolfo di Cambio. It rests on nine columns of granite, porphyry and marble. The outer ones stand on bases or on figures of lions, while the foot of the middle column is decorated with allegories of the seven liberal arts and philosophy. Above the capitals are personifications of the Christian virtues; prophets are in the arch spandrels. The facing has outstanding reliefs in the style of ancient sarcophaguses.

DUOMO SANTA MARIA

✳ ✳ **The stately cathedral of Santa Maria towers at the highest point of the city with Romanesque and Gothic elements in its façade. Below the choir is the baptistery of San Giovanni, and the remains of the »new cathedral«, which was to have enlarged the building in the 14th century, can be seen at the side.**

🕐 Hours:
Nov–mid-March daily 7.30am–1pm and 2.30–5pm, mid-March–Oct daily 9am–7.30pm, advance tickets tel. 05 77 28 30 48

① **Marble façade**
In the late 13th century Giovanni Pisano designed the façade of the cathedral, inspired by French Gothic style.

② **Libreria Piccolomini**
The Piccolomini library was founded by Cardinal Francesco Piccolomini (later Pius III) in honour of his uncle Pius II. Pinturicchio's famous frescoes with scenes from the life of the later pope and a collection of choir books are here.

③ **Capella di San Giovanni**
The works in the Renaissance chapel include a fresco cycle by Pinturicchio and a bronze statue of John the Baptist by Donatello (1457).

The typical black and white marble decorations can also be found inside. The lack of pews is also noticeable.

④ **Pulpit by Nicola Pisano**
Among all the art treasures, the octagonal pulpit by Nicola Pisano (1266–1268) stands out. It rests on pillars which are in turn supported by lions.

⑤ **Battistero di San Giovanni**
The enlargement of the choir in 1316 was an opportunity to build a lower church, the baptistery.

⑥ **Museo dell'Opera Metropolitana**
The works on the ground floor of the cathedral museum include the larger-than-life-size sculptures for the façade by Pisano and his assistants, which were replaced by copies in the course of time.

⑦ **Il Facciatone**
The expansion plans of Siena's city fathers were stopped by the outbreak of the plague in 1348. The partially completed outer wall called Il Facciatone (the big façade) is a reminder of this.

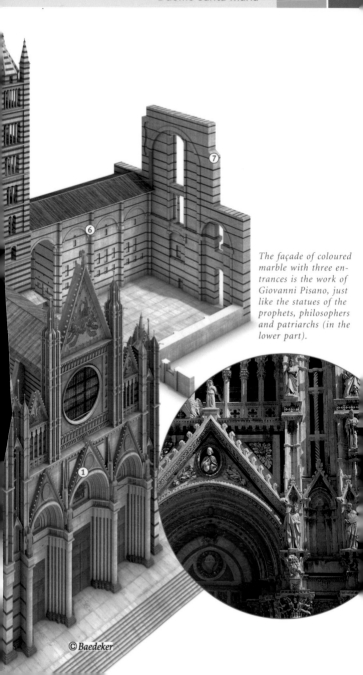

The façade of coloured marble with three entrances is the work of Giovanni Pisano, just like the statues of the prophets, philosophers and patriarchs (in the lower part).

© Baedeker

The high, pointed bell tower of the cathedral with its black-and-white decorative stripes rises above the city.

The floor of the cathedral of Siena is decorated with unique marble intarsia work (here: the »Mountain of Wisdom«). In order to protect them, most works are covered and exposed only for special occasions. A picture in the cathedral museum shows the entire floor.

Choir The dominant feature in the choir is the large marble high altar by Baldassare Peruzzi (1532). Two angels flank the bronze ciborium (1472) by Vecchietta. At the top of the choir wall is a large round window with probably the oldest preserved stained glass in Italy, dating from 1288. The painter Duccio designed it. The **choir stalls** of 1363–1397 are worth a closer look. Of more than 90 seats originally here, 36 have been preserved. The intarsia work on the backs of the seats (1503) gives a view from a window into the distance or into a cabinet of musical instruments – all an illusion, a masterly design with abundant detail, achieved with the help of perspective. A wonderful deception!

Cappella Chigi In the southern transept is the entrance to the Chigi chapel, constructed by the famous Baroque artist Gian Lorenzo Bernini between 1659 and 1662. The statues of St Jerome and St Mary Magdalene are dramatic late works of Bernini.

Campanile The bell tower originally stood in a corner between the nave and transept, but the expansion of the cathedral brought it inside the church. Above the door that leads into the base of the tower is the tomb of Bishop Tommaso Piccolomini del Testa (1484).

✳

Battistero di San Giovanni
⏱

Opening hours:
Mid-March–Sept
9am–7.30pm,
Oct 9am–6pm,
Nov–mid-March
10am–1pm and
2.30–5pm

The baptistery lies under the choir of the cathedral. In order to see it leave the church and climb down the steps to Piazza San Giovanni. The tall church with its own façade commands the small square. The baptistery was built from 1316 to 1327, when the choir was extended. The frescoes inside the main room are the work of several artists around 1450. The marble baptismal font, created from 1417 to 1430 probably by Jacopo della Quercia, stands on a six-sided pedestal. It is decorated with personifications of the virtues and bronze reliefs on the life of John the Baptist by Jacopo della Quercia (announcement of the birth of John to Zacharias), Giovanni di Turino (birth and preaching of John), Lorenzo Ghiberti (baptism of Christ, imprisonment) and Donatello (beheading of John, Herod's feast).

✳ ✳

Museo dell' Opera Metropolitana
⏱

Opening hours:
Mid-March–Sept
daily 9am–7.30pm;
Oct daily
9am–6pm, Nov–
mid-March daily
9am–1.30pm

The cathedral museum is housed under three bays of the nave of the unfinished »new cathedral« on Piazza del Duomo 8. The rich collection contains, in addition to a Roman marble group of the three graces, above all works of medieval sculpture including **reliefs by Nicola Pisano**, works by Giovanni Pisano or his workshop, a wonderful relief of the *Madonna with Child, St Anthony and Cardinal Casini* by Jacopo della Quercia and the high-quality sculptures by Giovanni Pisano for the cathedral façade.

Among the panel paintings the world-famous *Maestà* (1311), a painting of the Virgin by Duccio di Buoninsegna for the cathedral high altar, is the undisputed highlight. *The Birth of the Virgin* (1342) by Pietro Lorenzetti and the *Madonna degli Occhi Grossi*

(Madonna with the large eyes), a work of the early 13th century that still reflects Byzantine influence, are also interesting. On the second floor valuable reliquaries such as the gilded 13th-century head reliquary of St Galgano and other items from the cathedral treasury are on display. From the top floor stairs lead to the »great façade« (Il Facciatone), a giant panorama terrace with a beautiful view of Siena.

Opposite the cathedral façade the hospital founded in 823 and named after the steps (scala in Italian) of the cathedral retains its original form of the 13th and 14th centuries. The frescoes in the pilgrims' hall were executed from 1440 to 1443 by Domenico di Bartolo and show nuns caring for the sick (hours: in summer daily 10am–6pm, in winter daily 10.30am–4.30pm).

Spedale di Santa Maria della Scala ⊙

Since 1993 the left wing of the ospedale on Piazza del Duomo has housed the collections of the archaeological museum with finds from the surroundings of Siena from the Stone Age until the fall of the Roman Empire, with special emphasis on Etruscan civilization. Urns, bronze statuettes, sarcophagi and a large coin collection are on display (hours: see Spedale di S. Maria; one ticket is valid for both sites).

★ **Museo Archeologico Nazionale**

A Gothic masterpiece: the cathedral of Siena

Palazzo Arcivescovile   The Gothic forms of the archbishop's palace, which was built between 1718 and 1723 opposite the north wall of the cathedral nave, represent an early example of historicizing architecture. This return to an earlier style aimed to preserve the homogeneous appearance of the square. The bi-coloured marble covering of the cathedral has its counterpart on the ground floor of the palazzo.

✳ ✳ Pinacoteca Nazionale

🕐 Opening hours:
Mon and Sun
8.30am–1.30pm,
Tue–Sat
8.15am–7.15pm

The Pinacoteca Nazionale is not far to the south-east of the cathedral in Palazzo Buonsignori at Via San Pietro 29. The late Gothic building with a crenellated roof, one of the most elegant palaces in the region, dates from the 15th century. This important art gallery provides an excellent overview of Sienese painting from the 12th to the 16th century.

First floor   The main attraction on the first floor is the work of the high Renaissance painter Giovanni Antonio Bazzi, known as Sodoma, including the *Flagellation of Christ* (1511–1514) and *Deposition from the Cross* (around 1510), as well as paintings by Domenico Beccafumi, a representative of early Mannerism, including sketches for the floor decoration of the cathedral: *St Catherine of Siena Receives the Wounds of Christ* (around 1515) and *Birth of the Virgin* (around 1543).

For clothes, pastries, household items or terracotta –
Siena is without question a shopping paradise.

The highlights of the second floor, where the tour should begin, include in room 1 a damaged late 12th-century crucifix, one of the oldest works of Sienese art, as well as the altarpiece with *Christ in the Mandorla* from 1215 – the earliest dated example of Sienese painting.

The *Madonna and Child* (around 1262) by Guido da Siena in room 2 betrays Byzantine influences in the elongated bodies and the pronounced lines, while the retable with St John (around 1280) and the altar of St Peter (1280–1290) by anonymous masters demonstrate the transition from austere Byzantine forms to natural and colourful compositions. In room 2 there is also a diptych as well as five panels on the Passion of Christ, which were probably part of a *Maestà* in the Palazzo Pubblico, all from the workshop of Guido da Siena.

Rooms 3 and 4 contain two altar panels by Duccio di Buoninsegna, the founder of the great Gothic school of painting in Siena (around 1310): *Madonna between Saints Augustine, Paul, Peter and Dominic*, lifelike and with delicate layers of colour, as well as *Madonna between Saints Agnes, John the Evangelist, John the Baptist and Mary Magdalene* with clear figure forms and a small panel of the *Madonna dei Francescani* (around 1300) which combines sensitive lines with delicate colour nuances. Other works from Duccio's circle are also exhibited here.

Gothic panel paintings from the second half of the 14th century by Bartolo di Fredi (*Adoration of the Magi*, 1370/1380), Taddeo di Bartolo (*Annunciation, Adoration of the Shepherds*) and Luca di Tommè (including *Virgin and Child with St Anne*, 1367) are in room 5, while a panel painting by the great Sienese master Simone Martini depicts the *Blessed Agostino Novello* (1330).

The generation of painters that followed Duccio is represented by important works of the brothers Ambrogio and Pietro Lorenzetti, including in room 7 *Madonna Enthroned with Saints and Angels* and scenes from the history of the Carmelite order (1328–1329) with clear figures and perspective rendering of space by Pietro, while Ambrogio is represented by two small landscapes (around 1340), the *City on the Sea* and *Castle on the Lakeside*, as well as with a *Madonna in Glory* (around 1340) and an *Annunciation* (1344) with a lyrical use of colour and form.

The next rooms are devoted to painters from the circle of Simone Martini, including Lippo Memmi (*Madonna and Child*, around 1340) and Naddo Ceccarelli (*Madonna Polyptych*) with extreme Gothic use of form. Room 11 houses several works from around 1400 by Taddeo di Bartolo, including an *Enthroned Madonna* and an Annunciation altarpiece with signs of international Gothic style.

Room 12–13 Works by Giovanni di Paolo, a leading master of Sienese painting in the first half of the 15th century, are on display in rooms 12 and 13. He painted extremely attractive works using central perspective in connection with the rich colours of the Sienese tradition: *Madonna with Child Surrounded by Angels Making Music* (1433), *Madonna dell' Umiltà* (around 1455) and *Presentation in the Temple* (1447–1448). The work of Stefano di Giovanni, called Sassetta, was influential in the development of Sienese painting in the 15th century,. Unfortunately only the predella and crown of a polyptych painted between 1423 and 1426 are exhibited.

Rooms 14–19 The second half of the 15th century is represented in rooms 14–19 by Matteo di Giovanni's *Madonna among Saints* (1470), three Madonna panels (around 1476–1495) by Neroccio di Bartolomeo Landi in late Gothic-Mannerist style, and an *Annunciation* (around 1470) by Francesco di Giorgio Martini, partly with extremely delicate lines, partly with clearly modelled figures in front of landscape and architectural scenes.

The Nannini family own several pasticcerias in Siena.

The **third floor** holds the collection of the Sienese Spannocchi family with paintings from the 16th and 17th centuries, including works by Flemish masters as well as by Tintoretto and Albrecht Dürer.

To reach **Prato Sant'Agostino** and Sant'Agostino church, built in 1258 as part of an Augustinian monastery, walk out of town from the Pinacoteca. The works inside the church, which was altered in Baroque style, include a *Crucifixion* by Perugino dated 1506, late 15th-century frescoes attributed to Francesco di Giorgio Martini from the (*Birth of the Virgin*, an *Adoration of Christ*) and a *Maestà* fresco by Ambrogio Lorenzetti in the Cappella Piccolomini.

Museo di Storia Naturale, Orto Botanico The former Camaldolese monastery diagonally opposite Sant' Agostino now accommodates an interesting natural history museum. The neighbouring botanical garden (orto botanico) already existed in 1588 and is open to the public.

From the Cathedral Square to Forte di Santa Barbara

Go down the steps from the cathedral to Piazza San Giovanni and continue north on the narrow Via Diacceto. About 50 yards along there is a beautiful view of the church of San Domenico, which rises out of the jumble of houses. Via della Galluzza is covered by **high supporting arches** and becomes even narrower as it leads down from Via Diacceto into the area around the Dominican church.

Via Diacceto

In Via Santa Caterina, a narrow street which branches off to the left, is the birthplace of St Catherine of Siena (1347–1380) with a sanctuary built in 1464, three years after she was canonized. The beautiful Renaissance portal has the inscription: »Sponsae Kristi Catherinae Domus« (house of Catherine, bride of Christ). Catherine's intervention for the return of the pope from Avignon to Rome and her visions led to her canonization in 1461 by Pope Pius II, who came from Siena. Since her home became too small for the stream of pilgrims, the upper oratory was built in the 16th century and decorated with **frescoes from the life of St Catherine**. According to tradition she received the wounds of Christ in 1375 in front of the Romanesque crucifix now in the Oratorio del Crocefisso.

✳ Casa di Santa Caterina

🕐 Opening hours: Daily 9am–12.30pm, 3.30–6pm

About 100m/110yd further to the west in Via Caterina is a large fountain with Siena's oldest stone inscription (1198) by Bellamino. The fountain was given its present form mainly by Giovanni di Stefano around 1246.

Fonte Branda

From the house of St Catherine it is not far to Piazza San Domenico near the city wall. Here stands the Dominican church of San Domenico, a massive plain brick building which was begun in 1226. The church has a nave without aisles and a square-ended choir as well as a tall transept from which two chapels extend to flank the choir. The fresco in the cross-vaulted chapel was painted by Andrea Vanni around 1370–1380, probably while Catherine was still alive, and is the oldest portrayal of the saint. The chapel of St Catherine also has two major works by Sodoma: the *Ecstasy of St Catherine* and *St Catherine Fainting* (both around 1525). There is also a marble tabernacle (1466) by Giovanni di Stefano, which holds the head of St Catherine, who died in Rome and was buried there in the church of Santa Maria sopra Minerva.

San Domenico

✳ ◀ Oldest portrait of St Catherine of Siena

On the other side of Viale dei Mille and north-west of San Domenico, beyond the athletics stadium, lies Forte di Santa Barbara, which Duke Cosimo I commissioned in 1560. The walls of the massive fortress give an attractive view of the city. In the old vaults of the first bastion on the left is the Enoteca Italiana (see shopping) with an excellent selection of wines and an exhibition on Italian winegrowing.

Forte di Santa Barbara

✳ ◀ Enoteca

The Palio begins with a parade of the standard bearers of the individual »contrade« and an impressive display of banner whirling.

GO, AND RETURN VICTORIOUS

This is easier said than done in the Palio, the famous Sienese horse race and Italy's traditional celebration par excellence. For the riders who take this blessing from the district priest risk life and limb on the campo. Without a saddle, with only reins and riding crop, the jockeys cling to the backs of their horses in order to be the first to cross the finish line at breakneck speed and carry away the coveted victor's ribbon.

Even though there is little evidence of the original procedure of the Palio, it is certain that it existed before 1310, the year when the city council officially confirmed the race: it was to take place every year on **16 August** in honour of the Holy Virgin, Siena's patron saint, but also as the symbol of the independent communes. The race on 2 July in honour of the Madonna di Provenzano has been held only since 1656.

17 City Districts Compete

In the Palio the 17 contrade of the various city districts of Siena compete. Their name probably comes from the Latin contrata, the place where contracts are made. The contrade are the small villages on the hills of the city, which in the 13th century in the face of the general decay of central government joined together into a local administration which would also serve as a defence in times of war. The militia of the contrade were lead by b**anner bearers** (gonfalonieri), whose commander-in-chief was the Capitano del Popolo. The names of the contrade were fixed in 1370. Apart from exceptions (like Torre for the district with the tower of the city hall and Onda with the wavy coat of arms for the persons responsible for the Sienese harbour Talamone) the names are almost all names of animals – eagle, panther, porcupine, turtle, she-wolf or goose. Next to their military and administrative duties the contrade soon took over important deci-

sion-making functions: they proposed laws, built streets, chose the heads of the guilds (priori) and organized the militia. Today they still play a role in the life of the city and for every Sienese, man or woman, it is a matter of course to belong to a contrada – they are born and remain contradialo even if they move away.

Coveted Flag

The **Palio** (Latin pallium = cloth) is actually the trophy, a silk flag commemorating the Virgin Mary which is designed new every year by an artist. The first unofficial discussions about the race and the training of the riders (fantini), who are mostly Sardinian, begin months beforehand. Four weeks before the start a draw officially decides which of the three contrade will compete in the Palio along with the seven that did not compete in the

previous year. Five days before the feast the wooden stands with expensive seats are erected. To watch the race sitting down, it is necessary to order tickets months ahead (through the tourist office). The centre of the piazza (nicchia), which is enclosed for the race with a wooden fence, can only be reached on the Via Malborghetto and has free admission. For the racetrack a special mixture of tuffstone and ochre-coloured sand is poured around the sloping Piazza del Campo to a depth of 20cm/8in and compacted to make a track 7.5m/25ft wide. When the sand is on the piazza the **excitement is at fever pitch**.

The Tension Mounts

The draw for the horses takes place under the supervision of the mayor on the day before the race on the town hall square. The lucky ones can

lead a swift Barbero to the stable, and the unlucky ones get a tired nag , a Brenna, and can only pray for the help of the patron saints. In the afternoon the qualifying races take place, three times around the square. In the meantime all of Siena is decorated with coats of arms and banners of the contrade and anxiously awaits the final moment.

On the evening before the Palio the participating contrade hold banquets on their squares, where everyone joins in and where final arrangements are made. Is there a realistic hope of winning the flag of the Virgin? Or if the horse drawn in the lottery has hardly a chance of winning, then it might at least make the race difficult for the rival contrade. On the morning of the race, horse and rider go to the **contrada church for a blessing**. »Va e torna vincitore – go, and return victorious« are the priest's closing words. Then the horses are presented to the mayor at noon, and at 3pm the contrade members assemble in the cathedral square for the **historic parade**. What the city has longed for, imagined and prepared for all year is delayed unbearably at the end. Without any haste, in fact particularly slowly, the residents of Siena move through the streets and alleys toward the Piazza del Campo to the monotone tolling of the bell of the Torre del Mangia. The colourful **Passeggiata Storica**, which reaches the overcrowded campo along Via del Casato, is accompanied by medieval banner throwers, drummers and pipers. At the front are the six staff bearers, and the town flag bearer rides whirling the black and white flag of Siena. Then come trumpeters and musicians, followed by banner bearers of the estates that once belonged to the city republic. They are followed by the three mercantile magistrates and representatives of the most important guilds. Now come the entourages of the ten participating and seven non-participant contrade: one drummer, two flag bearers, one captain, four

Spectacle for young and old: the enthusiasm of the Sienese at the Palio knows no bounds …

pages, another banner bearer, a rider on the parade horse and the stable master leading the racehorse for each contrade. The six historic contrade (bear, oak, rooster, lion, sword, viper) which were barred from the race forever in 1675 because of a riot are also represented. The parade can take up to two hours until finally the four Chianina oxen pull the decorated **triumphal wagon with the Martinella bell and the trophy** past the cheering crowd. Banners are thrown into the air one last time before the bell is silenced around 8pm, the horses trot nervously out of the inner courtyard of the Palazzo Pubblico and line up in the order that was drawn by lot amidst louder and louder cheers.

Decision in Seconds

Suddenly everything happens quickly. The rope (canapo) falls, the crowds roar and the spectacle takes its course. The horses have to circle the slanted oval piazza three times, and take about 100 seconds to do so. In the second round at the latest there is usually a spectacular and often dangerous fall at the notorious **Curva di San Martino**, which is padded with mattresses for this reason. Then one more round at breakneck speed until the first horse crosses the finish line, with or without a rider, to the frenetic shouts of the crowds. The first

… the unlucky ones get a tired nag and can only pray for the help of the patron saints …

spectators are already joyfully climbing over the barriers, pulling the winner from his horse and carrying him with the Palio on their shoulders in triumph to the thanksgiving Te Deum, on **2 July** in the Provenzano church and on 16 August in the cathedral. After a mere fifteen minutes the campo is almost empty, while the streets of Siena are quickly decorated with the colours of the winning contrada and everyone gathers around outdoor tables for an exuberant and opulent feast. **The head of the winners' table is reserved for the winning horse!**

From the Campo to the North-Eastern Old City

Croce di Travaglio

The walk begins at Piazza del Campo and heads first toward Via di Città. Near the Loggia di Mercanzia, at the so-called Croce di Travaglio, the »Cross of Troubles«, Via di Città meets the two other main shopping streets of the city centre: **Via Banchi di Sopra** and **Via Banchi di Sotto** (see shopping, p.379). The most elegant and oldest shops are here, especially in the slightly sloping Via Banchi di Sopra, but there are also many cafés and bars. Pasticceria Nannini in Via Banchi di Sopra 24 is a tempting place for a first coffee break.

Palazzo Tolomei, San Cristoforo

About 100 metres north of Croce di Travaglio, Via Banchi di Sopra opens into a pretty little square. On the left is one of the oldest palaces in Siena, Palazzo Tolomei, which was built in 1207 and reconstructed in 1267. The front has windows with pointed arches and Gothic tracery.

Opposite Palazzo Tolomei is the church of San Cristoforo, originally Romanesque but completely remodelled in the 18th century. It has a remarkable 14th-century crucifix.

After a long walk around town, Piazza Salimbeni is often the last stop.

Piazza Salimbeni is also a pretty square. It is dominated by a 14th-century fortified Gothic palazzo with a three-storey façade. Palazzo Salimbeni is the home of one of the oldest public credit institutions in Italy, Monte della Pietà which was established in 1472: the »money mountain of mercy«, offering low-interest loans to citizens who are in need. The banking house Monte dei Paschi – Monte loans are backed by income from the pastures (pascoli) of the Maremma – was established in 1624. To the right of the Salimbeni palace stands Palazzo Spannocchi, which was begun in 1470 for Ambrogio Spannocchi, treasurer of Pope Pius II of the Piccolomini family. The beautiful loggia was added to the elegant Renaissance building in 1880.

★ **Piazza Salimbeni**

◀ Piazza Spannocchi

Via dei Rossi, which turns off Via Banchi di Sopra just before Piazza Salimbeni, leads to the Gothic Franciscan church of San Francesco. The foundation stone was laid in 1326, but it was completed only in 1484. The church has characteristic features of the architecture of mendicant orders in the large nave for preaching to a numerous congregation and flat-ended choir. The campanile was added in 1765; the façade was remodelled in the years from 1894 until 1912. The interior has an open truss roof and imitates in its black and white walls the marble cladding of the cathedral. The banners of the old craft guilds hang on the nave walls. In the left transept a wonderfully expressive detached fresco *Crucifixion* (around 1336) by Pietro Lorenzetti is worth an extra look, as well as the two frescoes by his brother Ambrogio Lorenzetti from the same period: *St Louis of Toulouse before Pope Boniface VIII* and the *Martyrdom of the Seven Franciscans of Ceuta.*

San Francesco

A small two-storey oratory was built for St Bernard (1380–1444), a member of the order of St Francis, in the place where he usually preached. It stands next to the church and is worth visiting for its frescoes. They include works from the 16th century by Sodoma (St Louis, Mary in the Temple, St Anthony of Padua, St Francis of Assisi, Visitation, Assumption and Coronation of the Virgin), by Domenico Beccafumi (Marriage of the Virgin, Madonna with Angels, Death of the Virgin) and by Girolamo del Pacchia (Birth of the Virgin, St Bernard of Siena, Gabriel, Annunciation).

★ ★ **Oratorio di San Bernardino**

South-Eastern District

Via Banchi di Sotto, which runs from Croce di Travaglio, is the main axis of the south-east part of the city, the Terzo di San Martino. There are no great attractions here, but a lively atmosphere, small and less expensive shops – the further out the cheaper – and many cafés with a young crowd. In short it is obvious that the University of Siena and the renowned Università per Stranieri, the university for foreigners, are located here.

★ **Terzo di San Martino, Via Banchi di Sotto**

Loggia di Papa In Via Banchi di Sotto, not far east of Palazzo Piccolomini (see above), is the delicate Loggia di Papa, completed in 1462. This building with three arches by the architect Antonio Federighi takes its name from Pope Pius II (Enea Silvio Piccolomini), whose family had close ties to Siena.

Santa Maria dei Servi Follow Via Banchi di Sotto further out of town – it becomes Via Pantaneto and Via Roma – and turns off into Via San Clemente, which in turn leads to the church of Santa Maria dei Servi. This church of the Servite order was built in the 13th century and remodelled in contemporary style in the 15th and 16th centuries. The austere façade was not changed; next to it stands the 13th-century campanile. Points of interest inside are the *Madonna del Bordone*, a picture of Mary with child and two angels by Coppo di Marcovaldo (1261), and in the second chapel in the right-hand transept the famous **fresco *Massacre of the Innocents*** (around 1330) by Pietro Lorenzetti.

Porta Romana ▶ From Santa Maria dei Servi it is not far to the city wall with the Porta Romana, a simple gate built in 1327.

Around Siena

Chiesa dell'Osservanza Walk through Porta Ovile to the Chiesa dell'Osservanza 3km/2mi north of the old city. It was built in 1476 over an older church which was donated by St Bernard. After being almost completely destroyed in a bombing raid in 1944, the church was rebuilt in its original form. The nave has no aisles but eight side chapels. In the third chapel on the right is a reliquary of St Bernard, made in 1454 by Francesco d'Antonio; in the fourth chapel a beautiful triptych (*Madonna with Saints Ambrose and Jerome*, around 1436) by an unknown master. The **Annunciation scene of colourful terracotta** on the pillars of the triumphal arch between the nave and choir is by Andrea della Robbia; the *Pietà* (15th century) in the sacristy by Giacomo Cozzarelli.

Museo Aurelio Castelli In the adjacent Museo Aurelio Castelli there are valuable old prints and beautiful illuminated manuscripts (tours by appointment, tel. 057 73 32 44).

✳ **Monteriggioni** For the journey from Siena to Monteriggioni, the autostrada is much less attractive than the beautiful drive on a country road through woods, vineyards and fields of dark brown earth. The town, founded in 1203, lies about 10km/6mi north-west of Siena on a hill over the Elsa valley and is a popular tourist site. Park under the olive trees of the parking lot (fee charged) in front of the well-preserved medieval wall, which dates from the 13th century and is fortified with 14 towers mentioned in Dante's *Divine Comedy*. The pretty cobblestone main square is only a few paces from the Porta Romea, the main

Out of town – a trip into the countryside around Siena is definitely worthwhile.

gate. Compared to the size of the town its **wide range of culinary attractions** with several cafés, two restaurants, two bars and a gelateria is actually huge; the only accommodation so far is a good but expensive hotel.

2km/1.3mi west of Monteriggioni, on the way to Strove, is the Romanesque basilica of the beautifully situated Cistercian monastery Abbadia a Isola.

Abbadia a Isola

The region south-east of Siena, between Asciano and the Arbia valley, belies the adage that Tuscany consists only of beautiful landscape: this is Crete, a bizarre landscape of bare hills cut by valleys. The name comes from creta and means clay or chalk. The unwelcoming landscape, which is threatened by erosion, is the result of relentless deforestation and overgrazing. Where the topsoil has already been washed away, clay soil that tolerates only short grass for pastures or wheat is exposed.

✷
Crete Sienesi

✳
Murlo

The pretty town of Murlo lies on the SS 2 south of Siena. Just beyond Monteroni d'Arbia a country road branches off to the right to the small medieval fortified town, which can justly be called a jewel. The imposing Palazzo Vescovile houses an interesting Museo Etrusco. Finds from the nearby necropolis Poggio Civitate are on display here, including an almost completely preserved roof construction ⊕ and the gable of a building from the 5th century BC (hours: Nov–Feb. daily except Mon 10am–12.30pm, Sat–Sun also 2.30–5pm, March-Oct 9.30am–12.30pm and 3–5pm, April and Sept until 7.30pm, July–Aug until 11pm).

Asciano

In the Crete foothills, on the upper Ombrone River a good 25km/16mi south-east of Siena, lies the town of Asciano with a population of 6,000. Formerly the property of the counts of Sinalunga, Asciano was acquired by Siena in 1285 and defended against Florence until 1554. The Romanesque church of Sant'Agata was built of travertine stone in the 11th to 14th centuries. The neighbouring Museo di Arte Sacra on Piazza della Basilica shows Sienese paintings and sculptures from the 14th and 15th centuries. A visit to Corso Matteotti 46, the **Museo Civico Archeologico** in the former church of San Bernardino is worthwhile. Finds from five Etruscan chamber graves from the Poggio Pinco east of town as well as gold jewellery, bronze brooches ⊕ and urns are on display here (hours: Tue–Sun daily 10am–12.30pm, mid-June–mid-Sept also 4.30–6.30pm).

San Giovanni d'Asso

»White gold« or »kitchen diamonds« – hardly any other produce is prized as highly as white truffles. A short while ago, in the town of San Giovanni d'Asso only about 10km/6mi further south, white truffles found an official home. In the first Italian **truffle museum** visi- ⊕ tors get an insight into of the world of this delicacy (hours: Sat/Sun 10am–1pm and 2–6pm).

Rapolano Terme

The importance of olive groves and the processing of oil for the region is shown to visitors of Rapolano Terme, 10km/6mi north-east of Asciano. Here, in the village of Serre di Rapolano, an oil museum has opened in the rooms of a former oil press in an old building (Museo dell' Antica Grancia).

✳ ✳ San Galgano

Ruins of an important Cistercian abbey

It may only be a ruin – but what a ruin! The former abbey of San Galgano lies about 35km/22mi south-west of ► Siena, a little distance from the road to ► Massa Marittima. The monastery was founded in the 12th century by the nobleman Galgano Guidotti from nearby Chuisdino. According to legend the archangel Gabriel appeared to him in a dream and told him to look for the way to God and nature in a **hermitage on the hill Montesiepi**. As a sign of his renunciation of violence and arms Galgano is said to have thrust his

The church of the former Cistercian abbey of San Galgano is still impressive as a ruin.

sword into a cleft in the rocks – the shaft sticking out of the rock has since then been honoured as a cross. The young hermit died at the age of 33 and was canonized in 1185 by Pope Lucius III.

A few years after his death the Cistercians came to Montesiepi, but soon the monastery was too small for them and they decided to move to the fertile valley floor. The building of the Abbazia di San Galgano began in 1224. It was almost finished at the end of the 13th century. Through donations, papal and imperial support the monastery continued to gain influence and property until the end of the 14th century. But raids by Florentine mercenaries and the exploitation of the estates by the so-called commandery abbots in the 15th century ended the period of prosperity. The monastery closed in 1816.

The 69m/226ft-long church is a classic example of the Cistercian Gothic style that originated in Ile-de-France. The church is well preserved except for the roof and has the plan of a Latin cross. It is built partly of **travertine** and partly of brick. The older part of the nave is divided into four storeys with pointed arcades and clerestory windows; the newer part has only three storeys. The door lintels have artistic floral capitals, and the main doorway is decorated with a 13th-century frieze of acanthus leaves. The enormous interior is unforgettable with its beautiful apse and wonderful alignment of pointed arches and windows vaulted by the blue sky. Of the monastery the east wing and parts of the large cloister are preserved.

Monastery church

The original core of the Cistercian monastery is a small Romanesque rotunda, which was built in 1182 over the grave of St Galgano on Montesiepi. Above the natural stone base the walls consist of alternating layers of stone and fair-faced brickwork. The dome of San Galgano sul Monte Siepi recalls Etruscan grave monuments, while the tambour resembles the grave of Caecilia Metalla on the Via Appia in Rome. The countless spiralling stone rings are a medieval symbol

★
San Galgano sul Monte Siepi

★ ★
Fresco cycle
by Ambrogio
Lorenzetti ▶

for a person rising up to his maker. In the middle of the floor the sword of Galgano sticks out of a rock – however, it was placed here in the 19th century. The brick chapel was added in the 14th century and holds wonderful frescoes by the Sienese Ambrogio Lorenzetti. Parts of the two-row cycle are unfortunately in poor condition – the scenes from the life of St Galgano and the Annunciation, for example. The latter incorporates a window and the coffered ceiling into the composition, which gives a three-dimensional effect. A restoration revealed that the figure of the Virgin in a Maestà was painted over and was originally conceived as the queen of angels without a child. Eve, the original sinner, lies at Mary's feet; two kneeling women symbolize brotherly love (distributing fruits) and the love of God (offering a heart). The two Cistercian monks are presumably the founder of the order, Robert of Molesme, and St Bernard of Clairvaux.

Val di Chiana

I–L 13/14

Provinces: Siena (SI) and Arezzo (AR)

The broad Chiana valley, which stretches between Monte San Savino, ▶Arezzo, ▶Cortona and ▶Chiusi and from there to Latium, was swampland for many years. The Etruscans tried to drain it and planted grain.

With the fall of the western Roman Empire the Chiana valley reverted to swamp. Dante called it the »uninhabitable plague swamp«, and it was successfully drained only in the mid-18th century under the Habsburgs. Val di Chiana then quickly developed into the granary of Italy. Sugar beets, olives and wine are today part of the intensive agriculture of the region, which is also known for its Chianina cattle.

What to See in Val di Chiana

Castiglion
Fiorentino

About halfway between ▶Arezzo and ▶Cortona the town of Castiglion Fiorentino (population 11,500) is situated on a hill on the eastern edge of Val di Chiana. It is completely surrounded by a medieval wall and has a panoramic view. On the main square, Piazza del Municipio, the Vasari loggias from the second half of the 16th century also offer a wonderful view of the Chiana valley. The church of Sant'Angelo lies a little higher and leads to the former convent, which houses the art gallery today. Along with high-quality gold work there are masterpieces from the schools of Arezzo and Siena to be admired, including a panel by Margaritone d'Arezzo *St Francis* (around 1280), a *Madonna* by Taddeo Gaddi (around 1350) and panels by Bartolomeo della Gatta (15th century). The church of San Francesco was built in the 13th century on the threshold of Romanesque to Gothic style. St Francis is depicted on the lintel of the door. The cloister was added in the 15th century. Near the Porta San Michele is the two-storey pilgrimage church Madonna della Consolazione. The church was built in 1607 in late Renaissance style on an octagonal plan and has a Baroque high altar with a Madonna fresco attributed to Luca Signorelli.

About 3km/2mi to the south, the road to Cortona passes the hill of the 13th-century Castello di Montecchio Vesponi. It is largely intact with its impressive, almost 270m/295yd-long crenellated walls, massive defensive towers and a 30m/98ft-high keep. The castle was begun in the 11th century by the Guasconi family of Arezzo. At the end of the 13th century Florence took possession and gave it to the English mercenary John Hawkwood alias Giovanni Acuto as a fiefdom one hundred years later; he was the successful commander of the Florentine mounted forces from 1377 until 1394.

Castello di Montecchio Vesponi

Lucignano lies on the western edge of the valley about as far up as Cortona. Its harmonious medieval appearance makes it a pearl amongst Tuscan towns. Cobblestone streets just wide enough for a car to pass lead to the highest point of the town, which is crowned by the late 16th-century parish church San Michele. The Palazzo Comunale behind the church houses the museum, which is worth a visit. The Sala Tribunale was painted in the second half of the 15th century by an unknown master with a fine fresco cycle depicting Roman emperors, poets and clerics with equal status. The main attraction, however, is the Albero di San Francesco, a gold reliquary that was made in Arezzo in the 15th century.

✸ Lucignano

It may not have the charm of Lucignano, but 7km/4.5mi to the north the neighbouring town of Monte San Savino is also an attractive place for a short stop. The elongated main square, Piazza Gamurrini, is dominated by the Cassero. This fortified 14th-century building today houses the municipal museum and a ceramics collection. On Corso Antonio da Sangallo, which runs across the fortified town, there are several proud palazzi as well as a well-proportioned arcaded hall, the merchants' loggia (1520). It is the work of the town's most famous son, the architect and sculptor Andrea Sansovino (1460/ 67–1529), who together with his teacher Giuliano da Sangallo worked on the baptistery in Florence.

Monte San Savino

The massive Palazzo del Monte opposite the loggia was commissioned in the early 16th century by Cardinal Antonio del Monte. A look inside the palace is worthwhile; it is the seat of the town administration today. Walk through a pretty inner courtyard and go into the garden behind the building, which has been carefully laid out in terraces and which extends to the remains of a small amphitheatre.

Versilia

Province: Massa-Carrara and Lucca

Abundant sand and sea, with the white slopes of the ►Alpi Apuane as a backdrop: these are the attractions of the Versilia coast in north-west Tuscany between Viareggio and ► Carrara on the border to Liguria.

Tuscan Riviera For more than 30km/20mi with hardly a break, one bathing resort merges with the next along Route no. 1, the ancient Via Aurelia. When Viareggio was developed into a sophisticated seaside resort in the 19th century, the other seaside towns soon followed its lead. Today hundreds of hotels in all categories border the coast, and on every beach one sun-shade nudges the next during the high season. While the Tuscan hinterland gets most of its visitors in May, June and September, the coast is busiest during July and August.

Forte dei Marmi

Elegant seaside resort Forte dei Marmi (population 9,000) became the most exclusive resort on the Versilia coast in the 19th century – and it still is today. Since the beginning of the 20th century it has welcomed illustrious

Florida? Hawaii? No, the Versilia coast!

guests such as d'Annunzio and his muse Eleonora Duse, Thomas Mann and Aldous Huxley. Forte dei Marmi has kept up its high-class appearance. The holiday resort developed from a small fortress, which was built between 1782 and 1788 by Grand Duke Leopold I. Today there is an enjoyable **museum of caricature** (Museo della Caricatura, hours: June–Sept 5–8pm, 9pm–midnight, otherwise Fri– Sat 3.30–7.30pm, Sun and holidays also 10.30am until 1pm). The

 VISITING VERSILIA

INFORMATION

Viareggio, Piazza Mazzini 22
Tel. 058 44 88 81
Fax 058 44 74 06
www.versilia.turismo.toscana.it

EVENTS

Viareggio is a centre of carnival, which has been celebrated here every year in February since 1873. Thousands of masked revellers take part in the famous carnival parades, when extravagantly decorated floats and wagons move along the broad coastal road. In July and August the popular Puccini opera festival takes place at Lake Massaciuccoli (information and ticket sales: tel. 05 84 35 93 22, fax 05 84 35 02 77, www.puccinifestival.it).

WHERE TO EAT

► Moderate / expensive
L'Oca Bianca
Viareggio, Via Coppino 409
Tel. 05 84 38 84 77
Closed Mon and Sun midday.
Elegant restaurant with first-class fish, an incomparable dessert menu and a select wine list.

► Expensive
Da Lorenzo
Forte dei Marmi, Via Carducci 61
Tel. 05 84 87 40 30
Gourmet destination with first class service!

► Moderate
La Darsena
Via Virgilio 172
Tel. 05 84 39 27 85, closed Sun
Popular fish restaurant
steeped in tradition.

WHERE TO STAY

Viareggio is expensive, like the whole Versilia coast. The town has several fine traditional hotels, but also a large selection of small bed & breakfasts, especially along the city park.

► Luxury
Lord Byron
Forte dei Marmi, Viale A. Morin 46,
tel. 05 84 78 70 52
www.hotelbyron.net
Two enchanting early 20th-century villas on the sea.

► Mid-range / luxury
Plaza e de Russie
Viareggio, Piazza d'Azeglio 1
Tel. 058 44 44 49
Fax 058 44 40 31
www.plazaederussie.com, 52 rooms
Built in belle époque style in 1871 as the top hotel in Viareggio on the main square of the resort and still one of the best addresses. Meals are served on the roof terrace; the beach is about 100m away.

straight streets around Piazza Garibaldi have been converted for the most part into relaxed pedestrian zones with street cafés, the houses have been renovated and decorated with flowers and the shops are in the upper price range. The only thing that remains of the marble harbour is the 300m/330yd-long quay, which offers a wonderful view of the mountains. The slightly sloping beach of fine-grained sand makes Forte dei Marmi attractive above all to families.

Pietrasanta F 4

✱
Sculptors' town

Anyone interested in the artistic use of marble should go not just to Carrara (▸Carrara · Massa), but definitely to Pietrasanta (population 24,000) too. The capital of the Versilia has been home to sculptors' workshops and bronze foundries for centuries, and there are countless small studios and workshops where visitors can watch sculptors and stonemasons at work. The town was named after Guiscardo Pietrasanta, governor of Lucca, who founded the settlement in the mid-13th century.

Sightseeing

The heart of the old town centre at the foot of the castle hill with the ruins of a rocca from the 16th century is the spacious cathedral

Everything is paper maché: the popular figures are part of a typical Viareggio carnival float.

square. Broad steps lead up to the Duomo San Martino, which was begun in 1296. Its brick campanile is the landmark of the city. To the right the baptistery holds a baptismal font dated 1509 by Donato Bentis; diagonally opposite the Torre dell' Orologio has been striking the hours since 1534.

Further up the 16th-century Palazzo Moroni is the home of the local archaeological museum. The collection, which is closed until further notice, principally contains finds from the Versilia from the Bronze Age to the Renaissance.

The **birthplace of the poet Giosuè Carducci** (1835–1907) in Valdicastello has also been converted to a museum. Follow Via G. Mazzini north to the 14th-century former Augustinian monastery, which today houses the Luigi Rosso cultural centre. Its museum has more than 200 plaster models and sculptural designs by major artists, including works by Cesar, Alicia Penalba and Joan Mirò (hours: Tue–Sat, times vary, information tel. 05 84 79 11 22).

Viareggio   F 4

Viareggio (population 57,000) is the »city« beach of the Versilia coast, lined by villas, hotels and cafés, which were rebuilt in typical Italian **art nouveau** (stile liberty) or art deco style after the fire of 1917 that destroyed the earlier wooden houses. In the early 19th century Maria Luigia of Bourbon-Parma, the ruler of Lucca, promoted the development of the fishing village. It was laid out with a right-angled street grid and granted a town charter in 1820. In the second half of the century the first luxury hotels appeared around Piazza d'Azeglio with its pine trees, Piazza Mazzini and Piazza Puccini, which soon welcomed noble and prominent guests, including Thomas Mann, who was inspired here to write his novella *Mario and the Magician* (1930), Arnold Böcklin and Lord Byron.

★
Vibrant seaside resort

More than 200 hotels and guesthouses, the older ones with magnificent stucco façades, line Viareggio's miles-long, four-lane coast road. The broad **beach promenade** runs parallel with palm trees, jasmine bushes and pine trees. On the beach side of this promenade the art nouveau pavilions that are Viareggio's trademark stand in a row. The little houses are built close together and for the most part date from the 1920s and 1930s, following the fire that destroyed almost all of their wooden predecessors in 1917.

Take the air: Viareggio's beach promenade

But most of the high-class shops and cafés have had to make room for fast-food chains and souvenir shops, and on many of the pavilions not much of the art nouveau glamour is left. Exceptions are the **Magazzini Duilio building** (no. 48; from 1930) with its curved windows and the large, clearly visible house number above the façade which recalls Belgian art nouveau; also the former **Grand Caffè Margherita** with its two characteristic towers a few steps away (see photo p.56).

| Citta del Carnevale | The newest attraction in Viareggio is the Cittadella del Carnevale, giant halls on the northern edge of town where carnival floats are on display. |

✴ Parco Naturale and Lago di Massaciuccoli

| Nature reserve | South of Viareggio along the coast to Livorno lies Parco Naturale di Migliarino – San Rossore – Massaciuccoli, a 23,000 ha/56,830-acre nature reserve with deer and wild boar, herons, bitterns, avocets and birds of prey. The enchanting Lago di Massaciuccoli, at 7 sq km/2.7 sq mi the largest lake in the area, constitutes the last remains of a lagoon which silted up through the sediment transported by the rivers Arno and Serchio. One impressive attraction in the park is the farm San Rossore on Viale delle Cascine, which has a racetrack. The park can be explored on foot, by bus, by bike or on horseback. Riding arrangements at tel. 050 52 30 19. |

Lago di Massaciuccoli ▶

| Torre del Lago Puccini | Viareggio is about 6km/3.5mi from Torre del Lago on Lake Massaciuccoli , which got its nickname from Giacomo Puccini (▶Famous People), who composed most of his operas in his art nouveau villa here around 1900, including *La Bohème* and *Madame Butterfly*. The great composer found his final resting place in a chapel next to his study in the villa, which is a museum today. The Puccini opera festival is held every year in his honour (▶ Visiting Versilia, see also p.65). |

✶ ✶ Volterra

18

Province: Pisa (PI)
Population: 11,500

Altitude: 545m/1,788ft above sea level

About 50km/30mi from the coast and 60km/37mi south-east of ▶Pisa, the small town of Volterra, famous for its alabaster art, occupies a steep hill between the river valleys of Cecina and Era.

Excavacations have shown that the hill has been inhabited since the Neolithic period. When iron ore was discovered around the Etruscan city of Velathri, the settlement flourished from the 4th century BC onwards. It minted its own coins and was protected by a wall more than 7km/4.5mi long. In the Middle Ages Volterra developed into a wealthy free state, which was conquered in 1361 by Florence. Today the town lives mostly from tourism and the sale of alabaster arts and crafts. Most of the shops and workshops are in Via Matteotti, Via Guarnacci and Via Gramsci, which is called Via Don Minzoni behind Piazza XX Settembre.

Volterra Plan

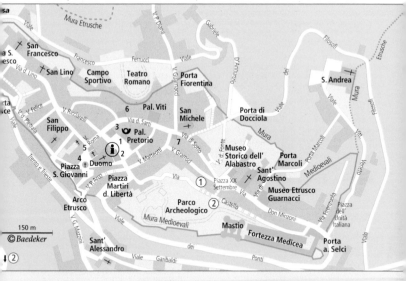

1 Piazza dei Priori
2 Palazzo dei Priori
3 Bishop's palace

4 Battistero
5 Museo Diocesano
 d'Arte Sacra

6 Museo Civico
 Pinacoteca
7 Casa-Torre Toscano

Where to eat
① Ombra della Sera
② Trattoria del Sacco Fiorentino

Where to stay
① Villa Nencini
② Villa Rioddi

What to See in Volterra

A fine place to begin a tour of Volterra is the southern approach to
the town on Viale dei Ponti (parking garage right before Piazza Mar-
tiri della Liberta). There is a beautiful view of the Cecina valley from
the panorama terrace near the bus station before the entrance to the
town.

✳
Observation point

In the heart of the old city Piazza dei Priori is surrounded by pretty
palazzi. It has been Volterra's market and assembly place since the
13th century. Today the Cooperativa Artieri Alabastro has a large
shop here. Coats of arms and inscriptions for Florentine governors
and commissioners decorate the façade of Palazzo dei Priori, which
was built between 1208 and 1254. It is the former residence and seat
of the podestà and the oldest preserved Tuscan city palace (hours:
10.30am–1pm, 2.30–6pm).
Its austere façade has only a few windows and is divided by narrow
cornices. On a clear day the sea is visible from the top of the town

✳
Piazza dei Priori

⏱

▶ VISITING VOLTERRA

INFORMATION

Piazza dei Priori 20
Tel. 058 88 72 57
www.volterratur.it

EVENTS

Volterra Medievale A.D. 1398
Medieval town festival. From the 3rd
until the 4th Sunday in August Volterra's old town returns to the year
1398!

WHERE TO EAT

▶ **Moderate**

① *Ombra della Sera*
Via Gramsci 70, tel. 058 88 66 63
This stylish little restaurant has been
open for more than 25 years. Two of
the many house specialties: zuppa alla
Volterrana and ravioli alla
Maremma. Closed Mon.

② *Trattoria del Sacco Fiorentino*
Piazza XX Settembre 18

Tel. 058 88 85 37
Elegant restaurant and rustic enoteca.
sophisticated seasonal cuisine and extensive wine list.
Closed Fri.

WHERE TO STAY

▶ **Moderate**

② *Villa Rioddi*
Loc. Rioddi
Tel. 058 88 80 53
Fax 058 88 80 74
www.hotelvillarioddi.it
Small comfortable hotel (9 rooms) in a
15th-century former coaching station.

▶ **Budget/mid-range**

① *Villa Nencini*
Borgo Santo Stefano 55
Tel. 058 88 63 86, fax 058 88 06 01
www.villanencini.it, 14 rooms
Hotel opposite Porta San Francesco
with a garden and swimming pool.

---

hall tower. The Palazzo Pretorio opposite was the seat of the Capitano del Popolo until 1511 and later the Florentine administration. The Torre del Podestà towers over this crenellated building, which is a combination of several structures going back to the 13th century. An alabaster pig nicknamed »Porcellino« looks down from the cornice.

✳ **Duomo Santa Maria Assunta**

Walk through the narrow Via Turazza to the cathedral, which was dedicated in 1120 and enlarged around 1254 in Pisan Romanesque style. The campanile was rebuilt after collapsing in 1493, but one storey had to be removed afterwards for structural reasons. The interior got its present appearance in Renaissance forms mainly in the 16th century, when the walls were adorned with stripes, the capitals and column shafts were redecorated and a wooden coffered ceiling by Francesco Capriano was added. The surviving **Romanesque furnishings** are the large wooden *Deposition from the Cross* in the right transept, with its slender figures from the time around 1250, a rarity in Italy, and an impressive pulpit which was assembled in the 17th century using fragments from the 12th and 13th centuries. Its 12th-century reliefs show scenes from the Old and New Testament. Wonderful examples of the transition from Mannerism to Baroque can be seen on the wings of the altars in the aisles, as in the *Immaculate Conception* by the Mannerist **Pomaranchio** (1592). The three dark paintings in the Capella Inghirani, depictions of the life and martyrdom of St Paul by Domenichino, embody Baroque drama by means of chiaroscuro effects. The marble ciborium from the year 1471 on the altar and, in the Cappella dell'Addolorata, the colourful terracotta group *Mary and Joseph with Child* in front of Benozzo Gozzoli's fresco depicting the arrival of the Magi are also of interest.

Battistero

The baptistery opposite the cathedral also dates from the 13th century. A dome was added about 300 years later. It faces the cathedral and is covered with white and green marble stripes and has a portal decorated with figures. The main attraction inside is the beautiful baptismal font by Andrea Sansovino (1502).

Arco Etrusco

From Palazzo dei Priori steps (Via Porta all'Arco) lead down to Arco Etrusco, the only preserved **Etruscan city gate** in the ancient wall. The masonry in the sides and the three weathered heads on the outer gate have been dated to the 4th–3rd century BC. The vaulted arch was renovated in the 1st century by the Romans, and the walls are medieval.

Museo Diocesano d'Arte Sacra

The diocesan museum is in the cloister just a few steps north-west of the cathedral (Via Roma 1). It displays religious art from the diocese of Volterra including glazed terracotta busts of St Linus, the first disciple of St Peter, by Andrea della Robbia, a bust reliquary of St Ottaviano of embossed silver (15th century) by Antonio del Pollaiuolo, a tabernacle with miniature painting (15th century) of the Umbrian school, a gilded bronze crucifix (16th century) by Giambologna as well as vestments from the 16th to the 18th centuries (hours: ⏱ March–Oct daily 9am–1pm, 3–6.30pm, otherwise 9am–1pm).

✸ Side trip to San Francesco Frescoes by Cenni di Francesco

A side trip goes to the north-west end of town to the 13th-century church of San Francesco. The chapel of the cross was added in 1315 and painted in 1410 by Cenni di Francesco with a fresco cycle on the *Legenda Aurea* and the childhood of Christ – about 25 years after Gaddi's cycle in Santa Croce in ►Florence and 50 years before Piero della Francesca created his famous cycle on the *Legend of the Holy Cross* in ►Arezzo.

Via Riccarelli, residential towers

Back in the centre walk through Via Ricarelli, where there are two beautiful examples of medieval residential towers (casa-torre) of the 12th and 13th centuries: Casa-Torre Buonparenti (at the intersection with Via Roma) and Casa Ricciarelli (no. 34–36). There is another tower in Via Matteotti: Casa-Torre Toscano.

WHITE AND VELVETY

Alabaster is to Volterra what marble is to Carrara. The processing of the white stone has provided jobs for the city since time immemorial – and any number of souvenirs for the tourists.

Alabaster has always been popular with artists, as it is so easy to work. In the course of history it has been used for many things: in the ancient Orient, for instance, white alabaster

»Today's selection in the alabaster shops lies somewhere between art and kitsch ...«

was used for containers or statuettes; the coarser, greenish alabaster was used in Assyria for large reliefs, steps, basins and the like. Vessels, lamps and canopic jars were the most popular objects in ancient Egypt, and in Roman times it was used most often for vases, urns and reliefs. The much-praised alabaster work of Volterra

flourished from the 6th until the 1st century BC under the **Etruscans**, who used this attractive natural stone along with tuff and terracotta to produce urns. After production all but stopped at the end of Roman rule, and the more resistant and precious ivory was more in demand in the Middle Ages, the processing of alabaster only began again during the Renaissance. The first artisan school for alabaster was started by Inghirami-Fei in the late 18th century. By the middle of the 19th century there were more than 60 workshops which increasingly used alabaster for mass production.

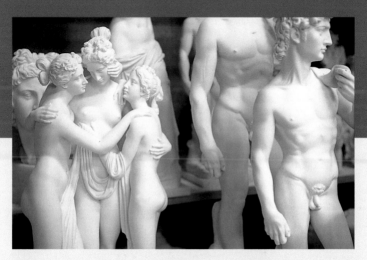

Kitsch or art? Alabaster from Volterra.

Today's selection in the alabaster shops lies somewhere between art and kitsch. Visitors will find everything here from valuable sculptures to decorative jars, knick-knacks, ashtrays, vases and other accessories.

A Type of Plaster

Alabaster is a hydrous calcium sulphate, a crystalline, fine-grained variety of plaster. Four different kinds can be found near Volterra. The white-grey **bardiglio** has many colour nuances and structures and is opaque; it is mined, and was used by the Etruscans for funeral urns. **Pietra a marmor**, twice as expensive and milky white with less structure, is extracted in surface mining near Siena and Volterra. **Scaglione** is translucent and slightly marbled. It is mined near Castellina Marittima in shafts up to 300m/1,000ft below ground and costs three times as much.

But the ultimate alabaster is the transparent **alabastro agatha**, a light-yellow to dark-brown stone with a very fine structure which occurs near Volterra and Siena and costs about four times as much as bardiglio. Anyone who is uncertain and wants to test whether an object is genuine alabaster can test it like this: try scratching it with a fingernail. Unlike artificial materials, alabaster can easily be scratched.

✴
Pinacoteca and Museo Civico

The next stage of the tour is the Renaissance palace Minucci-Solaini in Via dei Sarti (no. 1) with the Pinacoteca (art gallery) and Museo Civico. The high quality of the collection, which contains works by artists from Florence, Siena and Volterra, derives from such important pieces as the large wooden statues of the *Annunciation* group (around 1420) by Francesco di Domenico Valdambrino from the cathedral of Volterra, Luca Signorelli's graceful *Madonna and Child with Saints* (1491) and his *Annunciation* (1501), two triptychs from the 14th or 15th century by Taddeo di Bartolo, and Domenico Ghirlandaio's lifelike depiction of *Christ with Saints Attinea, Greciniana, Benedict and Romuald* (1492), which was made for the Benedictine convent San Giusto.

The highlight of the collection is the **Deposition** by Rosso Fiorentino, which glows in bright colours and was designed for the Cappella della Croce di Giorno of the church of San Francesco on Piazza Inghirami in 1521. This large-scale painting is a masterpiece of Florentine Mannerism and takes its appeal from its dynamic composition, in which the figures are connected with each other as in a net in front the ground of the pictue, and the light illuminates certain areas of the scene like a spotlight (hours: March–Oct daily 9am–7pm, otherwise 9am–2pm).

Natural stone is the trademark of Via all'Arco in Volterra

Viti Palace, a few steps further on Via del Sarti, was begun at the end of the 16th century on behalf of the nobleman Attilio Incontri. In the second half of the 19th century it was acquired by Benedetto Guiseppe Viti, a wealthy businessman whose alabaster workshop was one of the most important artisan businesses in Volterra before it closed in 1874. He supplied the sculptures in the stairwell as well as the chandeliers in the ballroom, among other things. There are also two magnificent alabaster candelabras which were intended for Emperor Maximilian of Habsburg, but which were never delivered because of his execution in 1867. In the cabinets are oriental birds of paradise, Chinese chess sets and a Bali temple of balsa wood, all Viti family souvenirs from their business trips. The Chinese drawings on rice paper in the dining room from the 18th and 19th centuries, two Lombard Louis XVI chests by Guiseppe Maggiolini and the gilded furniture in the Red Salon are also notable (hours: daily except Tue 10am–1pm and 2.30–6.30pm).

★
Palazzo Viti

Follow the busy Via Guarnacci downhill towards Porta Fiorentina. Below the medieval city wall are the ruins of a 1st-century Roman theatre, which was donated by the wealthy citizen Caecina and his son. The building materials come from the surroundings area: sandstone for the walls, tuff for the seats and lava for the steps. Some of the spectator seating and part of the two-storey stage wall have been partially reconstructed.
In the second half of the 3rd century the stone of the theatre was used to build the nearby thermal baths (hours: daily 10.30am–1pm, 2.30–6.45pm). In summer there is a market next to the Teatro Romano on Saturdays.

Teatro Romano

From the Roman theatre follow Via Guarnacci back to Via Gramsci, which opens up into the pretty Piazza XX Settembre. A former monastery, in the 19th century the home of one of the largest alabaster workshops in Volterra, today houses a private alabaster museum. The large collection, which includes not only decorative vases, busts, clocks and any number of small sculptures from the 18th to the 20th centuries, but also old furniture and paintings, is beautiful, even though the presentation is not very informative (hours: daily 9.30am–12.30pm and 2.30–6.30pm).

Museo Storico dell'Alabastro

In and around Volterra, Etruscan Velathri, astonishing finds from the Etruscan periods have come to light. The Guarnacci Museum in Via Don Minzoni 15 is considered to be one of the most important Etruscan museums in Italy. It owes its existence to the cleric Mario Guarnacci (1701–1785), who left his large collection to the city.
The exhibition gives an excellent impression of the culture and life of the Etruscans. It includes about 600 urns (cists), most from the 4th to the 1st century BC when Volterra was a centre of urn production. The lids of the urns were made of tuff, alabaster or terracotta and

★ ★
Museo Etrusco Guarnacci

shaped like boxes. They have figures of the dead, while the sides are decorated with mythological reliefs and were originally painted. The motifs cover hunting, battle and funerary scenes, taking leave of life, the journey into the after-life – which the Etruscans thought was populated by fearful demons – and scenes from Greek mythology. The Urna degli Sposi (urn of the bridal couple) is noteworthy for the expressions on the faces of the couple during the feast. The most important piece among the Etruscan bronze stele is the 57cm/22in statue of a naked youth from the late 3rd century BC called »ombra della sera« (evening shadow), which could easily be a modern sculpture.

The museum also has a wonderful black Volterran jug (4th century BC), a cyathos (cup with one handle) of Bucchero clay with a high decorated handle, fine bronze articles, votive stele, dishes and tools, marble heads and floor mosaics from the Roman imperial period as well as Etruscan jewellery and ancient coins (hours: March–Oct daily 9am–7pm, otherwise 9am–2pm).

Fortezza Medicea
On the highest point on the hill of Volterra stands the massive Medici fortress, today a high-security prison and not accessible. The proud stronghold is among the largest bulwarks of Renaissance architecture in Italy. The old castle in the east was built in the 14th century by the Duca d'Athene, the new castle between 1472 and 1475 for Lorenzo de Medici. The middle round tower of the new castle, built after 1472, was called »maschio« (little man), whereas the half-elliptical tower of the old castle is called »femmina« (little woman).

Parco Archeologica
At the western foot of the Medici fortress is the archaeological park. In 1926 during an excavation the remains of an ancient acropolis were exposed, including the foundations of two temples from the 2nd century BC and a cistern (piscina).

Etruscan walls
There are remains everywhere of the wall that the Etruscans built to defend the wealthy city of Velathri. The 7km/4.5mi-long wall encircled an area that was much larger than the medieval city. In the north and north-west especially it runs outside the old city. In some places the remains of the wall are 11m/36ft high. The remains are especially well preserved in the north-west near the small Santa Chiara church.

Around Volterra

Le Balze
The Balze (balza = cliff), an inhospitable landscape almost bare of vegetation whose hills are cut by deep fissures as a result of erosion, lies immediately north-west of the city and makes a deep impression. Etruscan necropolises, part of the ancient wall and a medieval church have all fallen victim to the continuous erosion of the soft

Alabaster creates many jobs in Volterra. Tourists are welcome to visit the workshops.

sedimentary stone. The former Camaldolese abbey (Badia) also had to be abandoned in 1861 because it was in danger of collapsing.

About 35km/22mi south, a little away from the road between Volterra and Massa Marittima and near the 691m/2,267ft-high Monte Cerboli, lies the geothermal centre of Larderello. Next to the area of ▶ Monte Amiata it is the largest plant of its kind in the world. The cooling towers of the steam power plant, which uses the heat of the earth (90–230°C/195–450°F) to produce electricity, are almost 75m/250ft high. In an area of 240 sq km/90 sq mi about 180 bore holes deliver steam to the power plants from volcanic sources up to 4,000m/13,000ft deep. These steam sources are called »soffioni« and also deliver boric acid, borax and ammonium sulphate for industry. The city also owes its name to a producer of ammonia derivates, the Frenchman François de Larderel, who built a factory here in 1818. In the Museo della Geotermia of the state electricity company E.N.E.L. the geology of the area and the technology used here are explained (hours: daily upon request tel. 058 86 77 24, fax ⊙ 058 86 73 72).

Larderello, geothermal power plant

INDEX

LIST OF MAPS AND ILLUSTRATIONS

PHOTO CREDITS

BLISHER'S INFORMATION

rations etc: 220 illustrations, 33 maps
iagrams, one large map

Eva Maria Blattner, Marlies Burget,
el Machatschek, Andreas März, Dr.
ard Paesler, Peter Peter, Dr. Madeleine
ke, Reinhard Strüber, Ursula Thurner,
a Wurth

ng: Baedeker editorial team
Sykes)

lation: Barbara Schmidt-Runkel

graphy: Franz Huber, Munich;
DUMONT/Falk Verlag, Ostfildern (map)

lustrations: jangled nerves, Stuttgart

gn: independent Medien-Design, Munich;
n Schemel

r-in-chief: Rainer Eisenschmid,
ker Ostfildern

lition 2008

Copyright: Karl Baedeker Verlag, Ostfildern
Publication rights: MAIRDUMONT GmbH & Co;
Ostfildern

Printed in China

DEAR READER,

We would like to thank you for choosing this Baedeker travel guide. It w
reliable companion on your travels and will not disappoint you.
This book describes the major sights, of course, but it also recommends
cafés, as well as hotels in the luxury and budget categories, and includ
about restaurants, shopping and much more, helping to make your trip
enjoyable experience. Our authors ensure the quality of this informatic
making regular journeys to Tuscany and putting all their know-how int
book.

Nevertheless, experience shows us that it is impossible to rule out errors a
changes made after the book goes to press, for which Baedeker accepts no
liability. Please send us your criticisms, corrections and suggestions for
improvement: we appreciate your contribution. Contact us by post or e-m
phone us:

► **Verlag Karl Baedeker GmbH**
Editorial department
Postfach 3162
73751 Ostfildern
Germany
Tel. 49-711-4502-262, fax -343
www.baedeker.com
E-Mail: baedeker@mairdumont.com

Baedeker Travel Guides in English at a glance:

► Andalusia

► Dubai · Emirates

► Egypt

► Ireland

► London

► Mexico

► New York

► Portugal

► Rome

► Thailand

► Tuscany

► Venice